DORK COVEN

The Collected Dork Tower, V

by John Kovalic

PUBLISHED BY DORK STORM PRESS

PO Box 45063,
Madison, WI 53744
E-mail: john@kovalic.com

Marketing and Advertising:
Liz Fulda, sales@DorkStorm.com
Phone: (608) 255-1348 • Fax: (608) 255-1352

PRINTED IN CANADA.
FIRST PRINTING, October 2000
ISBN1-930964-40-4

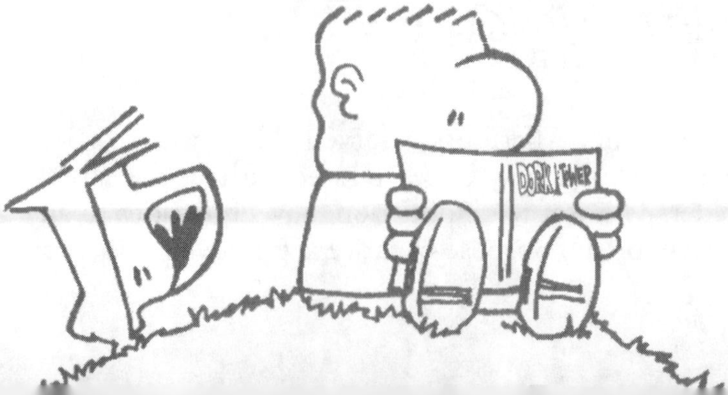
DORK TOWER

To the love of my life, my wife Judith, for believing in this, and in me.

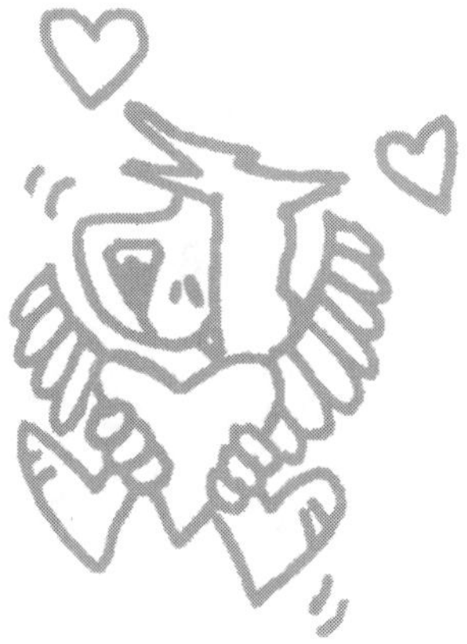

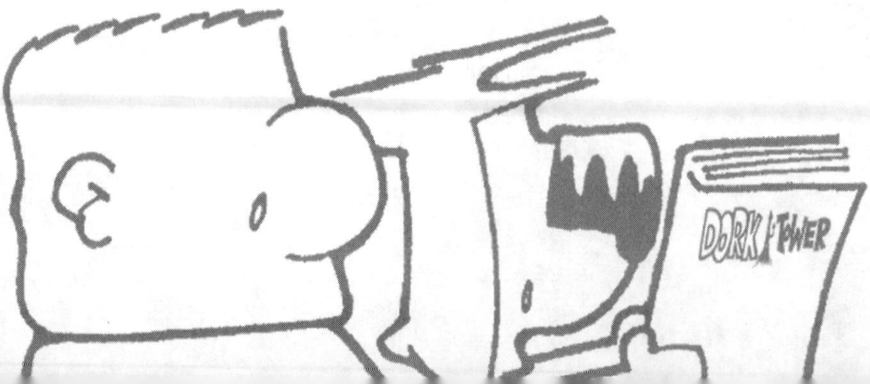
DORK TOWER

DORKS OF THE TOWER

"Hey, Marcia. Come and see the satanist."

That one still cracks me up.

I have no great affection for gaming, but then I'm always suspicious when a noun becomes a verb without warning. Like "party." It is interesting to me that, right around the time-that "party" became a verb (I party, you party, he/she/it parties, we party, you party, they party), what it was describing had virtually ceased to exist and the sort of characters that Kevin Smith has made a career out of documenting had taken over. In *my* day, when those fellows took over the keg, you knew that you should have left half an hour ago.

You might well ask what has this to do with John Kovalic and his excellent comic book, *Dork Tower.*

You might well ask what is wrong with the characters that Kevin Smith documents?

You would ask in vain, however, for I confine my closely reasoned arguments to the back pages of *Cerebus.*

Uh. *Cerebus?* The comic book that I draw?

Yes. Yes. Twenty-three years now (almost). A little over three years to go. Pardon? Yes, it's one long story that I started in ... Science fiction? No, no. It isn't *really* a... well, Cerebus *did* do a tour of the solar system in one of .. Fantasy? Uhh. Yeah. I mean, not as much as there was early on when it was mostly a *Conan parody. Conan.* Well, *before* the movies, Conan was a ... No, I'm not really interested in Hollywood myself. You mean, like a *Cerebus* animated cartoon or something? No, I really... Well, the loss of *control.* See, when you sign a contract with a studio, they... Pardon? Well, millions of dollars if everything goes right. But, you see, it only goes right once in a great while. Like with the *Teenage Mutant Ninja Turtles,* but then you have to stop writing and drawing and become the CEO full-time of whatever you... Well, I don't know how many millions the *Turtles* made, *exactly.* But millions and millions, yes. definitely... See, to me, when you self-publish your work, as I do with *Cerebus* and as John Kovalic is now doing with *Dork Tower,* the idea is to *reduce* the amount of outside interference and to limit the business side to turning the artwork into printed comic books and getting them to the...

No, comic *books.* The ones in the newspaper are *comic strips.*

Yes, it was very sad that Charles Schulz died.

JOHN KOVALIC GOT A LETTER FROM HIM ONCE.

Yes, that's right. *The* Charles Schulz. Oh, many millions of dollars ... maybe even a quarter of a *billion.*

Yes.

Yes. It *is* hard to imagine, Well, I think what impressed John was more the *quality* of the *strip* and that was why getting a letter from its creator was such a big deal to him... why he has the letter framed and up on his...

No. A *lot* of cartoonists do that, but Schulz didn't have ghosts. He wrote and drew and pencilled and inked and lettered *every Peanuts* strip that ever...

Yes, wasn't that great? Yes, I watch it every Christmas myself. And when Linus goes out into the spotlight and starts reciting from Luke's Gospel...

Well, it was first aired in 1965, so I guess it's made a lot of money since then. I don't really know how those things work. Whether the studio gets paid every time it's aired and pays Schulz's estate (now), or if someone bought the rights to it, you know, some big corporation like Time-Warner or ABC or something offered a lot of money for it at some point and Schulz (or whoever owned it) just decided...

A *Dork Tower* movie?

Well, I don't know. See, that's one of the funny things with self-publishers. Some of them are interested in Hollywood and some aren't. It seems to me that you don't really know *which* one you *are* until you get an actual offer from ... Pardon?

Well, I *did*--years and years ago--get a phone call from Lucasfilm... Yes. *Star Wars*. Definitely. *Star Wars* has made millions and *millions* of dollars... Well, no, just the one phone call. As I said, I'm not interested, so, you know, there wasn't much reason for them to call back. Regret it? No. No, uh, exactly the opposite. As I said, I don't really have any interest in Hollywood. As I said, the *loss of control* just...

Danny DeVito as Igor?

Well, Danny DeVito has got to be... what? Late forties, early fifties by now. I always got the impression that the characters in Dork Tower are... Well, yes, you're right. There *are* gamers who are in their late forties and early fifties. Yes, that's true. If you have characters of different ages, they *do* like that in Hollywood. Hit the different demographic groups. You could cast same hot twenty year-old as Matt and get that older brother-younger brother thing. Make Igor the sloppy one and Matt the neat one. Yeah, like the *Odd Couple*. No, no--exactly. The *first Odd Couple* movie or maybe even the *Odd Couple* television show. Or you could make Matt a girl. Jenna Elfman and Danny DeVito. Wouldn't that be something? Yeah, they're both really funny.

Speaking of really funny, have you ever *read Dork Tower?* The *Dork Tower* comic book? No?

You really should.

Yes,

Yes, it is.

It's very, very funny.

Dave Sim
Kitchener, Ontario
3 June 00

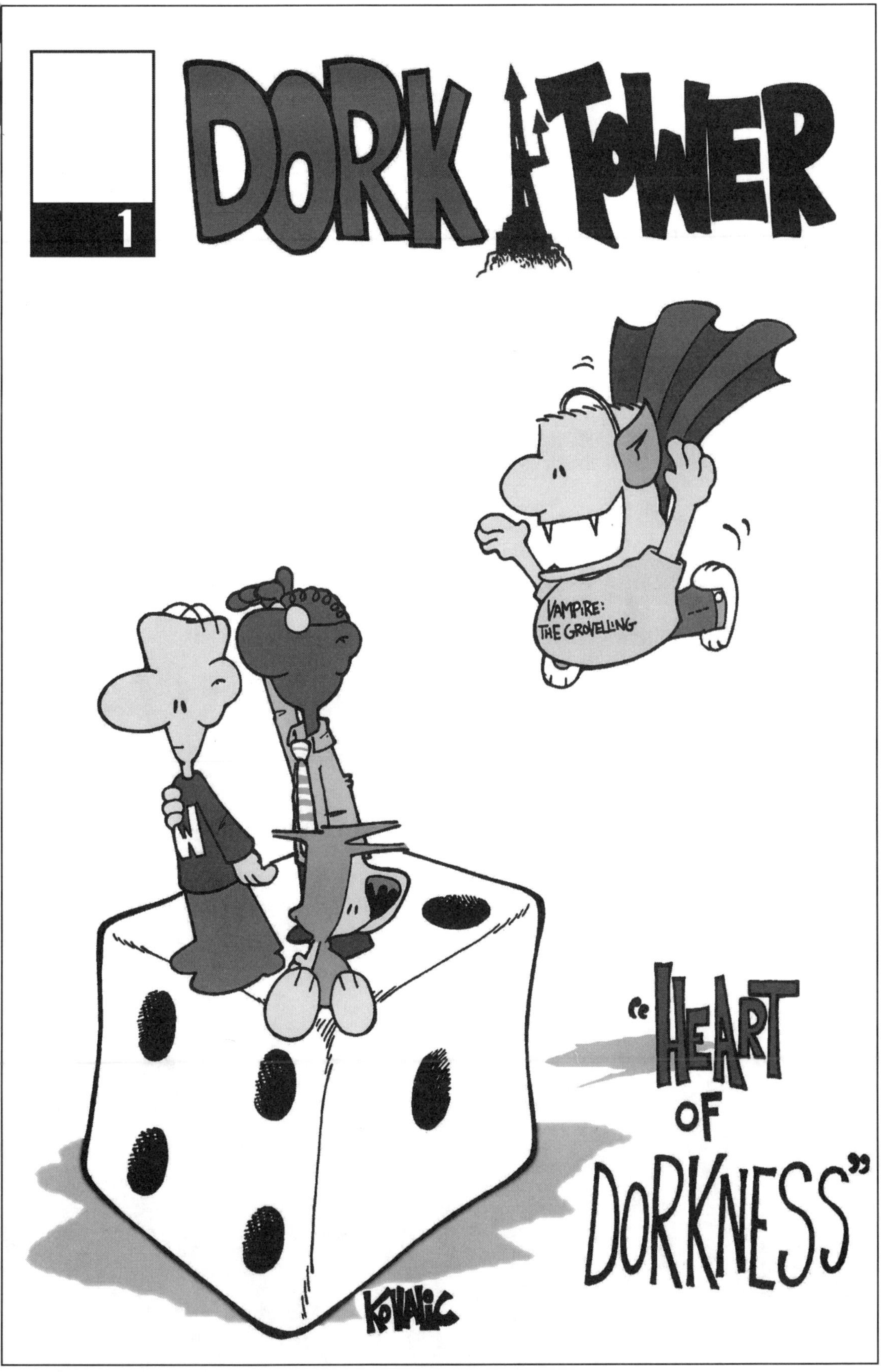
1
DORK TOWER
VAMPIRE: THE GROVELLING
"HEART OF DORKNESS"
KOVALIC

"Come on, Daddy needs a new sword of wounding."

-Langly in X-Files: "Unusual Suspects"

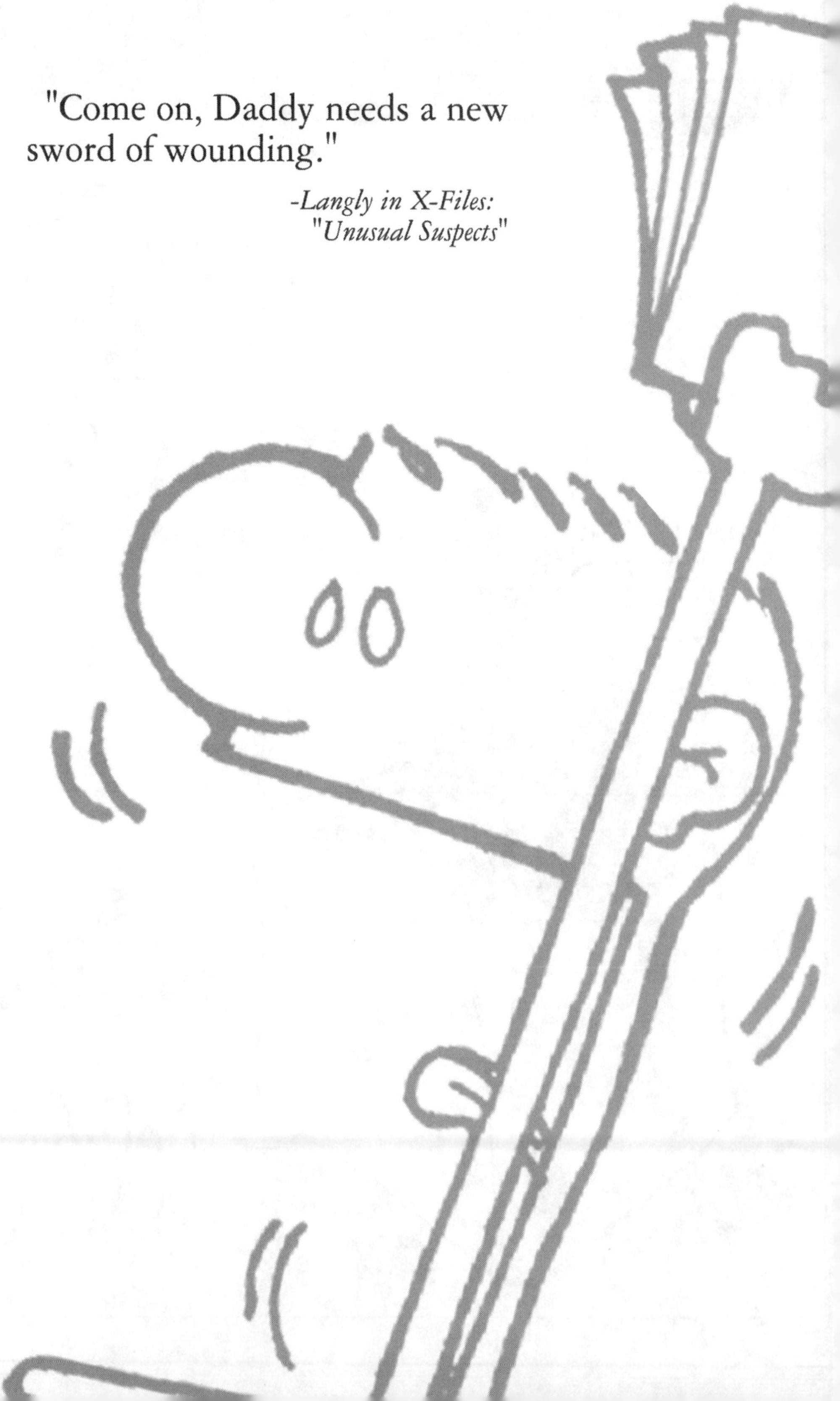

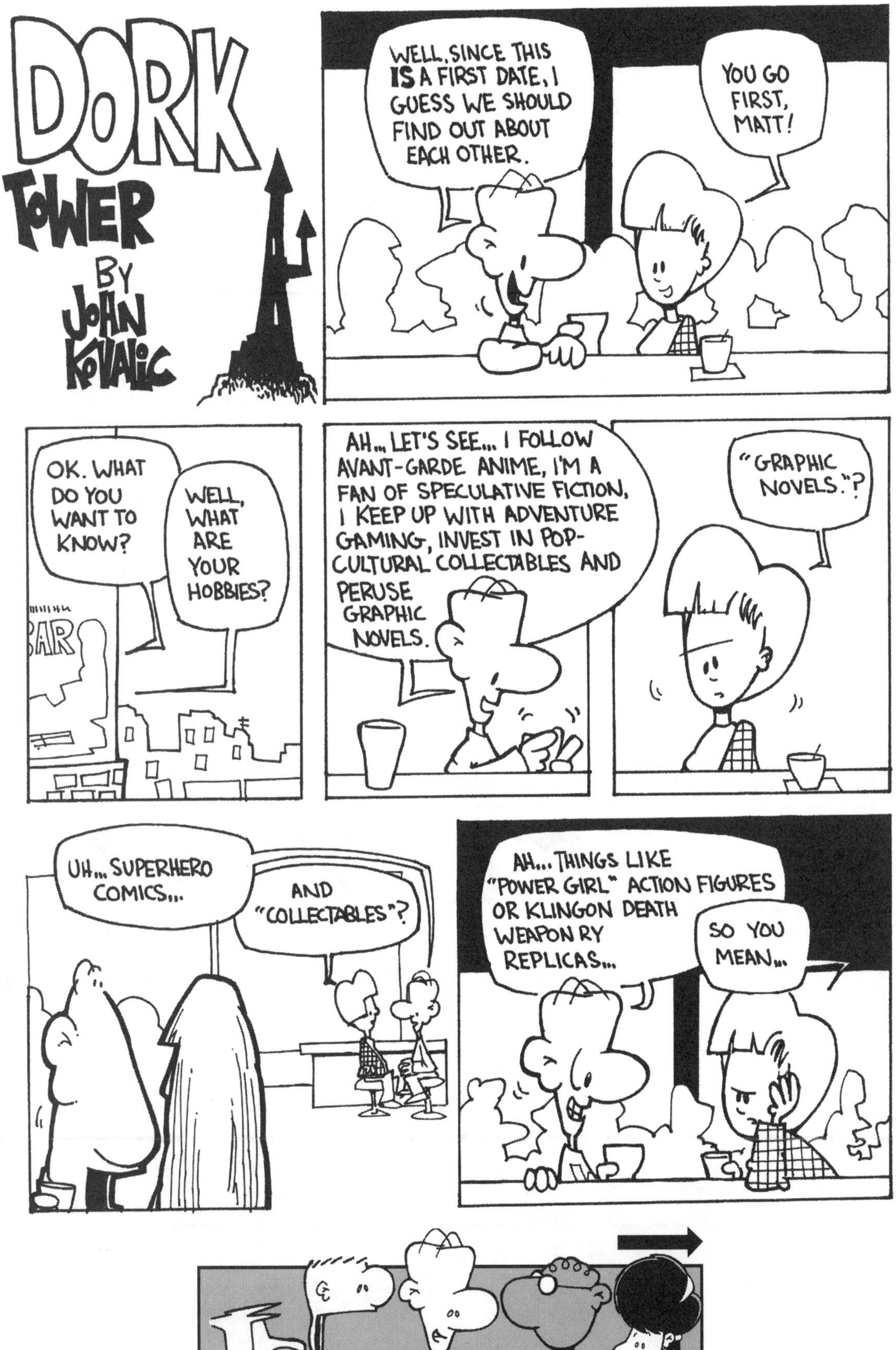
DORK TOWER
BY JOHN KOVALIC
WELL, SINCE THIS IS A FIRST DATE, I GUESS WE SHOULD FIND OUT ABOUT EACH OTHER.
YOU GO FIRST, MATT!
OK. WHAT DO YOU WANT TO KNOW?
WELL, WHAT ARE YOUR HOBBIES?
BAR
AH... LET'S SEE... I FOLLOW AVANT-GARDE ANIME, I'M A FAN OF SPECULATIVE FICTION, I KEEP UP WITH ADVENTURE GAMING, INVEST IN POP-CULTURAL COLLECTABLES AND PERUSE GRAPHIC NOVELS.
"GRAPHIC NOVELS."?
UH... SUPERHERO COMICS...
AND "COLLECTABLES"?
AH... THINGS LIKE "POWER GIRL" ACTION FIGURES OR KLINGON DEATH WEAPON RY REPLICAS...
SO YOU MEAN...

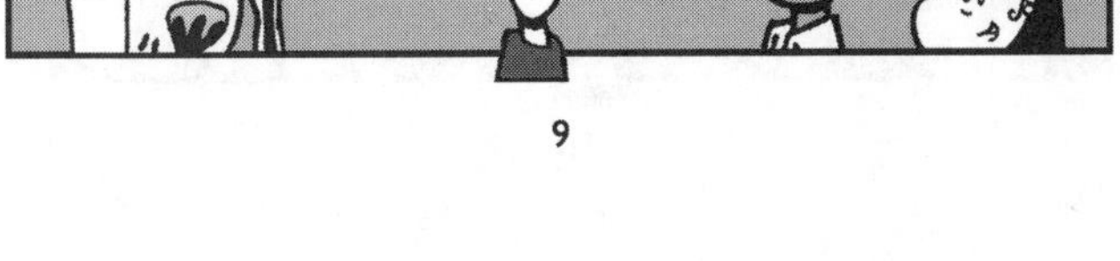

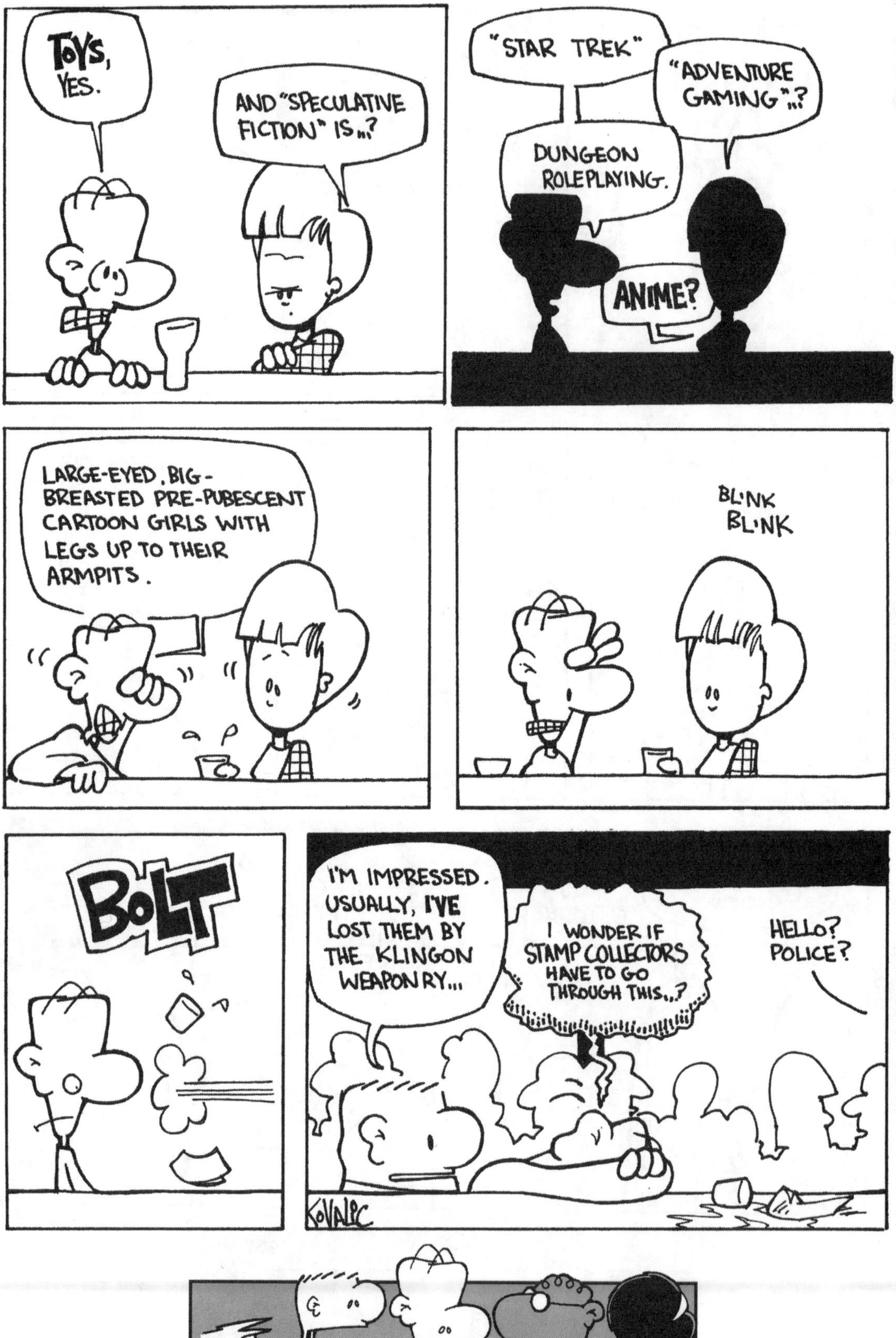
TOYS, YES.
AND "SPECULATIVE FICTION" IS...?
"STAR TREK"
"ADVENTURE GAMING"...?
DUNGEON ROLEPLAYING.
ANIME?
LARGE-EYED, BIG-BREASTED PRE-PUBESCENT CARTOON GIRLS WITH LEGS UP TO THEIR ARMPITS.
BLINK
BLINK
BOLT
I'M IMPRESSED. USUALLY, I'VE LOST THEM BY THE KLINGON WEAPONRY...
I WONDER IF STAMP COLLECTORS HAVE TO GO THROUGH THIS...?
HELLO? POLICE?
KOVALIC

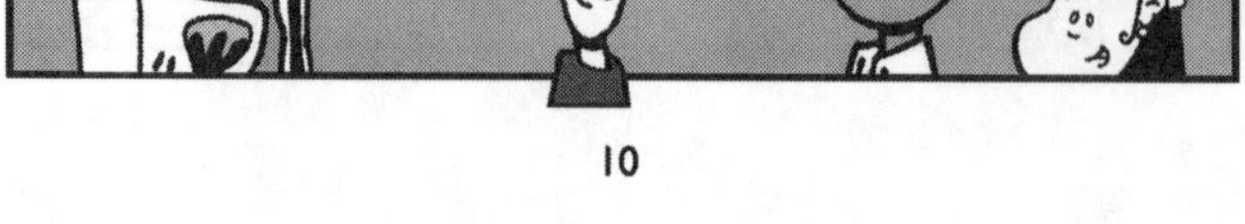

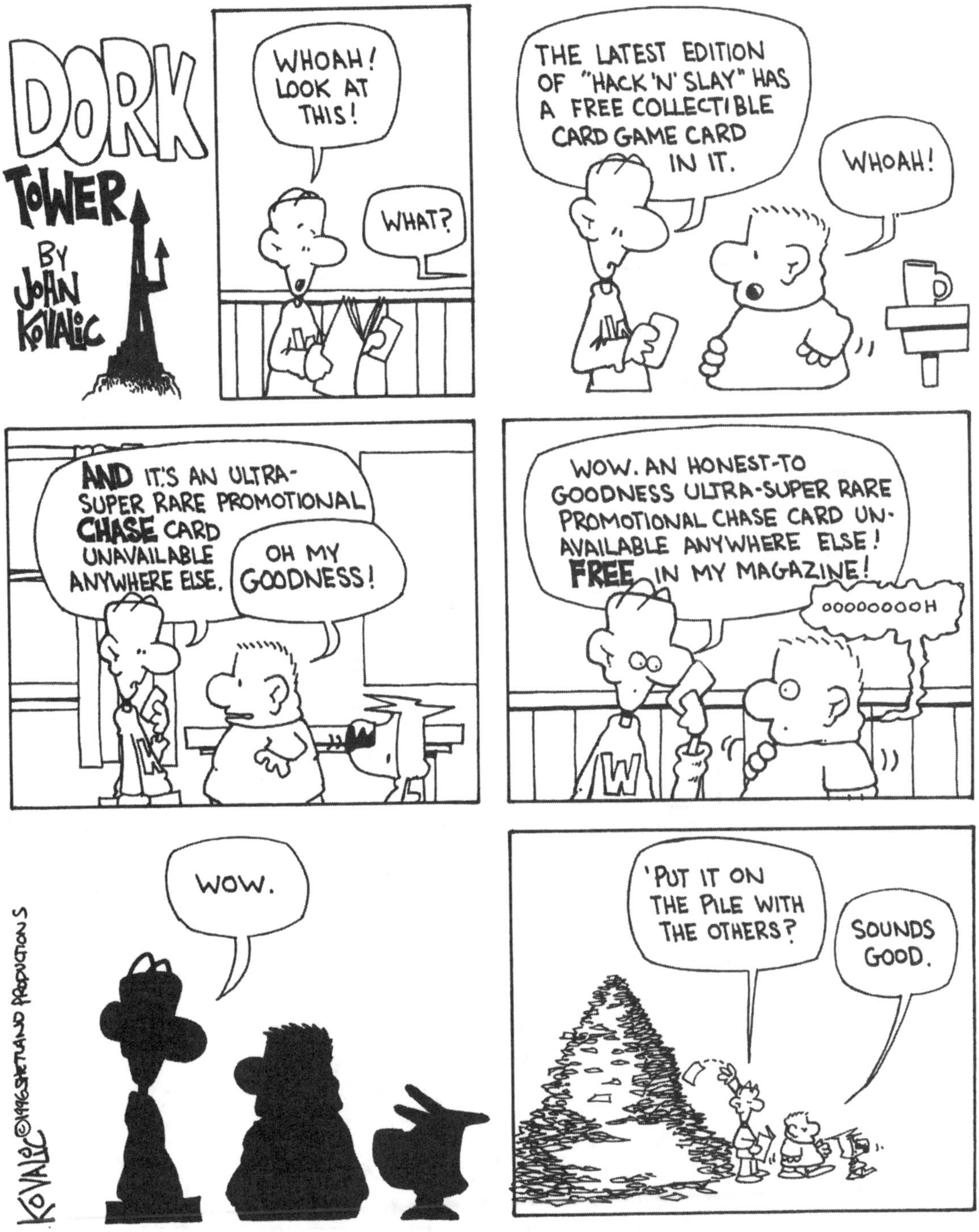
DORK TOWER
BY JOHN KOVALIC
WHOAH! LOOK AT THIS!
WHAT?
THE LATEST EDITION OF "HACK 'N' SLAY" HAS A FREE COLLECTIBLE CARD GAME CARD IN IT.
WHOAH!
AND IT'S AN ULTRA-SUPER RARE PROMOTIONAL CHASE CARD UNAVAILABLE ANYWHERE ELSE.
OH MY GOODNESS!
WOW. AN HONEST-TO GOODNESS ULTRA-SUPER RARE PROMOTIONAL CHASE CARD UN-AVAILABLE ANYWHERE ELSE! FREE IN MY MAGAZINE!
OOOOOOOOH
WOW.
'PUT IT ON THE PILE WITH THE OTHERS?
SOUNDS GOOD.
KOVALIC ©1996 SHETLAND PRODUCTIONS

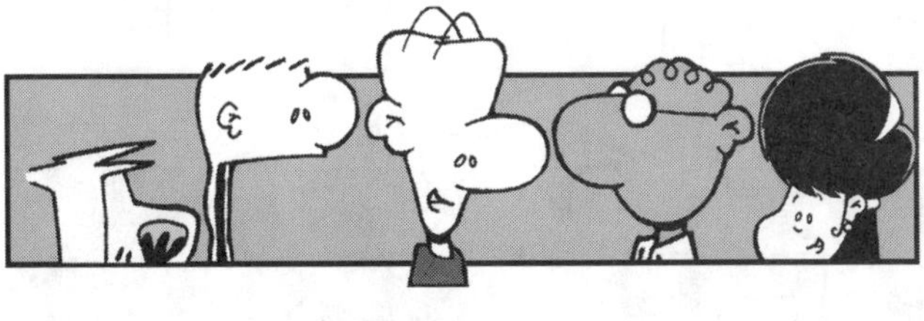

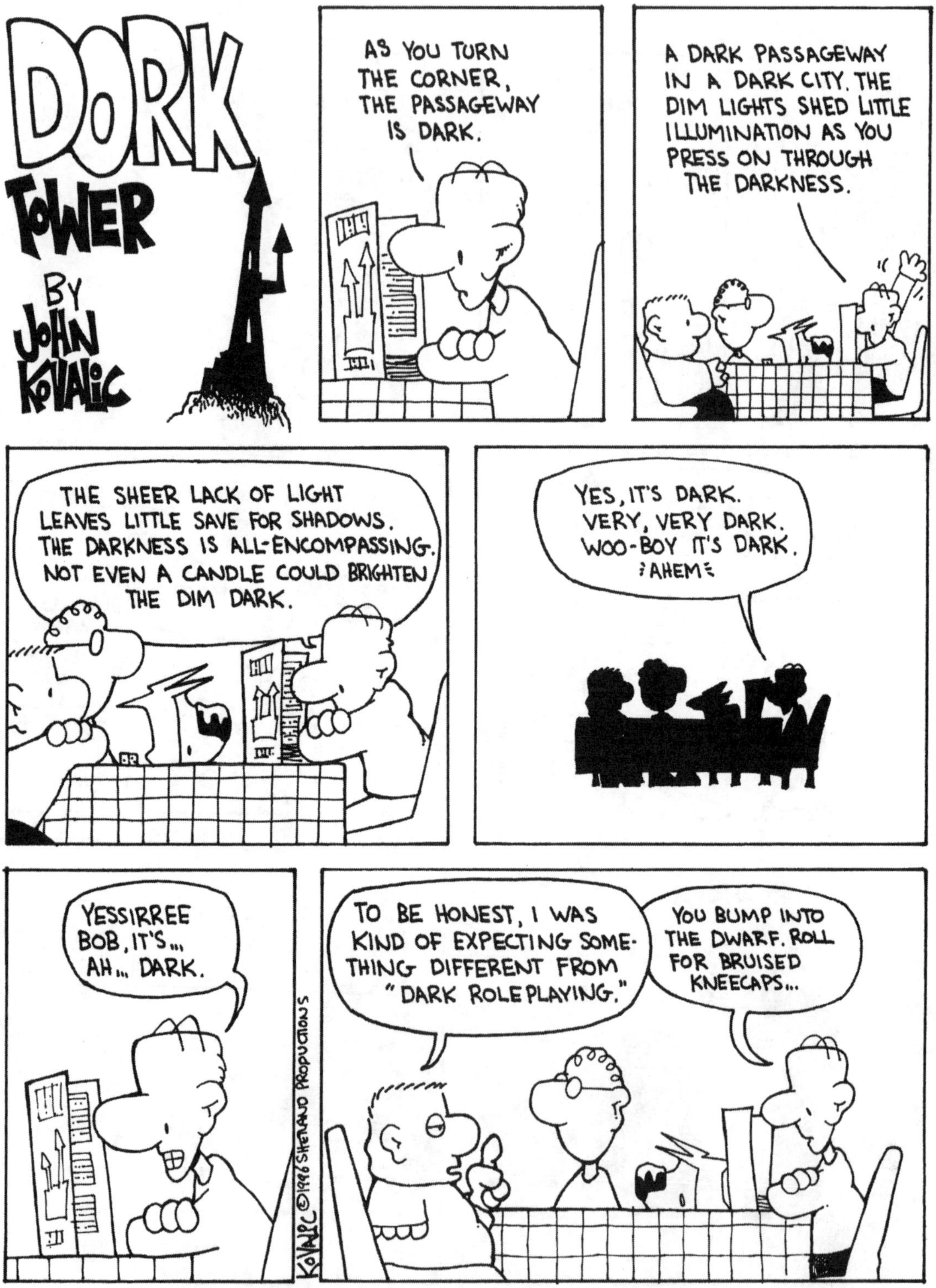
DORK TOWER
BY JOHN KOVALIC
AS YOU TURN THE CORNER, THE PASSAGEWAY IS DARK.
A DARK PASSAGEWAY IN A DARK CITY. THE DIM LIGHTS SHED LITTLE ILLUMINATION AS YOU PRESS ON THROUGH THE DARKNESS.
THE SHEER LACK OF LIGHT LEAVES LITTLE SAVE FOR SHADOWS. THE DARKNESS IS ALL-ENCOMPASSING. NOT EVEN A CANDLE COULD BRIGHTEN THE DIM DARK.
YES, IT'S DARK. VERY, VERY DARK. WOO-BOY IT'S DARK. AHEM
YESSIRREE BOB, IT'S... AH... DARK.
KOVALIC ©1996 SHETLAND PRODUCTIONS
TO BE HONEST, I WAS KIND OF EXPECTING SOMETHING DIFFERENT FROM "DARK ROLEPLAYING."
YOU BUMP INTO THE DWARF. ROLL FOR BRUISED KNEECAPS...

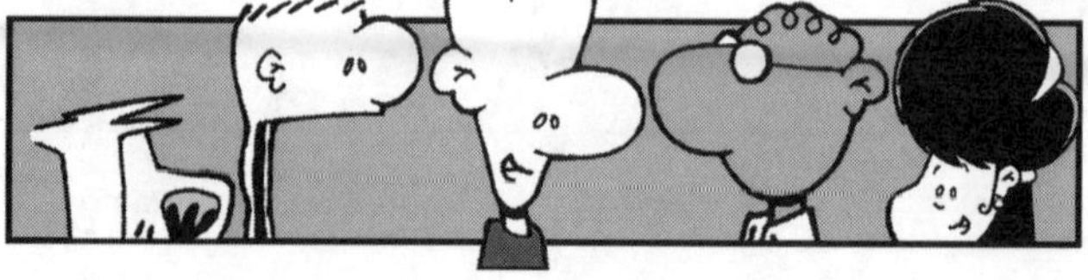

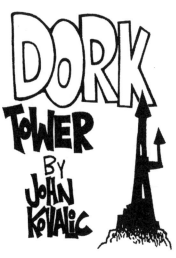

DORK TOWER
BY JOHN KOVALIC

MATT... I WAS THINKING ABOUT MAKING MY NEXT CHARACTER IN THE CAMPAIGN A WOMAN.

A WOMAN?

YOU WANT TO PLAY A WOMAN? WELL, THAT'S CERTAINLY GOING TO ADD TO THE GAME.

THAT'S WHAT I HOPED.

YOU KNOW, I'VE GOT TO ADMIRE YOUR ROLEPLAYING PROWESS.

I'LL SAY. WHAT SKILL IT MUST TAKE TO PLAY A DIFFERENT GENDER.

WHAT MASTERY OF THE FORM.

YOU THINK?

NOT TO MENTION THAT SUCH EXERCISES CAN BE A BRIDGE TO UNDERSTANDING BETWEEN THE SEXES.

A REAL NOBLE UNDERTAKING.

WOW

OH, YES. IT'S INSPIRATIONAL, IGOR.

A FEAT.

IMPRESSIVE.

WOW. THANKS

PERVERT.

DEVIANT.

FREAK.

DO YOU THINK DARK ELVES ARE INTO LEATHER?

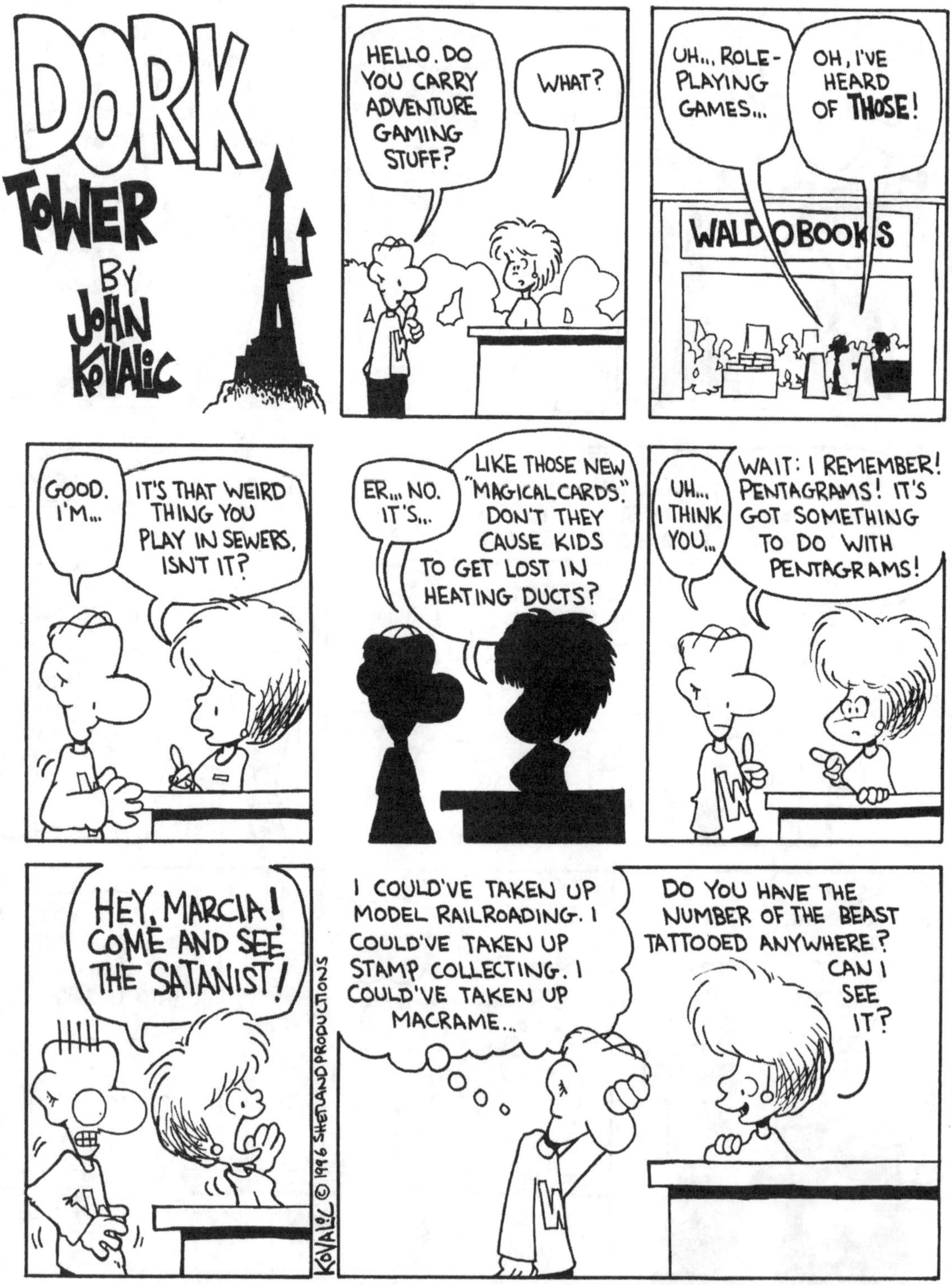
DORK TOWER
BY JOHN KOVALIC
HELLO. DO YOU CARRY ADVENTURE GAMING STUFF?
WHAT?
UH... ROLE-PLAYING GAMES...
OH, I'VE HEARD OF THOSE!
WALDOBOOKS
GOOD. I'M...
IT'S THAT WEIRD THING YOU PLAY IN SEWERS, ISN'T IT?
ER... NO. IT'S...
LIKE THOSE NEW "MAGICAL CARDS." DON'T THEY CAUSE KIDS TO GET LOST IN HEATING DUCTS?
UH... I THINK YOU...
WAIT: I REMEMBER! PENTAGRAMS! IT'S GOT SOMETHING TO DO WITH PENTAGRAMS!
HEY, MARCIA! COME AND SEE THE SATANIST!
KOVALIC © 1996 SHETLAND PRODUCTIONS
I COULD'VE TAKEN UP MODEL RAILROADING. I COULD'VE TAKEN UP STAMP COLLECTING. I COULD'VE TAKEN UP MACRAME...
DO YOU HAVE THE NUMBER OF THE BEAST TATTOOED ANYWHERE? CAN I SEE IT?

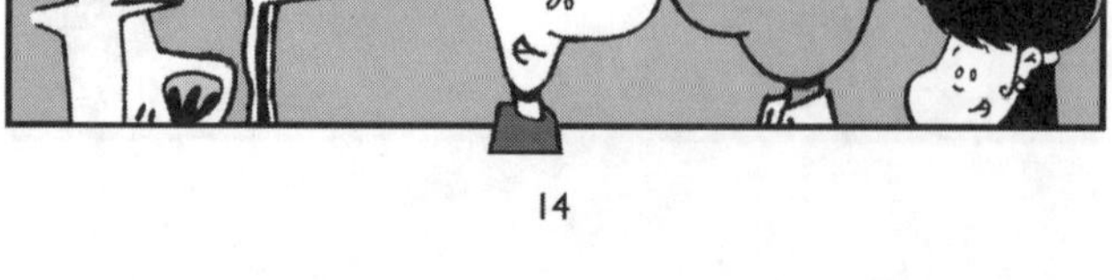

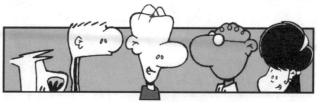

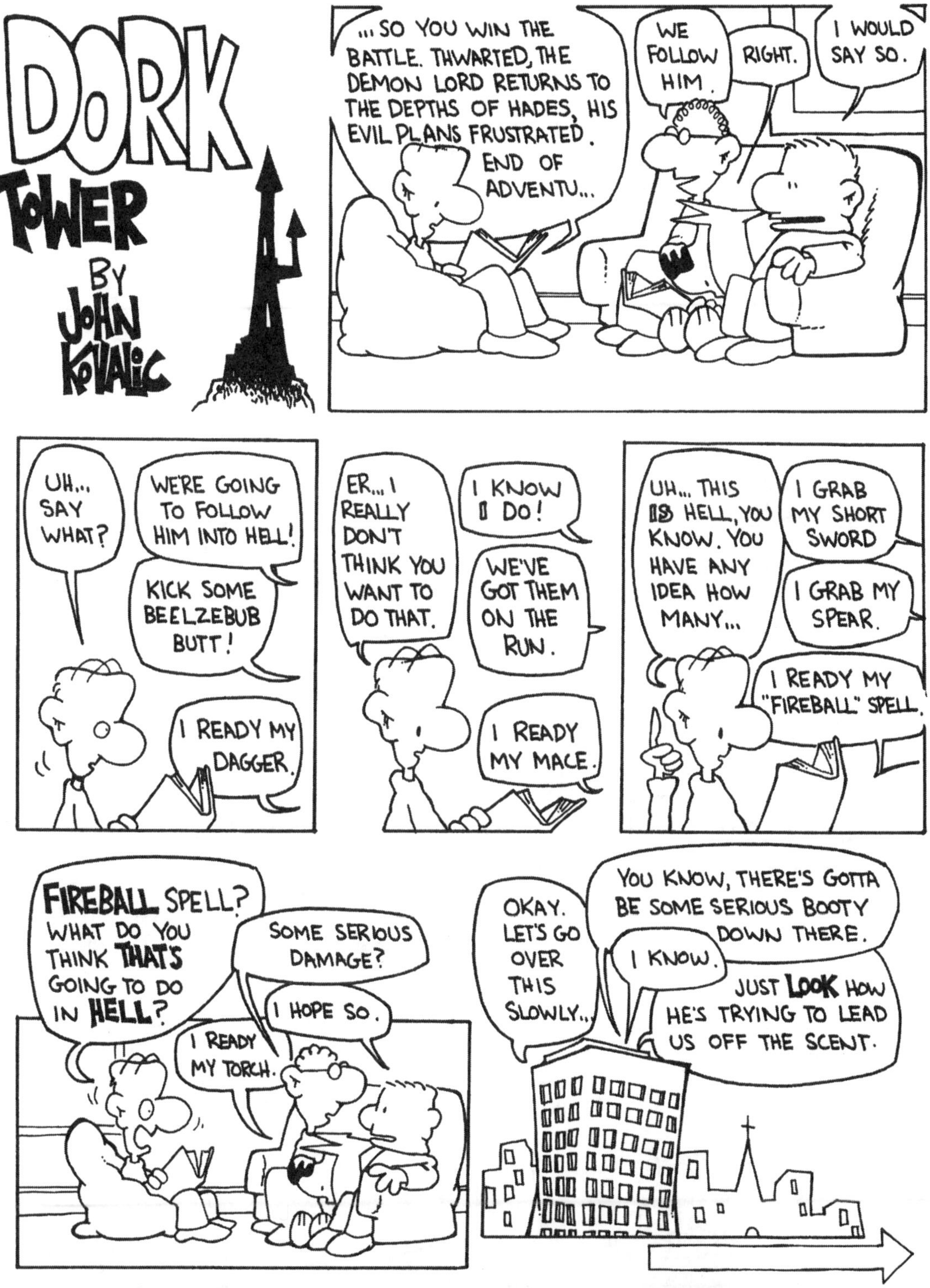
DORK TOWER
BY JOHN KOVALIC
...SO YOU WIN THE BATTLE. THWARTED, THE DEMON LORD RETURNS TO THE DEPTHS OF HADES, HIS EVIL PLANS FRUSTRATED. END OF ADVENTU...
WE FOLLOW HIM.
RIGHT.
I WOULD SAY SO.
UH... SAY WHAT?
WE'RE GOING TO FOLLOW HIM INTO HELL!
KICK SOME BEELZEBUB BUTT!
I READY MY DAGGER.
ER... I REALLY DON'T THINK YOU WANT TO DO THAT.
I KNOW I DO!
WE'VE GOT THEM ON THE RUN.
I READY MY MACE.
UH... THIS IS HELL, YOU KNOW. YOU HAVE ANY IDEA HOW MANY...
I GRAB MY SHORT SWORD
I GRAB MY SPEAR.
I READY MY "FIREBALL" SPELL.
FIREBALL SPELL? WHAT DO YOU THINK THAT'S GOING TO DO IN HELL?
SOME SERIOUS DAMAGE?
I HOPE SO.
I READY MY TORCH.
OKAY. LET'S GO OVER THIS SLOWLY...
YOU KNOW, THERE'S GOTTA BE SOME SERIOUS BOOTY DOWN THERE.
I KNOW.
JUST LOOK HOW HE'S TRYING TO LEAD US OFF THE SCENT.

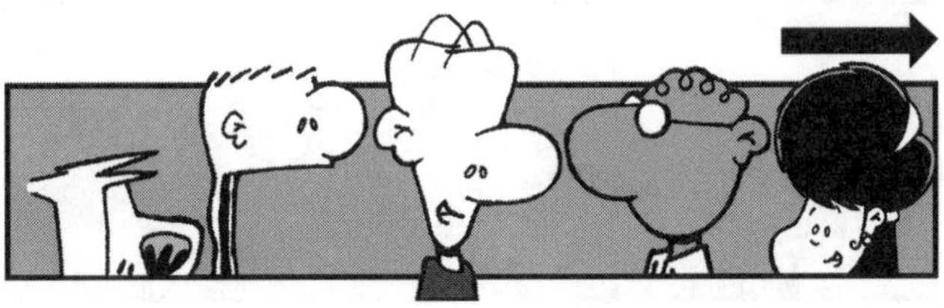

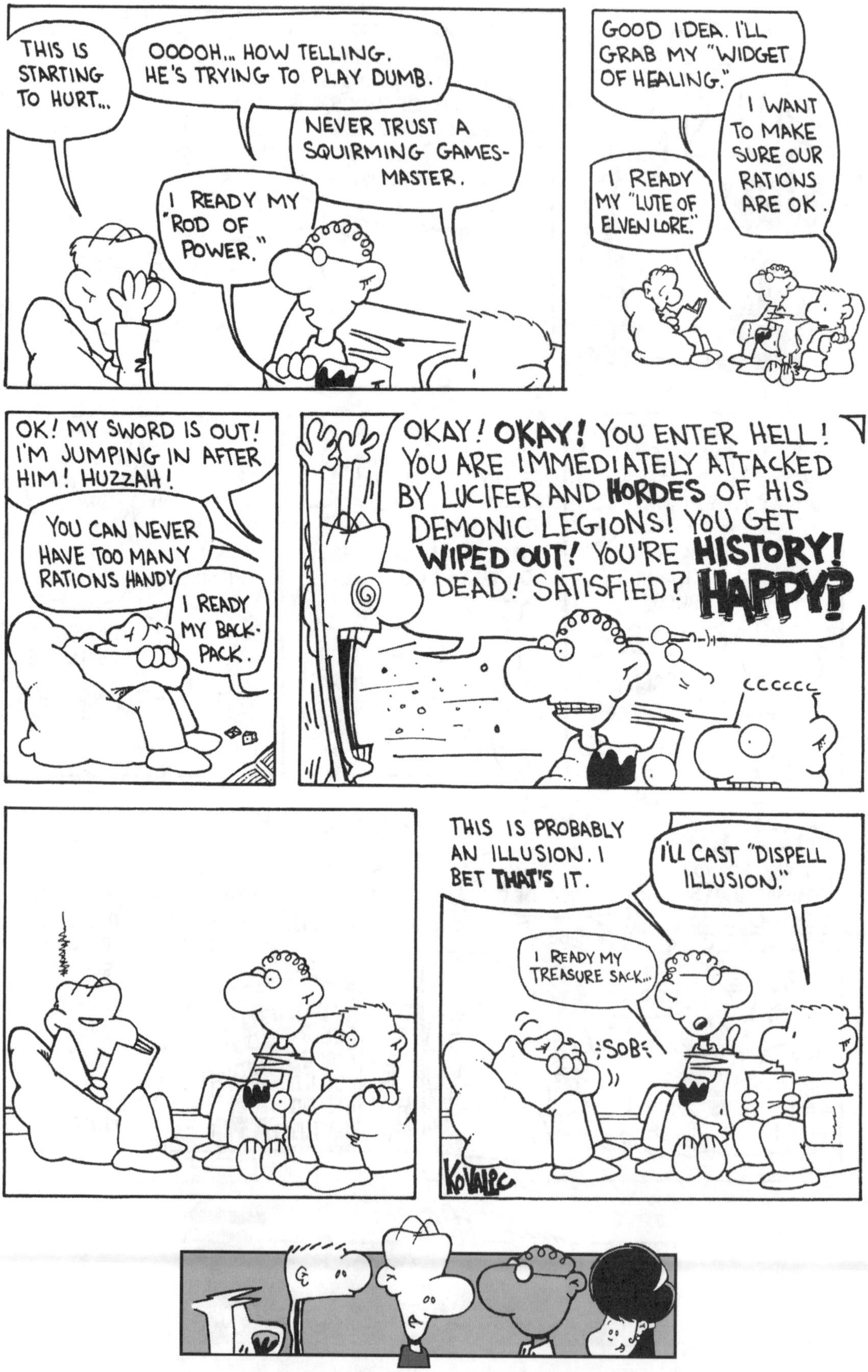
THIS IS STARTING TO HURT...
OOOOH... HOW TELLING. HE'S TRYING TO PLAY DUMB.
NEVER TRUST A SQUIRMING GAMES-MASTER.
I READY MY "ROD OF POWER."
GOOD IDEA. I'LL GRAB MY "WIDGET OF HEALING."
I WANT TO MAKE SURE OUR RATIONS ARE OK.
I READY MY "LUTE OF ELVEN LORE."
OK! MY SWORD IS OUT! I'M JUMPING IN AFTER HIM! HUZZAH!
YOU CAN NEVER HAVE TOO MANY RATIONS HANDY.
I READY MY BACK-PACK.
OKAY! OKAY! YOU ENTER HELL! YOU ARE IMMEDIATELY ATTACKED BY LUCIFER AND HORDES OF HIS DEMONIC LEGIONS! YOU GET WIPED OUT! YOU'RE HISTORY! DEAD! SATISFIED? HAPPY?
CCCCCC
THIS IS PROBABLY AN ILLUSION. I BET THAT'S IT.
I'LL CAST "DISPELL ILLUSION."
I READY MY TREASURE SACK...
SOB
KOVALIC

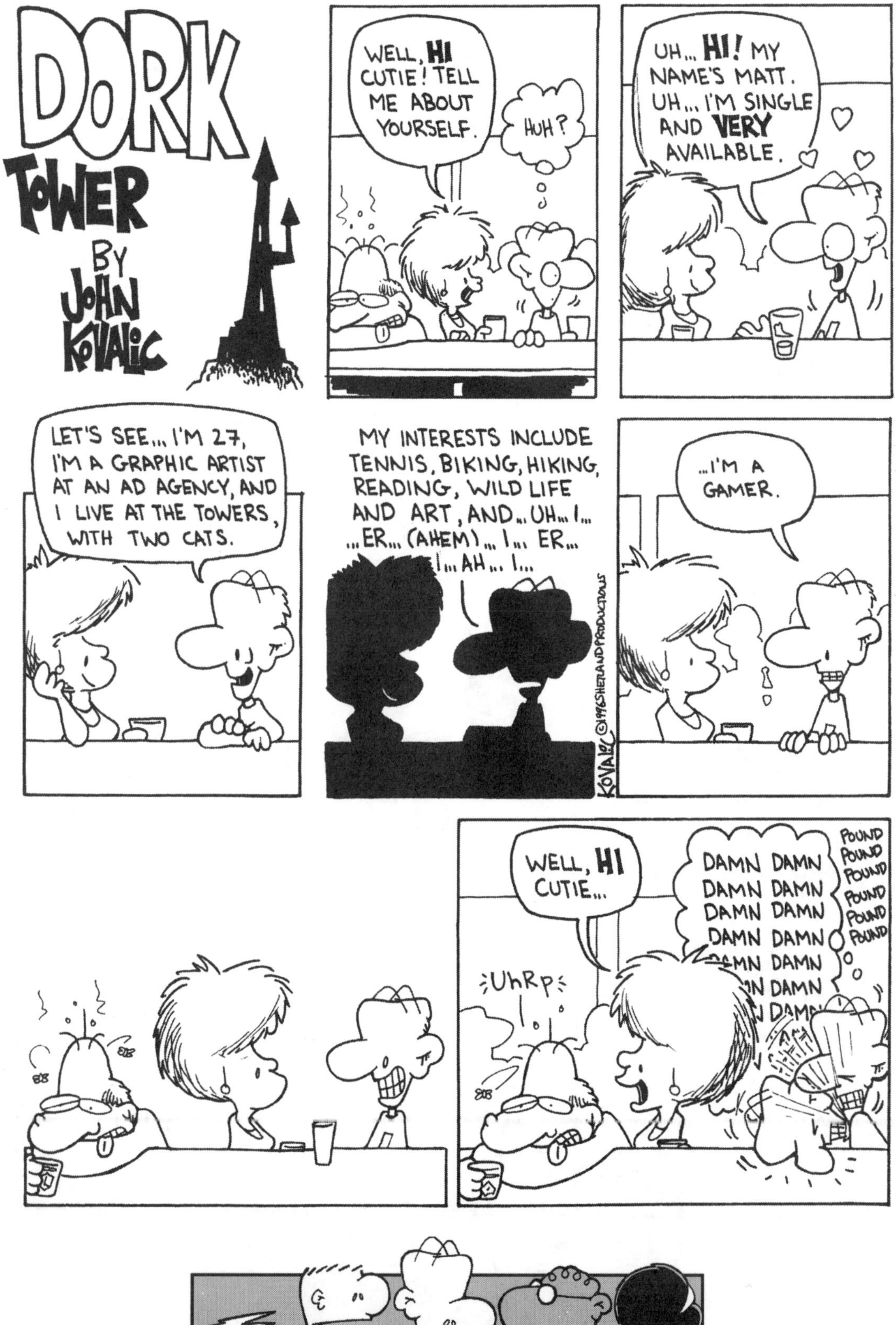
DORK TOWER
BY JOHN KOVALIC
WELL, HI CUTIE! TELL ME ABOUT YOURSELF.
HUH?
UH... HI! MY NAME'S MATT. UH... I'M SINGLE AND VERY AVAILABLE.
LET'S SEE... I'M 27, I'M A GRAPHIC ARTIST AT AN AD AGENCY, AND I LIVE AT THE TOWERS, WITH TWO CATS.
MY INTERESTS INCLUDE TENNIS, BIKING, HIKING, READING, WILD LIFE AND ART, AND... UH... I... ...ER... (AHEM)... I... ER... I... AH... I...
KOVALIC ©1996 SHETLAND PRODUCTIONS
...I'M A GAMER.
UhRp
WELL, HI CUTIE...
DAMN DAMN
DAMN DAMN
DAMN DAMN
DAMN DAMN
DAMN
POUND
POUND
POUND
POUND
POUND
POUND

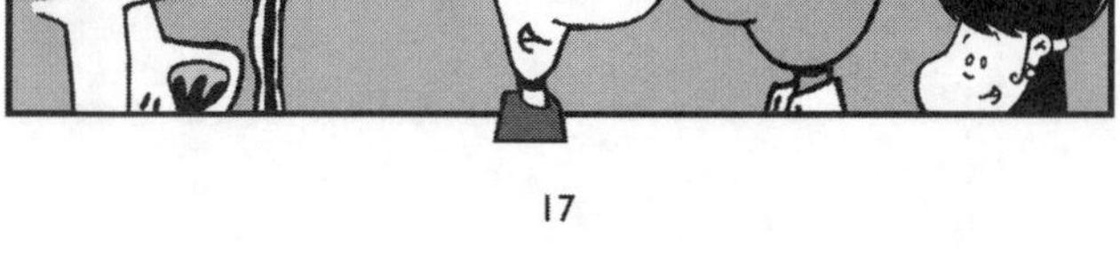

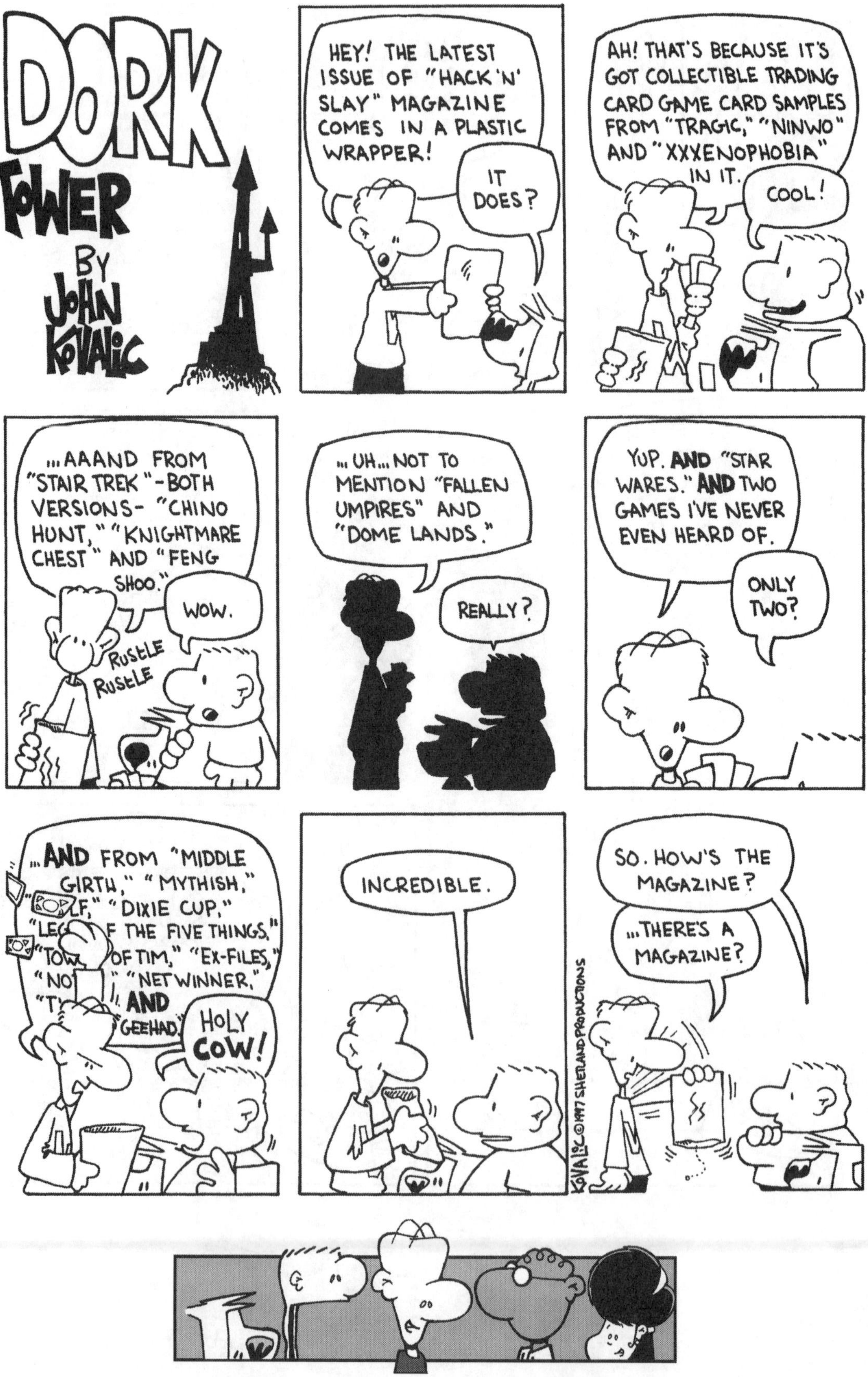
DORK TOWER
BY JOHN KOVALIC
HEY! THE LATEST ISSUE OF "HACK 'N' SLAY" MAGAZINE COMES IN A PLASTIC WRAPPER!
IT DOES?
AH! THAT'S BECAUSE IT'S GOT COLLECTIBLE TRADING CARD GAME CARD SAMPLES FROM "TRAGIC," "NINWO" AND "XXXENOPHOBIA" IN IT.
COOL!
...AAAND FROM "STAIR TREK" - BOTH VERSIONS - "CHINO HUNT," "KNIGHTMARE CHEST" AND "FENG SHOO."
WOW.
RUSTLE RUSTLE
...UH... NOT TO MENTION "FALLEN UMPIRES" AND "DOME LANDS."
REALLY?
YUP. AND "STAR WARES." AND TWO GAMES I'VE NEVER EVEN HEARD OF.
ONLY TWO?
...AND FROM "MIDDLE GIRTH," "MYTHISH," "DIXIE CUP," "F THE FIVE THINGS," "OF TIM," "EX-FILES," "NETWINNER," AND "GEEHAD."
HOLY COW!
INCREDIBLE.
KOVALIC ©1997 SHETLAND PRODUCTIONS
SO. HOW'S THE MAGAZINE?
...THERE'S A MAGAZINE?

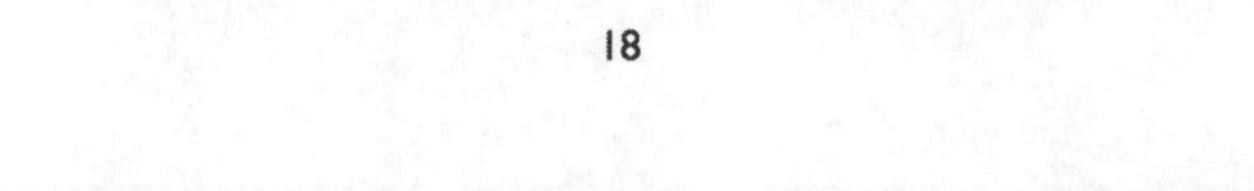

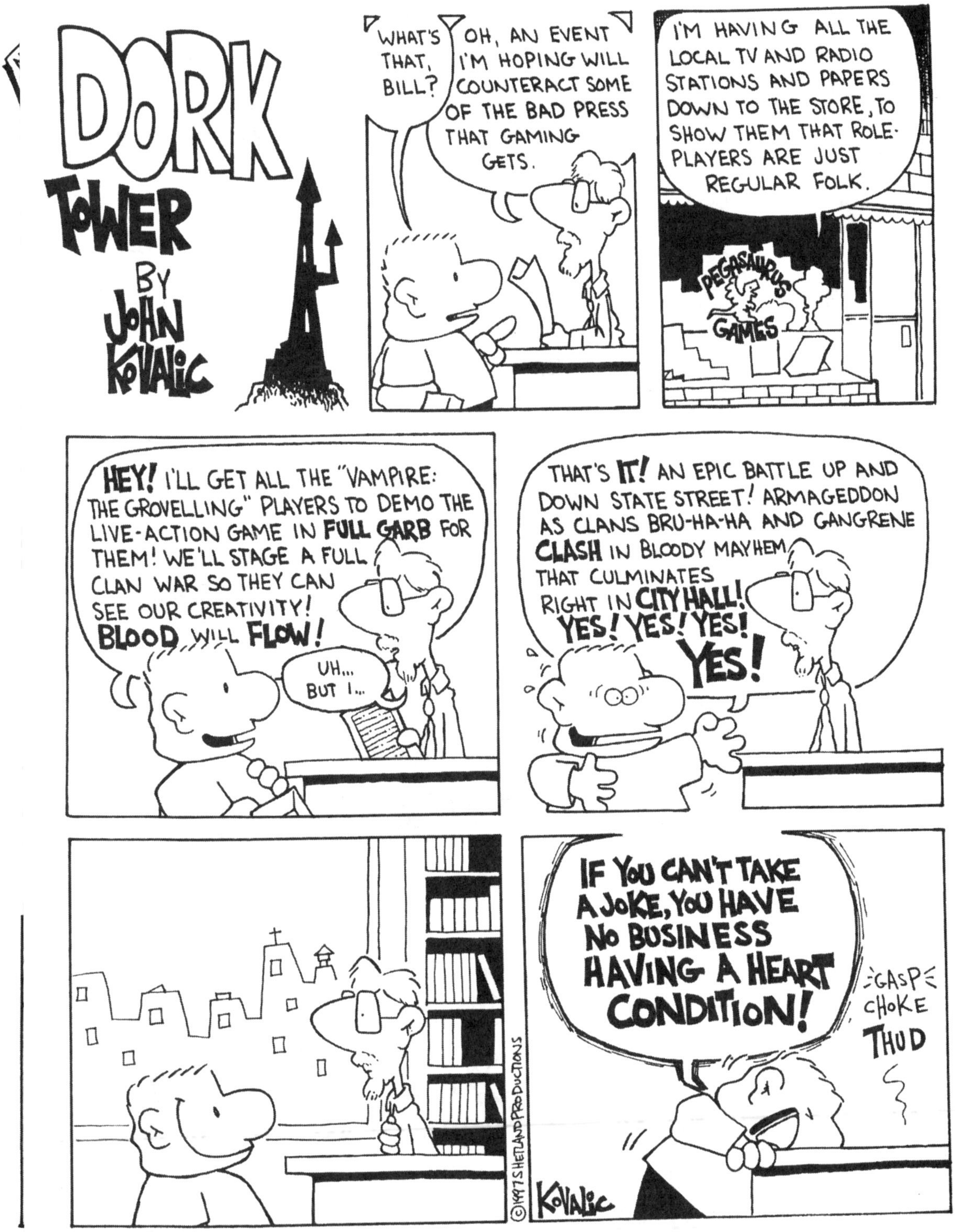
DORK TOWER BY JOHN KOVALIC
WHAT'S THAT, BILL?
OH, AN EVENT I'M HOPING WILL COUNTERACT SOME OF THE BAD PRESS THAT GAMING GETS.
I'M HAVING ALL THE LOCAL TV AND RADIO STATIONS AND PAPERS DOWN TO THE STORE, TO SHOW THEM THAT ROLE-PLAYERS ARE JUST REGULAR FOLK.
PEGASAURUS GAMES
HEY! I'LL GET ALL THE "VAMPIRE: THE GROVELLING" PLAYERS TO DEMO THE LIVE-ACTION GAME IN FULL GARB FOR THEM! WE'LL STAGE A FULL CLAN WAR SO THEY CAN SEE OUR CREATIVITY! BLOOD WILL FLOW!
UH... BUT I...
THAT'S IT! AN EPIC BATTLE UP AND DOWN STATE STREET! ARMAGEDDON AS CLANS BRU-HA-HA AND GANGRENE CLASH IN BLOODY MAYHEM THAT CULMINATES RIGHT IN CITY HALL! YES! YES! YES! YES!
IF YOU CAN'T TAKE A JOKE, YOU HAVE NO BUSINESS HAVING A HEART CONDITION!
GASP
CHOKE
THUD
©1997 SHETLAND PRODUCTIONS
KOVALIC

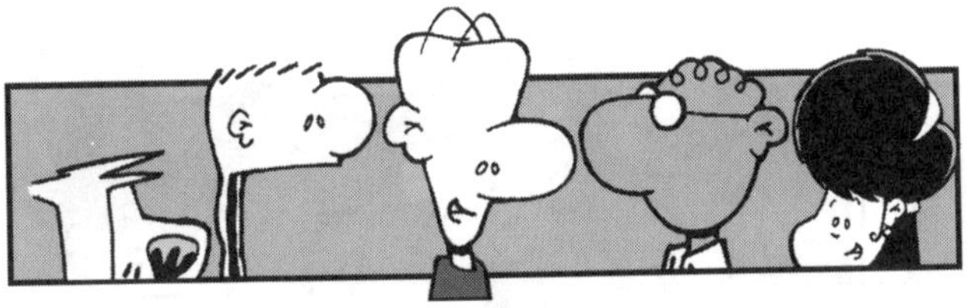

"Perky, a little bouncy, not too bouncy..."

-Brittany in Daria: "Malled"

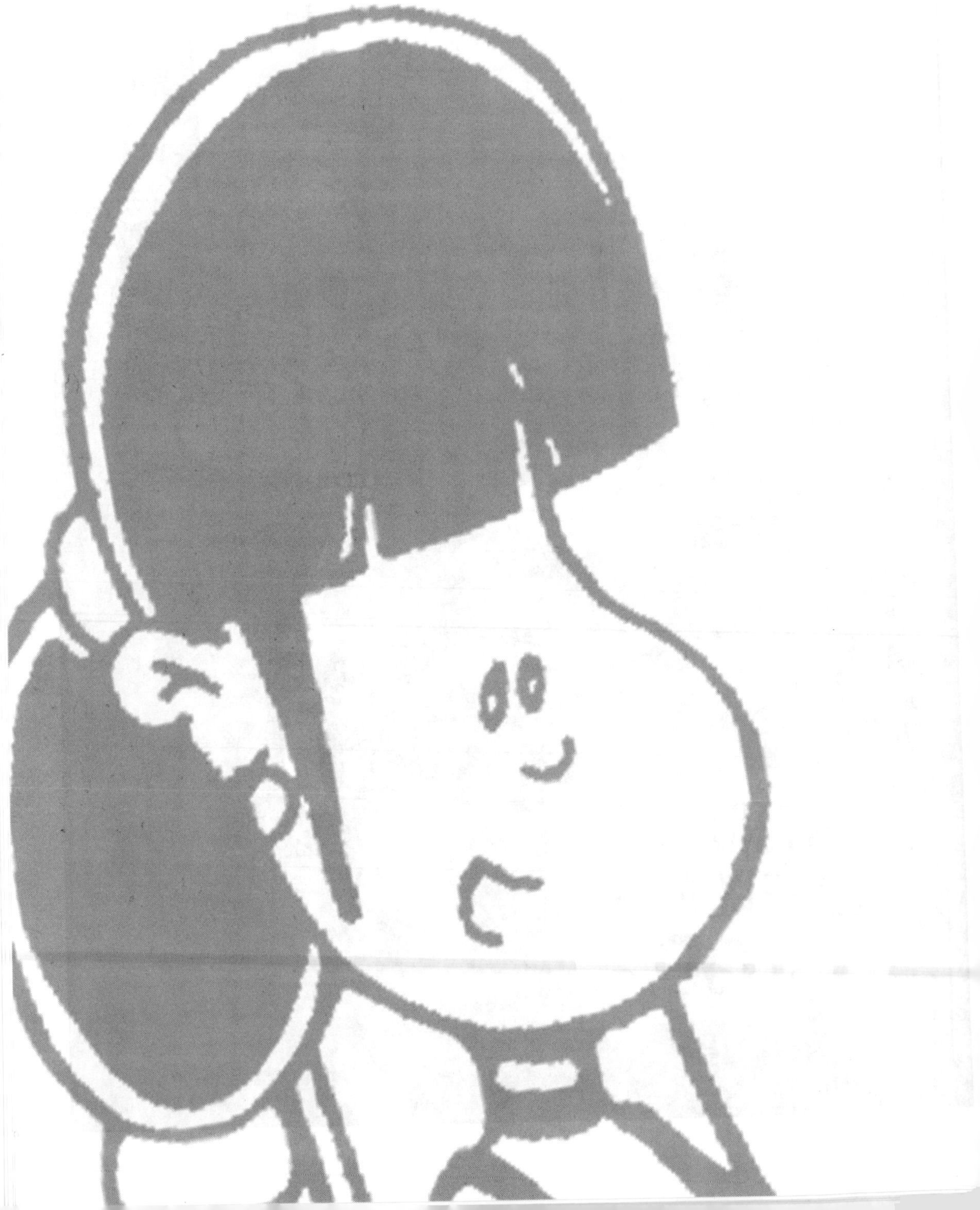

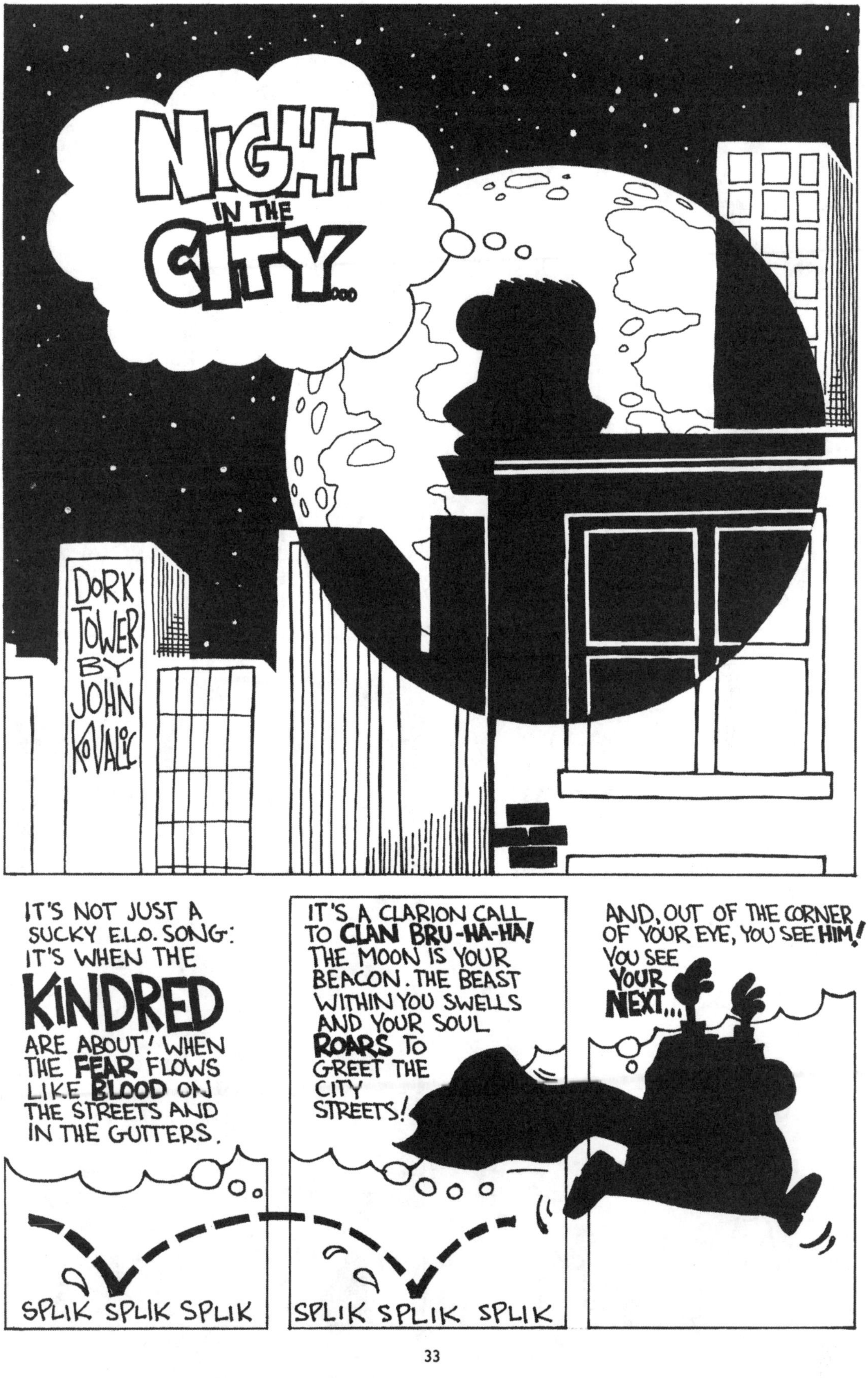
NIGHT IN THE CITY...
DORK TOWER BY JOHN KOVALIC
IT'S NOT JUST A SUCKY E.L.O. SONG: IT'S WHEN THE KINDRED ARE ABOUT! WHEN THE FEAR FLOWS LIKE BLOOD ON THE STREETS AND IN THE GUTTERS.
SPLIK SPLIK SPLIK
IT'S A CLARION CALL TO CLAN BRU-HA-HA! THE MOON IS YOUR BEACON. THE BEAST WITHIN YOU SWELLS AND YOUR SOUL ROARS TO GREET THE CITY STREETS!
SPLIK SPLIK SPLIK
AND, OUT OF THE CORNER OF YOUR EYE, YOU SEE HIM! YOU SEE YOUR NEXT...

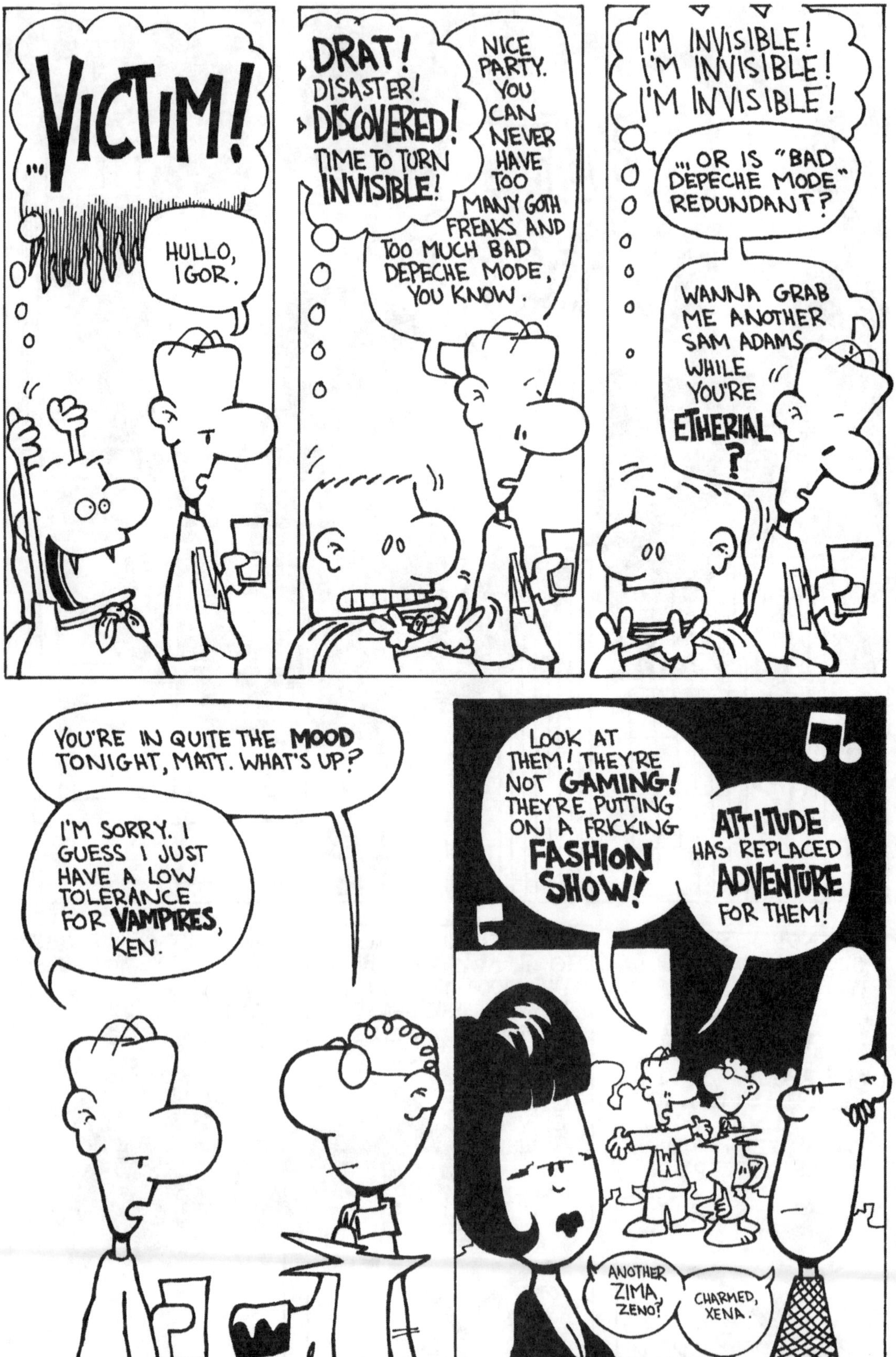
...VICTIM!
HULLO, IGOR.
DRAT! DISASTER! DISCOVERED! TIME TO TURN INVISIBLE!
NICE PARTY. YOU CAN NEVER HAVE TOO MANY GOTH FREAKS AND TOO MUCH BAD DEPECHE MODE, YOU KNOW.
I'M INVISIBLE! I'M INVISIBLE! I'M INVISIBLE!
...OR IS "BAD DEPECHE MODE" REDUNDANT?
WANNA GRAB ME ANOTHER SAM ADAMS WHILE YOU'RE ETHERIAL?
YOU'RE IN QUITE THE MOOD TONIGHT, MATT. WHAT'S UP?
I'M SORRY. I GUESS I JUST HAVE A LOW TOLERANCE FOR VAMPIRES, KEN.
LOOK AT THEM! THEY'RE NOT GAMING! THEY'RE PUTTING ON A FRICKING FASHION SHOW!
ATTITUDE HAS REPLACED ADVENTURE FOR THEM!
ANOTHER ZIMA, ZENO?
CHARMED, XENA.

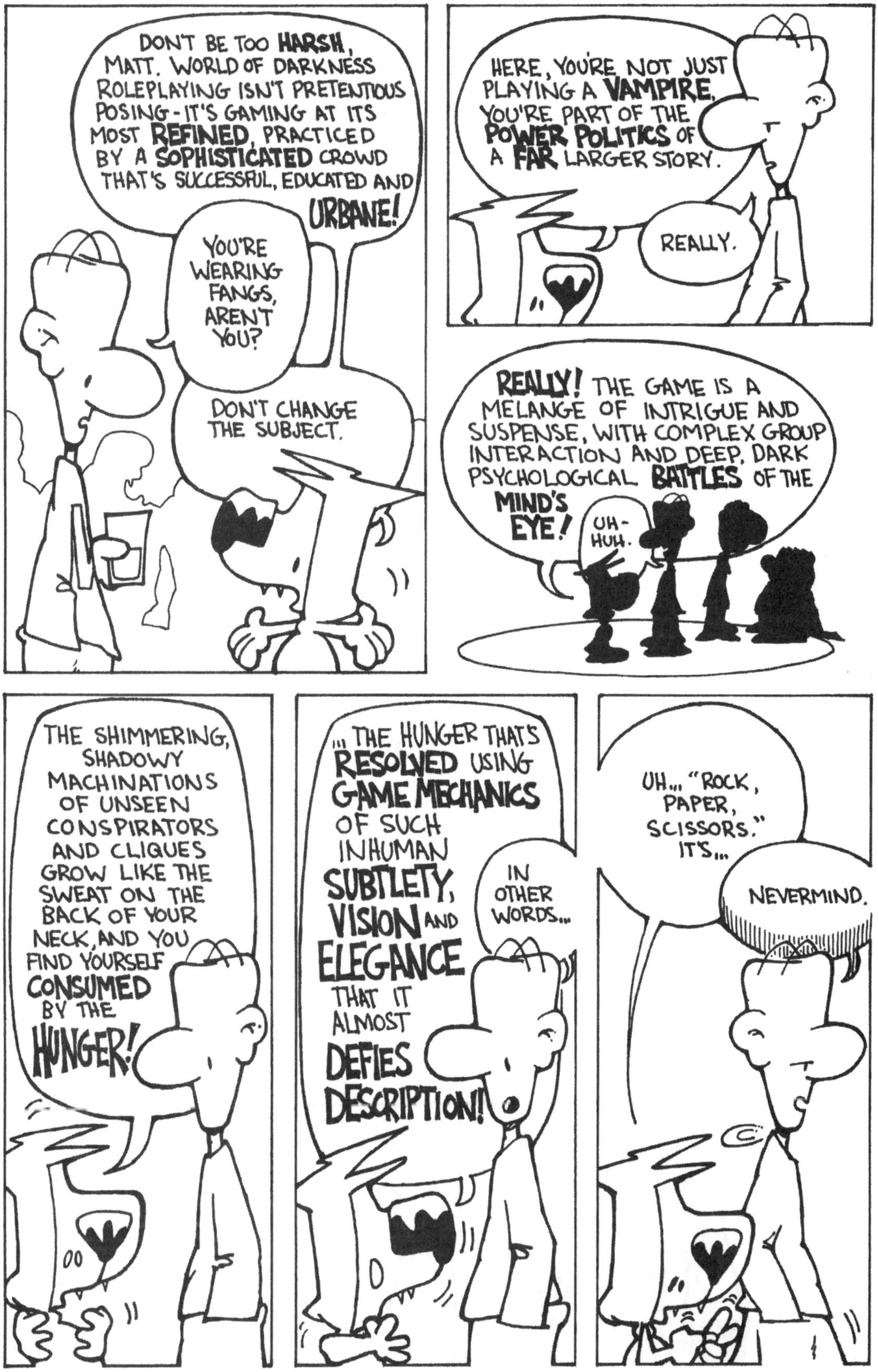
DON'T BE TOO HARSH, MATT. WORLD OF DARKNESS ROLEPLAYING ISN'T PRETENTIOUS POSING - IT'S GAMING AT ITS MOST REFINED, PRACTICED BY A SOPHISTICATED CROWD THAT'S SUCCESSFUL, EDUCATED AND URBANE!
YOU'RE WEARING FANGS, AREN'T YOU?
DON'T CHANGE THE SUBJECT.
HERE, YOU'RE NOT JUST PLAYING A VAMPIRE, YOU'RE PART OF THE POWER POLITICS OF A FAR LARGER STORY.
REALLY.
REALLY! THE GAME IS A MELANGE OF INTRIGUE AND SUSPENSE, WITH COMPLEX GROUP INTERACTION AND DEEP, DARK PSYCHOLOGICAL BATTLES OF THE MIND'S EYE!
UH-HUH.
THE SHIMMERING, SHADOWY MACHINATIONS OF UNSEEN CONSPIRATORS AND CLIQUES GROW LIKE THE SWEAT ON THE BACK OF YOUR NECK, AND YOU FIND YOURSELF CONSUMED BY THE HUNGER!
... THE HUNGER THAT'S RESOLVED USING GAME MECHANICS OF SUCH INHUMAN SUBTLETY, VISION AND ELEGANCE THAT IT ALMOST DEFIES DESCRIPTION!
IN OTHER WORDS...
UH... "ROCK, PAPER, SCISSORS." IT'S...
NEVERMIND.

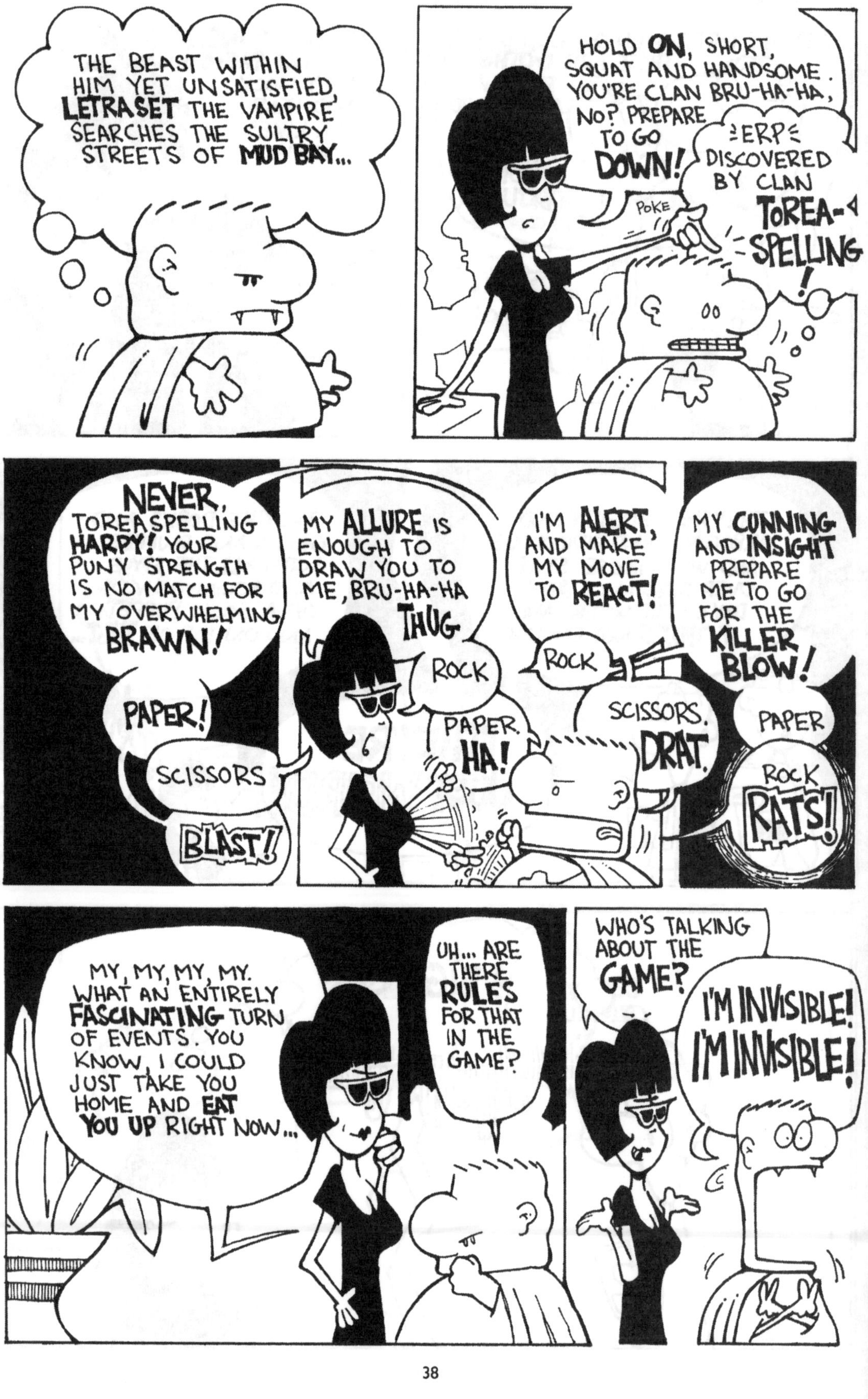
THE BEAST WITHIN HIM YET UNSATISFIED, LETRASET THE VAMPIRE SEARCHES THE SULTRY STREETS OF MUD BAY...
HOLD ON, SHORT, SQUAT AND HANDSOME. YOU'RE CLAN BRU-HA-HA, NO? PREPARE TO GO DOWN!
POKE
ERP DISCOVERED BY CLAN TOREA-SPELLING!
NEVER, TOREASPELLING HARPY! YOUR PUNY STRENGTH IS NO MATCH FOR MY OVERWHELMING BRAWN!
PAPER!
SCISSORS
BLAST!
MY ALLURE IS ENOUGH TO DRAW YOU TO ME, BRU-HA-HA THUG
ROCK
PAPER. HA!
I'M ALERT, AND MAKE MY MOVE TO REACT!
ROCK
SCISSORS. DRAT.
MY CUNNING AND INSIGHT PREPARE ME TO GO FOR THE KILLER BLOW!
PAPER
ROCK
RATS!
MY, MY, MY, MY. WHAT AN ENTIRELY FASCINATING TURN OF EVENTS. YOU KNOW, I COULD JUST TAKE YOU HOME AND EAT YOU UP RIGHT NOW...
UH... ARE THERE RULES FOR THAT IN THE GAME?
WHO'S TALKING ABOUT THE GAME?
I'M INVISIBLE! I'M INVISIBLE!

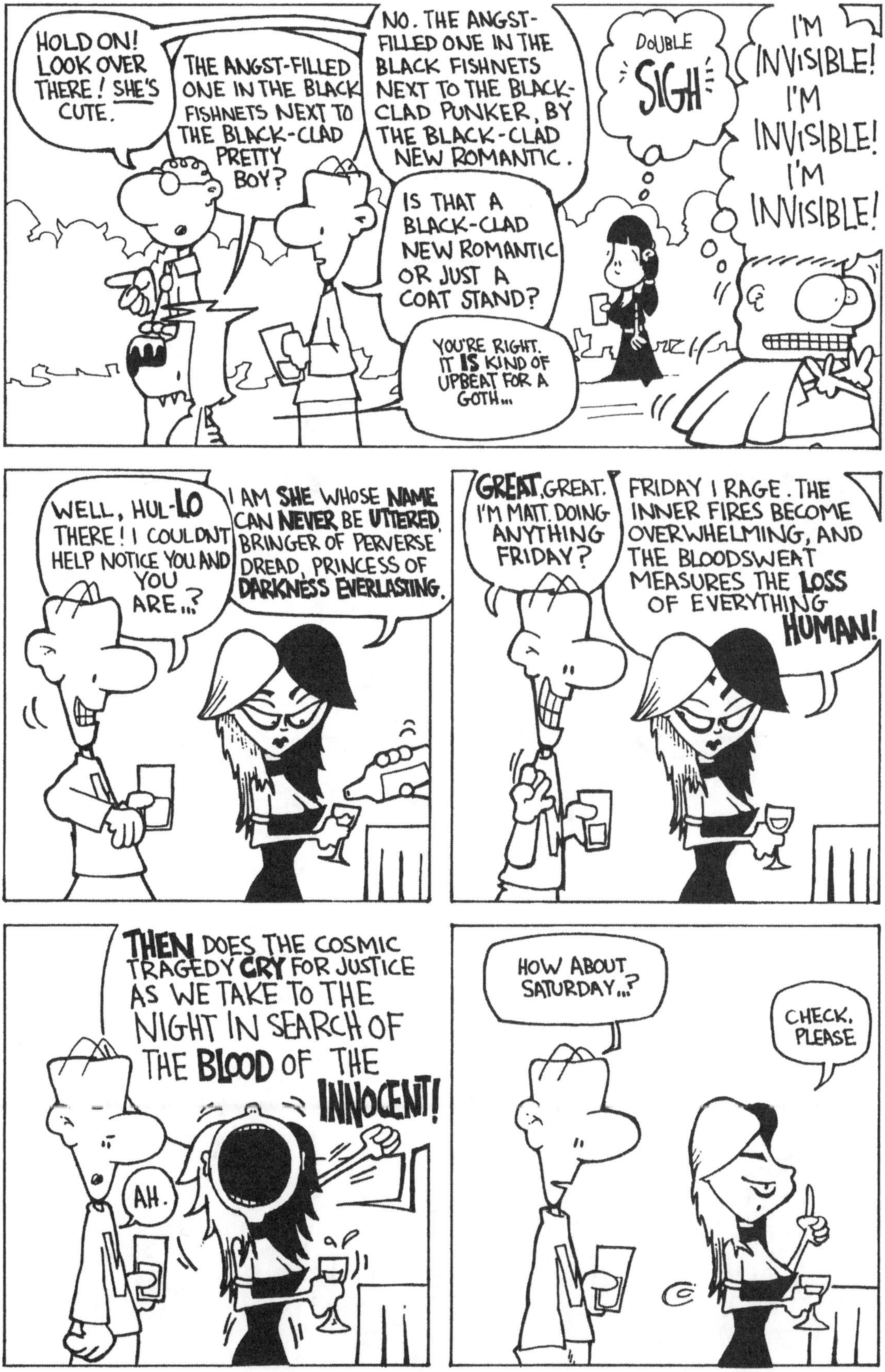
HOLD ON! LOOK OVER THERE! SHE'S CUTE.
THE ANGST-FILLED ONE IN THE BLACK FISHNETS NEXT TO THE BLACK-CLAD PRETTY BOY?
NO. THE ANGST-FILLED ONE IN THE BLACK FISHNETS NEXT TO THE BLACK-CLAD PUNKER, BY THE BLACK-CLAD NEW ROMANTIC.
IS THAT A BLACK-CLAD NEW ROMANTIC OR JUST A COAT STAND?
YOU'RE RIGHT. IT IS KIND OF UPBEAT FOR A GOTH...
DOUBLE SIGH
I'M INVISIBLE! I'M INVISIBLE! I'M INVISIBLE!
WELL, HUL-LO THERE! I COULDN'T HELP NOTICE YOU. AND YOU ARE...?
I AM SHE WHOSE NAME CAN NEVER BE UTTERED, BRINGER OF PERVERSE DREAD, PRINCESS OF DARKNESS EVERLASTING.
GREAT, GREAT. I'M MATT. DOING ANYTHING FRIDAY?
FRIDAY I RAGE. THE INNER FIRES BECOME OVERWHELMING, AND THE BLOODSWEAT MEASURES THE LOSS OF EVERYTHING HUMAN!
THEN DOES THE COSMIC TRAGEDY CRY FOR JUSTICE AS WE TAKE TO THE NIGHT IN SEARCH OF THE BLOOD OF THE INNOCENT!
AH.
HOW ABOUT SATURDAY...?
CHECK, PLEASE

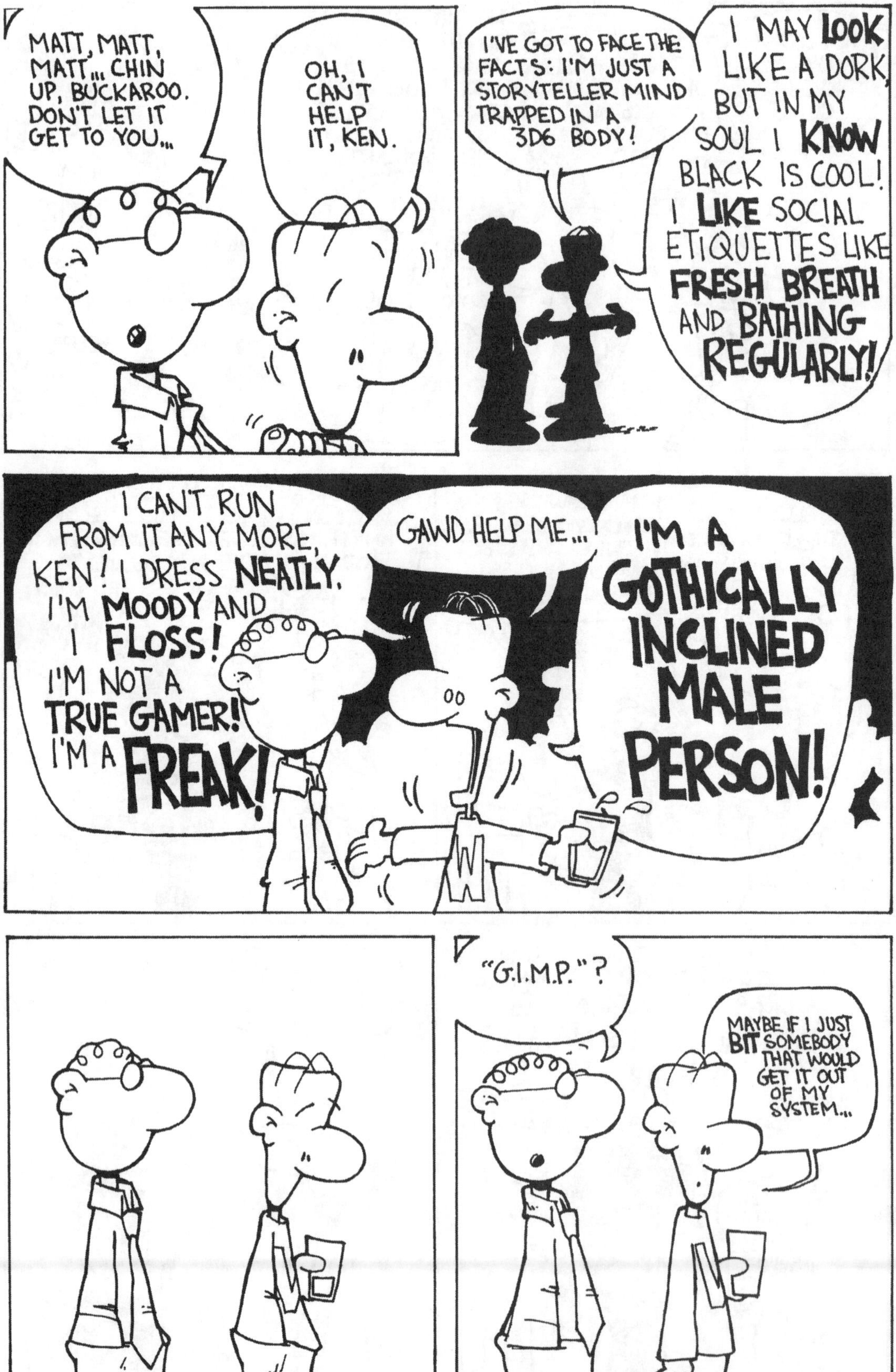

MATT, MATT, MATT... CHIN UP, BUCKAROO. DON'T LET IT GET TO YOU...
OH, I CAN'T HELP IT, KEN.
I'VE GOT TO FACE THE FACTS: I'M JUST A STORYTELLER MIND TRAPPED IN A 3D6 BODY!
I MAY **LOOK** LIKE A DORK, BUT IN MY SOUL I **KNOW** BLACK IS COOL! I **LIKE** SOCIAL ETIQUETTES LIKE **FRESH BREATH** AND **BATHING REGULARLY!**
I CAN'T RUN FROM IT ANY MORE, KEN! I DRESS **NEATLY**. I'M **MOODY** AND I **FLOSS!** I'M NOT A **TRUE GAMER!** I'M A **FREAK!**
GAWD HELP ME...
I'M A GOTHICALLY INCLINED MALE PERSON!
"G.I.M.P."?
MAYBE IF I JUST **BIT** SOMEBODY THAT WOULD GET IT OUT OF MY SYSTEM...

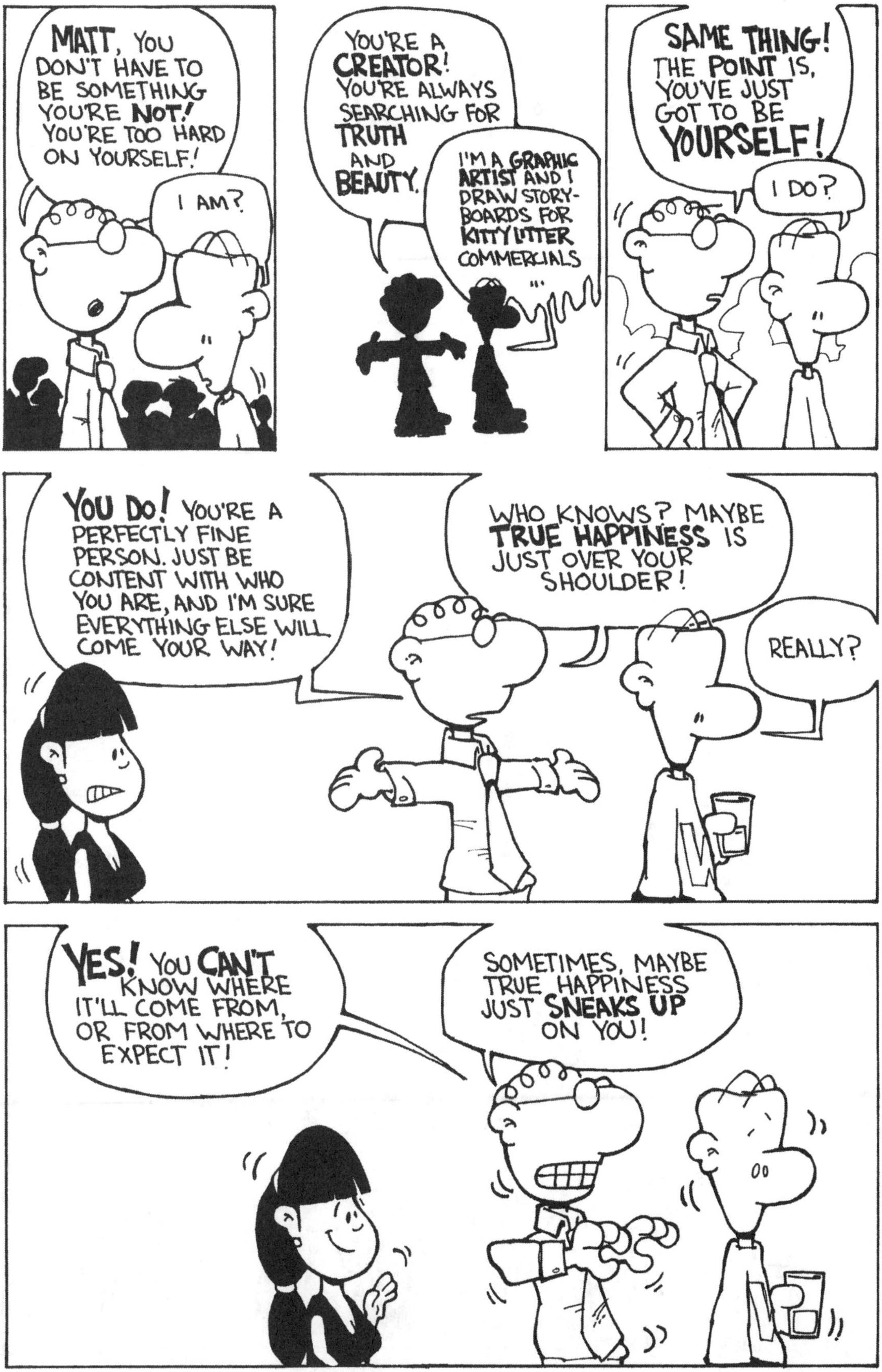
MATT, YOU DON'T HAVE TO BE SOMETHING YOU'RE NOT! YOU'RE TOO HARD ON YOURSELF!
I AM?
YOU'RE A CREATOR! YOU'RE ALWAYS SEARCHING FOR TRUTH AND BEAUTY.
I'M A GRAPHIC ARTIST AND I DRAW STORY-BOARDS FOR KITTY LITTER COMMERCIALS ...
SAME THING! THE POINT IS, YOU'VE JUST GOT TO BE YOURSELF!
I DO?
YOU DO! YOU'RE A PERFECTLY FINE PERSON. JUST BE CONTENT WITH WHO YOU ARE, AND I'M SURE EVERYTHING ELSE WILL COME YOUR WAY!
WHO KNOWS? MAYBE TRUE HAPPINESS IS JUST OVER YOUR SHOULDER!
REALLY?
YES! YOU CAN'T KNOW WHERE IT'LL COME FROM, OR FROM WHERE TO EXPECT IT!
SOMETIMES, MAYBE TRUE HAPPINESS JUST SNEAKS UP ON YOU!

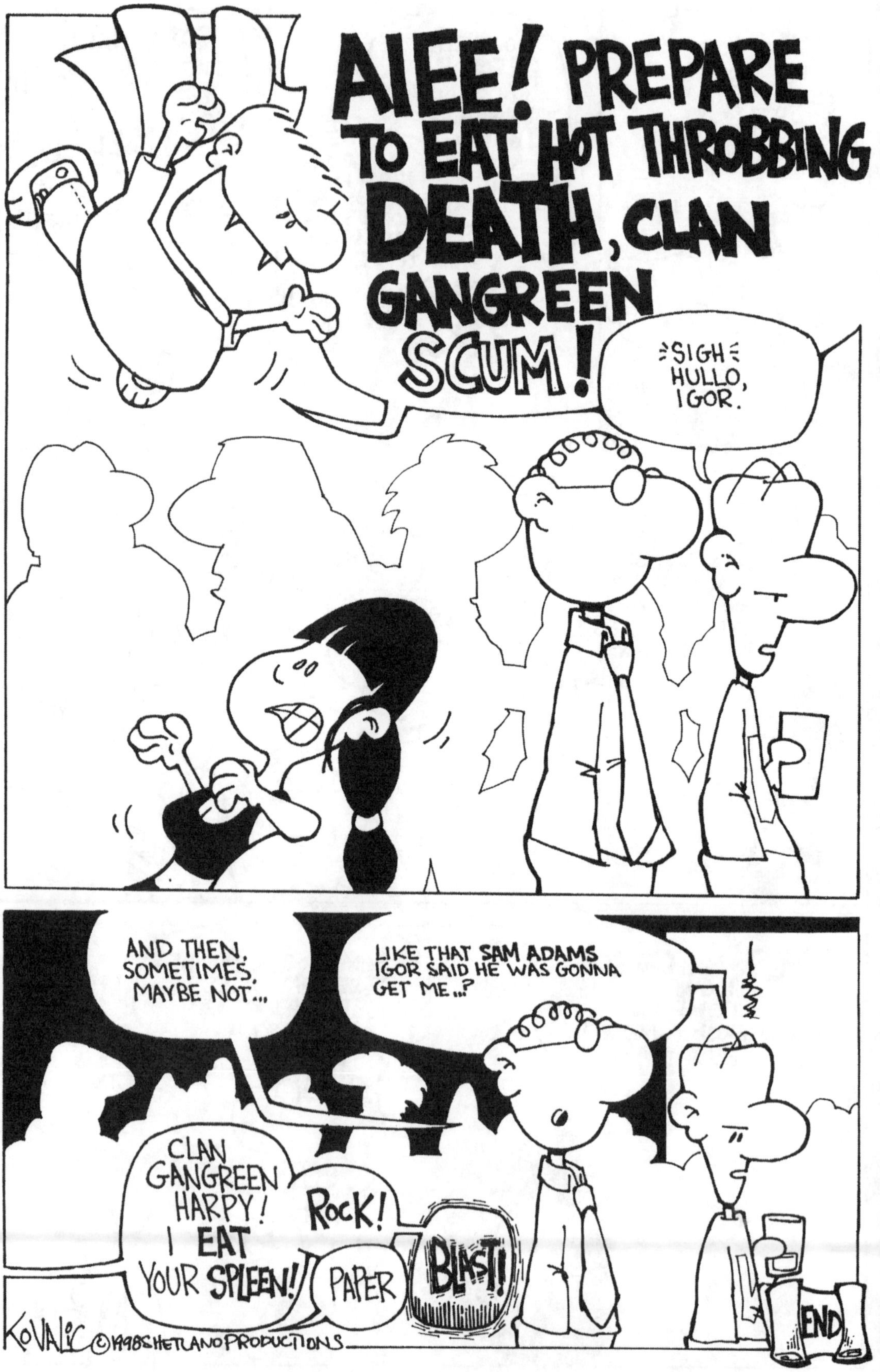
AIEE! PREPARE TO EAT HOT THROBBING DEATH, CLAN GANGREEN SCUM!
SIGH HULLO, IGOR.
AND THEN, SOMETIMES, MAYBE NOT...
LIKE THAT SAM ADAMS IGOR SAID HE WAS GONNA GET ME..?
CLAN GANGREEN HARPY! I EAT YOUR SPLEEN!
ROCK!
PAPER
BLAST!
END
KOVALIC ©1998 SHETLAND PRODUCTIONS

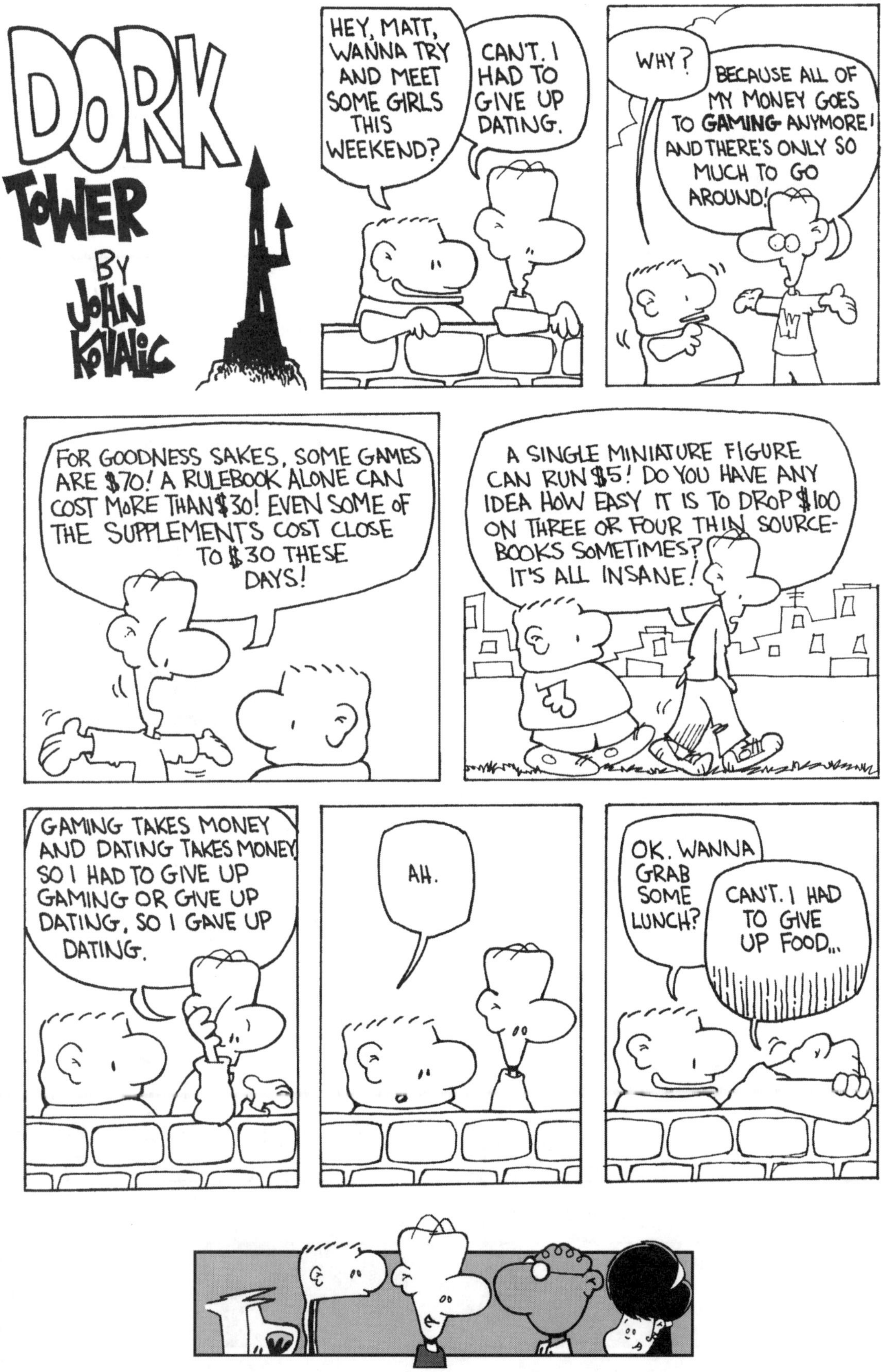
DORK TOWER
BY JOHN KOVALIC
HEY, MATT, WANNA TRY AND MEET SOME GIRLS THIS WEEKEND?
CAN'T. I HAD TO GIVE UP DATING.
WHY?
BECAUSE ALL OF MY MONEY GOES TO GAMING ANYMORE! AND THERE'S ONLY SO MUCH TO GO AROUND!
FOR GOODNESS SAKES, SOME GAMES ARE $70! A RULEBOOK ALONE CAN COST MORE THAN $30! EVEN SOME OF THE SUPPLEMENTS COST CLOSE TO $30 THESE DAYS!
A SINGLE MINIATURE FIGURE CAN RUN $5! DO YOU HAVE ANY IDEA HOW EASY IT IS TO DROP $100 ON THREE OR FOUR THIN SOURCE-BOOKS SOMETIMES? IT'S ALL INSANE!
GAMING TAKES MONEY AND DATING TAKES MONEY SO I HAD TO GIVE UP GAMING OR GIVE UP DATING, SO I GAVE UP DATING.
AH.
OK. WANNA GRAB SOME LUNCH?
CAN'T. I HAD TO GIVE UP FOOD...

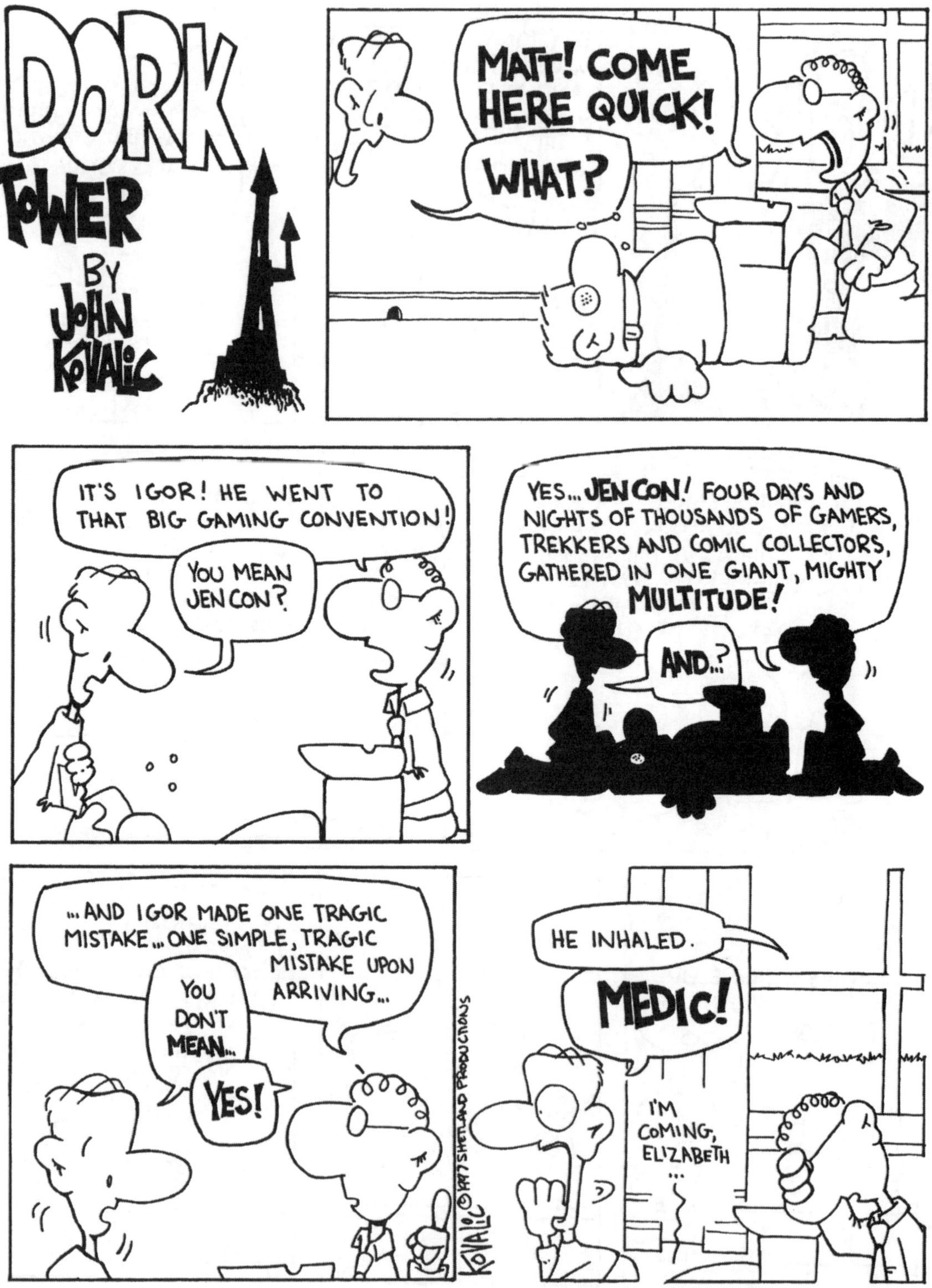
DORK TOWER
BY JOHN KOVALIC
MATT! COME HERE QUICK!
WHAT?
IT'S IGOR! HE WENT TO THAT BIG GAMING CONVENTION!
YOU MEAN JEN CON?
YES... JEN CON! FOUR DAYS AND NIGHTS OF THOUSANDS OF GAMERS, TREKKERS AND COMIC COLLECTORS, GATHERED IN ONE GIANT, MIGHTY MULTITUDE!
AND..?
...AND IGOR MADE ONE TRAGIC MISTAKE... ONE SIMPLE, TRAGIC MISTAKE UPON ARRIVING...
YOU DON'T MEAN...
YES!
KOVALIC ©1997 SHETLAND PRODUCTIONS
HE INHALED.
MEDIC!
I'M COMING, ELIZABETH ...

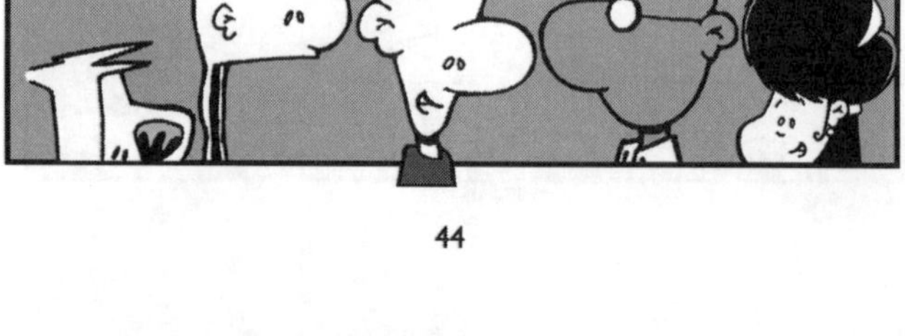

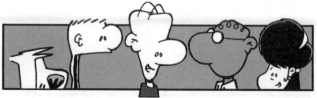

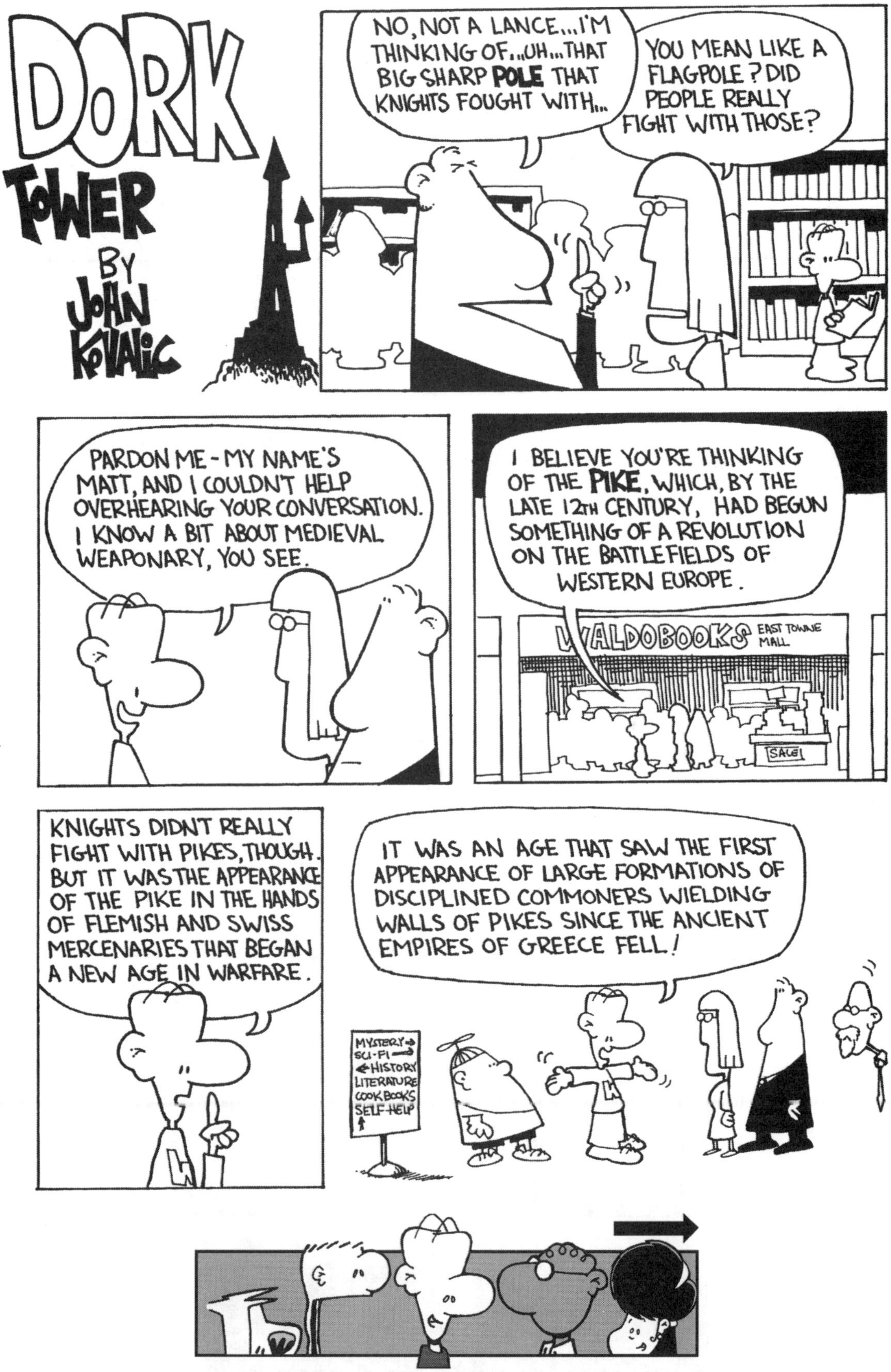
DORK TOWER
BY JOHN KOVALIC
NO, NOT A LANCE... I'M THINKING OF... UH... THAT BIG SHARP POLE THAT KNIGHTS FOUGHT WITH...
YOU MEAN LIKE A FLAGPOLE? DID PEOPLE REALLY FIGHT WITH THOSE?
PARDON ME - MY NAME'S MATT, AND I COULDN'T HELP OVERHEARING YOUR CONVERSATION. I KNOW A BIT ABOUT MEDIEVAL WEAPONARY, YOU SEE.
I BELIEVE YOU'RE THINKING OF THE PIKE, WHICH, BY THE LATE 12TH CENTURY, HAD BEGUN SOMETHING OF A REVOLUTION ON THE BATTLEFIELDS OF WESTERN EUROPE.
WALDOBOOKS
EAST TOWNE MALL
SALE
KNIGHTS DIDN'T REALLY FIGHT WITH PIKES, THOUGH. BUT IT WAS THE APPEARANCE OF THE PIKE IN THE HANDS OF FLEMISH AND SWISS MERCENARIES THAT BEGAN A NEW AGE IN WARFARE.
IT WAS AN AGE THAT SAW THE FIRST APPEARANCE OF LARGE FORMATIONS OF DISCIPLINED COMMONERS WIELDING WALLS OF PIKES SINCE THE ANCIENT EMPIRES OF GREECE FELL!
MYSTERY
SCI-FI
HISTORY
LITERATURE
COOKBOOKS
SELF-HELP

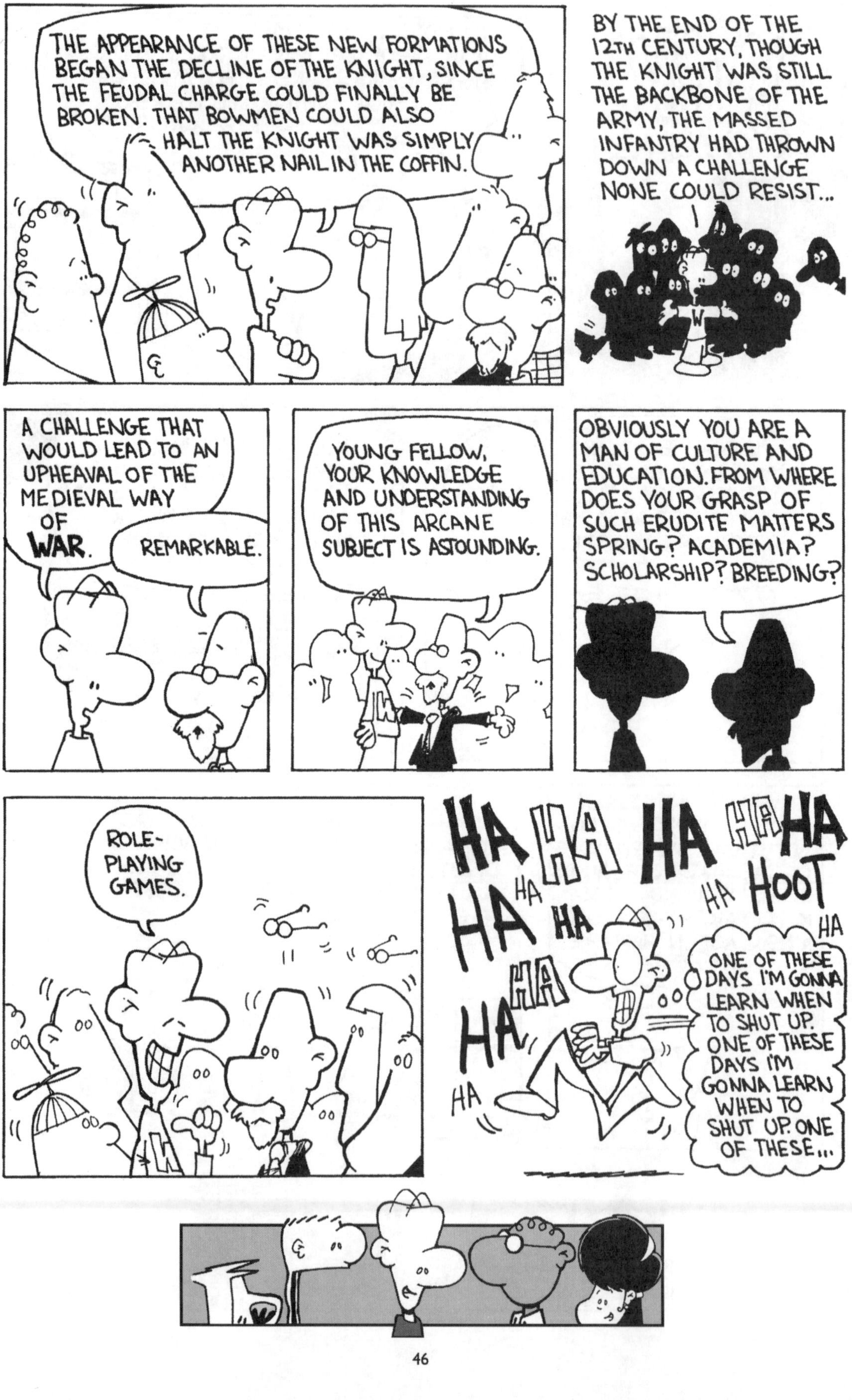
THE APPEARANCE OF THESE NEW FORMATIONS BEGAN THE DECLINE OF THE KNIGHT, SINCE THE FEUDAL CHARGE COULD FINALLY BE BROKEN. THAT BOWMEN COULD ALSO HALT THE KNIGHT WAS SIMPLY ANOTHER NAIL IN THE COFFIN.
BY THE END OF THE 12TH CENTURY, THOUGH THE KNIGHT WAS STILL THE BACKBONE OF THE ARMY, THE MASSED INFANTRY HAD THROWN DOWN A CHALLENGE NONE COULD RESIST...
W
A CHALLENGE THAT WOULD LEAD TO AN UPHEAVAL OF THE MEDIEVAL WAY OF WAR.
REMARKABLE.
YOUNG FELLOW, YOUR KNOWLEDGE AND UNDERSTANDING OF THIS ARCANE SUBJECT IS ASTOUNDING.
OBVIOUSLY YOU ARE A MAN OF CULTURE AND EDUCATION. FROM WHERE DOES YOUR GRASP OF SUCH ERUDITE MATTERS SPRING? ACADEMIA? SCHOLARSHIP? BREEDING?
ROLE-PLAYING GAMES.
HA HA HA HA HA HA
HA HA HA HA HOOT
HA
HA HA
HA
ONE OF THESE DAYS I'M GONNA LEARN WHEN TO SHUT UP. ONE OF THESE DAYS I'M GONNA LEARN WHEN TO SHUT UP. ONE OF THESE...

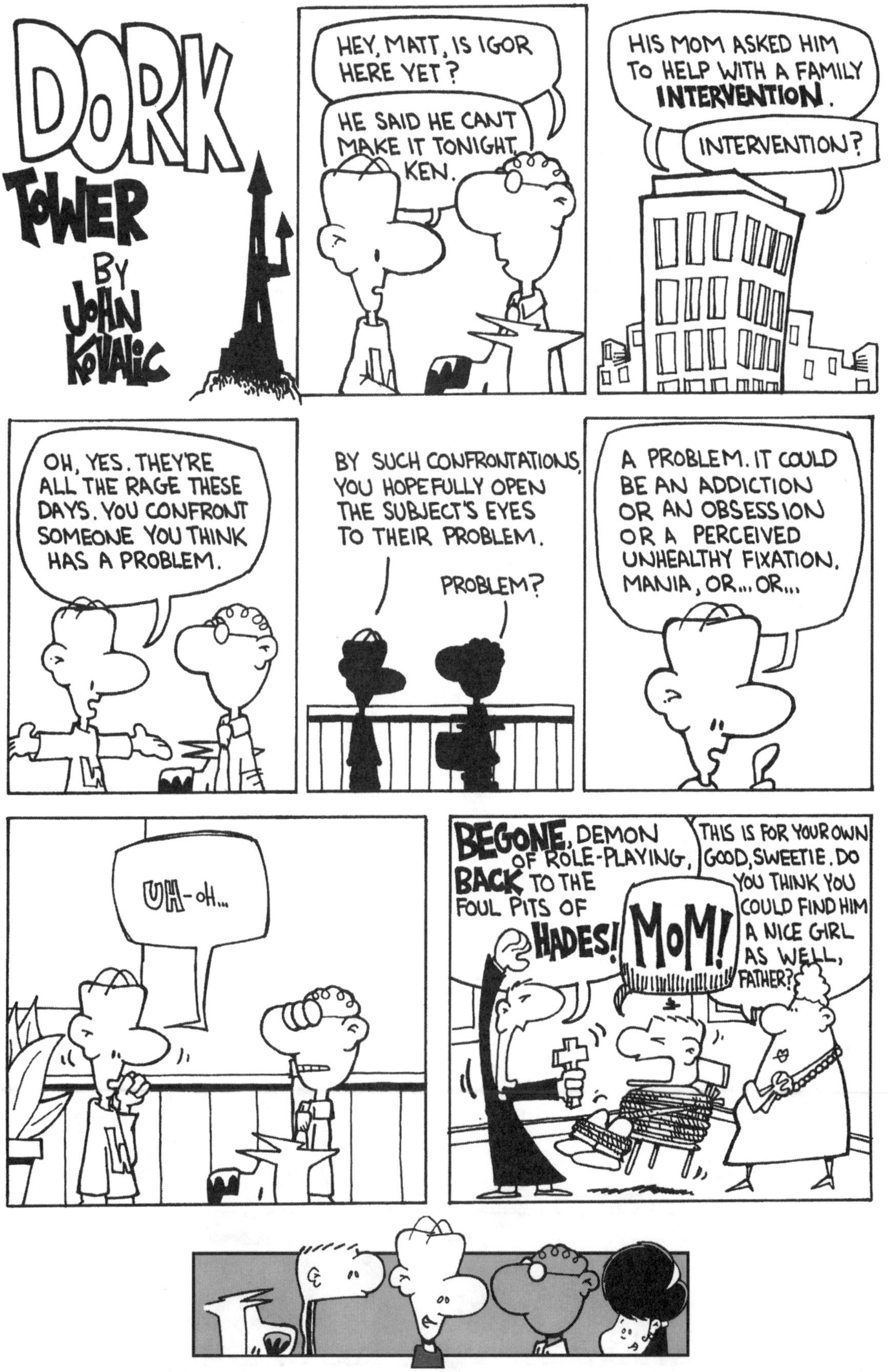
DORK TOWER
BY JOHN KOVALIC
HEY, MATT, IS IGOR HERE YET?
HE SAID HE CAN'T MAKE IT TONIGHT, KEN.
HIS MOM ASKED HIM TO HELP WITH A FAMILY INTERVENTION.
INTERVENTION?
OH, YES. THEY'RE ALL THE RAGE THESE DAYS. YOU CONFRONT SOMEONE YOU THINK HAS A PROBLEM.
BY SUCH CONFRONTATIONS, YOU HOPEFULLY OPEN THE SUBJECT'S EYES TO THEIR PROBLEM.
PROBLEM?
A PROBLEM. IT COULD BE AN ADDICTION OR AN OBSESSION OR A PERCEIVED UNHEALTHY FIXATION. MANIA, OR... OR...
UH-OH...
BEGONE, DEMON OF ROLE-PLAYING, BACK TO THE FOUL PITS OF HADES!
MOM!
THIS IS FOR YOUR OWN GOOD, SWEETIE. DO YOU THINK YOU COULD FIND HIM A NICE GIRL AS WELL, FATHER?

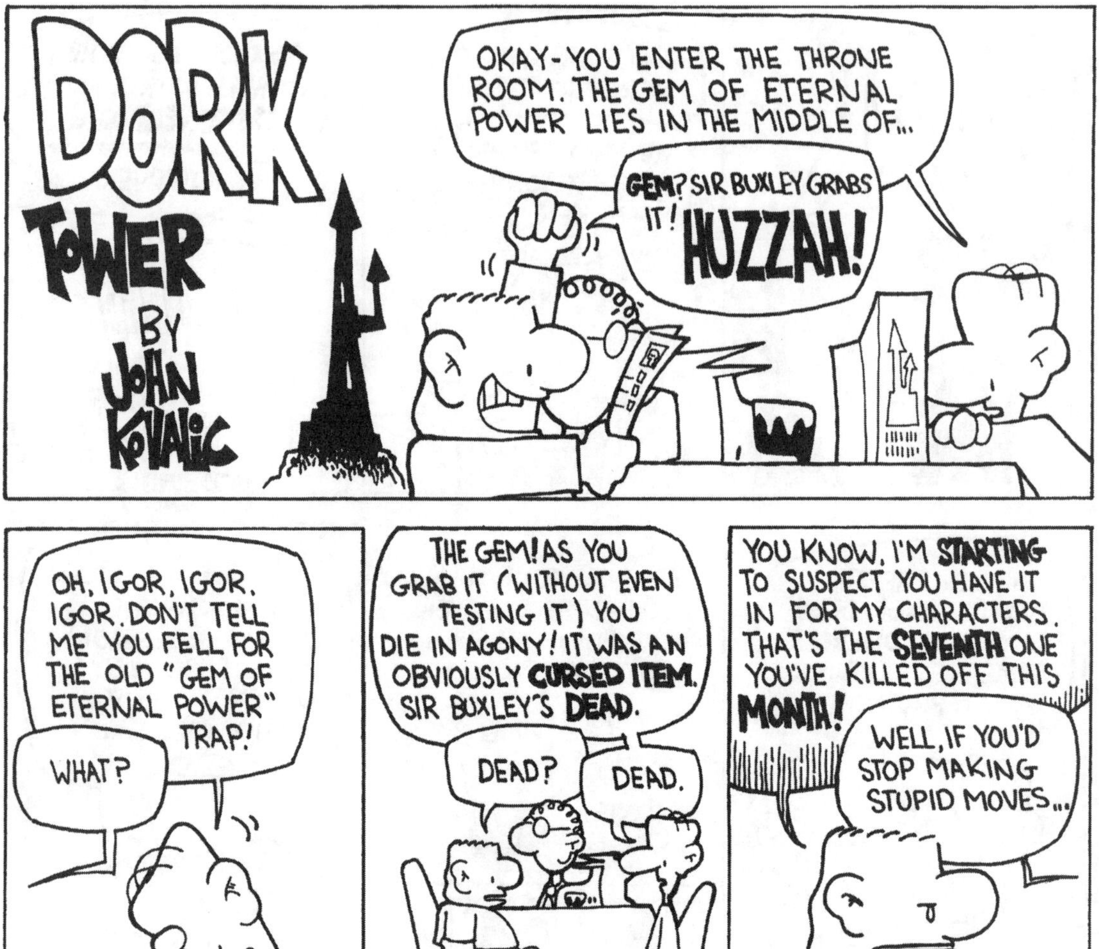
DORK TOWER
BY JOHN KOVALIC
OKAY- YOU ENTER THE THRONE ROOM. THE GEM OF ETERNAL POWER LIES IN THE MIDDLE OF...
GEM? SIR BUXLEY GRABS IT! HUZZAH!
THE GEM! AS YOU GRAB IT (WITHOUT EVEN TESTING IT) YOU DIE IN AGONY! IT WAS AN OBVIOUSLY CURSED ITEM. SIR BUXLEY'S DEAD.
DEAD?
DEAD.
OH, IGOR, IGOR. IGOR. DON'T TELL ME YOU FELL FOR THE OLD "GEM OF ETERNAL POWER" TRAP!
WHAT?
YOU KNOW, I'M STARTING TO SUSPECT YOU HAVE IT IN FOR MY CHARACTERS. THAT'S THE SEVENTH ONE YOU'VE KILLED OFF THIS MONTH!
WELL, IF YOU'D STOP MAKING STUPID MOVES...
"STUPID"?
OF COURSE.
IGOR, DO YOU REMEMBER SIR BILLINGSLY?
YOU SEALED HIS FATE WHEN HE ATTACKED AN ORC GARRISON SINGLE-HANDEDLY, IN HIS UNDERWEAR!

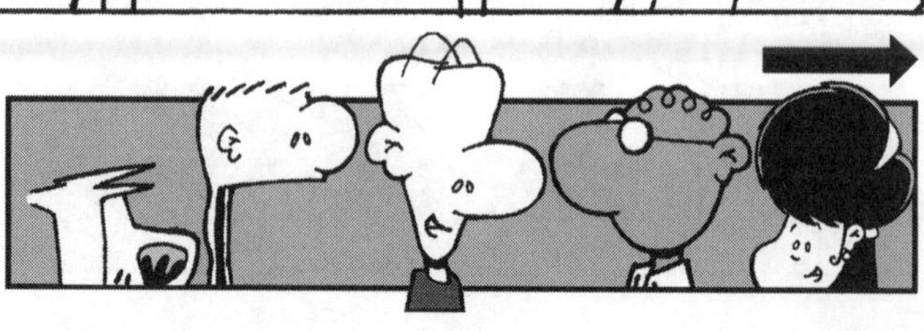

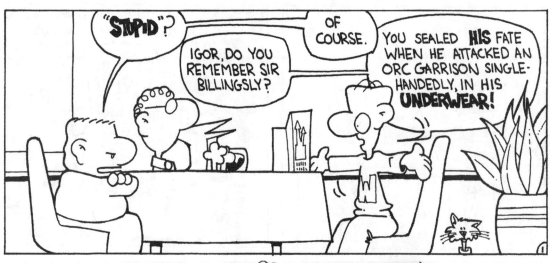

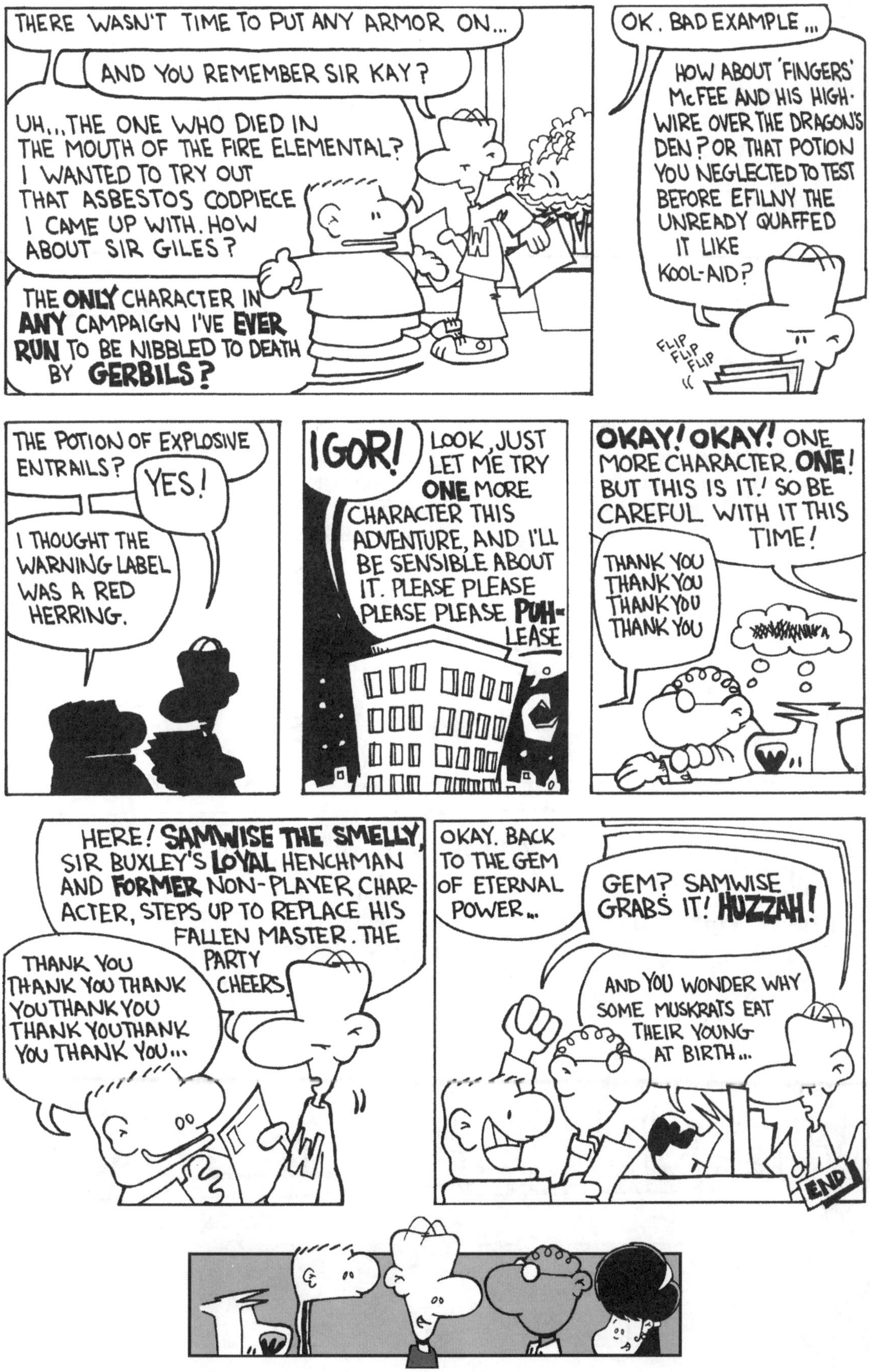
THERE WASN'T TIME TO PUT ANY ARMOR ON...
AND YOU REMEMBER SIR KAY?
UH...THE ONE WHO DIED IN THE MOUTH OF THE FIRE ELEMENTAL? I WANTED TO TRY OUT THAT ASBESTOS CODPIECE I CAME UP WITH. HOW ABOUT SIR GILES?
THE ONLY CHARACTER IN ANY CAMPAIGN I'VE EVER RUN TO BE NIBBLED TO DEATH BY GERBILS?
OK. BAD EXAMPLE...
HOW ABOUT 'FINGERS' McFEE AND HIS HIGH-WIRE OVER THE DRAGON'S DEN? OR THAT POTION YOU NEGLECTED TO TEST BEFORE EFILNY THE UNREADY QUAFFED IT LIKE KOOL-AID?
FLIP FLIP FLIP
THE POTION OF EXPLOSIVE ENTRAILS?
YES!
I THOUGHT THE WARNING LABEL WAS A RED HERRING.
IGOR!
LOOK, JUST LET ME TRY ONE MORE CHARACTER THIS ADVENTURE, AND I'LL BE SENSIBLE ABOUT IT. PLEASE PLEASE PLEASE PLEASE PUH-LEASE
OKAY! OKAY! ONE MORE CHARACTER. ONE! BUT THIS IS IT! SO BE CAREFUL WITH IT THIS TIME!
THANK YOU THANK YOU THANK YOU THANK YOU
HERE! SAMWISE THE SMELLY, SIR BUXLEY'S LOYAL HENCHMAN AND FORMER NON-PLAYER CHARACTER, STEPS UP TO REPLACE HIS FALLEN MASTER. THE PARTY CHEERS.
THANK YOU THANK YOU THANK YOU THANK YOU THANK YOU THANK YOU THANK YOU...
OKAY. BACK TO THE GEM OF ETERNAL POWER...
GEM? SAMWISE GRABS IT! HUZZAH!
AND YOU WONDER WHY SOME MUSKRATS EAT THEIR YOUNG AT BIRTH...
END

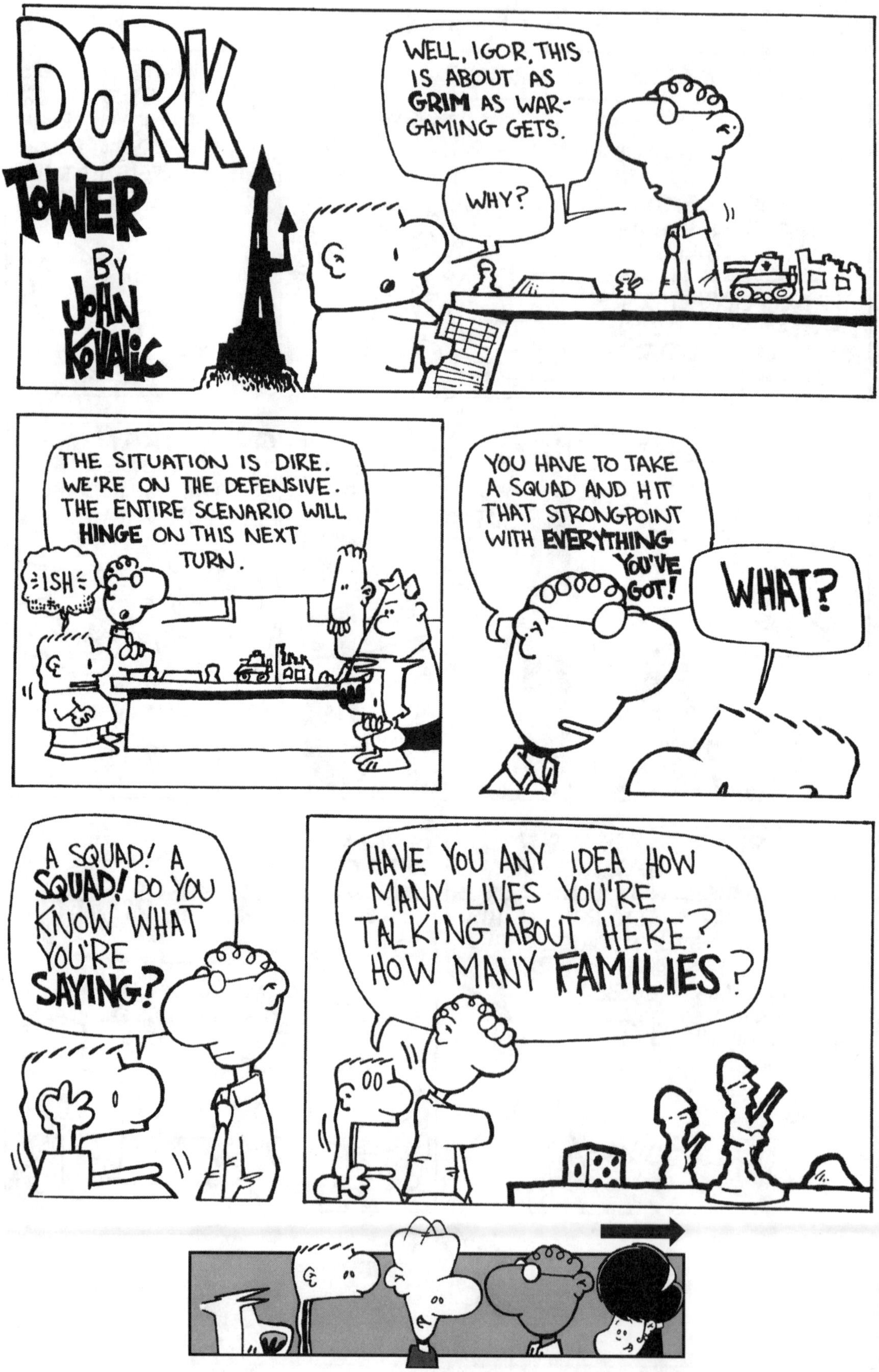
DORK TOWER
BY JOHN KOVALIC
WELL, IGOR, THIS IS ABOUT AS GRIM AS WAR-GAMING GETS.
WHY?
THE SITUATION IS DIRE. WE'RE ON THE DEFENSIVE. THE ENTIRE SCENARIO WILL HINGE ON THIS NEXT TURN.
ISH
YOU HAVE TO TAKE A SQUAD AND HIT THAT STRONGPOINT WITH EVERYTHING YOU'VE GOT!
WHAT?
A SQUAD! A SQUAD! DO YOU KNOW WHAT YOU'RE SAYING?
HAVE YOU ANY IDEA HOW MANY LIVES YOU'RE TALKING ABOUT HERE? HOW MANY FAMILIES?

...FAMILIES THAT WILL BE FOREVER **TORN** AS SONS AND FATHERS NEVER RETURN !!!

YES, YOU HEARD RIGHT: **NEVER RETURN!** NEVER SEE WIVES, GIRLFRIENDS OR GRAY-HAIRED MOTHERS **AGAIN!**

THERE **HAS** TO BE A BETTER WAY! WHEN, OH WHEN, WILL THIS MADNESS **END?**

LOOK AT THIS PERSON YOU SO GLIBLY ORDER INTO **HELL'S HEART!** LOOK AT THIS **LIFE!**

THE HORROR! THE HORROR! **THE HORROR!**

ISN'T THERE A **LAW** AGAINST GAMING JUST AFTER SEEING "SAVING PRIVATE RYAN"?

ALL WE ARE SAYYYYING IS GIVE PEACE A CHANCE!

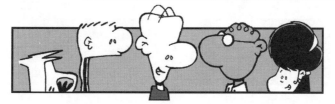

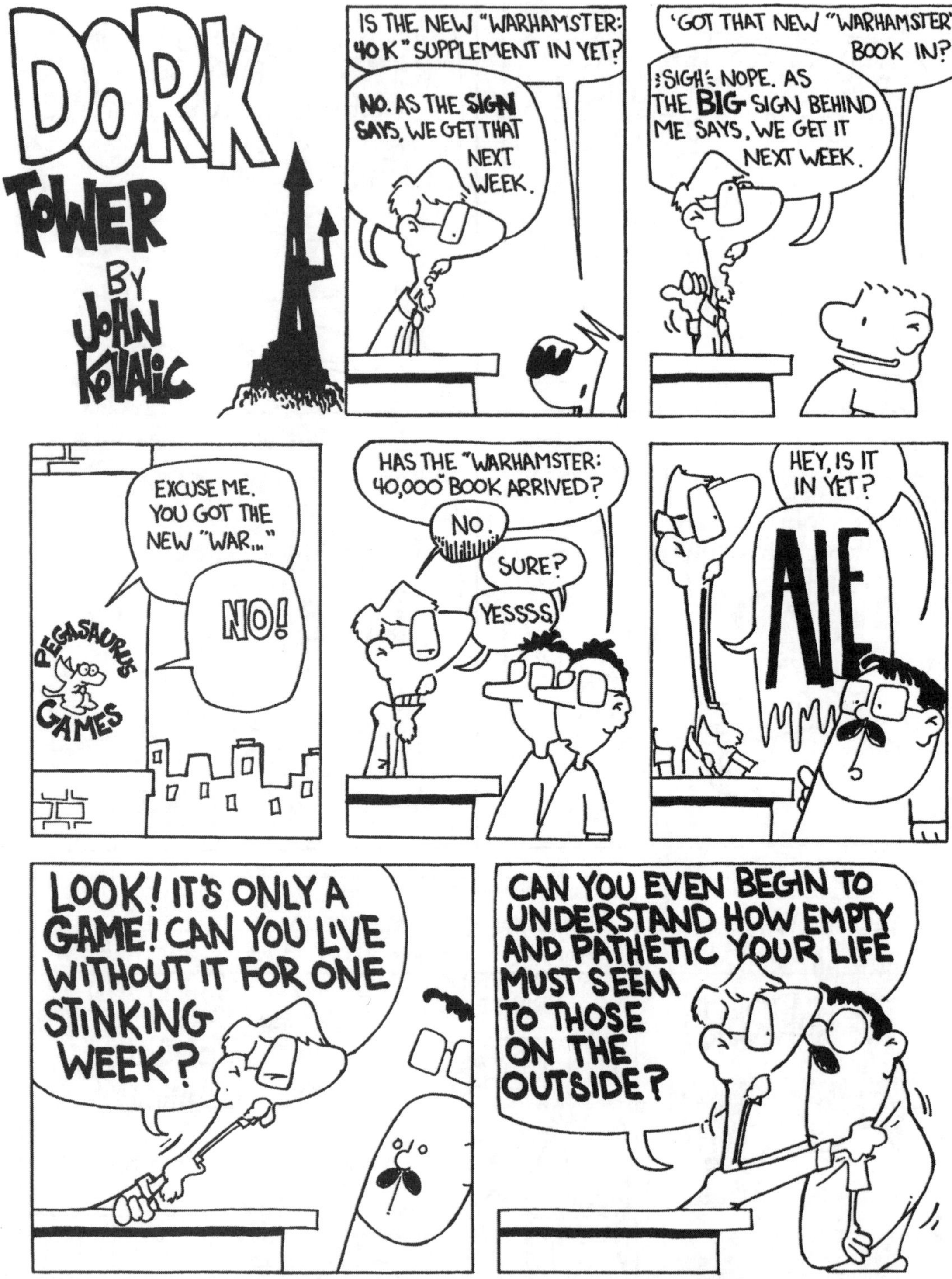
DORK TOWER
BY JOHN KOVALIC
IS THE NEW "WARHAMSTER: 40 K" SUPPLEMENT IN YET?
NO. AS THE SIGN SAYS, WE GET THAT NEXT WEEK.
'GOT THAT NEW "WARHAMSTER" BOOK IN?
:SIGH: NOPE. AS THE BIG SIGN BEHIND ME SAYS, WE GET IT NEXT WEEK.
EXCUSE ME. YOU GOT THE NEW "WAR..."
NO!
PEGASAURUS GAMES
HAS THE "WARHAMSTER: 40,000" BOOK ARRIVED?
NO.
SURE?
YESSSS.
HEY, IS IT IN YET?
AIE
LOOK! IT'S ONLY A GAME! CAN YOU LIVE WITHOUT IT FOR ONE STINKING WEEK?
CAN YOU EVEN BEGIN TO UNDERSTAND HOW EMPTY AND PATHETIC YOUR LIFE MUST SEEM TO THOSE ON THE OUTSIDE?

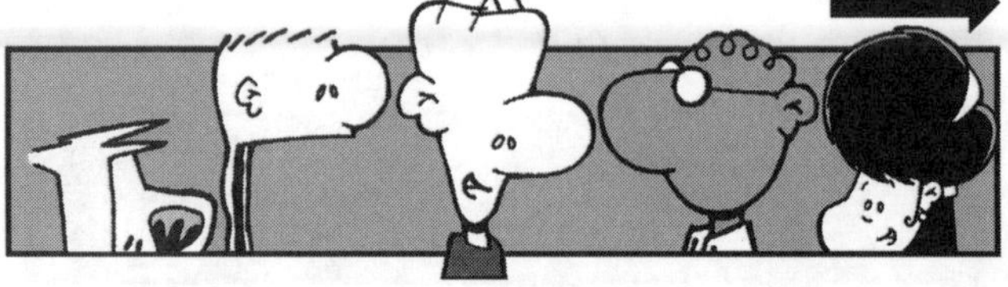

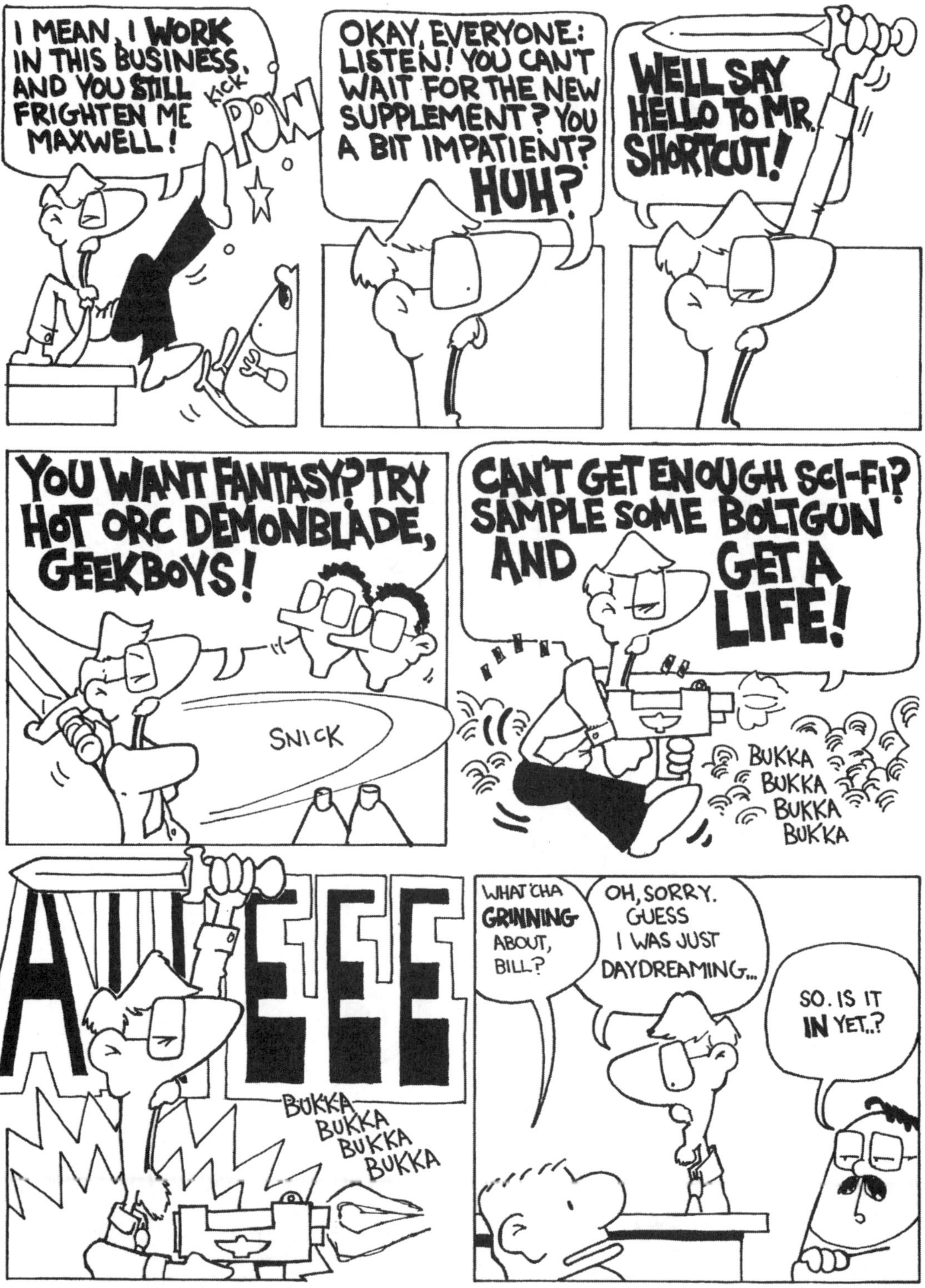
I MEAN, I WORK IN THIS BUSINESS, AND YOU STILL FRIGHTEN ME MAXWELL!
KICK
POW
OKAY, EVERYONE: LISTEN! YOU CAN'T WAIT FOR THE NEW SUPPLEMENT? YOU A BIT IMPATIENT? HUH?
WELL SAY HELLO TO MR. SHORTCUT!
YOU WANT FANTASY? TRY HOT ORC DEMONBLADE, GEEKBOYS!
SNICK
CAN'T GET ENOUGH SCI-FI? SAMPLE SOME BOLTGUN AND GET A LIFE!
BUKKA BUKKA BUKKA BUKKA
AIIEEE
BUKKA BUKKA BUKKA BUKKA
WHAT'CHA GRINNING ABOUT, BILL?
OH, SORRY. GUESS I WAS JUST DAYDREAMING...
SO. IS IT IN YET..?
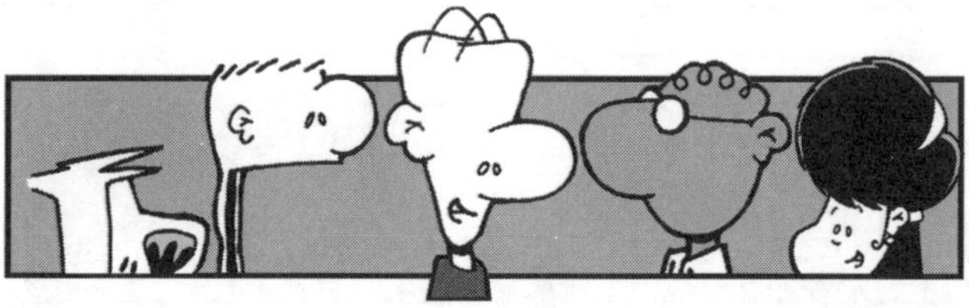

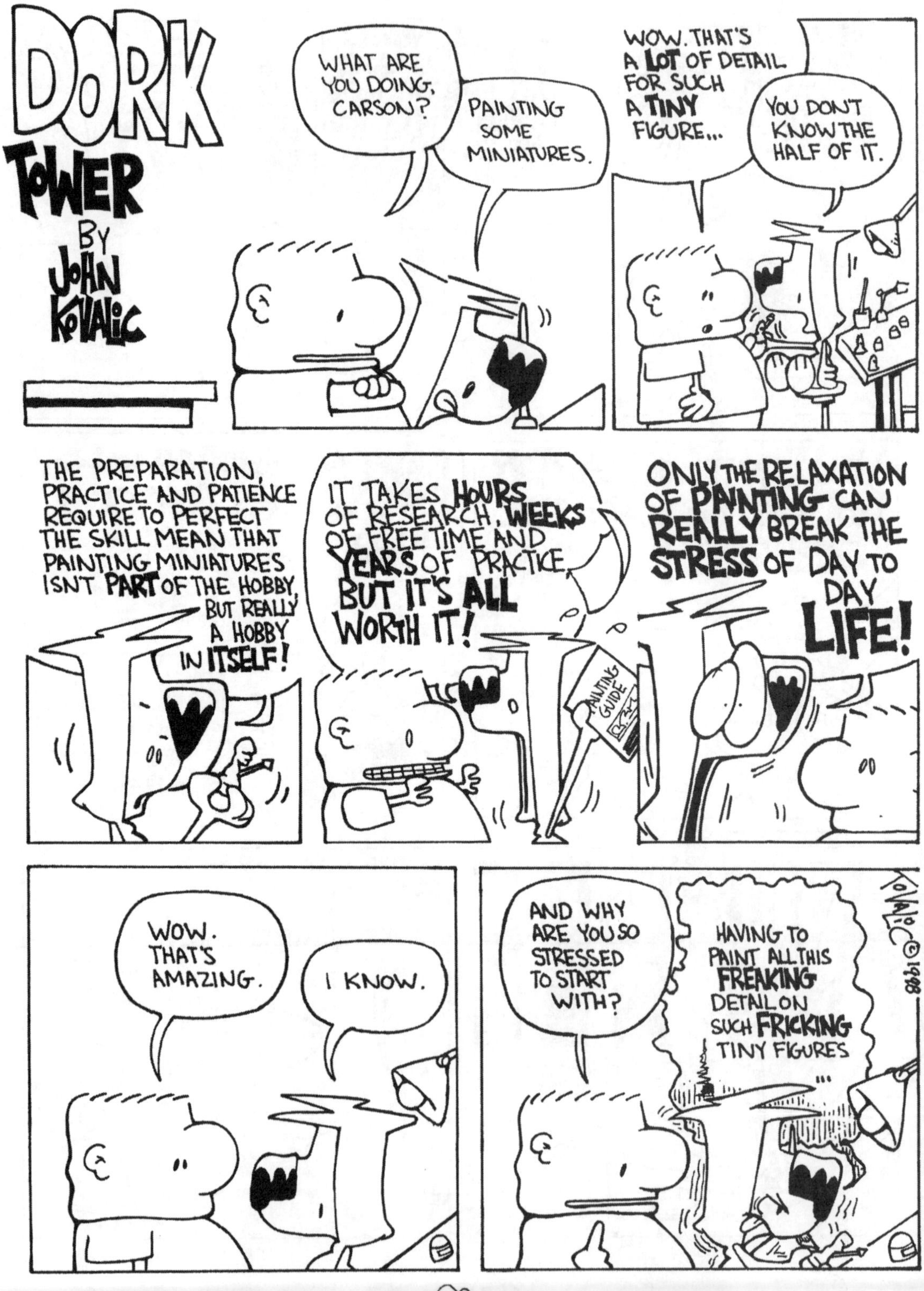
DORK TOWER
BY JOHN KOVALIC
WHAT ARE YOU DOING, CARSON?
PAINTING SOME MINIATURES.
WOW. THAT'S A LOT OF DETAIL FOR SUCH A TINY FIGURE...
YOU DON'T KNOW THE HALF OF IT.
THE PREPARATION, PRACTICE AND PATIENCE REQUIRE TO PERFECT THE SKILL MEAN THAT PAINTING MINIATURES ISN'T PART OF THE HOBBY, BUT REALLY A HOBBY IN ITSELF!
IT TAKES HOURS OF RESEARCH, WEEKS OF FREE TIME AND YEARS OF PRACTICE, BUT IT'S ALL WORTH IT!
PAINTING GUIDE
ONLY THE RELAXATION OF PAINTING CAN REALLY BREAK THE STRESS OF DAY TO DAY LIFE!
WOW. THAT'S AMAZING.
I KNOW.
AND WHY ARE YOU SO STRESSED TO START WITH?
HAVING TO PAINT ALL THIS FREAKING DETAIL ON SUCH FRICKING TINY FIGURES...
KOVALIC ©1998

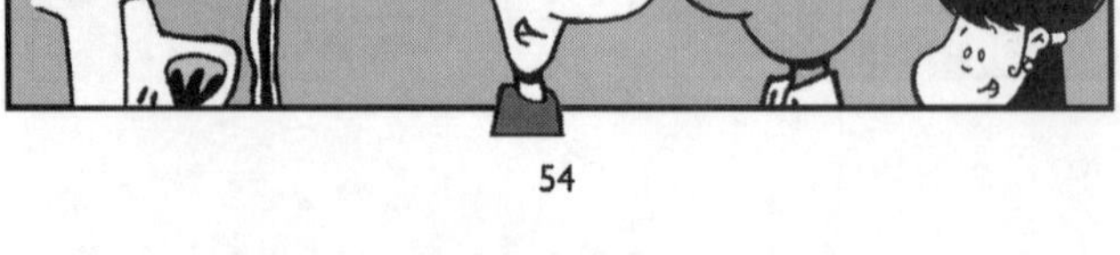

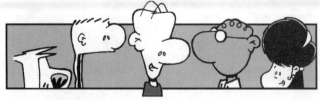

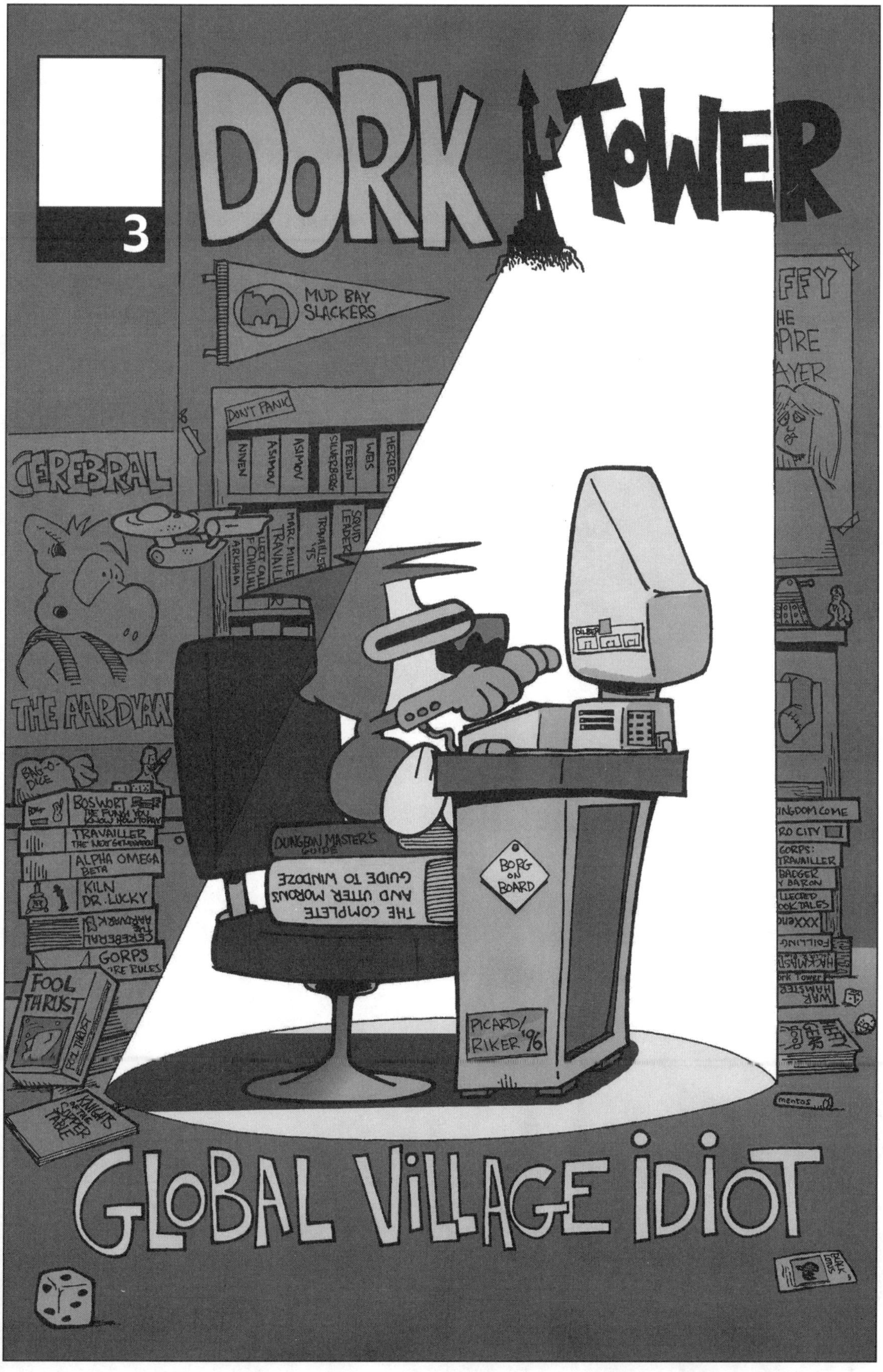
3
DORK TOWER
MUD BAY SLACKERS
DON'T PANIC
CEREBRAL
THE AARDVARK
DUNGEON MASTER'S GUIDE
THE COMPLETE AND UTTER MORON'S GUIDE TO WINDOZE
BORG ON BOARD
PICARD/RIKER '96
ALPHA OMEGA
FOOL THRUST
KNIGHTS OF THE COFFEE TABLE
mentos
GLOBAL VILLAGE IDIOT

“The trouble with computers, of course,
is that they're very sophisticated idiots.”

-The Doctor (Tom Baker) in
Doctor Who: “The Robot”

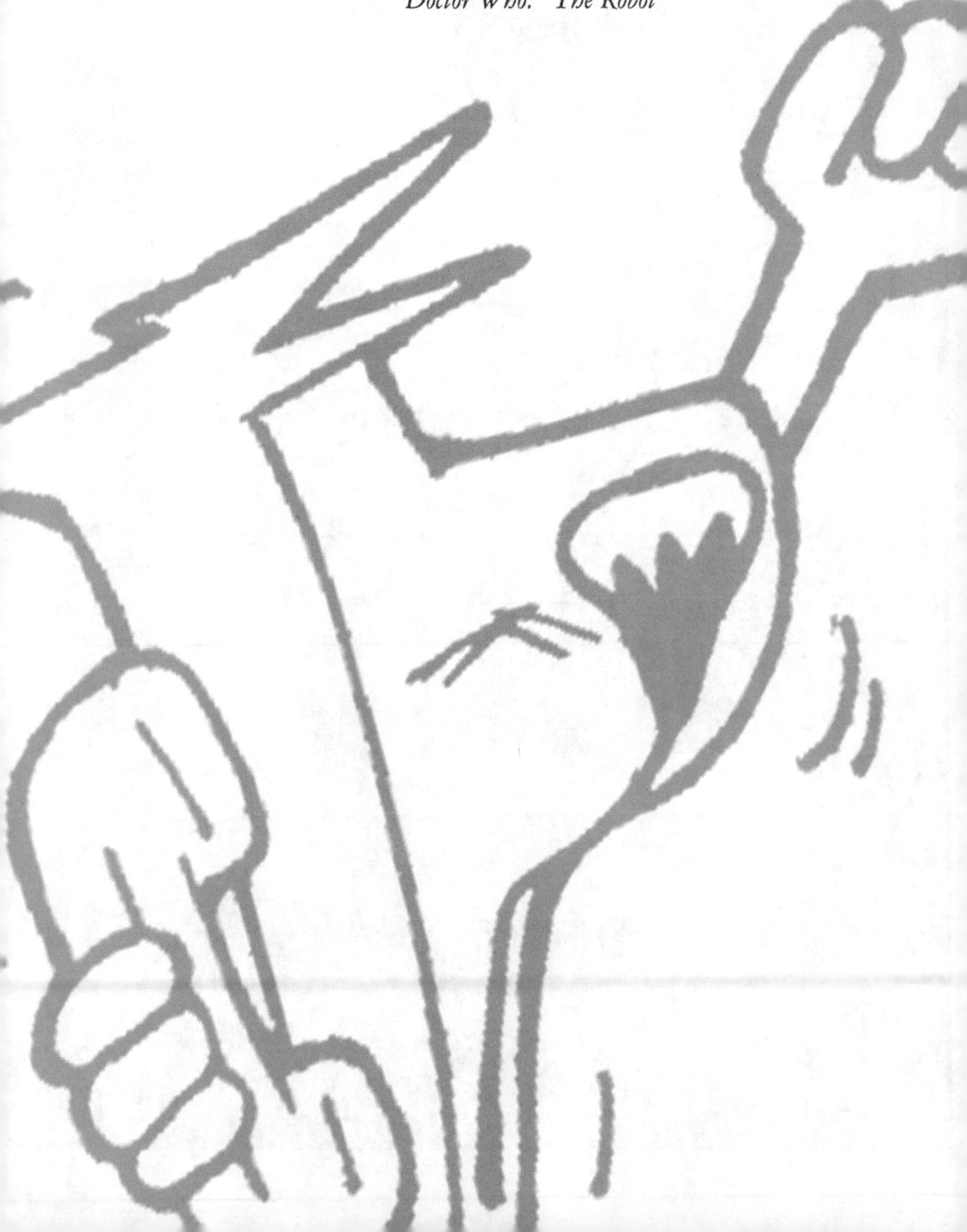

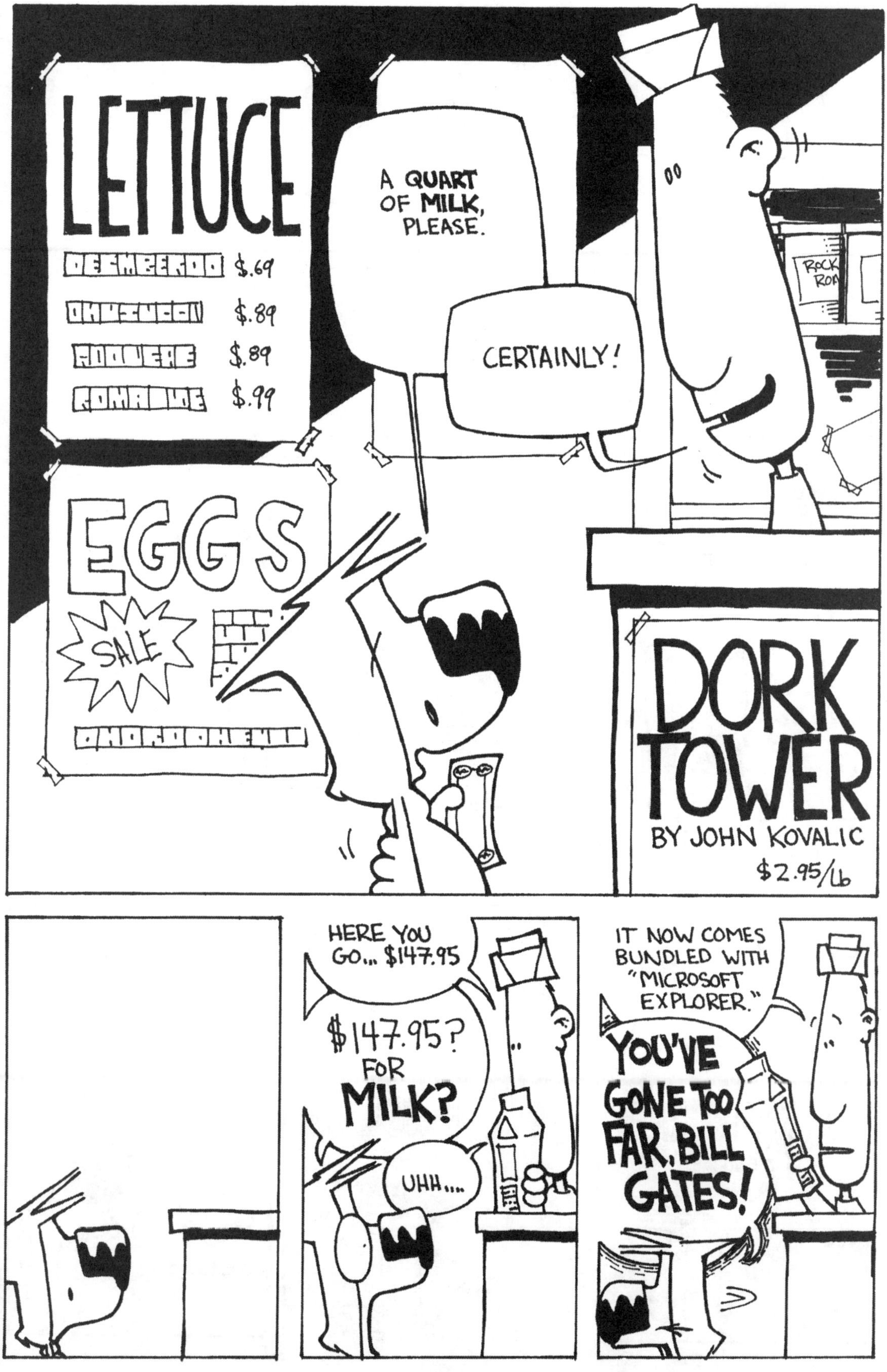
LETTUCE
$.69
$.89
$.89
$.99
EGGS
SALE
A QUART OF MILK, PLEASE.
CERTAINLY!
ROCK
DORK TOWER
BY JOHN KOVALIC
$2.95/Lb
HERE YOU GO... $147.95
$147.95? FOR MILK?
UHH....
IT NOW COMES BUNDLED WITH "MICROSOFT EXPLORER."
YOU'VE GONE TOO FAR, BILL GATES!

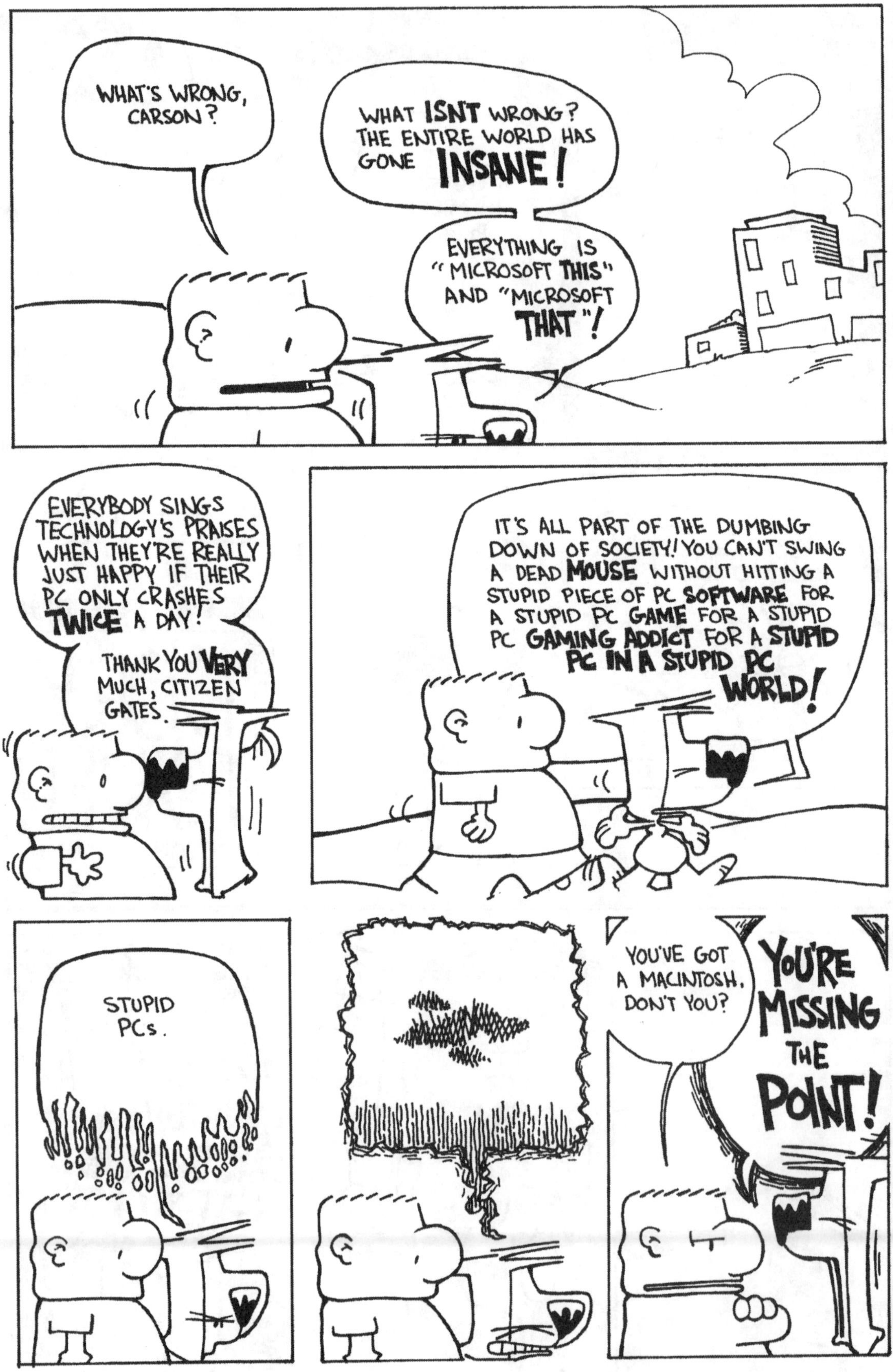
WHAT'S WRONG, CARSON?
WHAT ISN'T WRONG? THE ENTIRE WORLD HAS GONE INSANE!
EVERYTHING IS "MICROSOFT THIS" AND "MICROSOFT THAT"!
EVERYBODY SINGS TECHNOLOGY'S PRAISES WHEN THEY'RE REALLY JUST HAPPY IF THEIR PC ONLY CRASHES TWICE A DAY!
THANK YOU VERY MUCH, CITIZEN GATES.
IT'S ALL PART OF THE DUMBING DOWN OF SOCIETY! YOU CAN'T SWING A DEAD MOUSE WITHOUT HITTING A STUPID PIECE OF PC SOFTWARE FOR A STUPID PC GAME FOR A STUPID PC GAMING ADDICT FOR A STUPID PC IN A STUPID PC WORLD!
STUPID PCs.
YOU'VE GOT A MACINTOSH, DON'T YOU?
YOU'RE MISSING THE POINT!

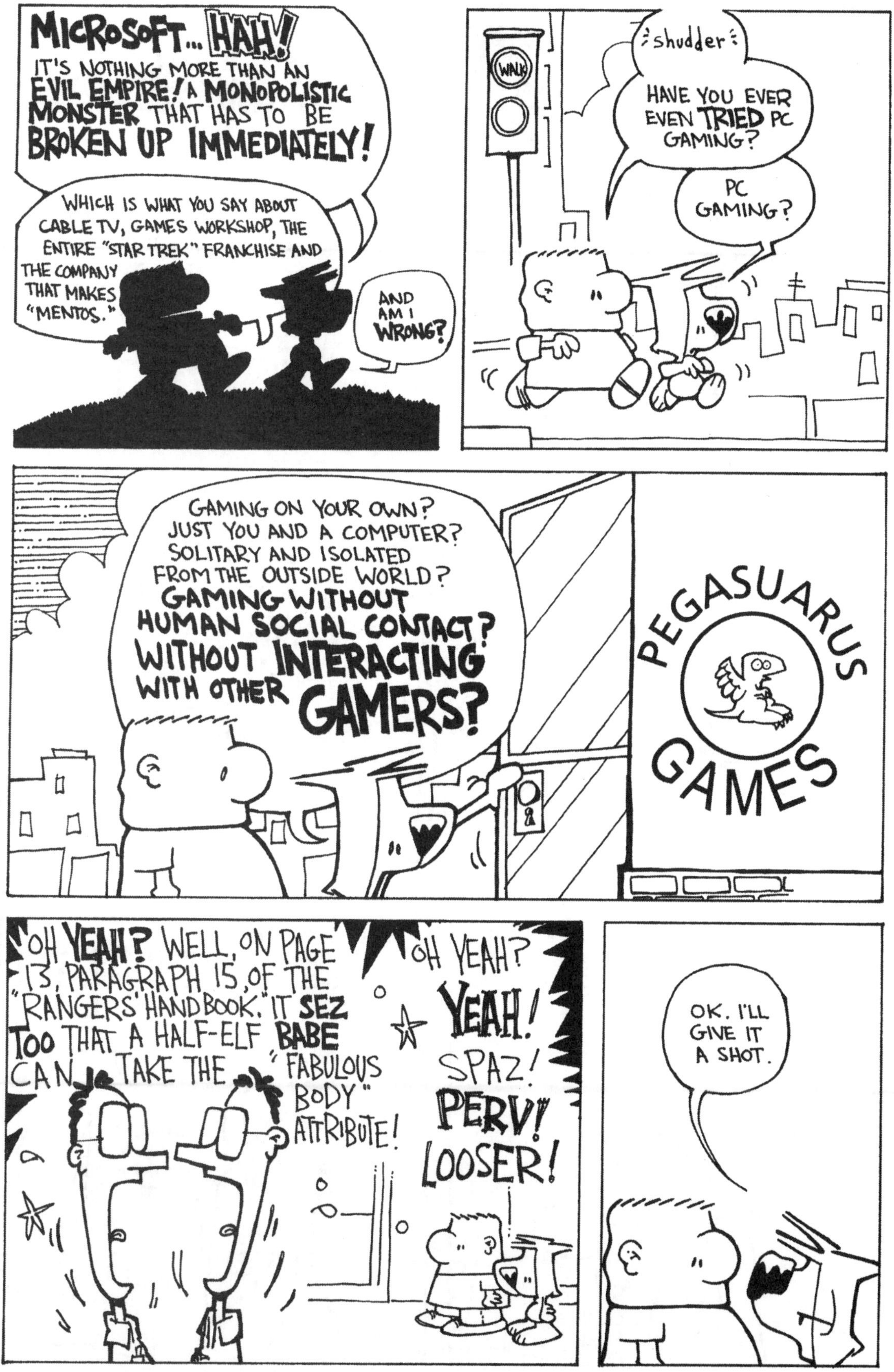
MICROSOFT... HAH! IT'S NOTHING MORE THAN AN EVIL EMPIRE! A MONOPOLISTIC MONSTER THAT HAS TO BE BROKEN UP IMMEDIATELY!
WHICH IS WHAT YOU SAY ABOUT CABLE TV, GAMES WORKSHOP, THE ENTIRE "STAR TREK" FRANCHISE AND THE COMPANY THAT MAKES "MENTOS."
AND AM I WRONG?
WALK
shudder
HAVE YOU EVER EVEN TRIED PC GAMING?
PC GAMING?
GAMING ON YOUR OWN? JUST YOU AND A COMPUTER? SOLITARY AND ISOLATED FROM THE OUTSIDE WORLD? GAMING WITHOUT HUMAN SOCIAL CONTACT? WITHOUT INTERACTING WITH OTHER GAMERS?
PEGASUARUS GAMES
OH YEAH? WELL, ON PAGE 13, PARAGRAPH 15, OF THE "RANGERS' HANDBOOK," IT SEZ TOO THAT A HALF-ELF BABE CAN TAKE THE "FABULOUS BODY" ATTRIBUTE!
OH YEAH?
YEAH!
SPAZ!
PERV!
LOOSER!
OK. I'LL GIVE IT A SHOT.

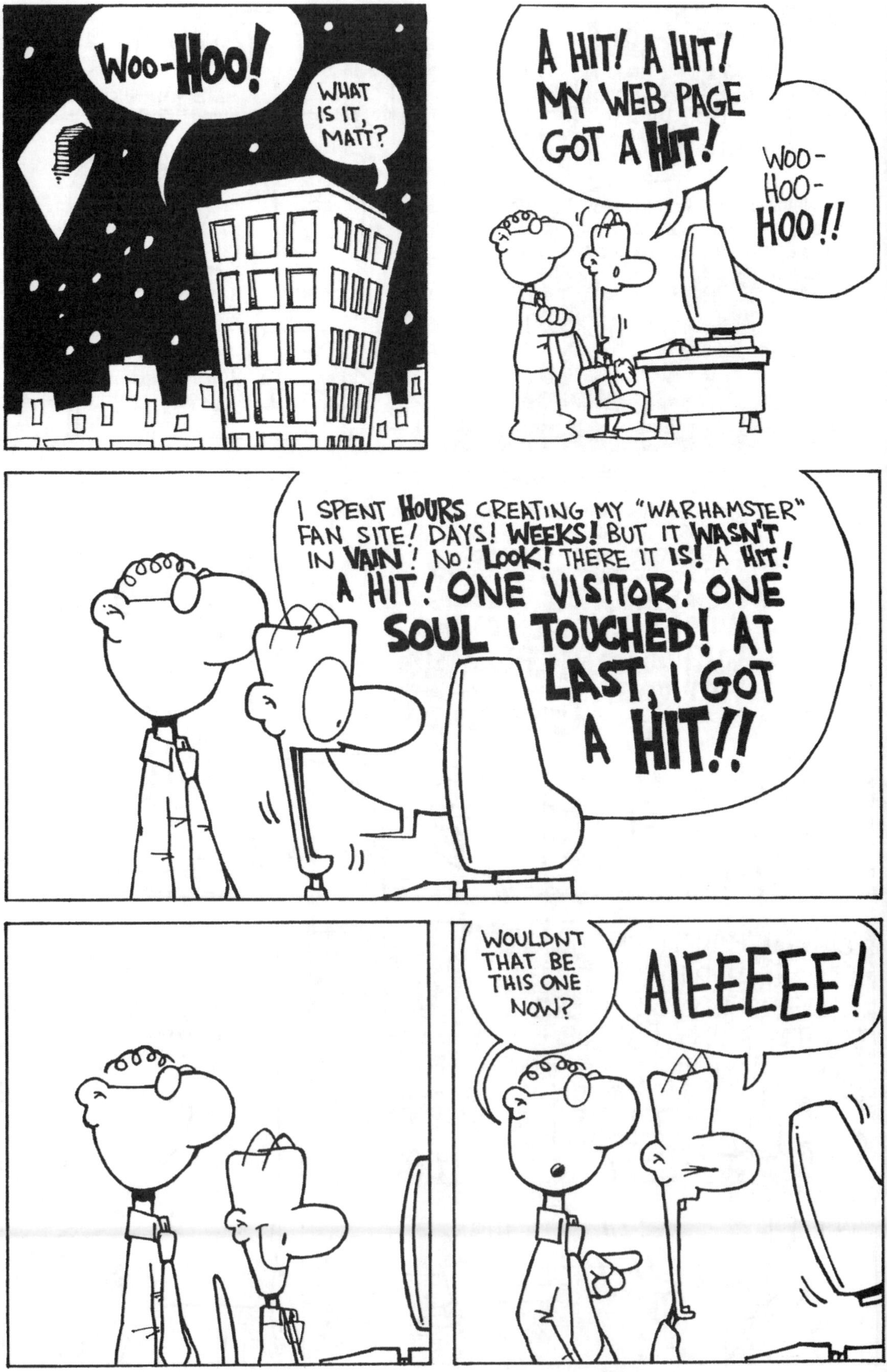
WOO-HOO!
WHAT IS IT, MATT?
A HIT! A HIT! MY WEB PAGE GOT A HIT!
WOO-HOO-HOO!!
I SPENT HOURS CREATING MY "WARHAMSTER" FAN SITE! DAYS! WEEKS! BUT IT WASN'T IN VAIN! NO! LOOK! THERE IT IS! A HIT!
A HIT! ONE VISITOR! ONE SOUL I TOUCHED! AT LAST, I GOT A HIT!!
WOULDNT THAT BE THIS ONE NOW?
AIEEEEE!

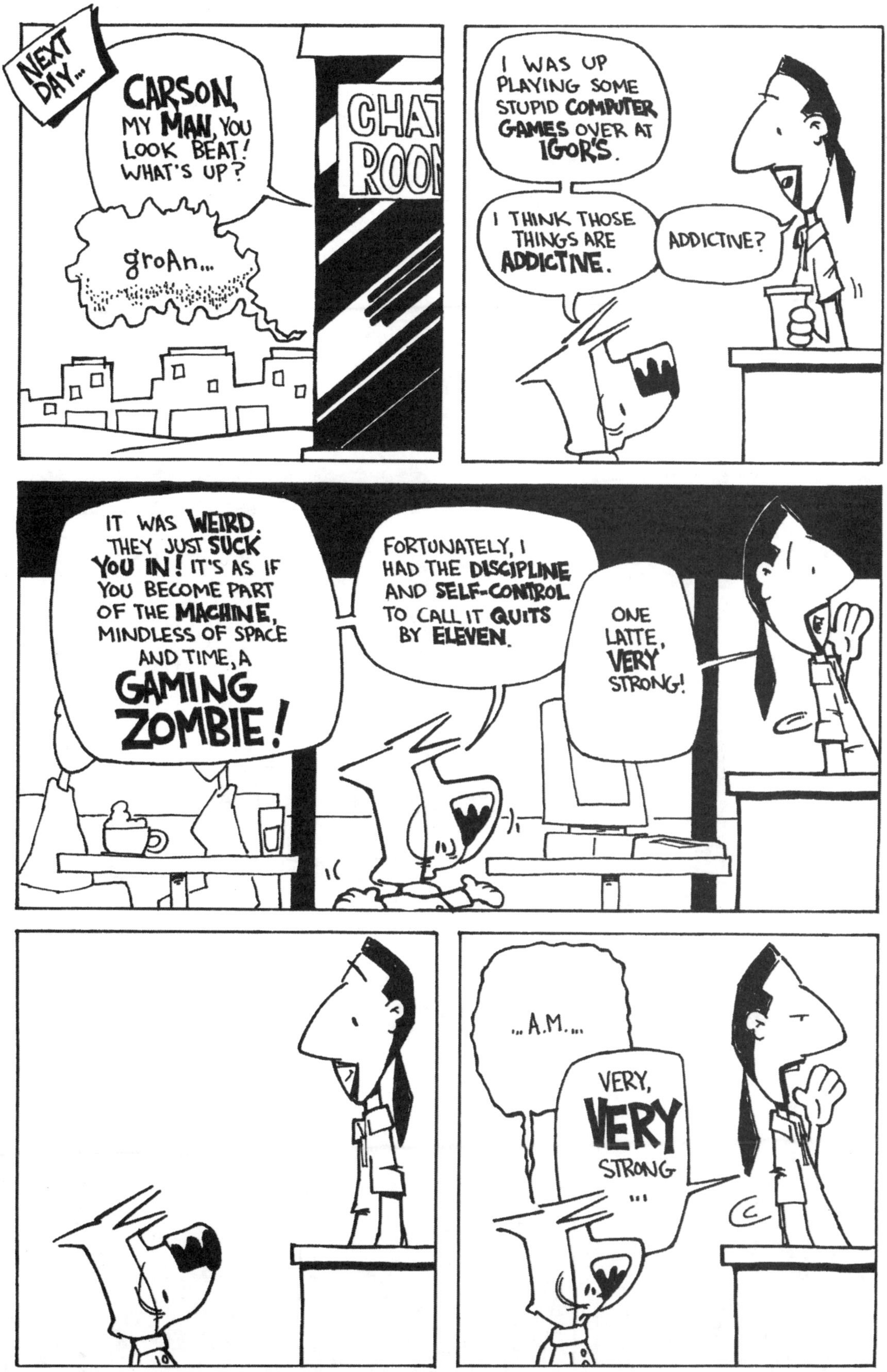
NEXT DAY...
CARSON, MY MAN, YOU LOOK BEAT! WHAT'S UP?
groAn...
CHAT ROOM
I WAS UP PLAYING SOME STUPID COMPUTER GAMES OVER AT IGOR'S.
I THINK THOSE THINGS ARE ADDICTIVE.
ADDICTIVE?
IT WAS WEIRD. THEY JUST SUCK YOU IN! IT'S AS IF YOU BECOME PART OF THE MACHINE, MINDLESS OF SPACE AND TIME, A GAMING ZOMBIE!
FORTUNATELY, I HAD THE DISCIPLINE AND SELF-CONTROL TO CALL IT QUITS BY ELEVEN.
ONE LATTE, VERY STRONG!
...A.M....
VERY, VERY STRONG ...

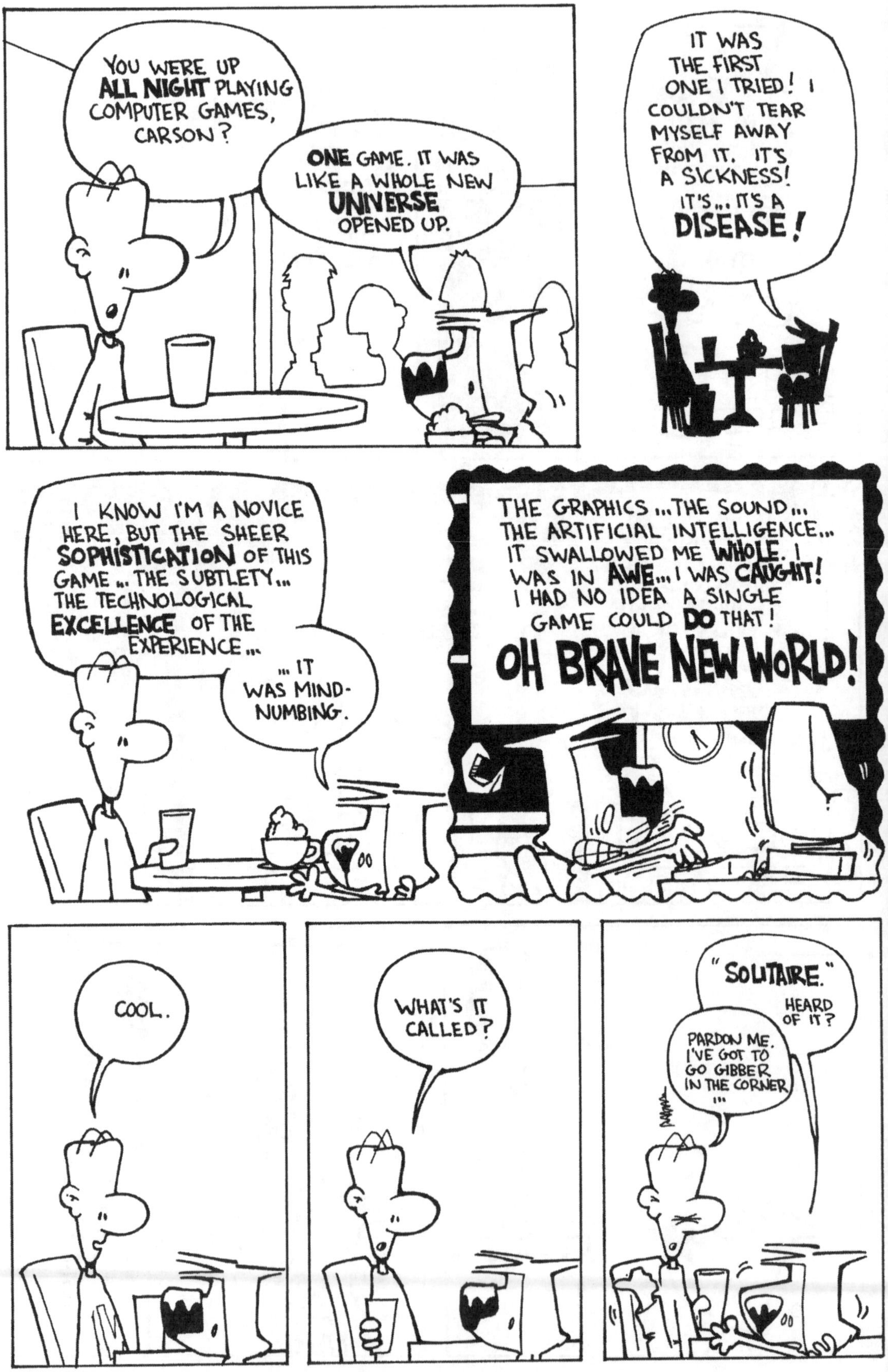
YOU WERE UP ALL NIGHT PLAYING COMPUTER GAMES, CARSON?
ONE GAME. IT WAS LIKE A WHOLE NEW UNIVERSE OPENED UP.
IT WAS THE FIRST ONE I TRIED! I COULDN'T TEAR MYSELF AWAY FROM IT. IT'S A SICKNESS! IT'S... IT'S A DISEASE!
I KNOW I'M A NOVICE HERE, BUT THE SHEER SOPHISTICATION OF THIS GAME... THE SUBTLETY... THE TECHNOLOGICAL EXCELLENCE OF THE EXPERIENCE...
...IT WAS MIND-NUMBING.
THE GRAPHICS... THE SOUND... THE ARTIFICIAL INTELLIGENCE... IT SWALLOWED ME WHOLE. I WAS IN AWE... I WAS CAUGHT! I HAD NO IDEA A SINGLE GAME COULD DO THAT!
OH BRAVE NEW WORLD!
COOL.
WHAT'S IT CALLED?
"SOLITAIRE." HEARD OF IT?
PARDON ME. I'VE GOT TO GO GIBBER IN THE CORNER...

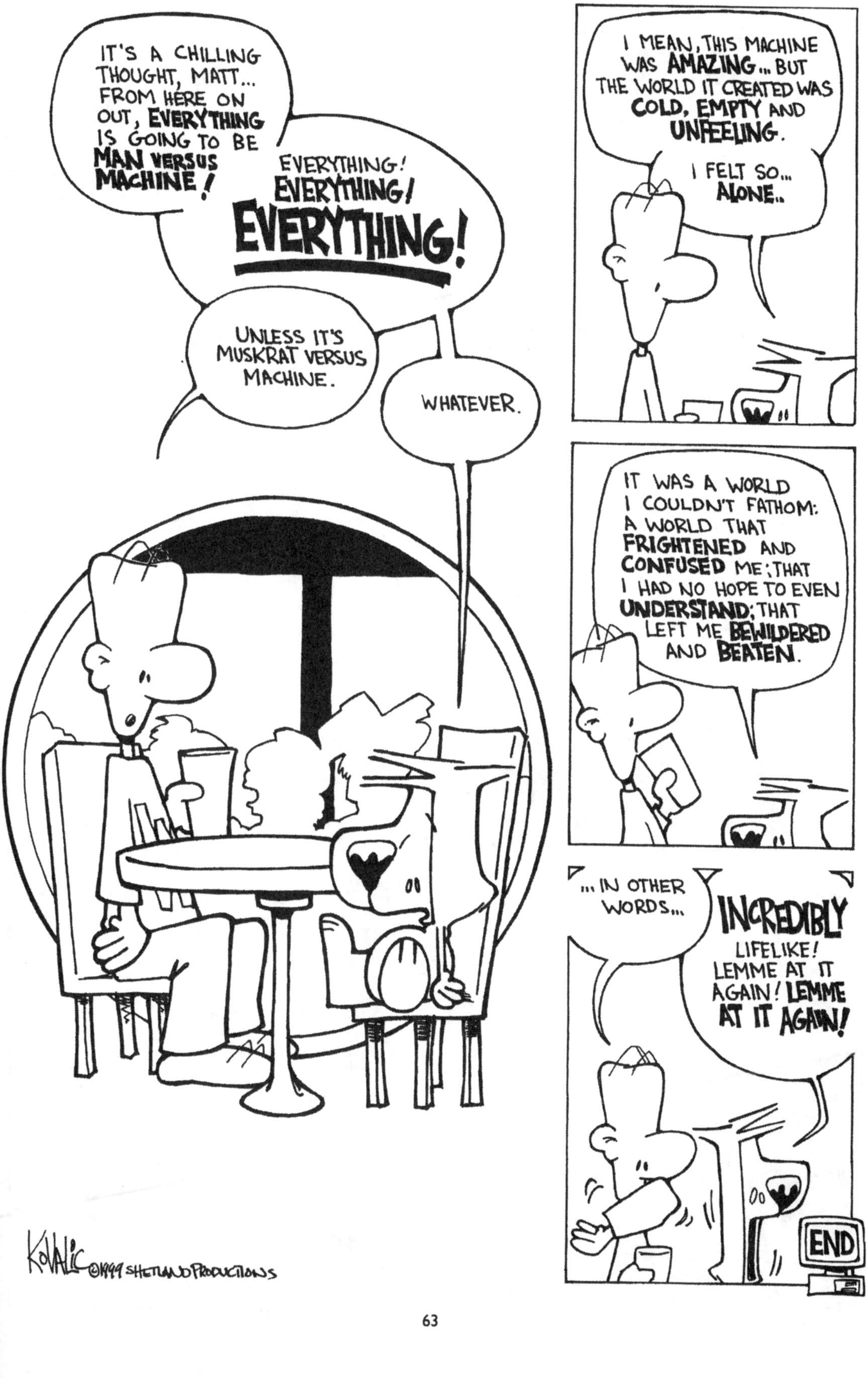

IT'S A CHILLING THOUGHT, MATT... FROM HERE ON OUT, EVERYTHING IS GOING TO BE MAN VERSUS MACHINE!
EVERYTHING! EVERYTHING! EVERYTHING!
UNLESS IT'S MUSKRAT VERSUS MACHINE.
WHATEVER.
I MEAN, THIS MACHINE WAS AMAZING... BUT THE WORLD IT CREATED WAS COLD, EMPTY AND UNFEELING.
I FELT SO... ALONE..
IT WAS A WORLD I COULDN'T FATHOM: A WORLD THAT FRIGHTENED AND CONFUSED ME; THAT I HAD NO HOPE TO EVEN UNDERSTAND; THAT LEFT ME BEWILDERED AND BEATEN.
... IN OTHER WORDS...
INCREDIBLY LIFELIKE! LEMME AT IT AGAIN! LEMME AT IT AGAIN!
END
KOVALIC ©1999 SHETLAND PRODUCTIONS

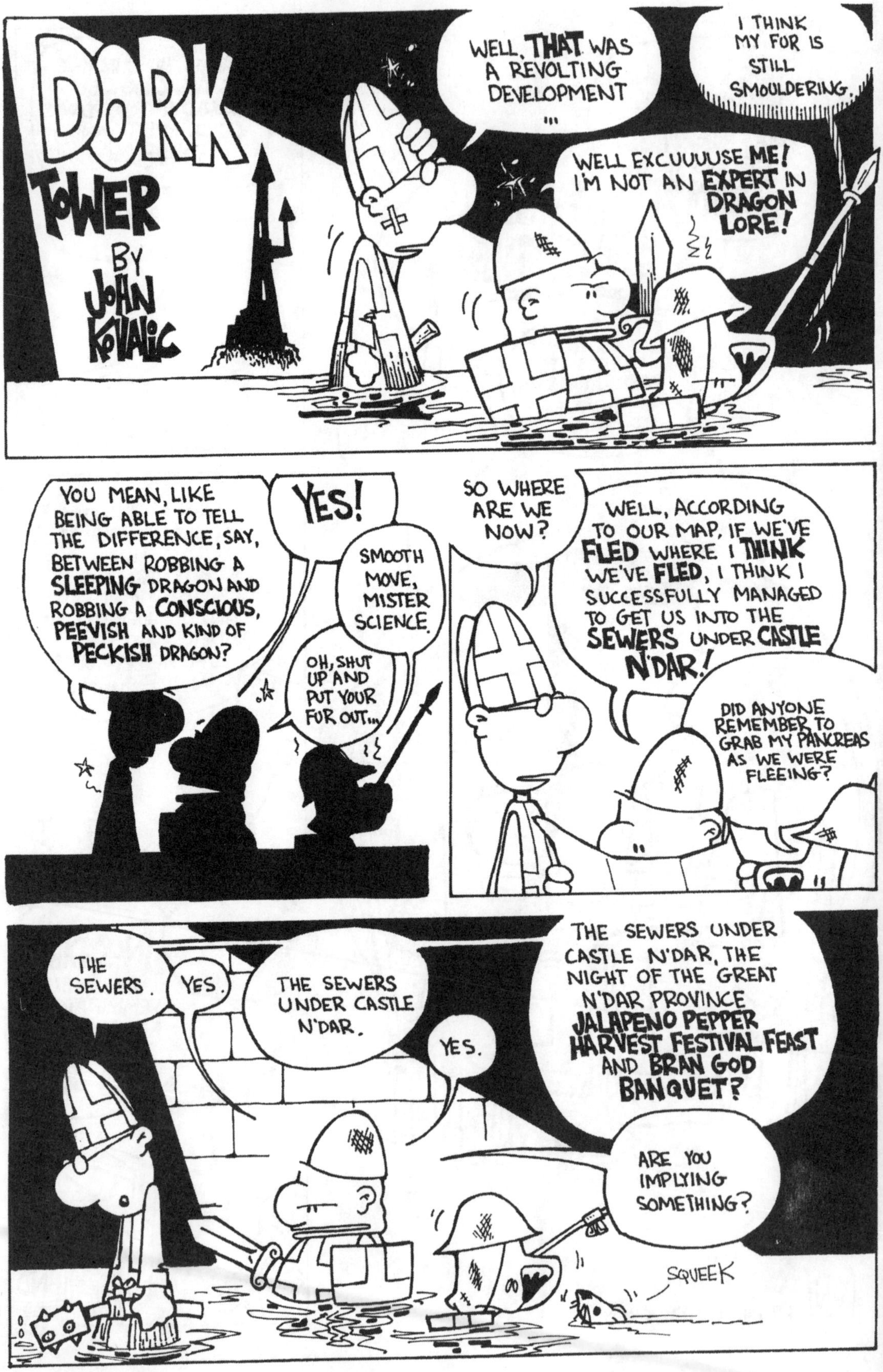
DORK TOWER
BY JOHN KOVALIC
WELL, THAT WAS A REVOLTING DEVELOPMENT...
I THINK MY FUR IS STILL SMOULDERING.
WELL EXCUUUUSE ME! I'M NOT AN EXPERT IN DRAGON LORE!
YOU MEAN, LIKE BEING ABLE TO TELL THE DIFFERENCE, SAY, BETWEEN ROBBING A SLEEPING DRAGON AND ROBBING A CONSCIOUS, PEEVISH AND KIND OF PECKISH DRAGON?
YES!
SMOOTH MOVE, MISTER SCIENCE.
OH, SHUT UP AND PUT YOUR FUR OUT...
SO WHERE ARE WE NOW?
WELL, ACCORDING TO OUR MAP, IF WE'VE FLED WHERE I THINK WE'VE FLED, I THINK I SUCCESSFULLY MANAGED TO GET US INTO THE SEWERS UNDER CASTLE N'DAR!
DID ANYONE REMEMBER TO GRAB MY PANCREAS AS WE WERE FLEEING?
THE SEWERS.
YES.
THE SEWERS UNDER CASTLE N'DAR.
YES.
THE SEWERS UNDER CASTLE N'DAR, THE NIGHT OF THE GREAT N'DAR PROVINCE JALAPENO PEPPER HARVEST FESTIVAL FEAST AND BRAN GOD BANQUET?
ARE YOU IMPLYING SOMETHING?
SQUEEK

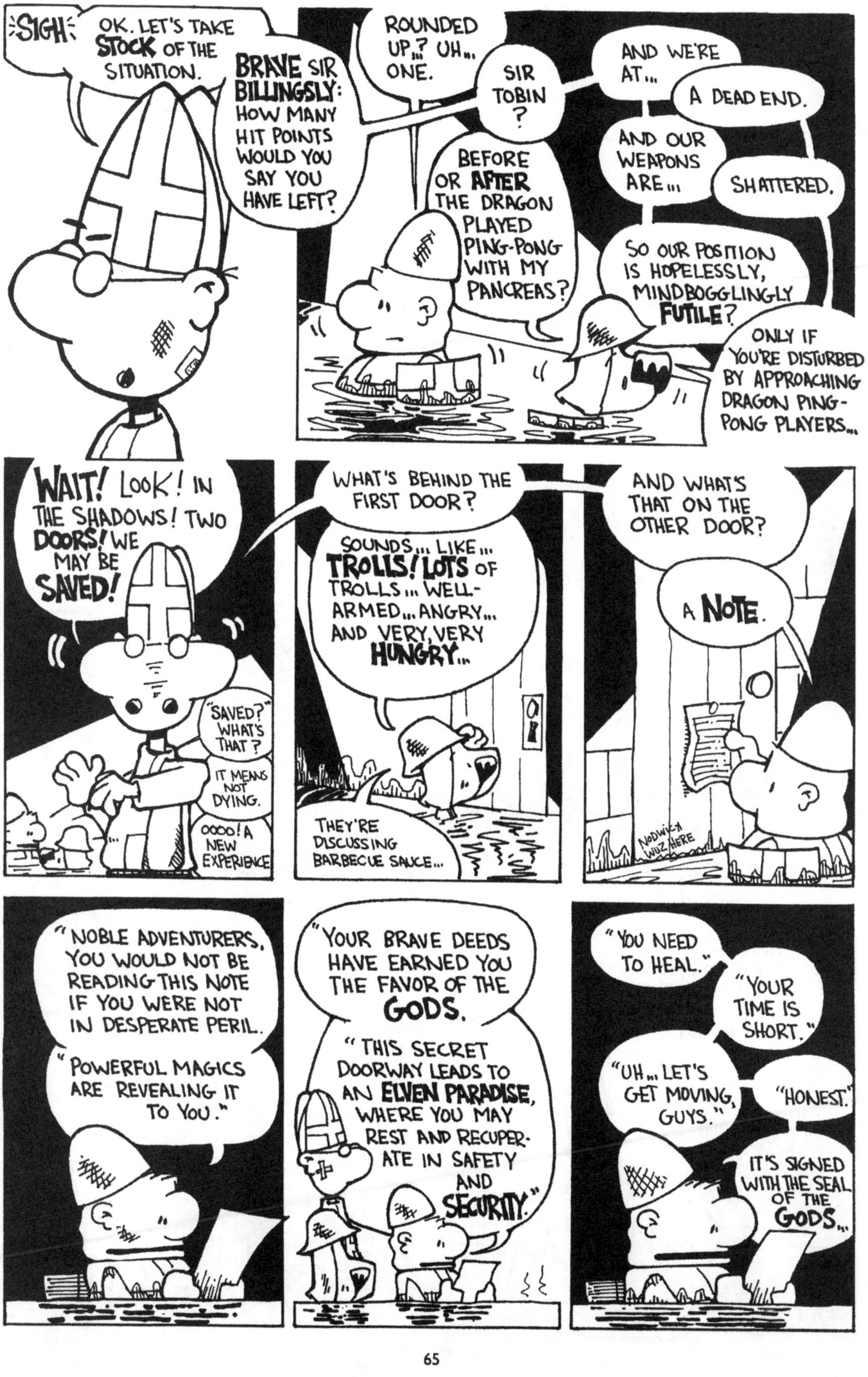

SIGH
OK. LET'S TAKE STOCK OF THE SITUATION.
BRAVE SIR BILLINGSLY: HOW MANY HIT POINTS WOULD YOU SAY YOU HAVE LEFT?
ROUNDED UP...? UH... ONE.
BEFORE OR AFTER THE DRAGON PLAYED PING-PONG WITH MY PANCREAS?
SIR TOBIN?
AND WE'RE AT...
A DEAD END.
AND OUR WEAPONS ARE...
SHATTERED.
SO OUR POSITION IS HOPELESSLY, MINDBOGGLINGLY FUTILE?
ONLY IF YOU'RE DISTURBED BY APPROACHING DRAGON PING-PONG PLAYERS...
WAIT! LOOK! IN THE SHADOWS! TWO DOORS! WE MAY BE SAVED!
"SAVED?" WHAT'S THAT?
IT MEANS NOT DYING.
OOOO! A NEW EXPERIENCE
WHAT'S BEHIND THE FIRST DOOR?
SOUNDS... LIKE... TROLLS! LOTS OF TROLLS... WELL-ARMED... ANGRY... AND VERY, VERY HUNGRY...
THEY'RE DISCUSSING BARBECUE SAUCE...
AND WHAT'S THAT ON THE OTHER DOOR?
A NOTE.
NODWICK WUZ HERE
"NOBLE ADVENTURERS, YOU WOULD NOT BE READING THIS NOTE IF YOU WERE NOT IN DESPERATE PERIL.
"POWERFUL MAGICS ARE REVEALING IT TO YOU."
"YOUR BRAVE DEEDS HAVE EARNED YOU THE FAVOR OF THE GODS.
"THIS SECRET DOORWAY LEADS TO AN ELVEN PARADISE, WHERE YOU MAY REST AND RECUPERATE IN SAFETY AND SECURITY."
"YOU NEED TO HEAL."
"YOUR TIME IS SHORT."
"UH... LET'S GET MOVING, GUYS."
"HONEST."
IT'S SIGNED WITH THE SEAL OF THE GODS...

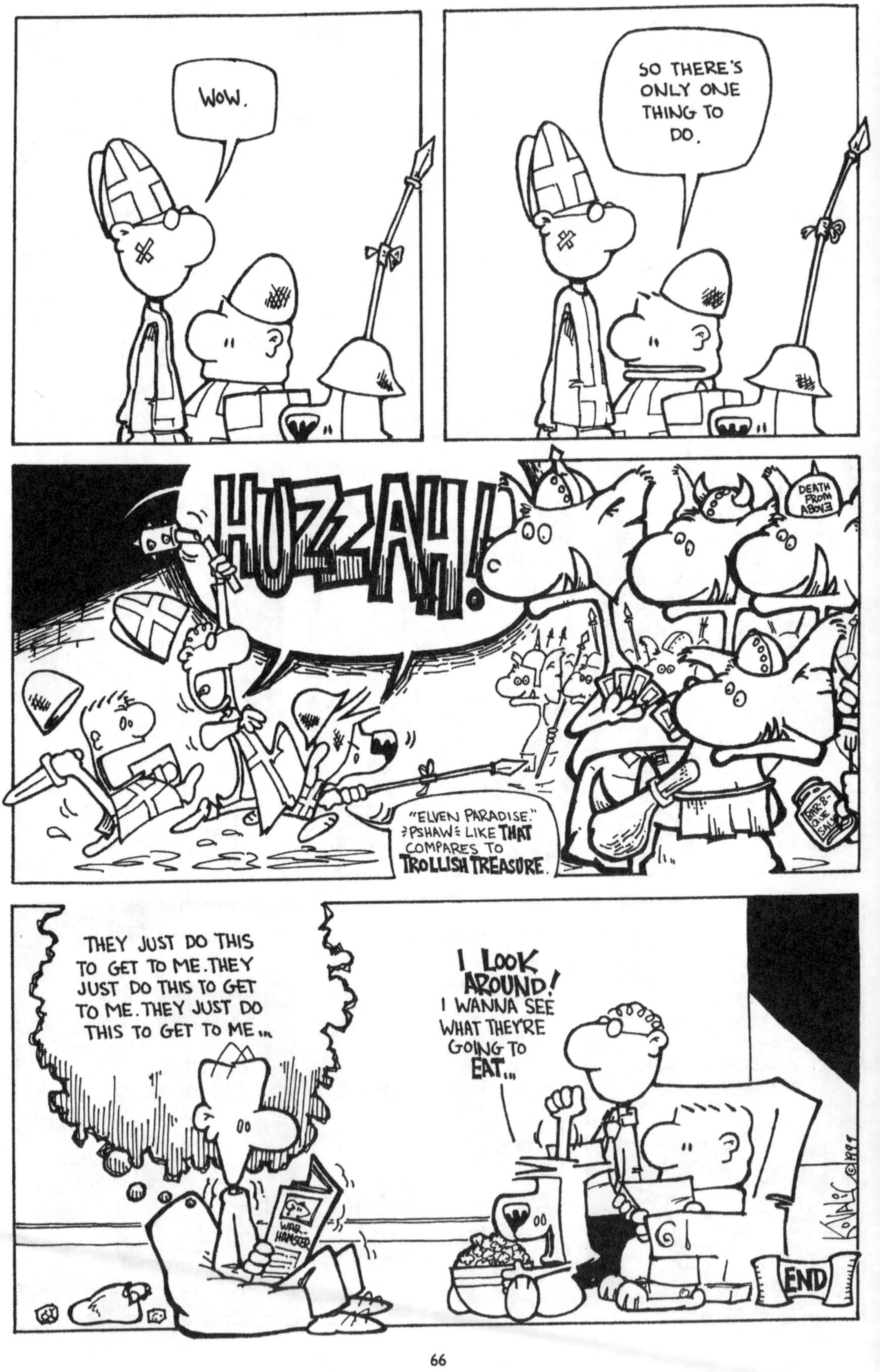
WOW.
SO THERE'S ONLY ONE THING TO DO.
HUZZAH!
DEATH FROM ABOVE
"ELVEN PARADISE." PSHAW! LIKE THAT COMPARES TO TROLLISH TREASURE.
BAR-B-QUE SAUCE
THEY JUST DO THIS TO GET TO ME. THEY JUST DO THIS TO GET TO ME. THEY JUST DO THIS TO GET TO ME...
WAR-HAMSTER
I LOOK AROUND! I WANNA SEE WHAT THEY'RE GOING TO EAT...
KOVALIC ©1999
END

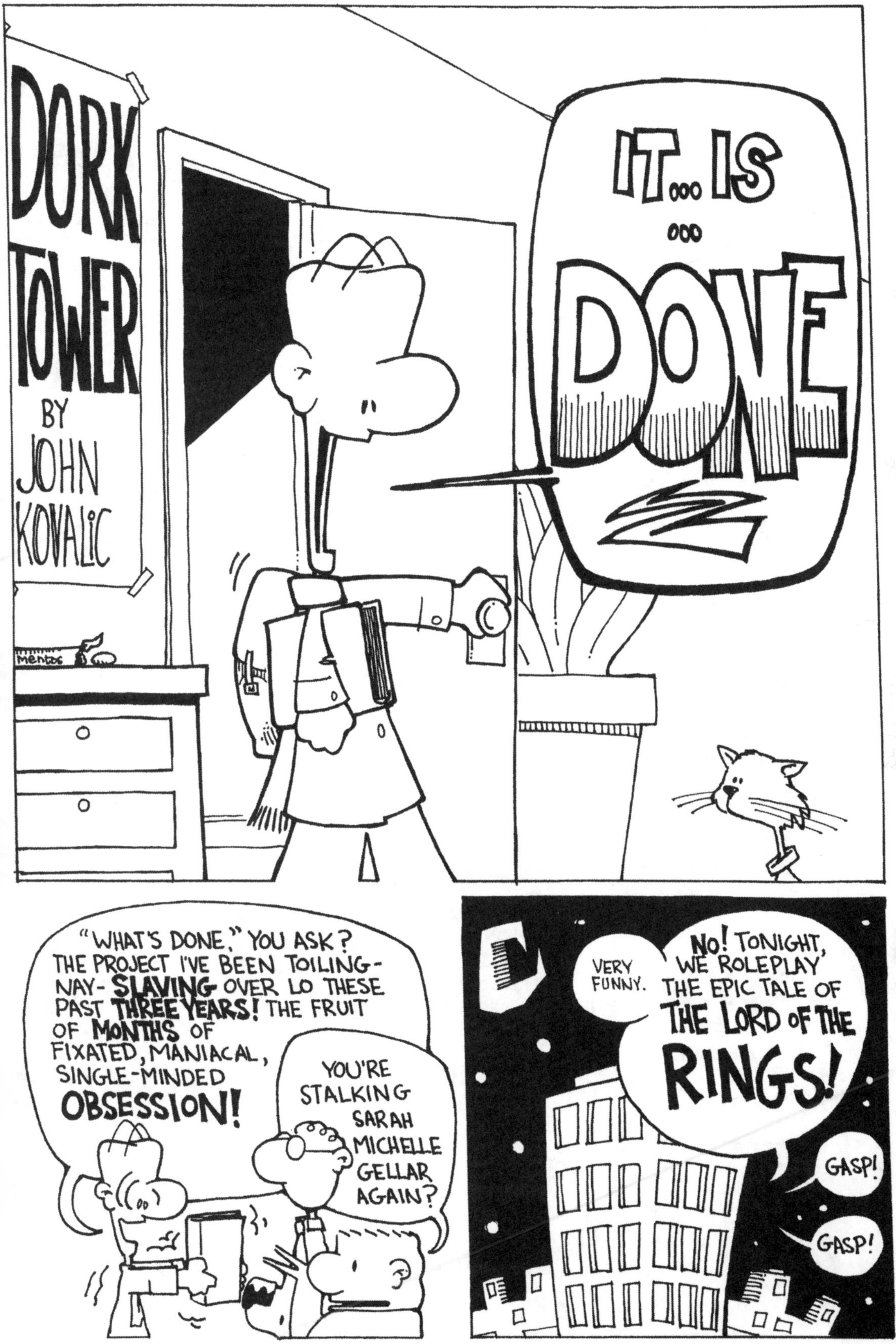
DORK TOWER
BY JOHN KOVALIC
mentos
IT... IS ... DONE
"WHAT'S DONE," YOU ASK? THE PROJECT I'VE BEEN TOILING- NAY- SLAVING OVER LO THESE PAST THREE YEARS! THE FRUIT OF MONTHS OF FIXATED, MANIACAL, SINGLE-MINDED OBSESSION!
YOU'RE STALKING SARAH MICHELLE GELLAR AGAIN?
VERY FUNNY.
NO! TONIGHT, WE ROLEPLAY THE EPIC TALE OF THE LORD OF THE RINGS!
GASP!
GASP!

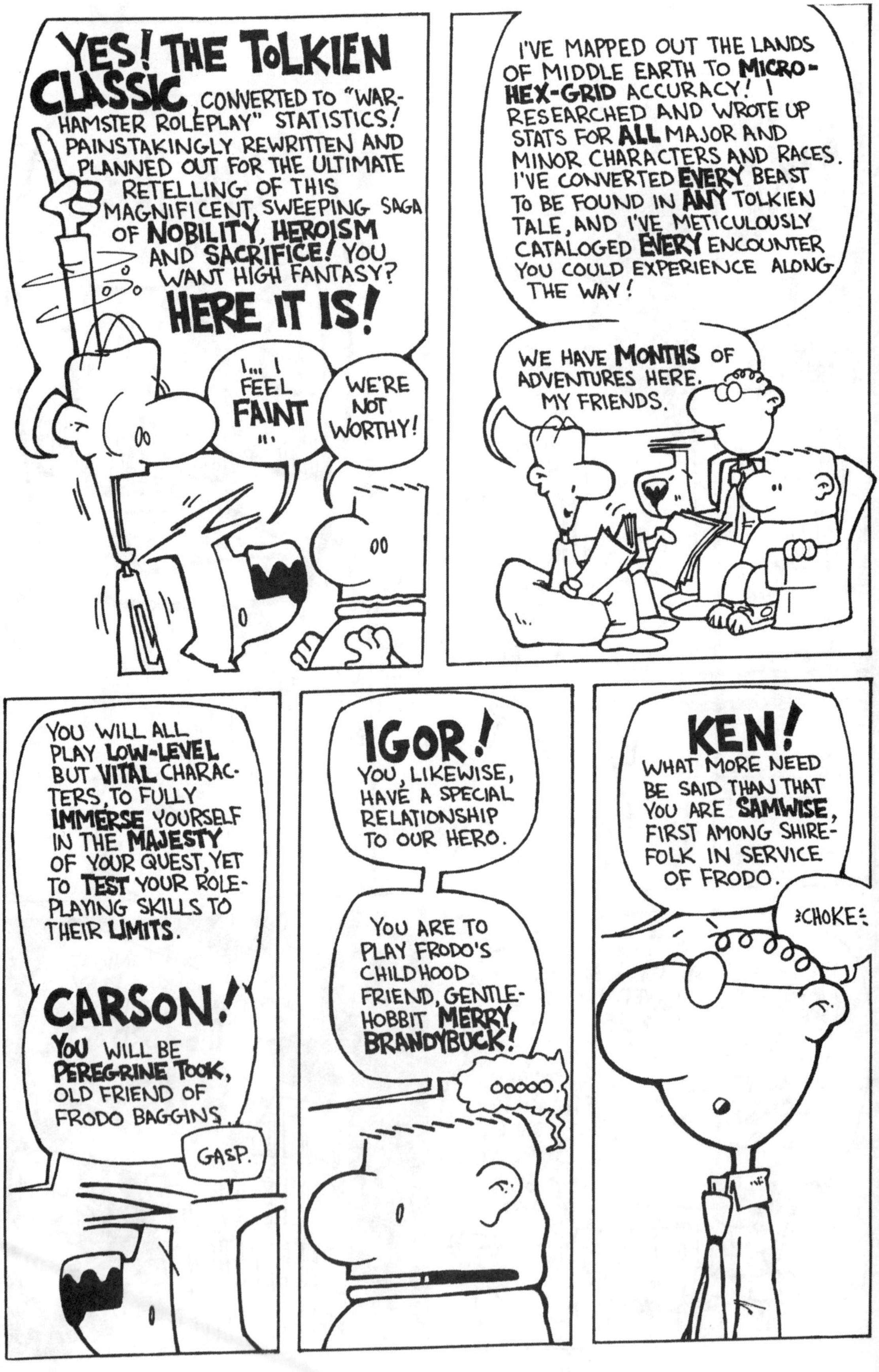
YES! THE TOLKIEN CLASSIC, CONVERTED TO "WAR-HAMSTER ROLEPLAY" STATISTICS! PAINSTAKINGLY REWRITTEN AND PLANNED OUT FOR THE ULTIMATE RETELLING OF THIS MAGNIFICENT, SWEEPING SAGA OF NOBILITY, HEROISM AND SACRIFICE! YOU WANT HIGH FANTASY? HERE IT IS!
I... I FEEL FAINT ...
WE'RE NOT WORTHY!
I'VE MAPPED OUT THE LANDS OF MIDDLE EARTH TO MICRO-HEX-GRID ACCURACY! I RESEARCHED AND WROTE UP STATS FOR ALL MAJOR AND MINOR CHARACTERS AND RACES. I'VE CONVERTED EVERY BEAST TO BE FOUND IN ANY TOLKIEN TALE, AND I'VE METICULOUSLY CATALOGED EVERY ENCOUNTER YOU COULD EXPERIENCE ALONG THE WAY!
WE HAVE MONTHS OF ADVENTURES HERE, MY FRIENDS.
YOU WILL ALL PLAY LOW-LEVEL BUT VITAL CHARACTERS, TO FULLY IMMERSE YOURSELF IN THE MAJESTY OF YOUR QUEST, YET TO TEST YOUR ROLE-PLAYING SKILLS TO THEIR LIMITS.
CARSON! YOU WILL BE PEREGRINE TOOK, OLD FRIEND OF FRODO BAGGINS.
GASP.
IGOR! YOU, LIKEWISE, HAVE A SPECIAL RELATIONSHIP TO OUR HERO.
YOU ARE TO PLAY FRODO'S CHILDHOOD FRIEND, GENTLE-HOBBIT MERRY BRANDYBUCK!
OOOOO.
KEN! WHAT MORE NEED BE SAID THAN THAT YOU ARE SAMWISE, FIRST AMONG SHIRE-FOLK IN SERVICE OF FRODO.
CHOKE

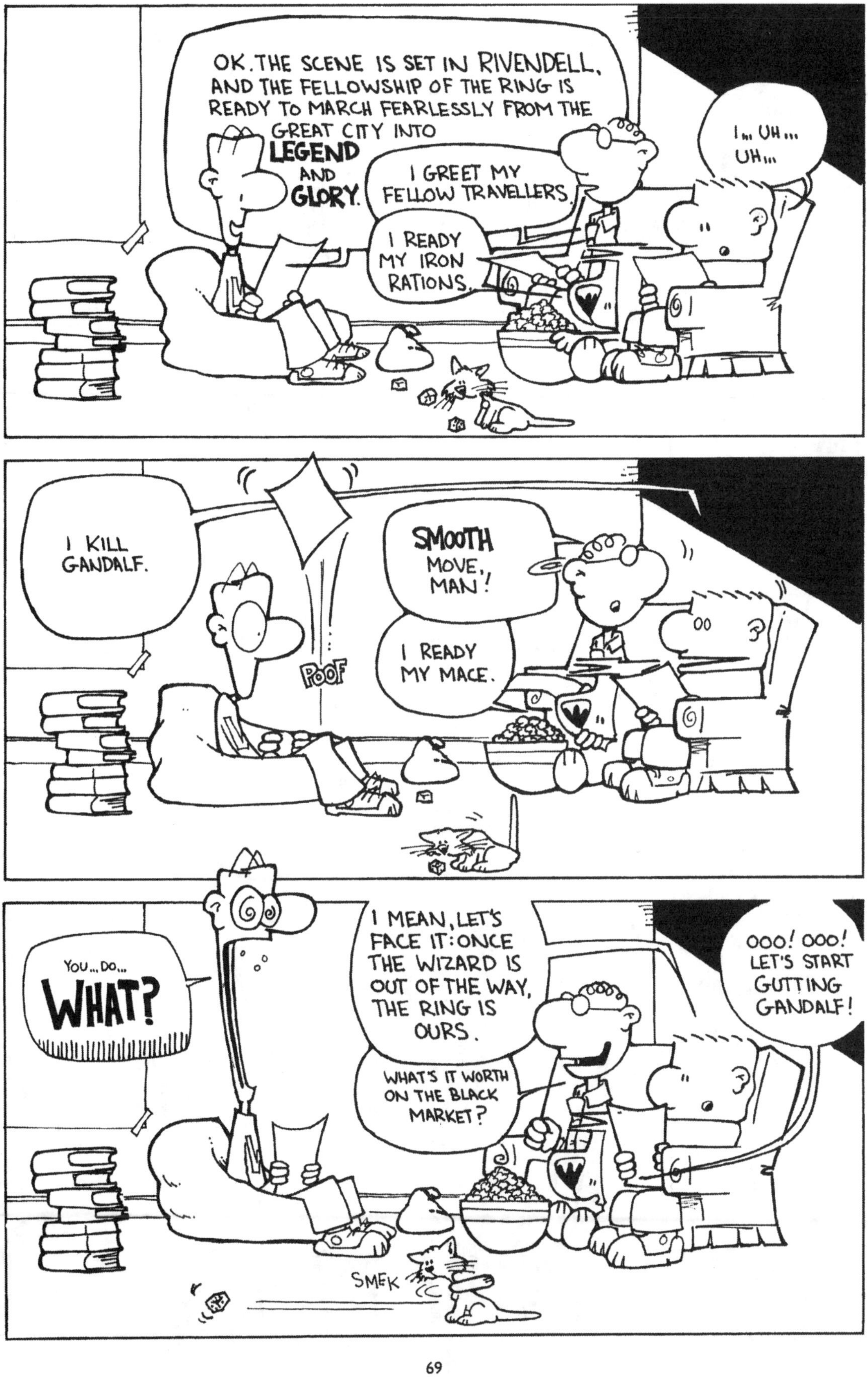
OK. THE SCENE IS SET IN RIVENDELL, AND THE FELLOWSHIP OF THE RING IS READY TO MARCH FEARLESSLY FROM THE GREAT CITY INTO LEGEND AND GLORY.
I GREET MY FELLOW TRAVELLERS.
I READY MY IRON RATIONS.
I... UH... UH...
I KILL GANDALF.
POOF
SMOOTH MOVE, MAN!
I READY MY MACE.
YOU... DO... WHAT?
I MEAN, LET'S FACE IT: ONCE THE WIZARD IS OUT OF THE WAY, THE RING IS OURS.
WHAT'S IT WORTH ON THE BLACK MARKET?
OOO! OOO! LET'S START GUTTING GANDALF!
SMEK

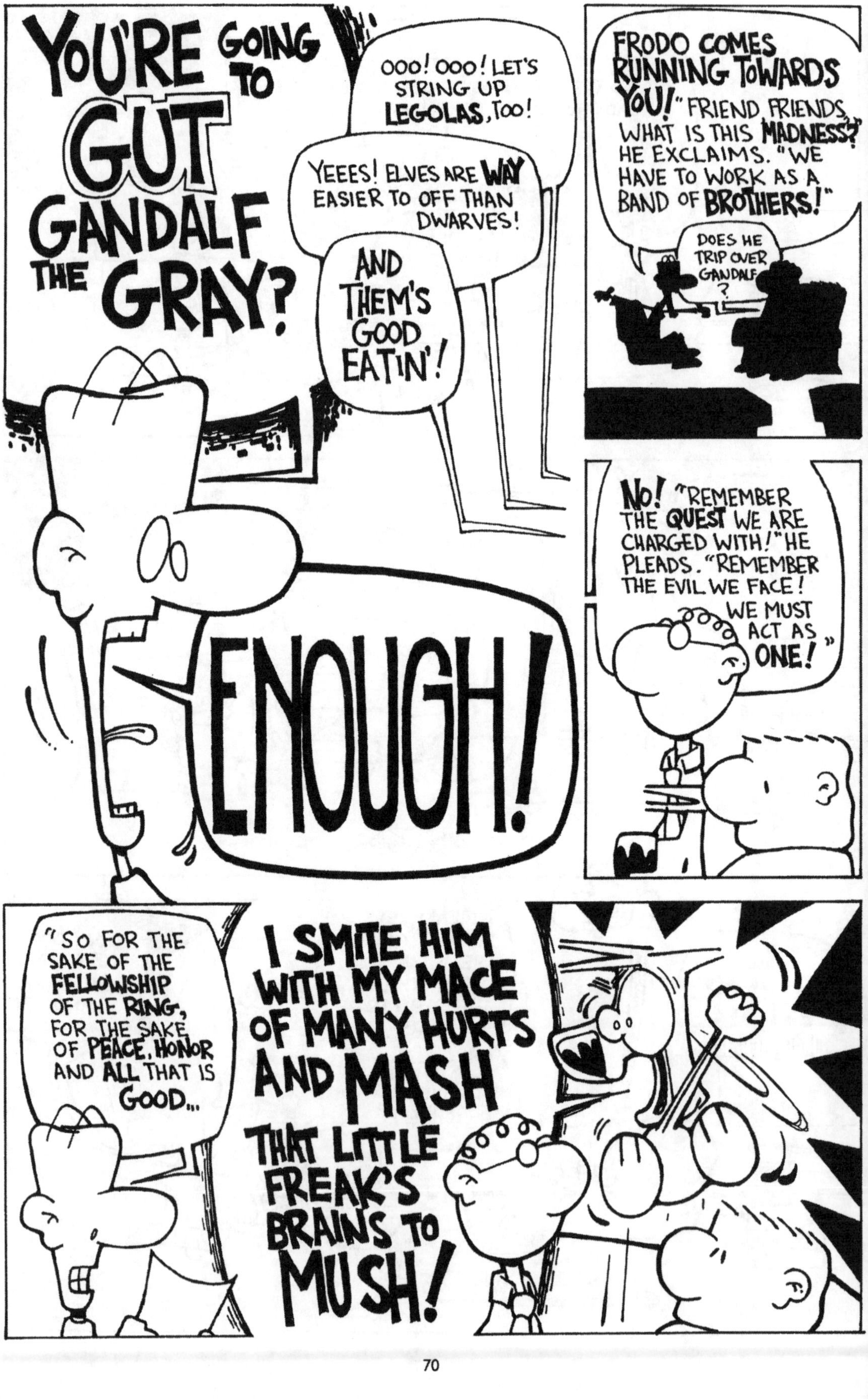
YOU'RE GOING TO GUT GANDALF THE GRAY?
OOO! OOO! LET'S STRING UP LEGOLAS, TOO!
YEEES! ELVES ARE WAY EASIER TO OFF THAN DWARVES!
AND THEM'S GOOD EATIN'!
ENOUGH!
FRODO COMES RUNNING TOWARDS YOU! "FRIEND FRIENDS, WHAT IS THIS MADNESS?" HE EXCLAIMS. "WE HAVE TO WORK AS A BAND OF BROTHERS!"
DOES HE TRIP OVER GANDALF?
NO! "REMEMBER THE QUEST WE ARE CHARGED WITH!" HE PLEADS. "REMEMBER THE EVIL WE FACE! WE MUST ACT AS ONE!"
"SO FOR THE SAKE OF THE FELLOWSHIP OF THE RING, FOR THE SAKE OF PEACE, HONOR AND ALL THAT IS GOOD...
I SMITE HIM WITH MY MACE OF MANY HURTS AND MASH THAT LITTLE FREAK'S BRAINS TO MUSH!

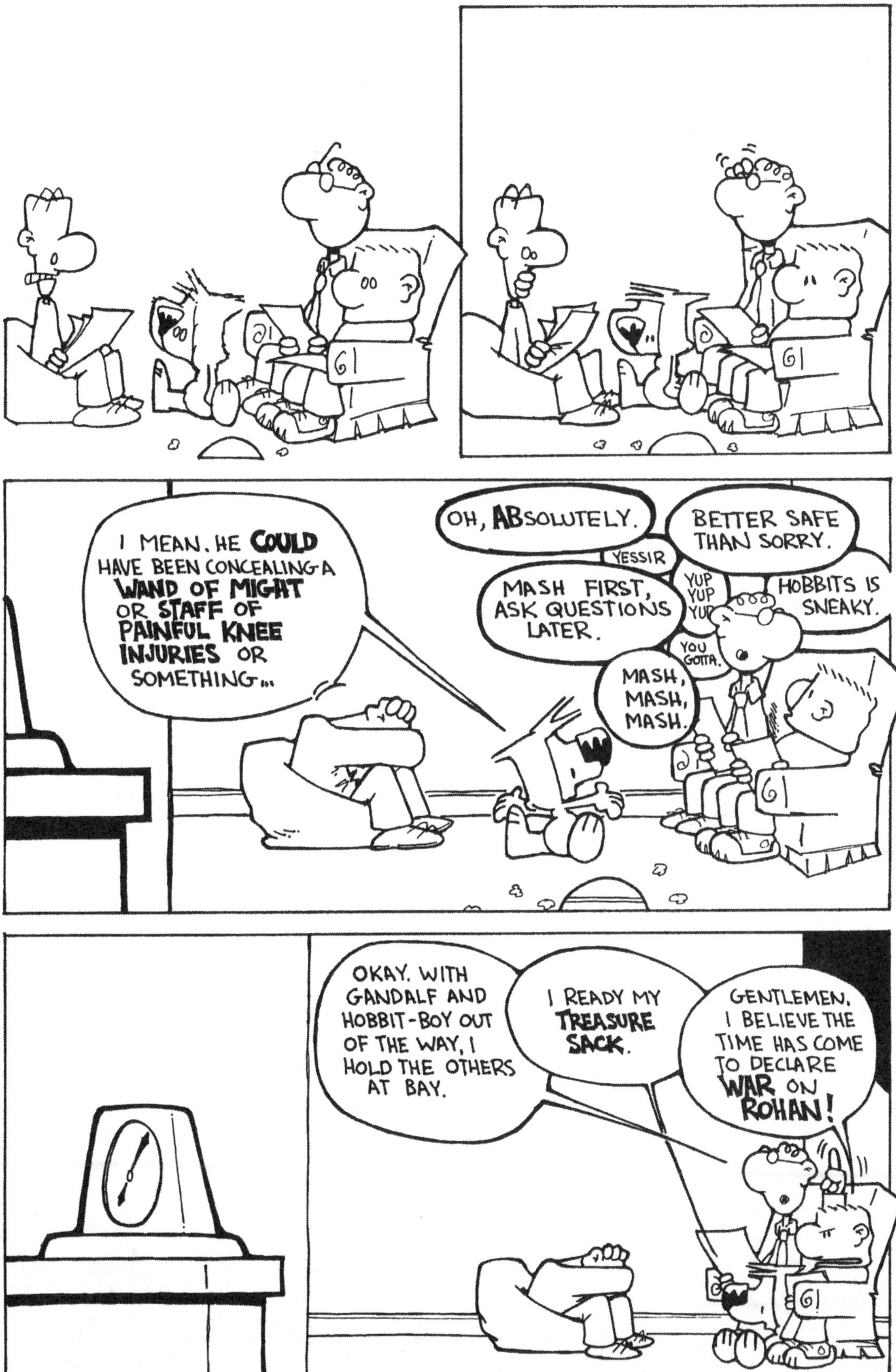
I MEAN. HE COULD HAVE BEEN CONCEALING A WAND OF MIGHT OR STAFF OF PAINFUL KNEE INJURIES OR SOMETHING...
OH, ABSOLUTELY.
BETTER SAFE THAN SORRY.
YESSIR
MASH FIRST, ASK QUESTIONS LATER.
YUP YUP YUP
HOBBITS IS SNEAKY.
YOU GOTTA.
MASH, MASH, MASH.
OKAY. WITH GANDALF AND HOBBIT-BOY OUT OF THE WAY, I HOLD THE OTHERS AT BAY.
I READY MY TREASURE SACK.
GENTLEMEN. I BELIEVE THE TIME HAS COME TO DECLARE WAR ON ROHAN!

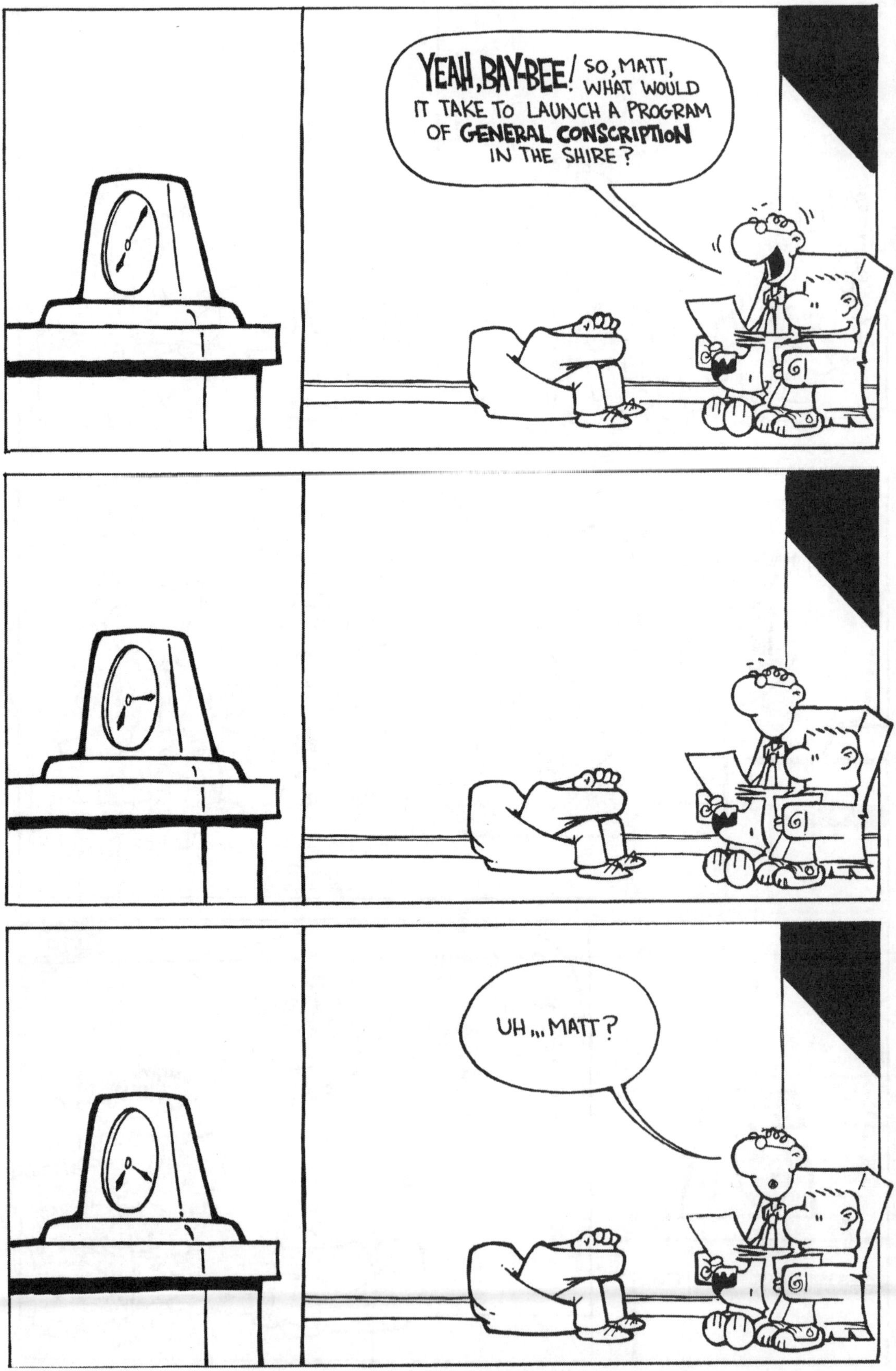
YEAH, BAY-BEE! SO, MATT, WHAT WOULD IT TAKE TO LAUNCH A PROGRAM OF GENERAL CONSCRIPTION IN THE SHIRE?
UH... MATT?

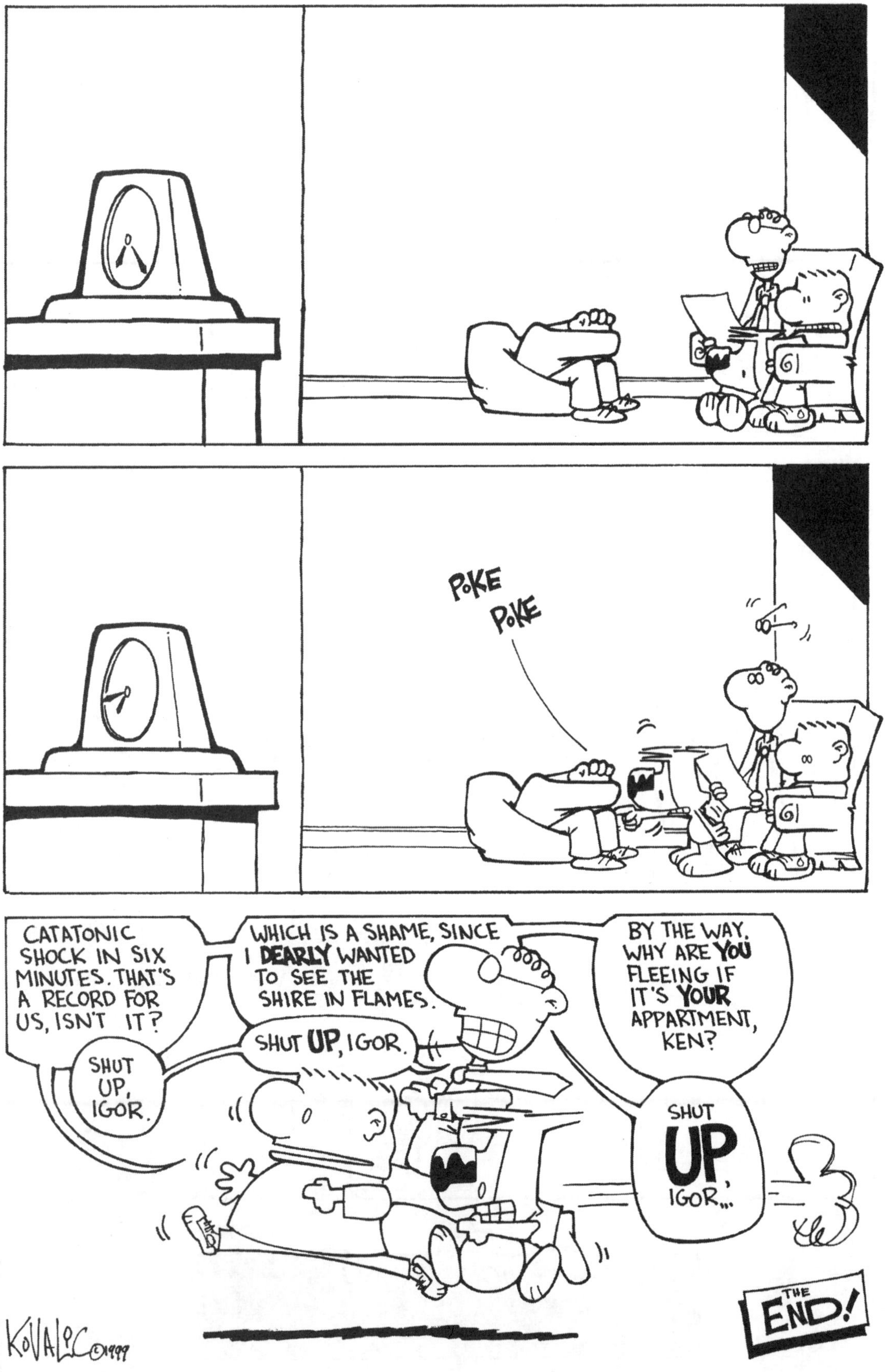
POKE
POKE
CATATONIC SHOCK IN SIX MINUTES. THAT'S A RECORD FOR US, ISN'T IT?
SHUT UP, IGOR.
WHICH IS A SHAME, SINCE I DEARLY WANTED TO SEE THE SHIRE IN FLAMES.
SHUT UP, IGOR.
BY THE WAY, WHY ARE YOU FLEEING IF IT'S YOUR APPARTMENT, KEN?
SHUT UP, IGOR...
THE END!
KOVALIC ©1999

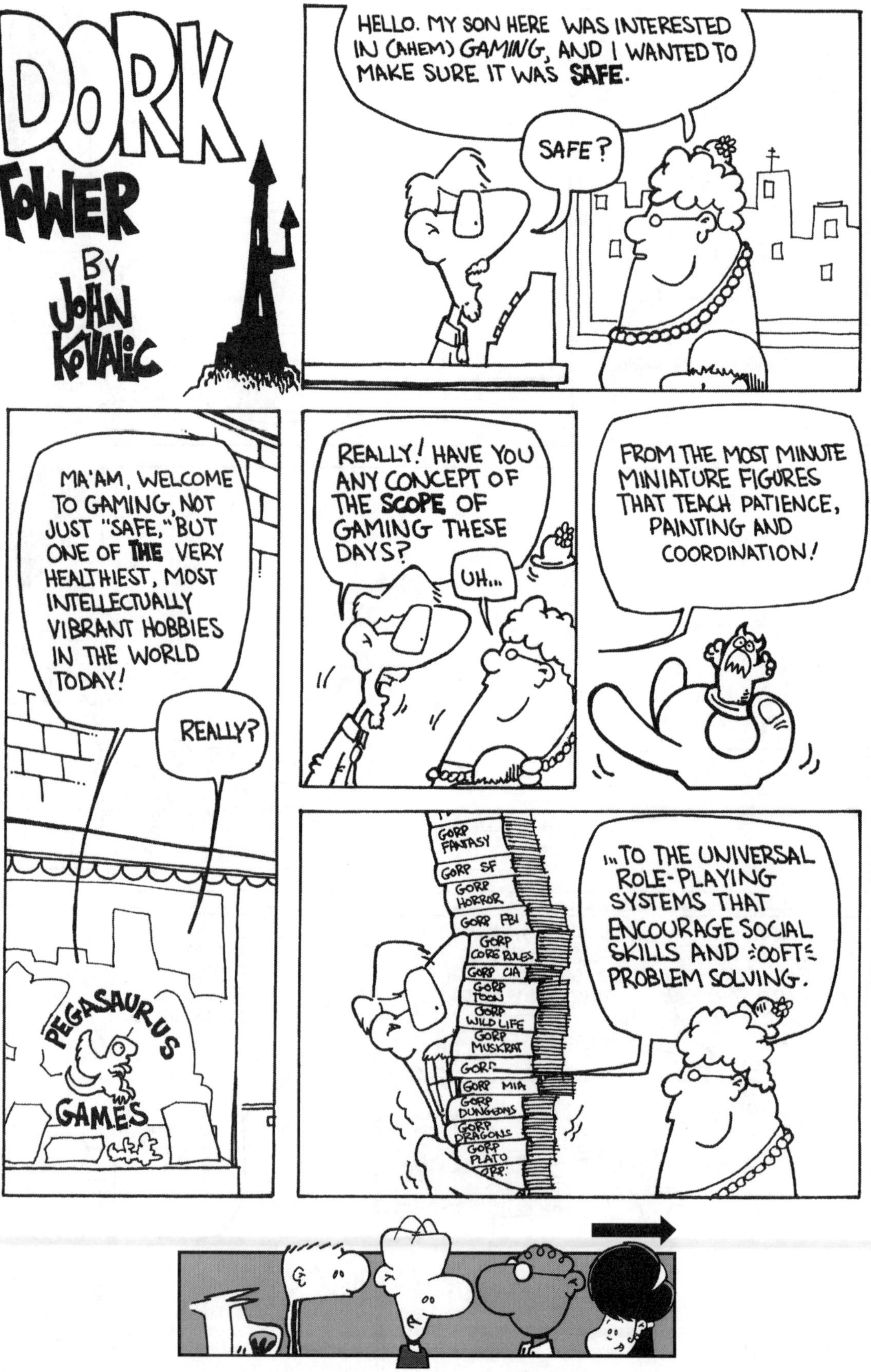
DORK TOWER
BY JOHN KOVALIC
HELLO. MY SON HERE WAS INTERESTED IN (AHEM) GAMING, AND I WANTED TO MAKE SURE IT WAS SAFE.
SAFE?
MA'AM, WELCOME TO GAMING, NOT JUST "SAFE," BUT ONE OF THE VERY HEALTHIEST, MOST INTELLECTUALLY VIBRANT HOBBIES IN THE WORLD TODAY!
REALLY?
PEGASAURUS GAMES
REALLY! HAVE YOU ANY CONCEPT OF THE SCOPE OF GAMING THESE DAYS?
UH...
FROM THE MOST MINUTE MINIATURE FIGURES THAT TEACH PATIENCE, PAINTING AND COORDINATION!
...TO THE UNIVERSAL ROLE-PLAYING SYSTEMS THAT ENCOURAGE SOCIAL SKILLS AND OOF! PROBLEM SOLVING.
GORP FANTASY
GORP SF
GORP HORROR
GORP FBI
GORP CORE RULES
GORP CIA
GORP TOON
GORP WILD LIFE
GORP MUSKRAT
GORP MIA
GORP DUNGEONS
GORP DRAGONS
GORP PLATO

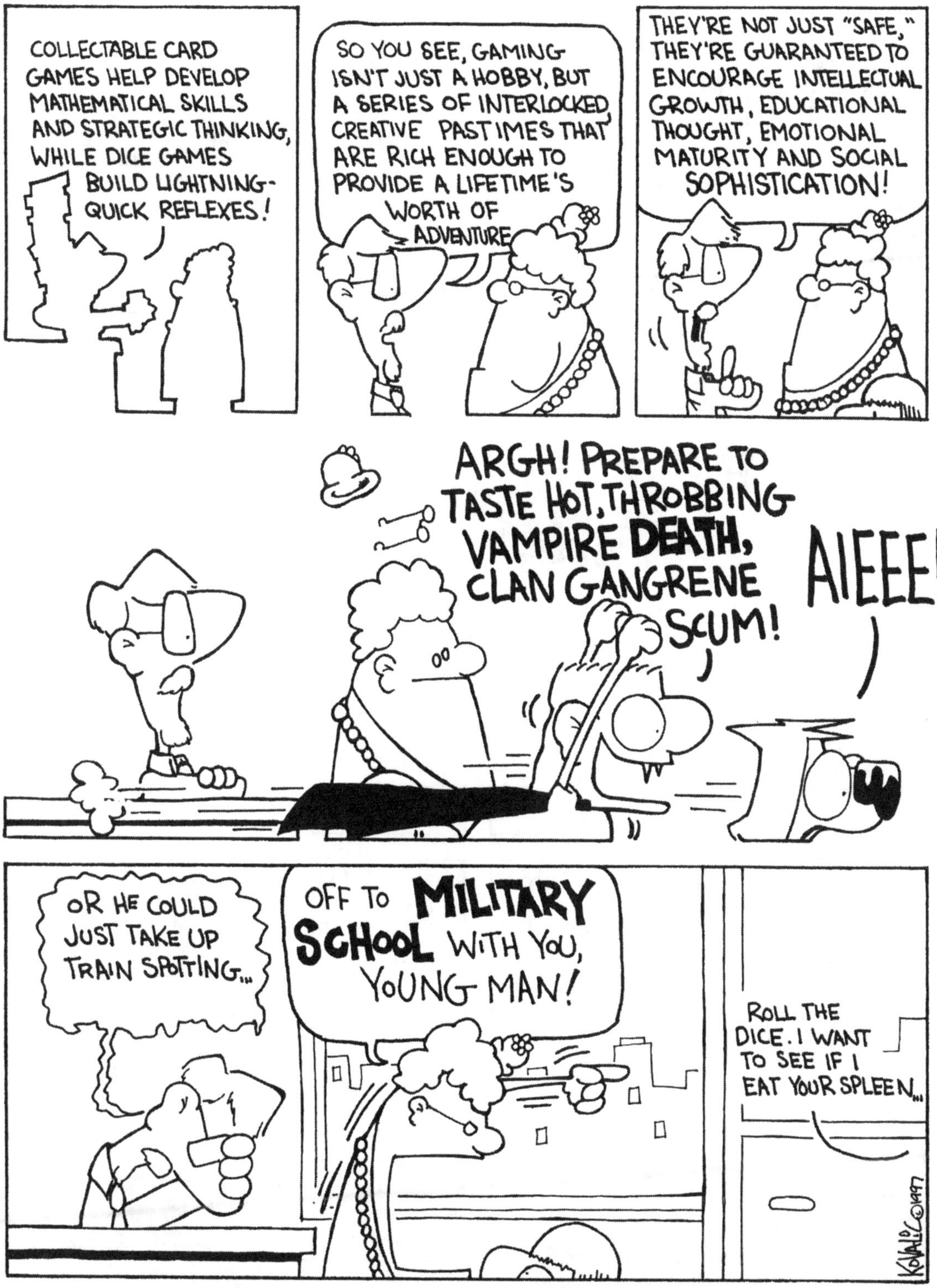
COLLECTABLE CARD GAMES HELP DEVELOP MATHEMATICAL SKILLS AND STRATEGIC THINKING, WHILE DICE GAMES BUILD LIGHTNING-QUICK REFLEXES!
SO YOU SEE, GAMING ISN'T JUST A HOBBY, BUT A SERIES OF INTERLOCKED, CREATIVE PASTIMES THAT ARE RICH ENOUGH TO PROVIDE A LIFETIME'S WORTH OF ADVENTURE.
THEY'RE NOT JUST "SAFE," THEY'RE GUARANTEED TO ENCOURAGE INTELLECTUAL GROWTH, EDUCATIONAL THOUGHT, EMOTIONAL MATURITY AND SOCIAL SOPHISTICATION!
ARGH! PREPARE TO TASTE HOT, THROBBING VAMPIRE DEATH, CLAN GANGRENE SCUM!
AIEEE!
OR HE COULD JUST TAKE UP TRAIN SPOTTING...
OFF TO MILITARY SCHOOL WITH YOU, YOUNG MAN!
ROLL THE DICE. I WANT TO SEE IF I EAT YOUR SPLEEN...
KOVALIC ©1997

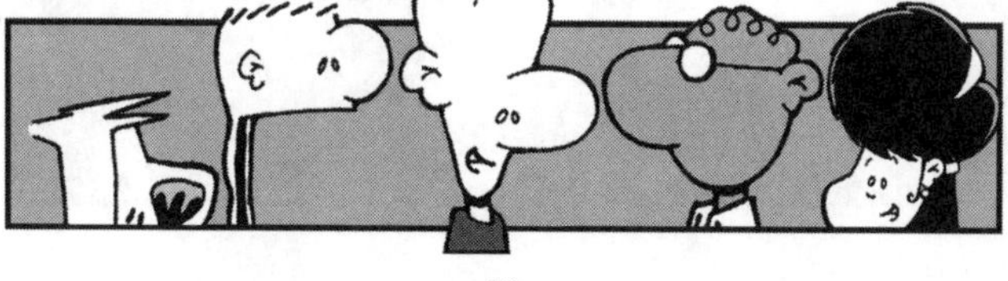

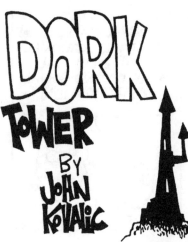

DORK TOWER
BY JOHN KOVALIC

HEY, IGOR! WE JUST GOT "WARHAMSTER 40,000" SUPPLEMENT **TEN** IN WITH THE NEW RELEASES.

¡GASP¿

IT MUST BE **MINE!**

OOOOOO... "WARHAMSTER" SUPPLEMENT **TEN**! HOW I'VE WAITED FOR THIS TO BE RELEASED! WAITED, PINED, **PRAYED**! **HUZZAH!**

NIRVANA! JOY! AT LAST! THE SUPPLEMENT OF SUPPLEMENTS! THE RELEASE OF THE **YEAR** — NAY, OF THE **DECADE!**

OF ALL THE BOOKS IN ALL THE WAREHOUSES IN ALL THE WORLD THAT COULD HAVE COME IN TODAY, **THIS** CAME IN FROM ON **HIGH!** OH BRAVE NEW WORLD! OH **BLISS!**

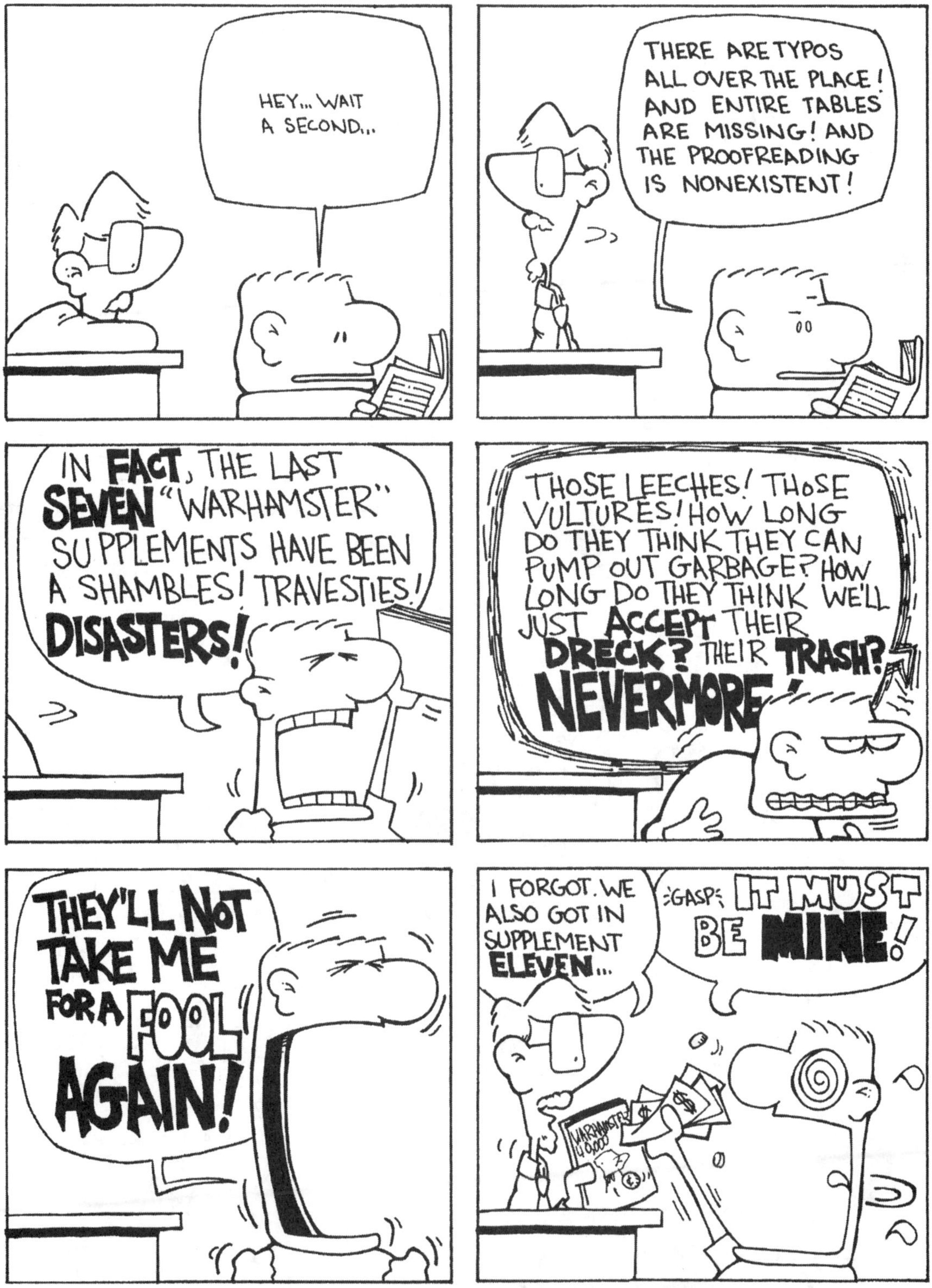
HEY... WAIT A SECOND...
THERE ARE TYPOS ALL OVER THE PLACE! AND ENTIRE TABLES ARE MISSING! AND THE PROOFREADING IS NONEXISTENT!
IN FACT, THE LAST SEVEN "WARHAMSTER" SUPPLEMENTS HAVE BEEN A SHAMBLES! TRAVESTIES! DISASTERS!
THOSE LEECHES! THOSE VULTURES! HOW LONG DO THEY THINK THEY CAN PUMP OUT GARBAGE? HOW LONG DO THEY THINK WE'LL JUST ACCEPT THEIR DRECK? THEIR TRASH? NEVERMORE!
THEY'LL NOT TAKE ME FOR A FOOL AGAIN!
I FORGOT. WE ALSO GOT IN SUPPLEMENT ELEVEN...
:GASP: IT MUST BE MINE!
WARHAMSTER 40,000

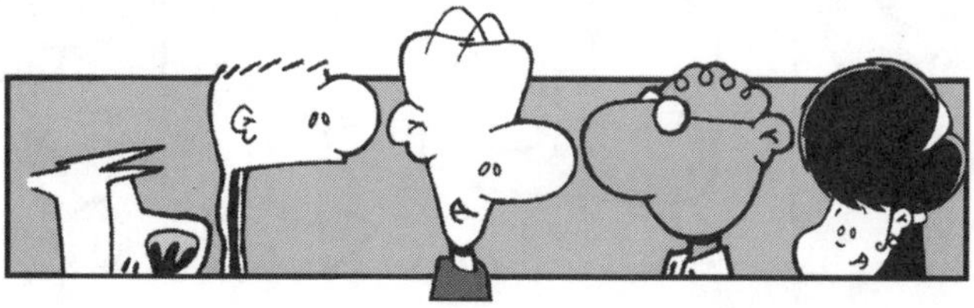

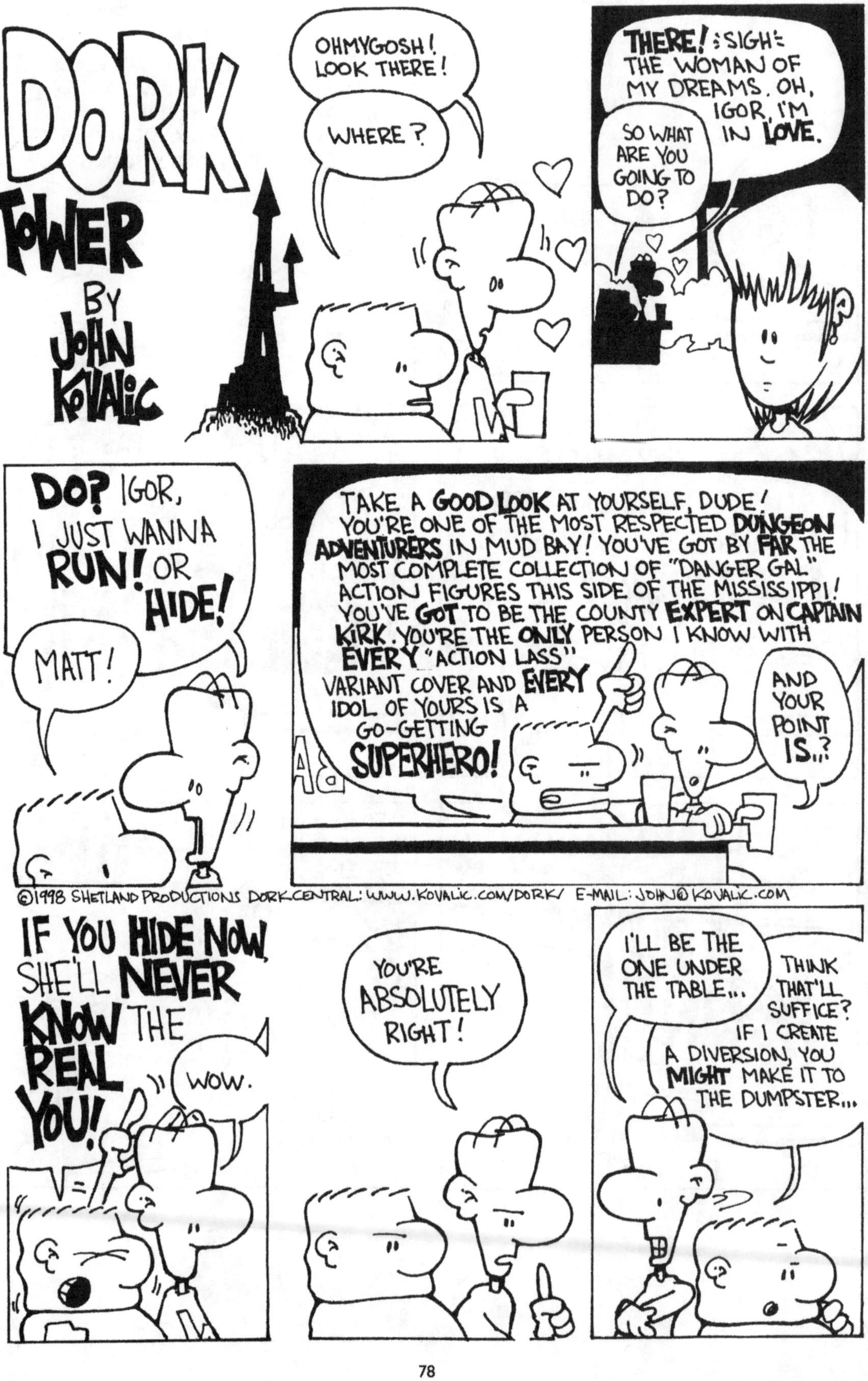
DORK TOWER
BY JOHN KOVALIC
OHMYGOSH! LOOK THERE!
WHERE?
THERE! :SIGH: THE WOMAN OF MY DREAMS. OH, IGOR, I'M IN LOVE.
SO WHAT ARE YOU GOING TO DO?
DO? IGOR, I JUST WANNA RUN! OR HIDE!
MATT!
TAKE A GOOD LOOK AT YOURSELF, DUDE! YOU'RE ONE OF THE MOST RESPECTED DUNGEON ADVENTURERS IN MUD BAY! YOU'VE GOT BY FAR THE MOST COMPLETE COLLECTION OF "DANGER GAL" ACTION FIGURES THIS SIDE OF THE MISSISSIPPI! YOU'VE GOT TO BE THE COUNTY EXPERT ON CAPTAIN KIRK. YOU'RE THE ONLY PERSON I KNOW WITH EVERY "ACTION LASS" VARIANT COVER AND EVERY IDOL OF YOURS IS A GO-GETTING SUPERHERO!
AND YOUR POINT IS..?
©1998 SHETLAND PRODUCTIONS DORK CENTRAL: WWW.KOVALIC.COM/DORK/ E-MAIL: JOHN@KOVALIC.COM
IF YOU HIDE NOW, SHE'LL NEVER KNOW THE REAL YOU!
WOW.
YOU'RE ABSOLUTELY RIGHT!
I'LL BE THE ONE UNDER THE TABLE...
THINK THAT'LL SUFFICE? IF I CREATE A DIVERSION, YOU MIGHT MAKE IT TO THE DUMPSTER...

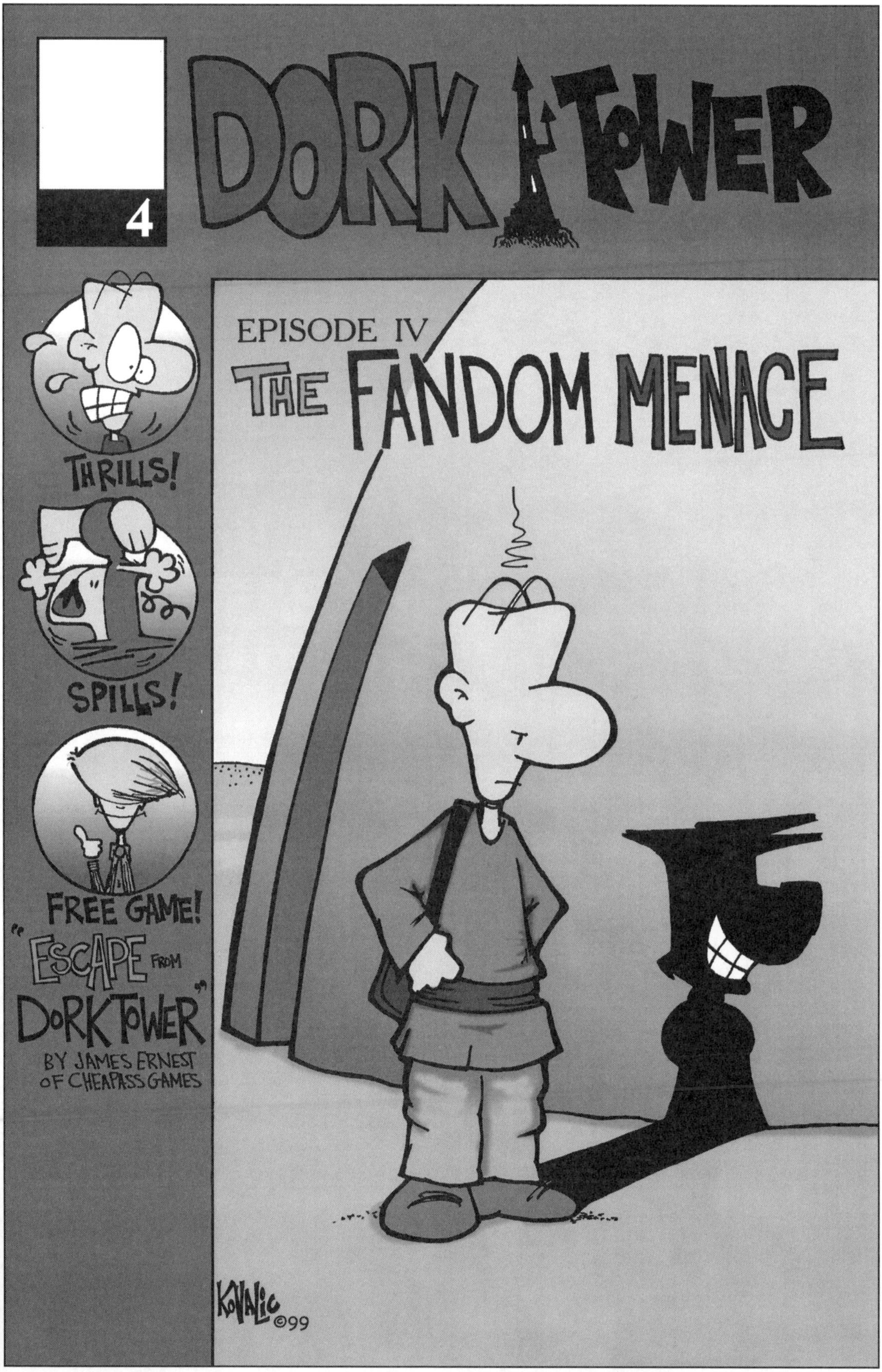
4
DORK TOWER
THRILLS!
SPILLS!
FREE GAME!
"ESCAPE FROM DORK TOWER"
BY JAMES ERNEST OF CHEAPASS GAMES
EPISODE IV
THE FANDOM MENACE
KOVALIC ©99

"Laugh it up, fuzzball."

-Han Solo to Chewbacca in
Star Wars: The Empire
Strikes Back

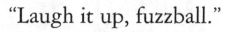

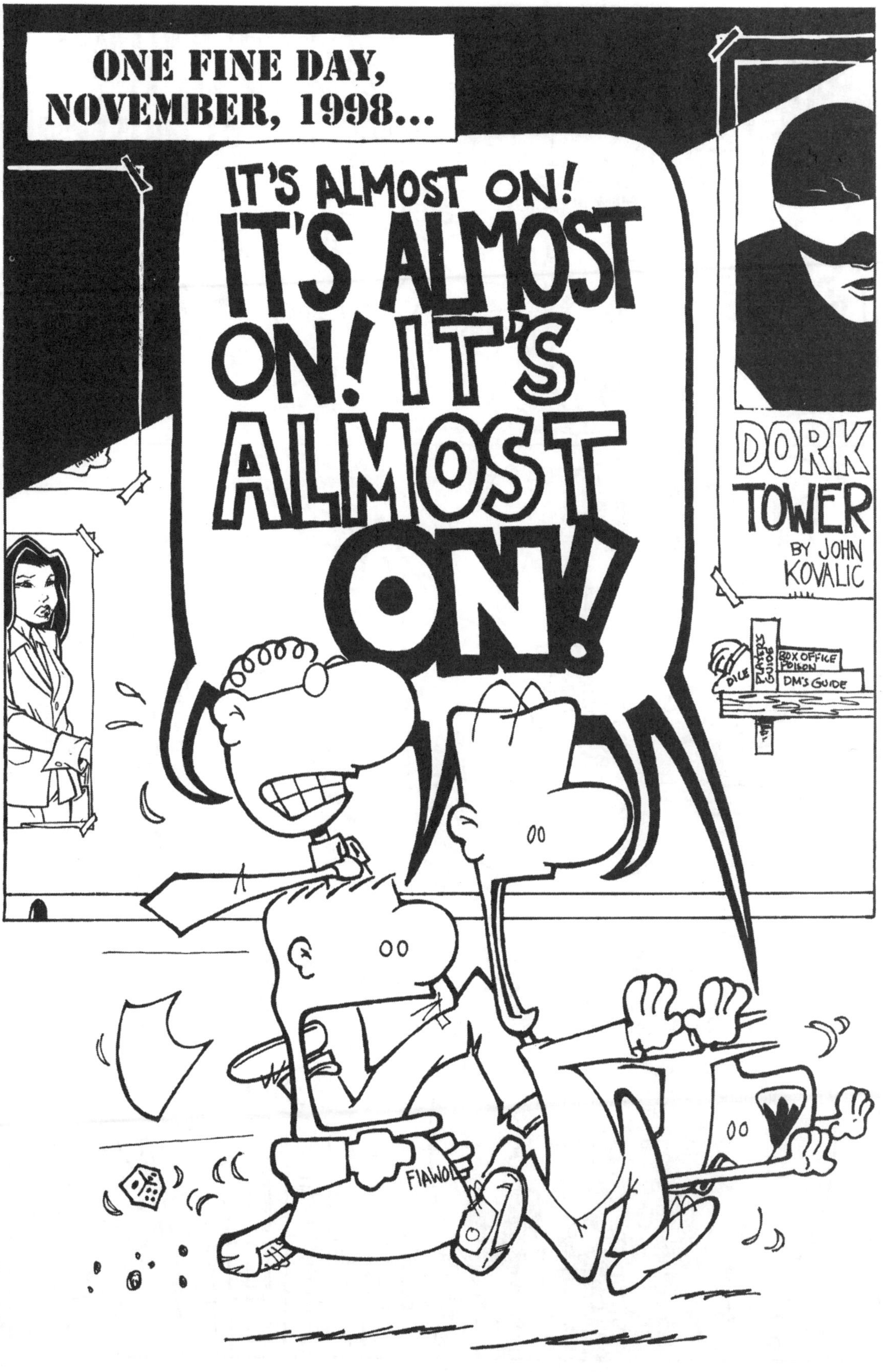
ONE FINE DAY, NOVEMBER, 1998...
IT'S ALMOST ON! IT'S ALMOST ON! IT'S ALMOST ON!
DORK TOWER
BY JOHN KOVALIC
DICE
PLAYERS GUIDE
BOX OFFICE POISON
DM'S GUIDE
FIAWOL

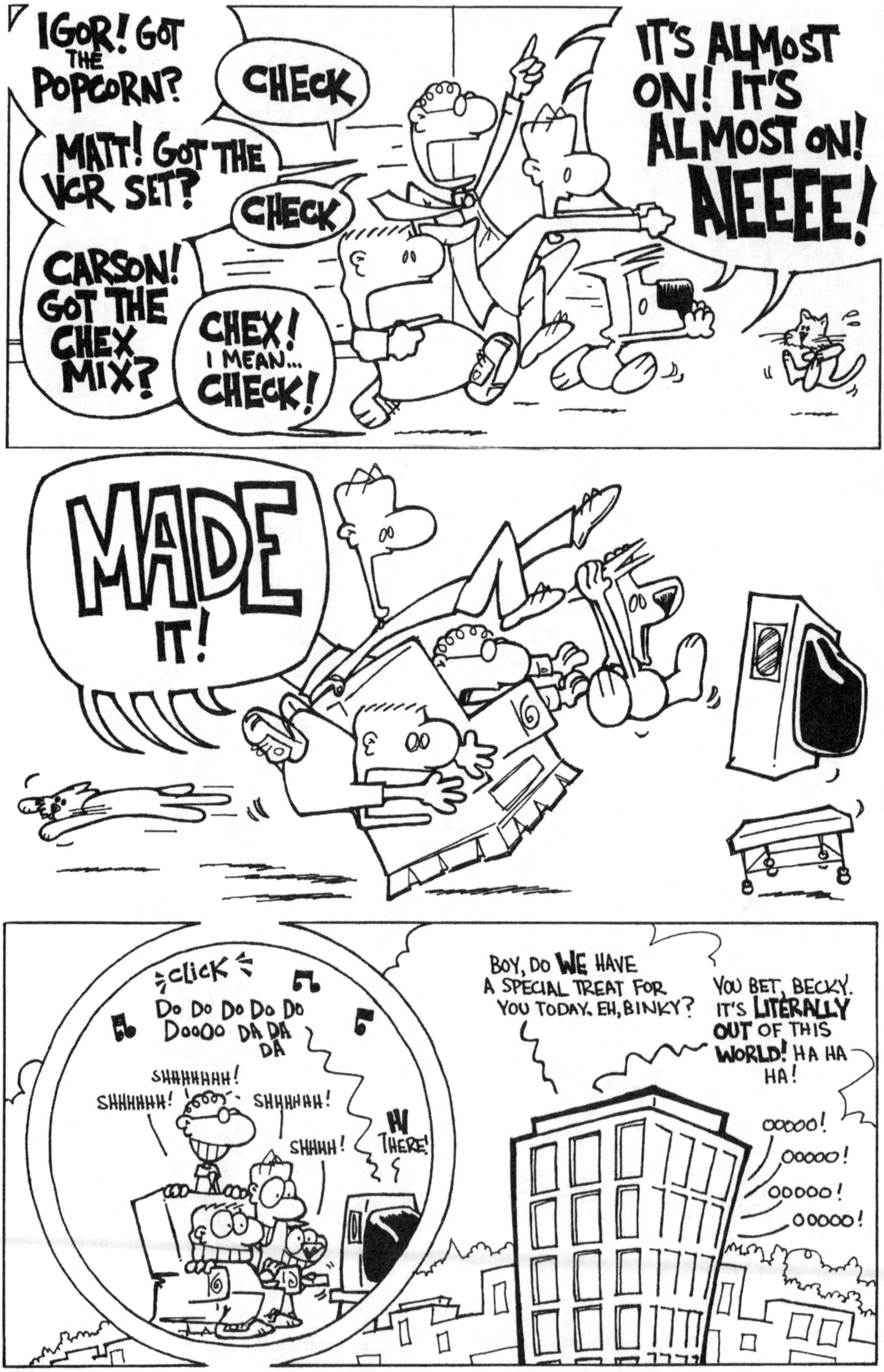
IGOR! GOT THE POPCORN?
CHECK
MATT! GOT THE VCR SET?
CHECK
CARSON! GOT THE CHEX MIX?
CHEX! I MEAN... CHECK!
IT'S ALMOST ON! IT'S ALMOST ON! AIEEEE!
MADE IT!
CLICK
Do Do Do Do Do Doooo DA DA DA
SHHHHHHH!
SHHHHHH!
SHHHHHH!
SHHHH!
HI THERE!
BOY, DO WE HAVE A SPECIAL TREAT FOR YOU TODAY. EH, BINKY?
YOU BET, BECKY. IT'S LITERALLY OUT OF THIS WORLD! HA HA HA!
OOOOO!
OOOOO!
OOOOO!
OOOOO!

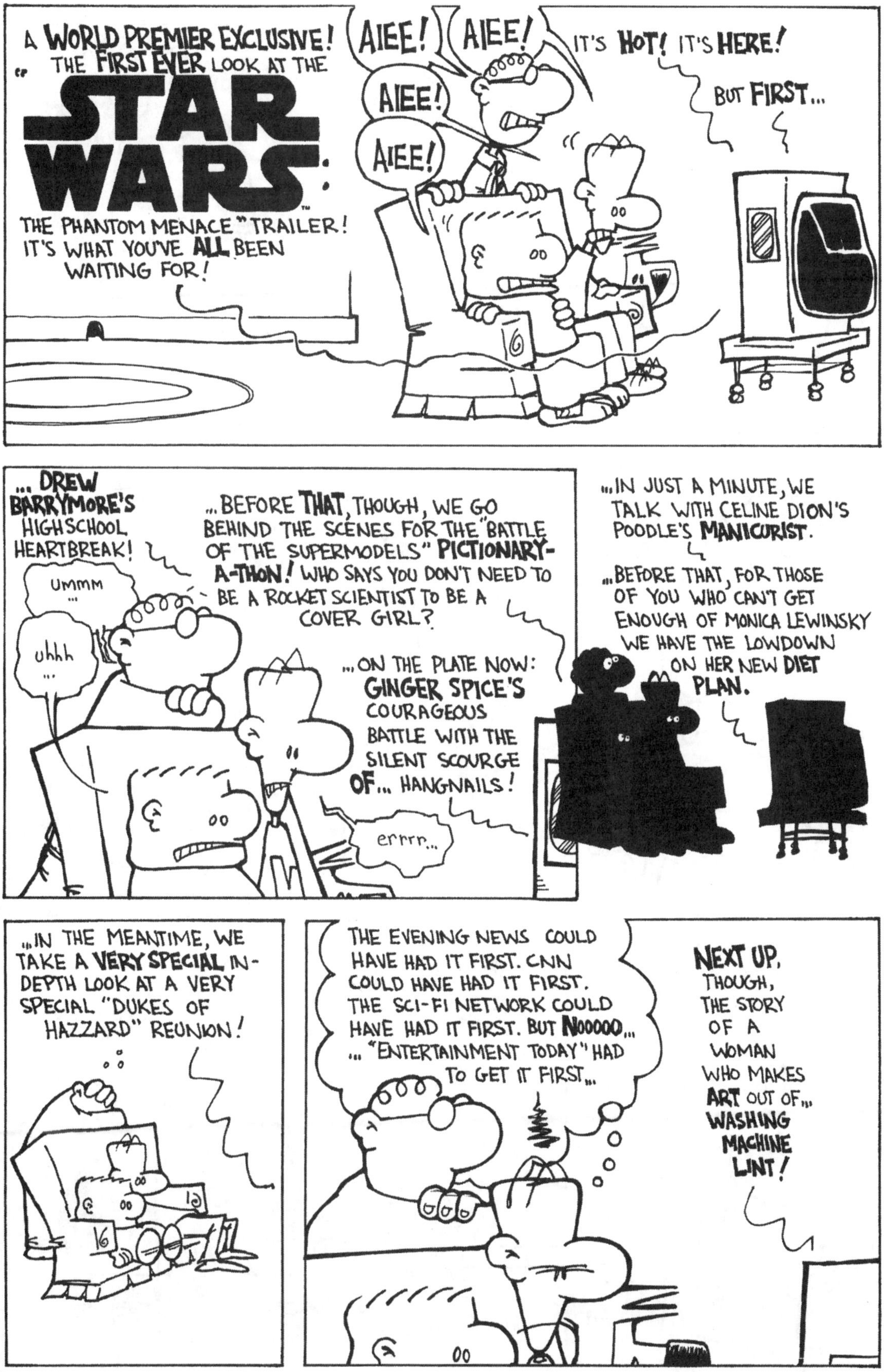
A WORLD PREMIER EXCLUSIVE! THE FIRST EVER LOOK AT THE "STAR WARS: THE PHANTOM MENACE" TRAILER! IT'S WHAT YOU'VE ALL BEEN WAITING FOR!
AIEE!
AIEE!
AIEE!
AIEE!
IT'S HOT! IT'S HERE!
BUT FIRST...
... DREW BARRYMORE'S HIGHSCHOOL HEARTBREAK!
UMMM ...
uhhh ...
... BEFORE THAT, THOUGH, WE GO BEHIND THE SCENES FOR THE "BATTLE OF THE SUPERMODELS" PICTIONARY-A-THON! WHO SAYS YOU DON'T NEED TO BE A ROCKET SCIENTIST TO BE A COVER GIRL?
... ON THE PLATE NOW: GINGER SPICE'S COURAGEOUS BATTLE WITH THE SILENT SCOURGE OF... HANGNAILS!
errrr...
... IN JUST A MINUTE, WE TALK WITH CELINE DION'S POODLE'S MANICURIST.
... BEFORE THAT, FOR THOSE OF YOU WHO CAN'T GET ENOUGH OF MONICA LEWINSKY WE HAVE THE LOWDOWN ON HER NEW DIET PLAN.
... IN THE MEANTIME, WE TAKE A VERY SPECIAL IN-DEPTH LOOK AT A VERY SPECIAL "DUKES OF HAZZARD" REUNION!
THE EVENING NEWS COULD HAVE HAD IT FIRST. CNN COULD HAVE HAD IT FIRST. THE SCI-FI NETWORK COULD HAVE HAD IT FIRST. BUT NOOOOO... ... "ENTERTAINMENT TODAY" HAD TO GET IT FIRST...
NEXT UP, THOUGH, THE STORY OF A WOMAN WHO MAKES ART OUT OF... WASHING MACHINE LINT!

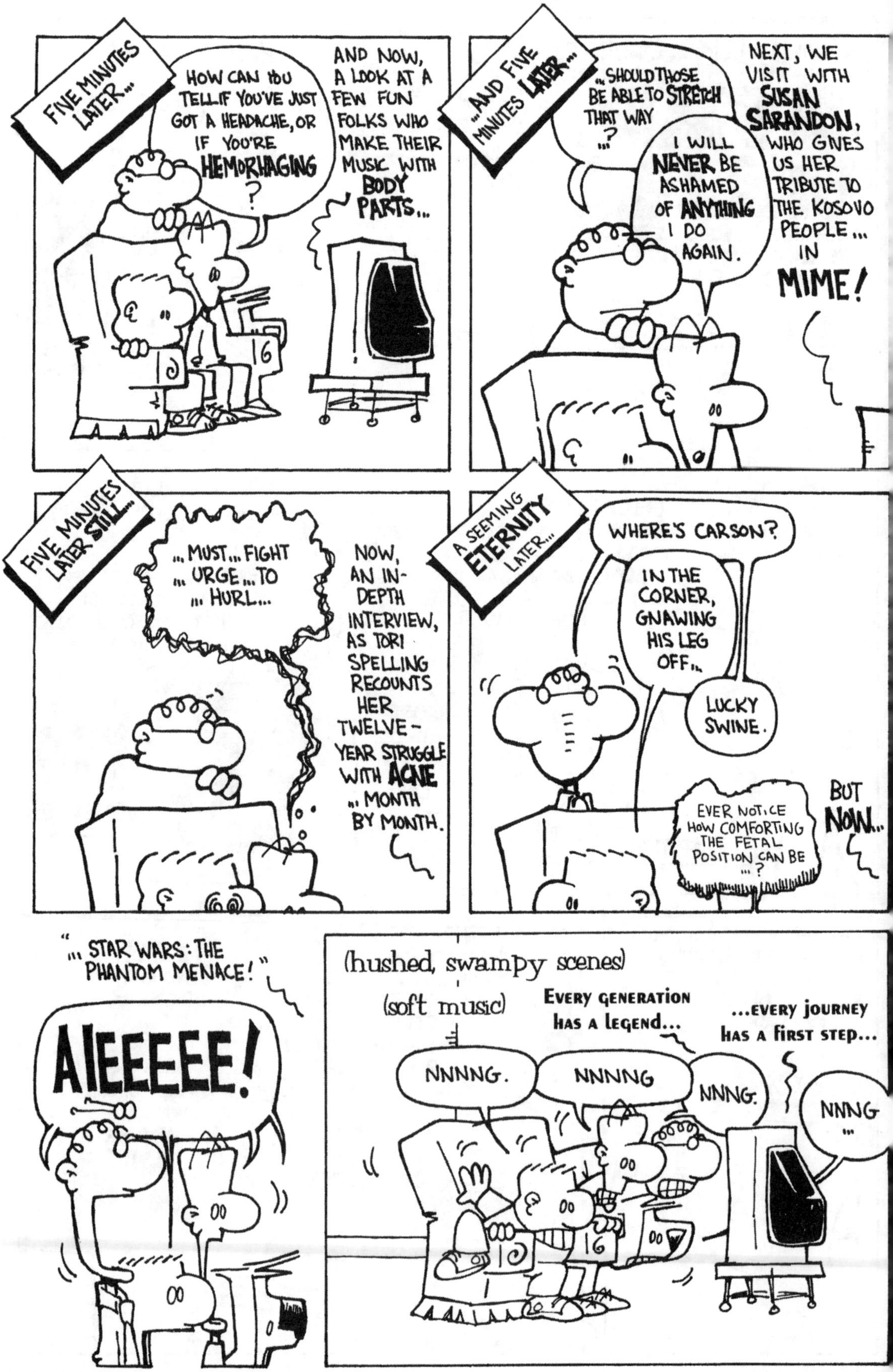
FIVE MINUTES LATER...
HOW CAN YOU TELL IF YOU'VE JUST GOT A HEADACHE, OR IF YOU'RE HEMORHAGING ?
AND NOW, A LOOK AT A FEW FUN FOLKS WHO MAKE THEIR MUSIC WITH BODY PARTS...
...AND FIVE MINUTES LATER...
...SHOULD THOSE BE ABLE TO STRETCH THAT WAY ...?
I WILL NEVER BE ASHAMED OF ANYTHING I DO AGAIN.
NEXT, WE VISIT WITH SUSAN SARANDON, WHO GIVES US HER TRIBUTE TO THE KOSOVO PEOPLE... IN MIME!
FIVE MINUTES LATER STILL...
... MUST... FIGHT ... URGE... TO ... HURL...
NOW, AN IN-DEPTH INTERVIEW, AS TORI SPELLING RECOUNTS HER TWELVE-YEAR STRUGGLE WITH ACNE ... MONTH BY MONTH.
A SEEMING ETERNITY LATER...
WHERE'S CARSON?
IN THE CORNER, GNAWING HIS LEG OFF...
LUCKY SWINE.
EVER NOTICE HOW COMFORTING THE FETAL POSITION CAN BE ...?
BUT NOW...
"... STAR WARS: THE PHANTOM MENACE!"
AIEEEEE!
(hushed, swampy scenes)
(soft music)
EVERY GENERATION HAS A LEGEND...
...EVERY JOURNEY HAS A FIRST STEP...
NNNNG.
NNNNG
NNNG.
NNNG ...

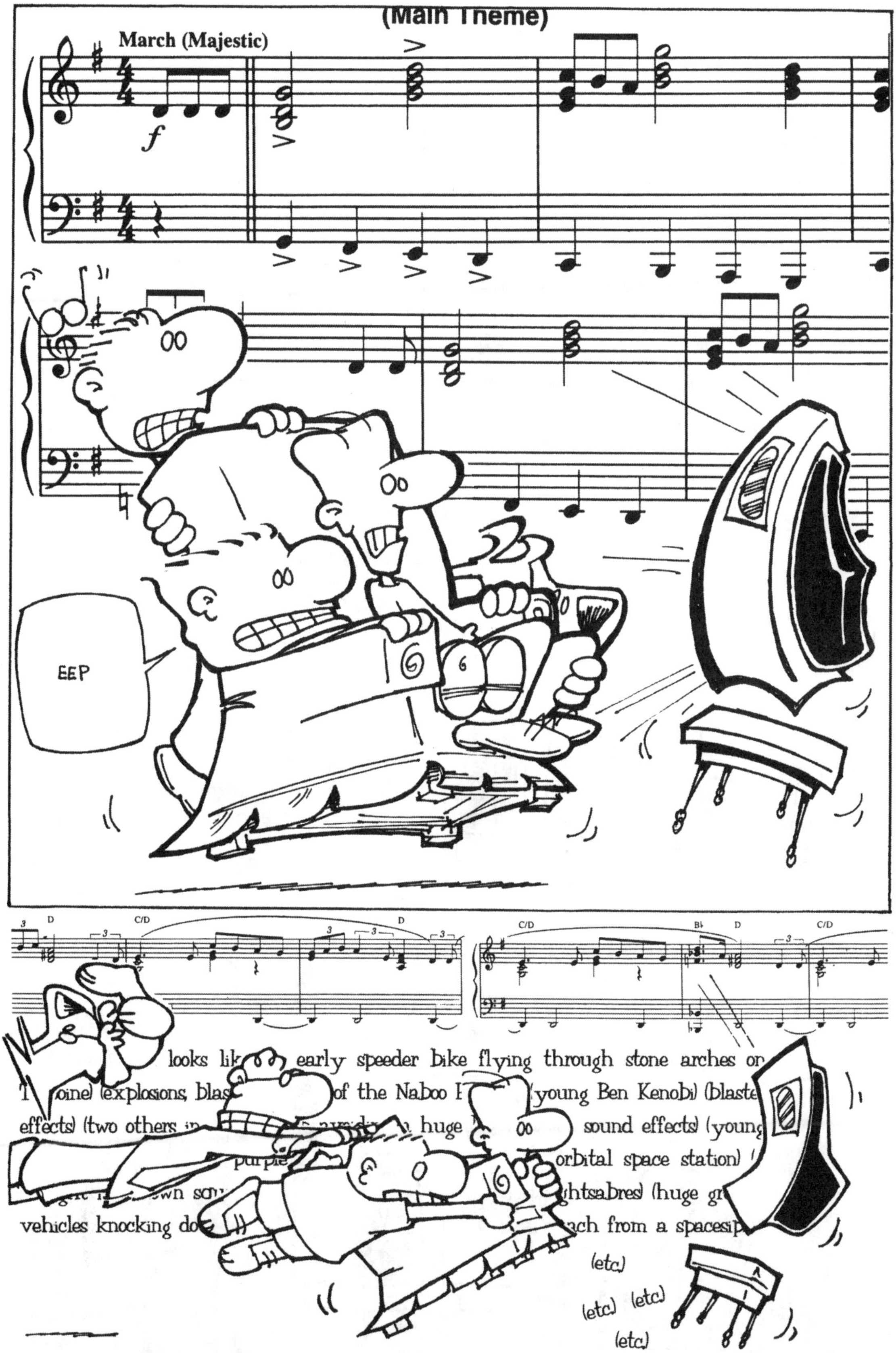
(Main Theme)
March (Majestic)
EEP
D
C/D
D
C/D
B♭
D
C/D
looks lik
early speeder bike flying through stone arches or
oine) (explosions, blas
of the Naboo
(young Ben Kenobi) (blaste
effects) (two others
huge
sound effects) (young
orbital space station)
ghtsabres) (huge gr
vehicles knocking do
ach from a spacesip
(etc.)
(etc.) (etc.)
(etc.)

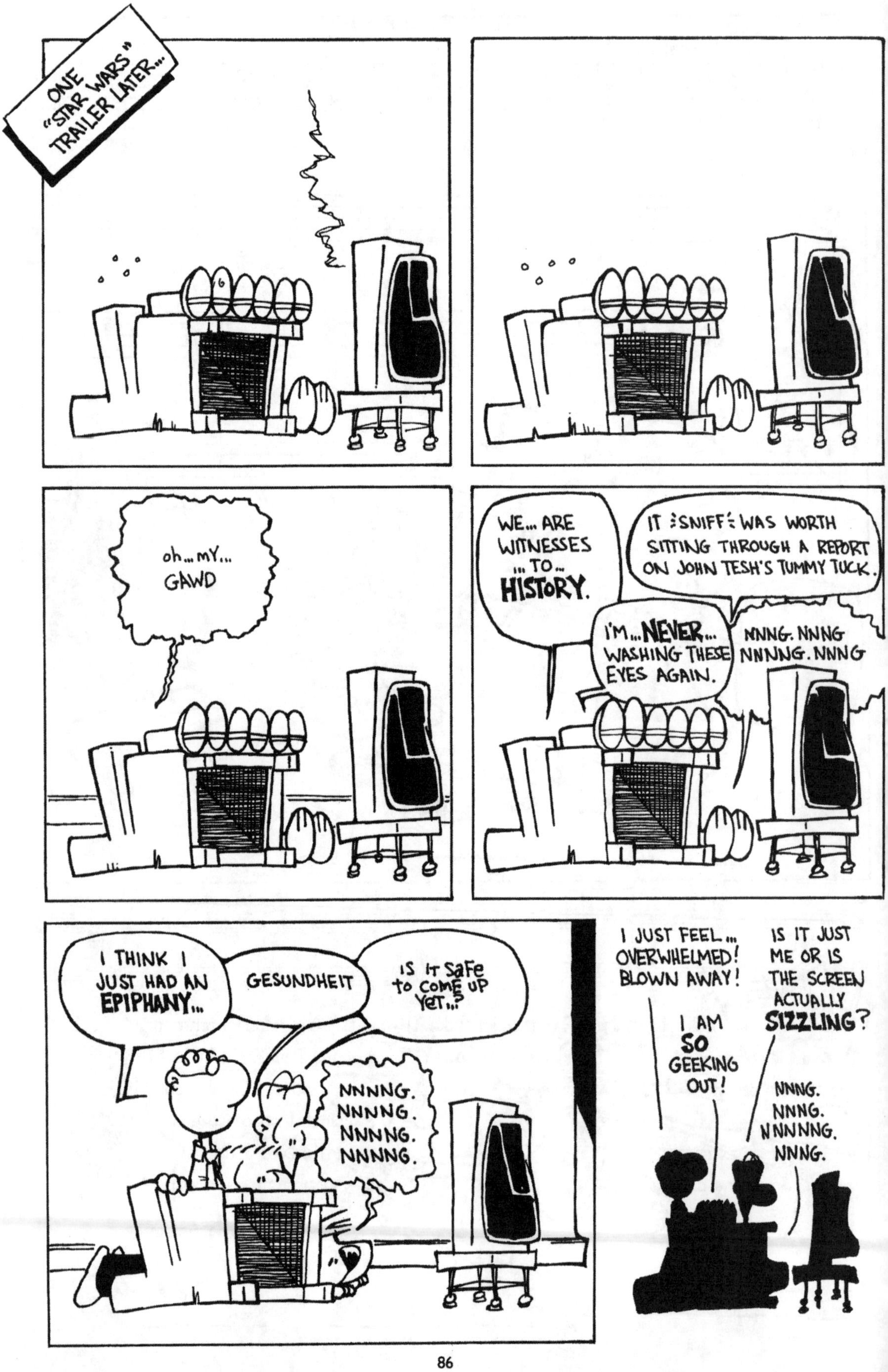
ONE "STAR WARS" TRAILER LATER...
oh... MY... GAWD
WE... ARE WITNESSES ... TO... HISTORY.
IT ⁝SNIFF⁝ WAS WORTH SITTING THROUGH A REPORT ON JOHN TESH'S TUMMY TUCK.
I'M... NEVER... WASHING THESE EYES AGAIN.
NNNG. NNNG NNNNG. NNNG
I THINK I JUST HAD AN EPIPHANY...
GESUNDHEIT
IS IT SAFE TO COME UP YET...?
NNNNG. NNNNG. NNNNG. NNNNG.
I JUST FEEL... OVERWHELMED! BLOWN AWAY!
I AM SO GEEKING OUT!
IS IT JUST ME OR IS THE SCREEN ACTUALLY SIZZLING?
NNNG. NNNG. NNNNNG. NNNG.

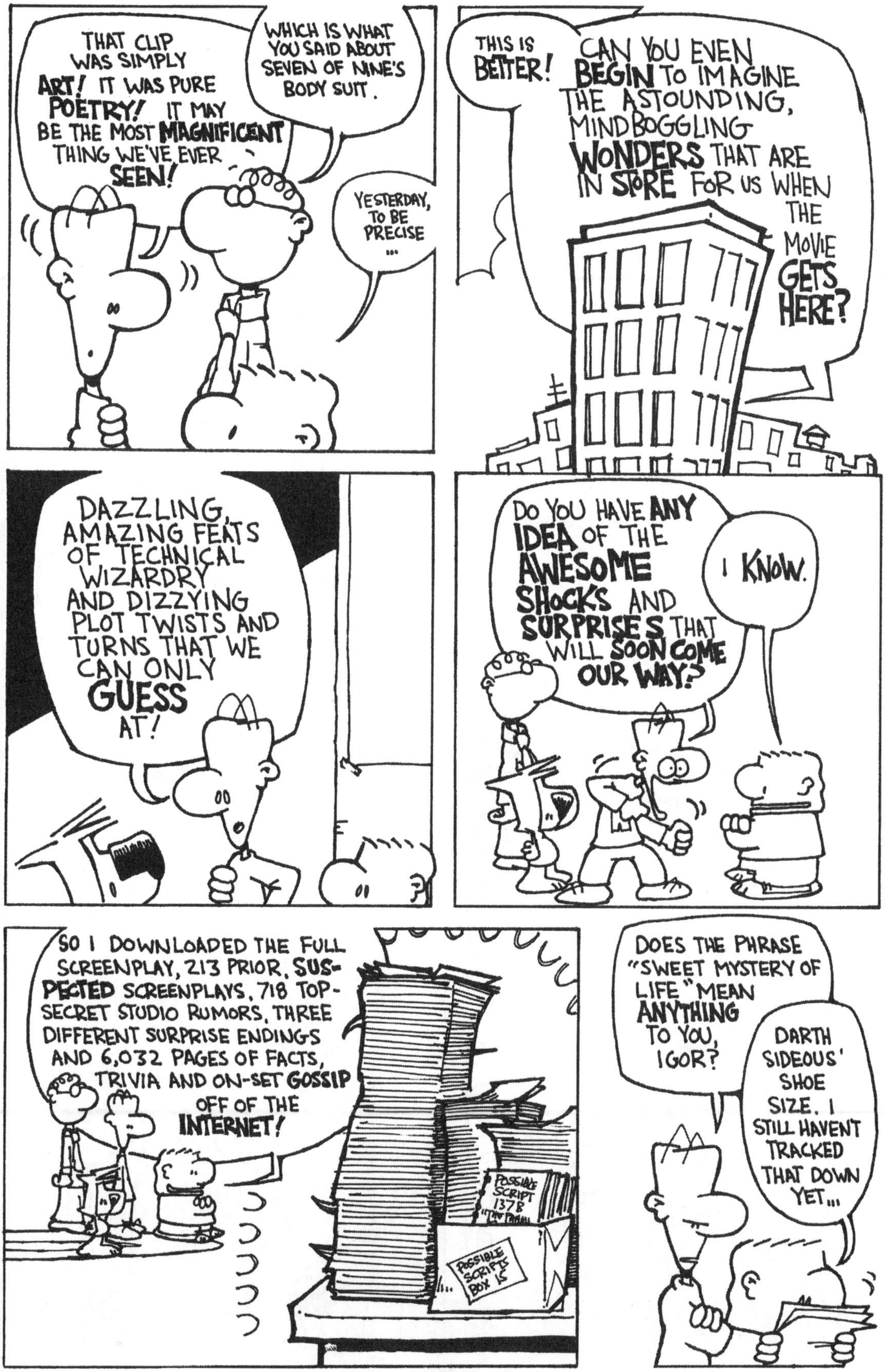
THAT CLIP WAS SIMPLY ART! IT WAS PURE POETRY! IT MAY BE THE MOST MAGNIFICENT THING WE'VE EVER SEEN!
WHICH IS WHAT YOU SAID ABOUT SEVEN OF NINE'S BODY SUIT.
YESTERDAY, TO BE PRECISE ...
THIS IS BETTER!
CAN YOU EVEN BEGIN TO IMAGINE THE ASTOUNDING, MINDBOGGLING WONDERS THAT ARE IN STORE FOR US WHEN THE MOVIE GETS HERE?
DAZZLING, AMAZING FEATS OF TECHNICAL WIZARDRY AND DIZZYING PLOT TWISTS AND TURNS THAT WE CAN ONLY GUESS AT!
DO YOU HAVE ANY IDEA OF THE AWESOME SHOCKS AND SURPRISES THAT WILL SOON COME OUR WAY?
I KNOW.
SO I DOWNLOADED THE FULL SCREENPLAY, 213 PRIOR, SUSPECTED SCREENPLAYS, 718 TOP-SECRET STUDIO RUMORS, THREE DIFFERENT SURPRISE ENDINGS AND 6,032 PAGES OF FACTS, TRIVIA AND ON-SET GOSSIP OFF OF THE INTERNET!
POSSIBLE SCRIPT 137B
POSSIBLE SCRIPTS BOX 15
DOES THE PHRASE "SWEET MYSTERY OF LIFE" MEAN ANYTHING TO YOU, IGOR?
DARTH SIDEOUS' SHOE SIZE. I STILL HAVEN'T TRACKED THAT DOWN YET...

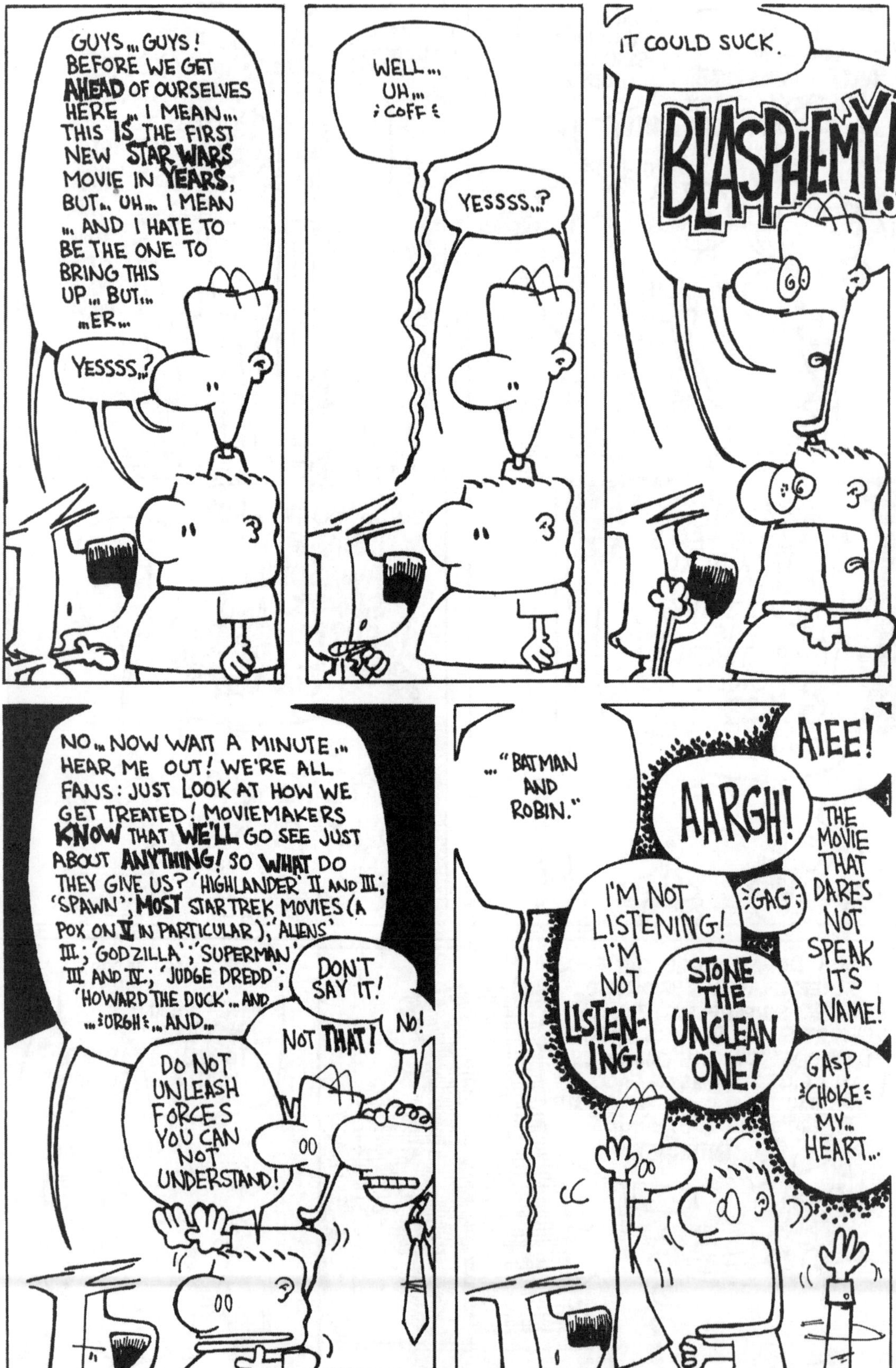

GUYS... GUYS! BEFORE WE GET AHEAD OF OURSELVES HERE... I MEAN... THIS IS THE FIRST NEW STAR WARS MOVIE IN YEARS, BUT... UH... I MEAN ... AND I HATE TO BE THE ONE TO BRING THIS UP... BUT... ...ER...
YESSSS..?
WELL... UH... ;COFF;
YESSSS..?
IT COULD SUCK.
BLASPHEMY!
NO... NOW WAIT A MINUTE... HEAR ME OUT! WE'RE ALL FANS: JUST LOOK AT HOW WE GET TREATED! MOVIEMAKERS KNOW THAT WE'LL GO SEE JUST ABOUT ANYTHING! SO WHAT DO THEY GIVE US? 'HIGHLANDER' II AND III; 'SPAWN'; MOST STAR TREK MOVIES (A POX ON V IN PARTICULAR); 'ALIENS' III; 'GODZILLA'; 'SUPERMAN' III AND IV; 'JUDGE DREDD'; 'HOWARD THE DUCK'... AND ...;URGH;... AND...
DON'T SAY IT!
NOT THAT!
NO!
DO NOT UNLEASH FORCES YOU CAN NOT UNDERSTAND!
..."BATMAN AND ROBIN."
AIEE!
AARGH!
THE MOVIE THAT DARES NOT SPEAK ITS NAME!
I'M NOT LISTENING! I'M NOT LISTENING!
;GAG;
STONE THE UNCLEAN ONE!
GASP ;CHOKE; MY... HEART...

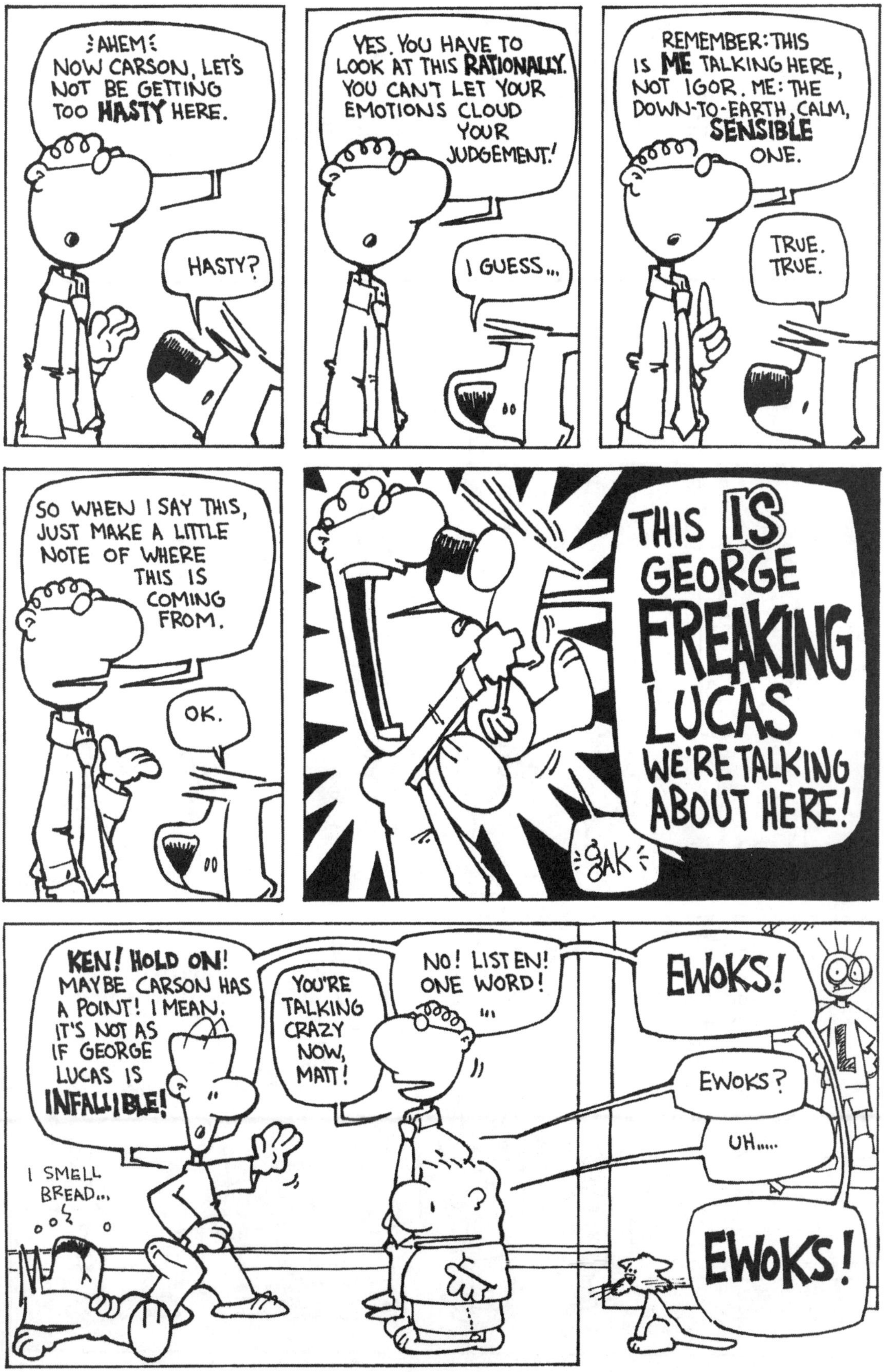

AHEM
NOW CARSON, LET'S NOT BE GETTING TOO HASTY HERE.
HASTY?
YES. YOU HAVE TO LOOK AT THIS RATIONALLY. YOU CAN'T LET YOUR EMOTIONS CLOUD YOUR JUDGEMENT!
I GUESS...
REMEMBER: THIS IS ME TALKING HERE, NOT IGOR. ME: THE DOWN-TO-EARTH, CALM, SENSIBLE ONE.
TRUE. TRUE.
SO WHEN I SAY THIS, JUST MAKE A LITTLE NOTE OF WHERE THIS IS COMING FROM.
OK.
THIS IS GEORGE FREAKING LUCAS WE'RE TALKING ABOUT HERE!
GAK
KEN! HOLD ON! MAYBE CARSON HAS A POINT! I MEAN, IT'S NOT AS IF GEORGE LUCAS IS INFALLIBLE!
YOU'RE TALKING CRAZY NOW, MATT!
NO! LISTEN! ONE WORD!
...
EWOKS!
EWOKS?
UH.....
EWOKS!
I SMELL BREAD...

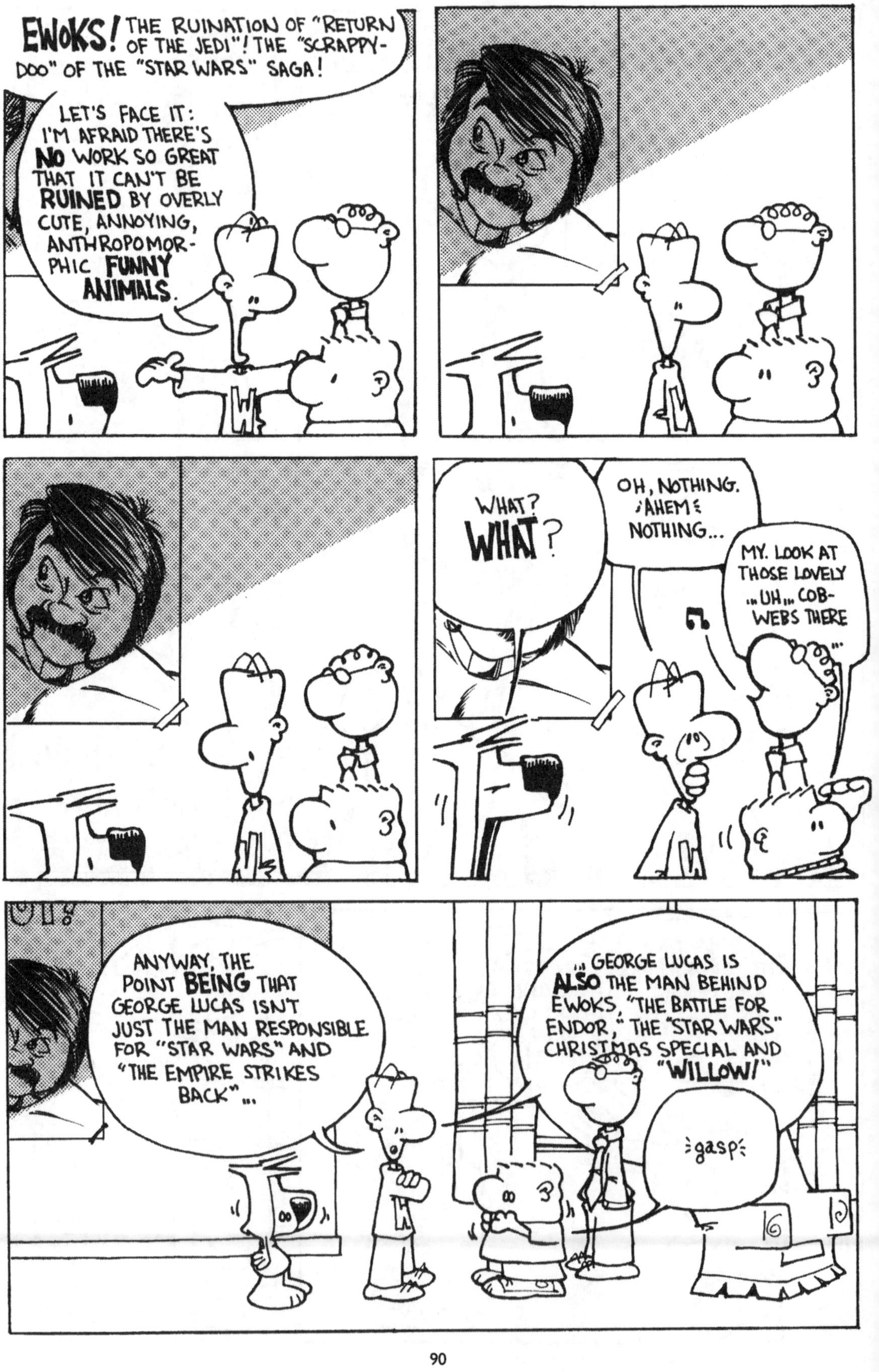
EWOKS! THE RUINATION OF "RETURN OF THE JEDI"! THE "SCRAPPY-DOO" OF THE "STAR WARS" SAGA!
LET'S FACE IT: I'M AFRAID THERE'S NO WORK SO GREAT THAT IT CAN'T BE RUINED BY OVERLY CUTE, ANNOYING, ANTHROPOMORPHIC FUNNY ANIMALS.
WHAT? WHAT?
OH, NOTHING. ¡AHEM! NOTHING...
MY. LOOK AT THOSE LOVELY ...UH... COBWEBS THERE...
ANYWAY, THE POINT BEING THAT GEORGE LUCAS ISN'T JUST THE MAN RESPONSIBLE FOR "STAR WARS" AND "THE EMPIRE STRIKES BACK"...
...GEORGE LUCAS IS ALSO THE MAN BEHIND EWOKS, "THE BATTLE FOR ENDOR," THE "STAR WARS" CHRISTMAS SPECIAL AND "WILLOW!"
gasp

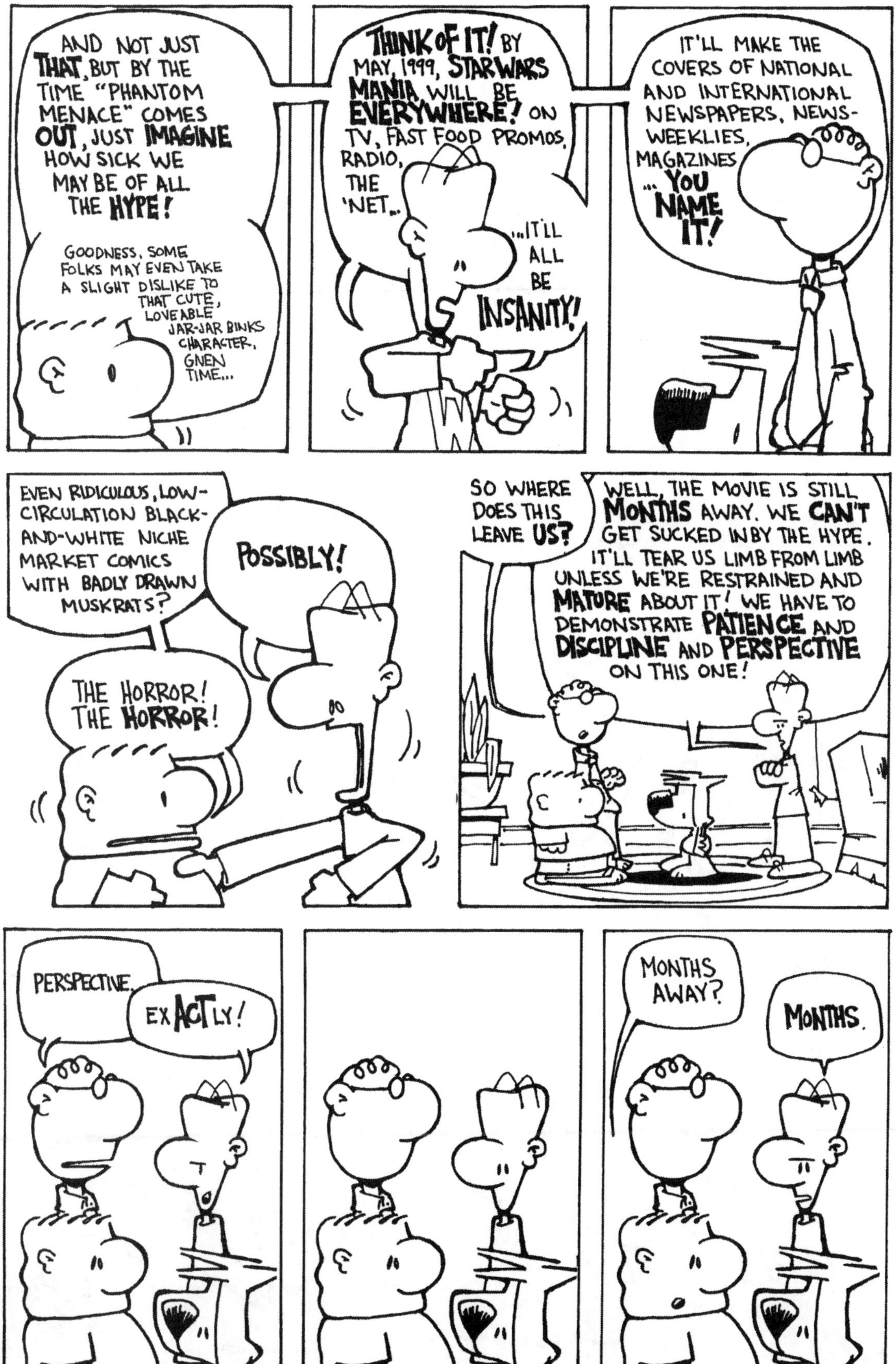
AND NOT JUST THAT, BUT BY THE TIME "PHANTOM MENACE" COMES OUT, JUST IMAGINE HOW SICK WE MAY BE OF ALL THE HYPE!
GOODNESS, SOME FOLKS MAY EVEN TAKE A SLIGHT DISLIKE TO THAT CUTE, LOVEABLE JAR-JAR BINKS CHARACTER, GIVEN TIME...
THINK OF IT! BY MAY, 1999, STAR WARS MANIA WILL BE EVERYWHERE! ON TV, FAST FOOD PROMOS, RADIO, THE 'NET...
...IT'LL ALL BE INSANITY!
IT'LL MAKE THE COVERS OF NATIONAL AND INTERNATIONAL NEWSPAPERS, NEWS-WEEKLIES, MAGAZINES ... YOU NAME IT!
EVEN RIDICULOUS, LOW-CIRCULATION BLACK-AND-WHITE NICHE MARKET COMICS WITH BADLY DRAWN MUSKRATS?
POSSIBLY!
THE HORROR! THE HORROR!
SO WHERE DOES THIS LEAVE US?
WELL, THE MOVIE IS STILL MONTHS AWAY. WE CAN'T GET SUCKED IN BY THE HYPE. IT'LL TEAR US LIMB FROM LIMB UNLESS WE'RE RESTRAINED AND MATURE ABOUT IT! WE HAVE TO DEMONSTRATE PATIENCE AND DISCIPLINE AND PERSPECTIVE ON THIS ONE!
PERSPECTIVE.
EXACTLY!
MONTHS AWAY?
MONTHS.

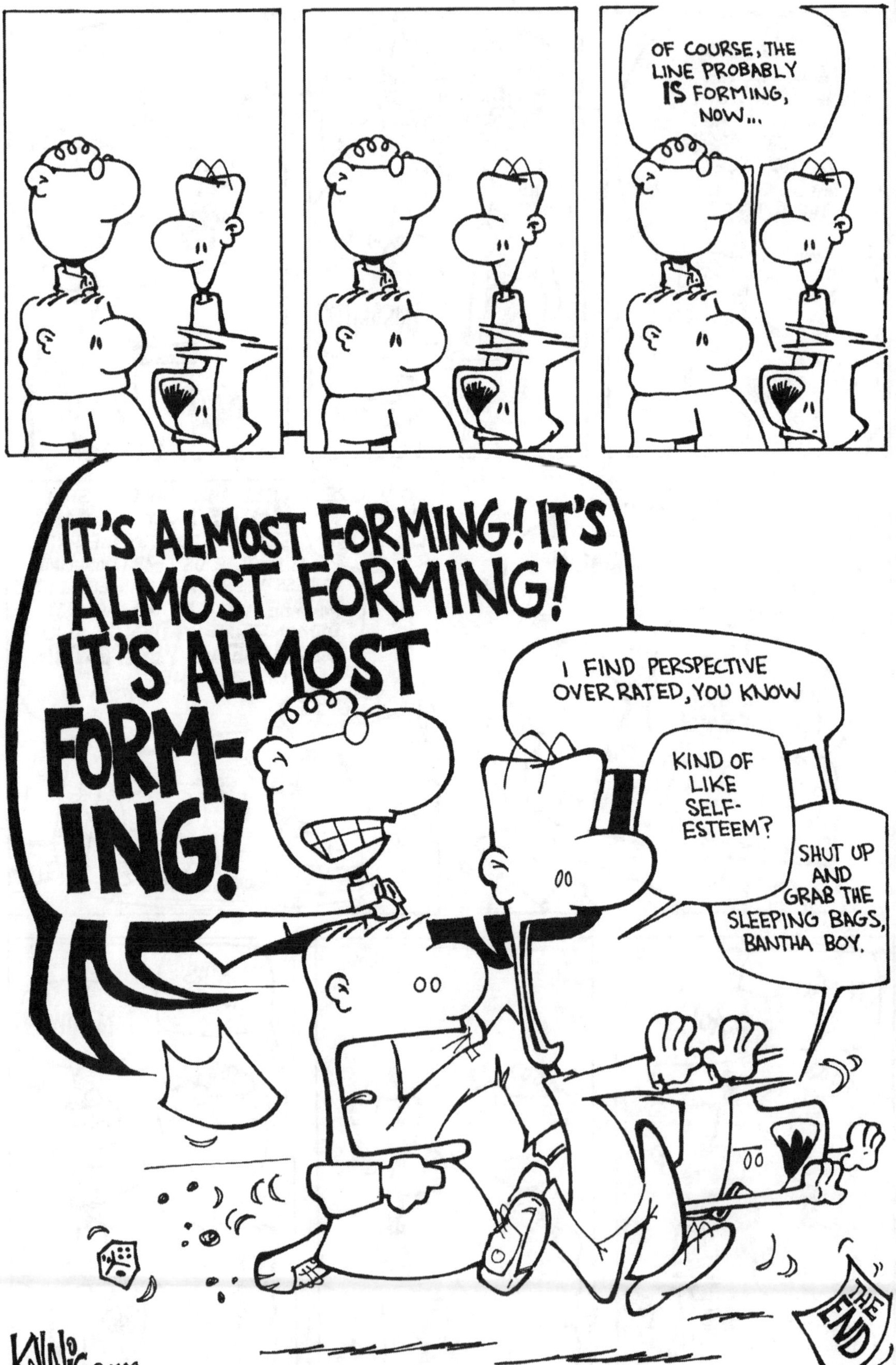
OF COURSE, THE LINE PROBABLY IS FORMING, NOW...
IT'S ALMOST FORMING! IT'S ALMOST FORMING! IT'S ALMOST FORM-ING!
I FIND PERSPECTIVE OVERRATED, YOU KNOW
KIND OF LIKE SELF-ESTEEM?
SHUT UP AND GRAB THE SLEEPING BAGS, BANTHA BOY.
THE END
KOVALIC © 1999

HEY, FAN-BOYS! DORK TOWER BY JOHN KOVALIC PRESENTS (ZAP! POW!) THE SUPER-SECRET ORIGINS OF CARSON THE MUSKRAT

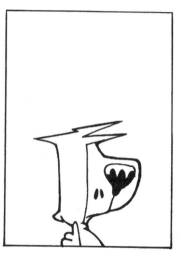

MY MOM AND DAD WERE MUSKRATS, THEREFORE I WAS A MUSKRAT.

REALLY.

ZAP! POW! THE END

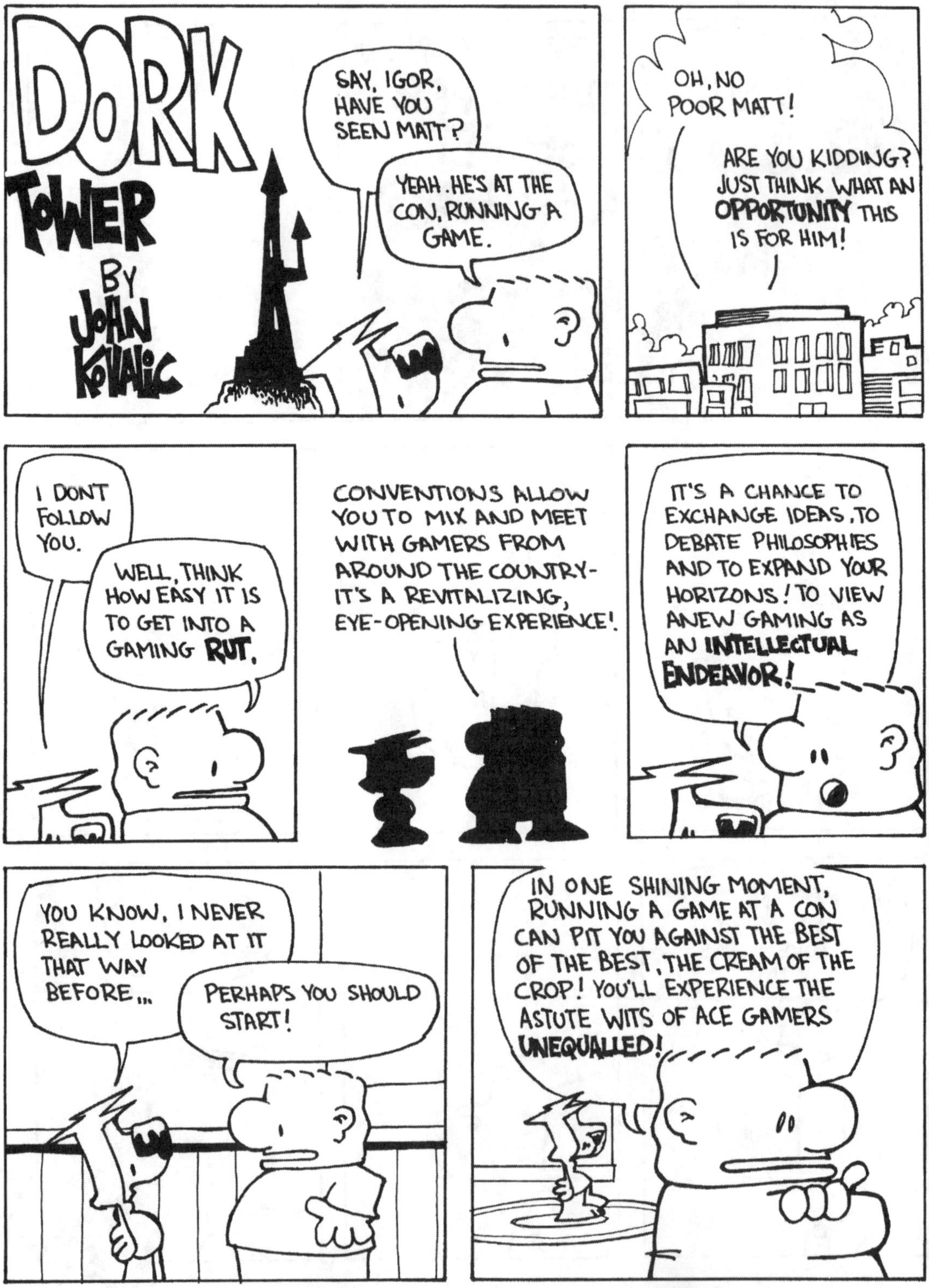
DORK TOWER BY JOHN KOVALIC
SAY, IGOR, HAVE YOU SEEN MATT?
YEAH. HE'S AT THE CON, RUNNING A GAME.
OH, NO POOR MATT!
ARE YOU KIDDING? JUST THINK WHAT AN OPPORTUNITY THIS IS FOR HIM!
I DONT FOLLOW YOU.
WELL, THINK HOW EASY IT IS TO GET INTO A GAMING RUT.
CONVENTIONS ALLOW YOU TO MIX AND MEET WITH GAMERS FROM AROUND THE COUNTRY- IT'S A REVITALIZING, EYE-OPENING EXPERIENCE!
IT'S A CHANCE TO EXCHANGE IDEAS, TO DEBATE PHILOSOPHIES AND TO EXPAND YOUR HORIZONS! TO VIEW ANEW GAMING AS AN INTELLECTUAL ENDEAVOR!
YOU KNOW, I NEVER REALLY LOOKED AT IT THAT WAY BEFORE...
PERHAPS YOU SHOULD START!
IN ONE SHINING MOMENT, RUNNING A GAME AT A CON CAN PIT YOU AGAINST THE BEST OF THE BEST, THE CREAM OF THE CROP! YOU'LL EXPERIENCE THE ASTUTE WITS OF ACE GAMERS UNEQUALLED!

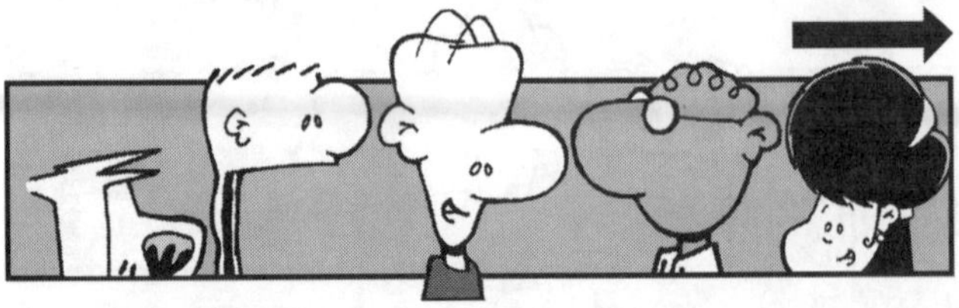

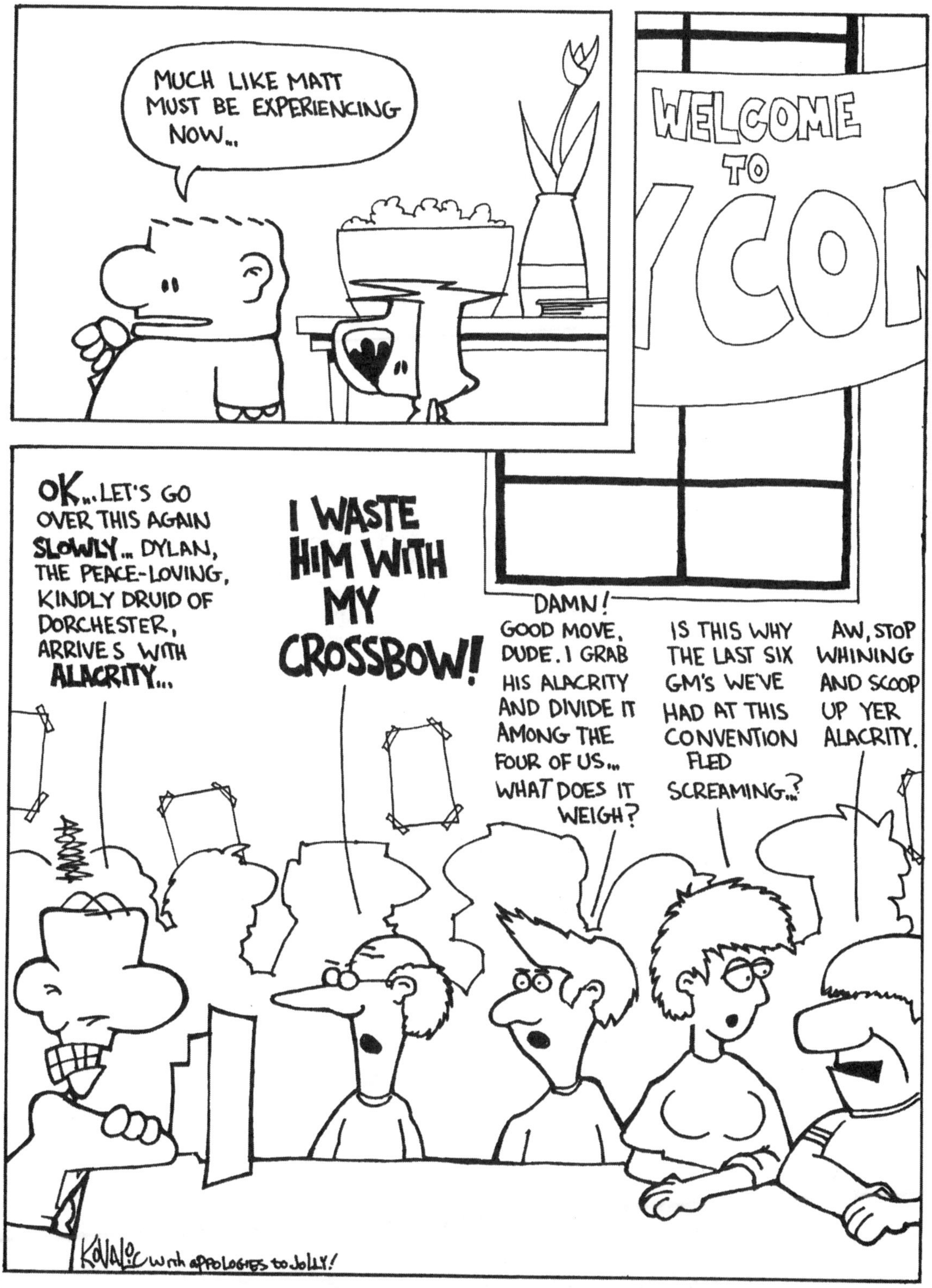
MUCH LIKE MATT MUST BE EXPERIENCING NOW...
WELCOME TO
OK... LET'S GO OVER THIS AGAIN SLOWLY... DYLAN, THE PEACE-LOVING, KINDLY DRUID OF DORCHESTER, ARRIVES WITH ALACRITY...
I WASTE HIM WITH MY CROSSBOW!
DAMN! GOOD MOVE, DUDE. I GRAB HIS ALACRITY AND DIVIDE IT AMONG THE FOUR OF US... WHAT DOES IT WEIGH?
IS THIS WHY THE LAST SIX GM'S WE'VE HAD AT THIS CONVENTION FLED SCREAMING...?
AW, STOP WHINING AND SCOOP UP YER ALACRITY.
KOVALIC with appologies to JOLLY!

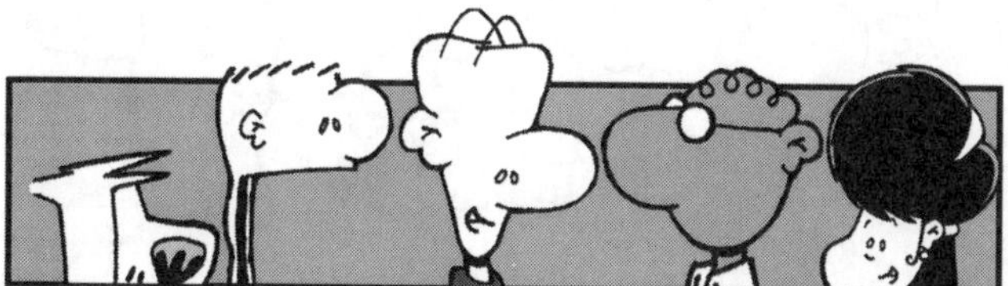

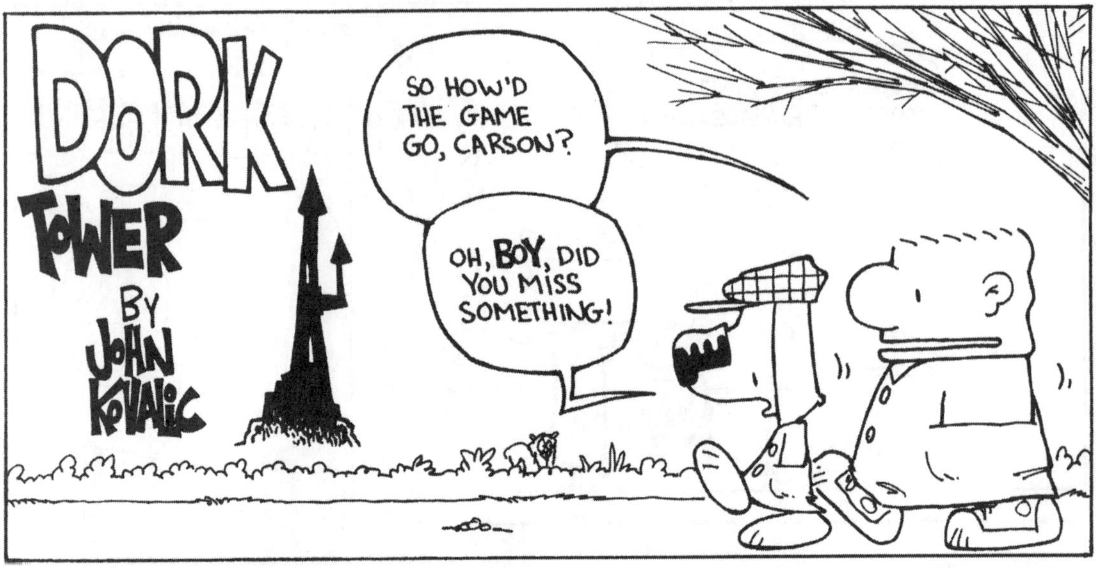
DORK TOWER
BY JOHN KOVALIC
SO HOW'D THE GAME GO, CARSON?
OH, BOY, DID YOU MISS SOMETHING!

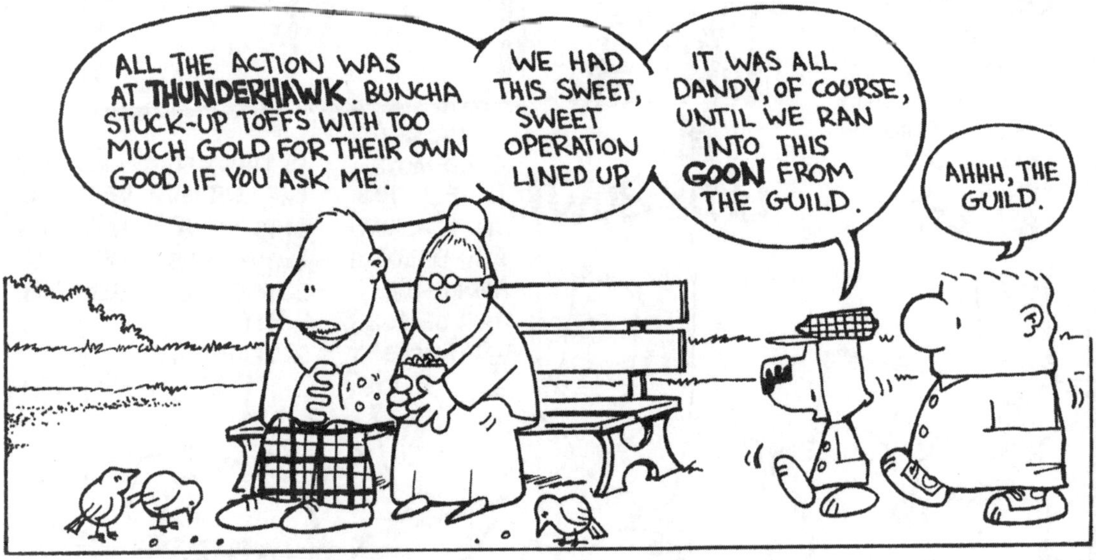
ALL THE ACTION WAS AT THUNDERHAWK. BUNCHA STUCK-UP TOFFS WITH TOO MUCH GOLD FOR THEIR OWN GOOD, IF YOU ASK ME.
WE HAD THIS SWEET, SWEET OPERATION LINED UP.
IT WAS ALL DANDY, OF COURSE, UNTIL WE RAN INTO THIS GOON FROM THE GUILD.
AHHH, THE GUILD.

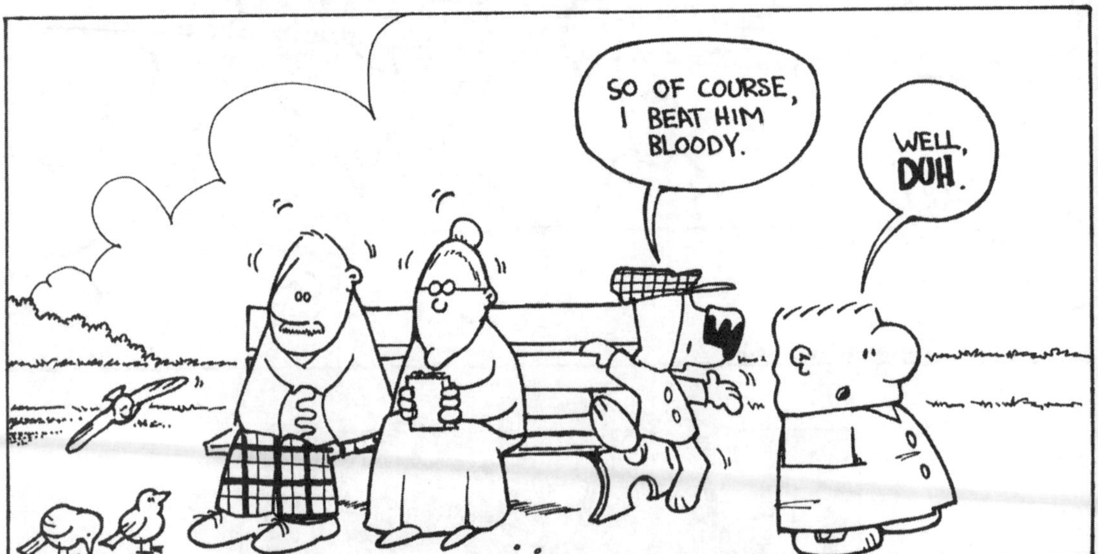
SO OF COURSE, I BEAT HIM BLOODY.
WELL, DUH.

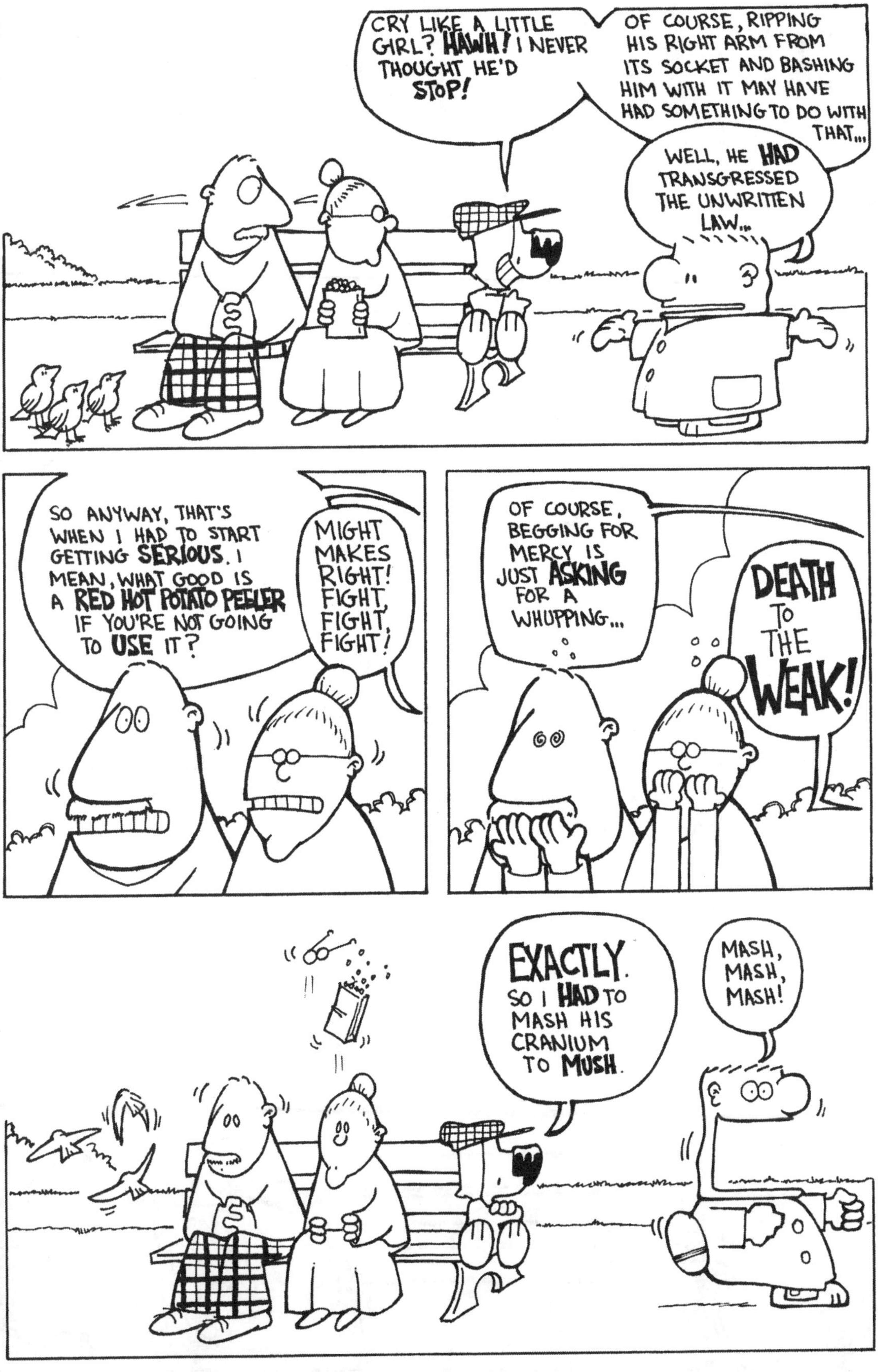
CRY LIKE A LITTLE GIRL? HAWH! I NEVER THOUGHT HE'D STOP!
OF COURSE, RIPPING HIS RIGHT ARM FROM ITS SOCKET AND BASHING HIM WITH IT MAY HAVE HAD SOMETHING TO DO WITH THAT...
WELL, HE HAD TRANSGRESSED THE UNWRITTEN LAW...
SO ANYWAY, THAT'S WHEN I HAD TO START GETTING SERIOUS. I MEAN, WHAT GOOD IS A RED HOT POTATO PEELER IF YOU'RE NOT GOING TO USE IT?
MIGHT MAKES RIGHT! FIGHT, FIGHT, FIGHT!
OF COURSE, BEGGING FOR MERCY IS JUST ASKING FOR A WHUPPING...
DEATH TO THE WEAK!
EXACTLY. SO I HAD TO MASH HIS CRANIUM TO MUSH.
MASH, MASH, MASH!

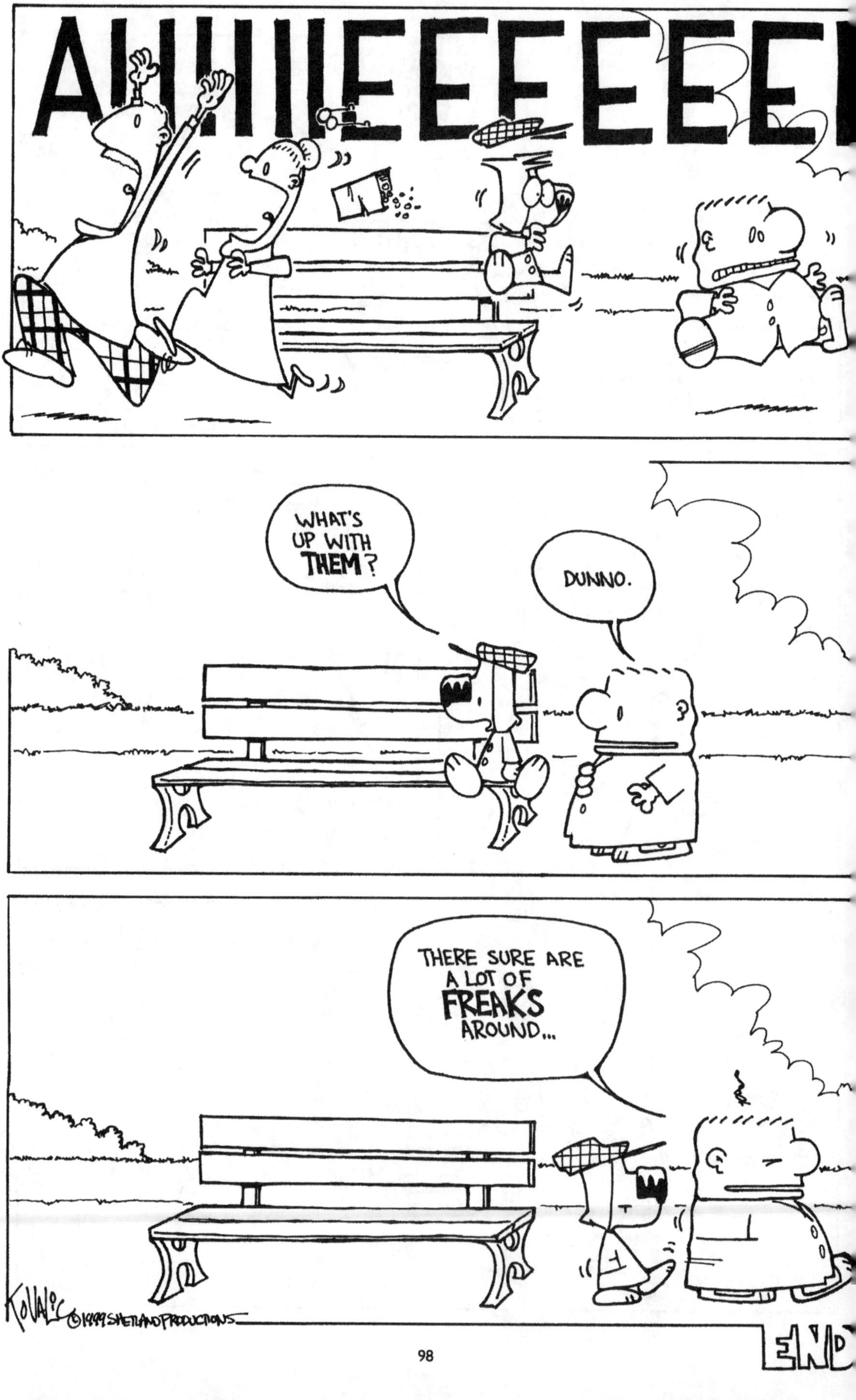
AIHHIEEEEEE
WHAT'S UP WITH THEM?
DUNNO.
THERE SURE ARE A LOT OF FREAKS AROUND...
KOVALIC ©1999 SHETLAND PRODUCTIONS
END

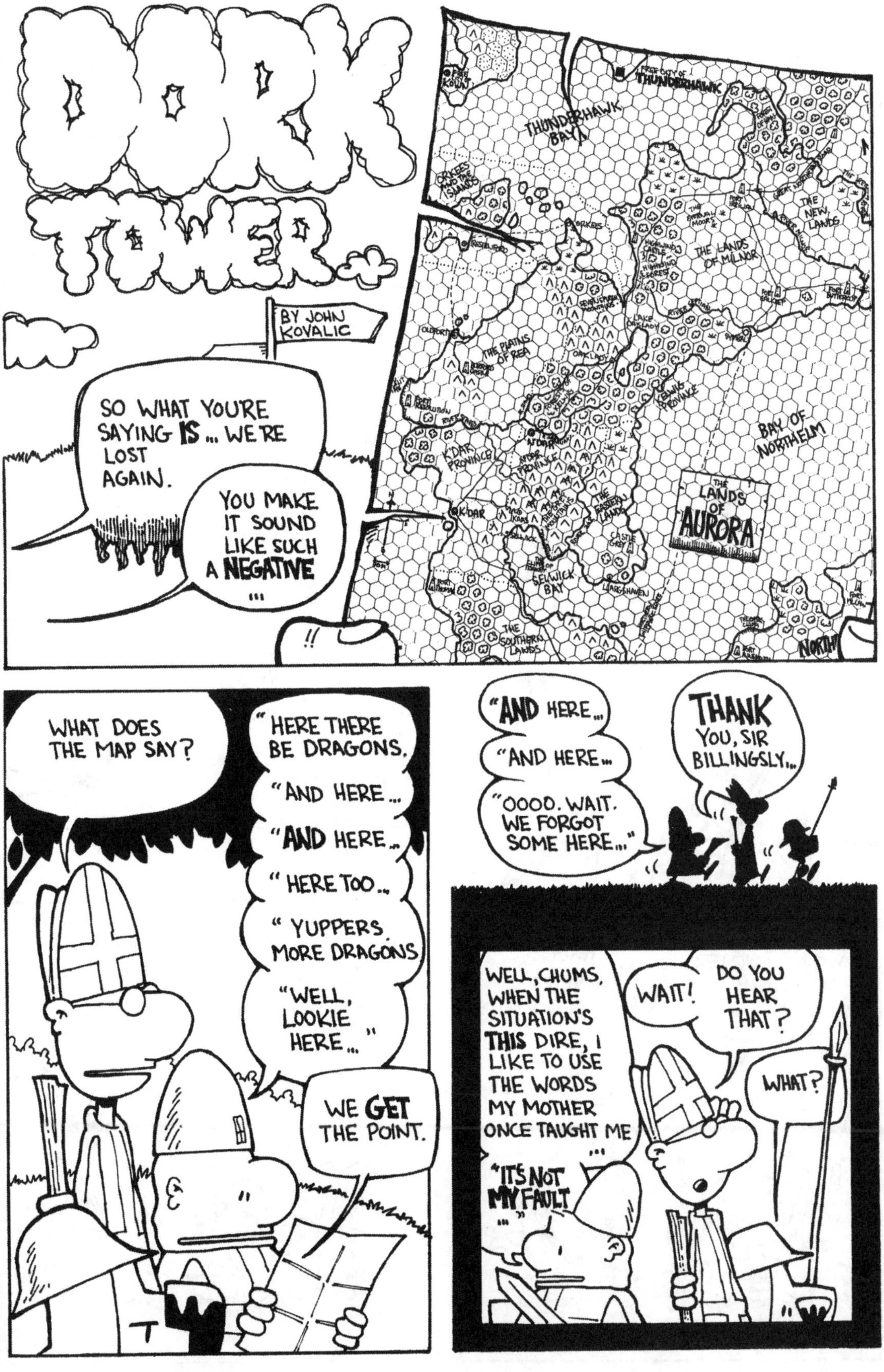
DORK TOWER
BY JOHN KOVALIC
THUNDERHAWK
THUNDERHAWK BAY
THE LANDS OF MILNOR
THE NEW LANDS
THE PLAINS OF REA
K'DAR PROVINCE
LEWIS PROVINCE
BAY OF NORTHELM
THE LANDS OF AURORA
THE EASTERN LANDS
CASTLE GREY
SELWICK BAY
THE SOUTHERN LANDS
SO WHAT YOU'RE SAYING IS... WE'RE LOST AGAIN.
YOU MAKE IT SOUND LIKE SUCH A NEGATIVE...
!!
WHAT DOES THE MAP SAY?
"HERE THERE BE DRAGONS.
"AND HERE...
"AND HERE...
"HERE TOO...
"YUPPERS. MORE DRAGONS.
"WELL, LOOKIE HERE..."
WE GET THE POINT.
"AND HERE...
"AND HERE...
"OOOO. WAIT. WE FORGOT SOME HERE..."
THANK YOU, SIR BILLINGSLY...
WELL, CHUMS, WHEN THE SITUATION'S THIS DIRE, I LIKE TO USE THE WORDS MY MOTHER ONCE TAUGHT ME...
"IT'S NOT MY FAULT..."
WAIT!
DO YOU HEAR THAT?
WHAT?

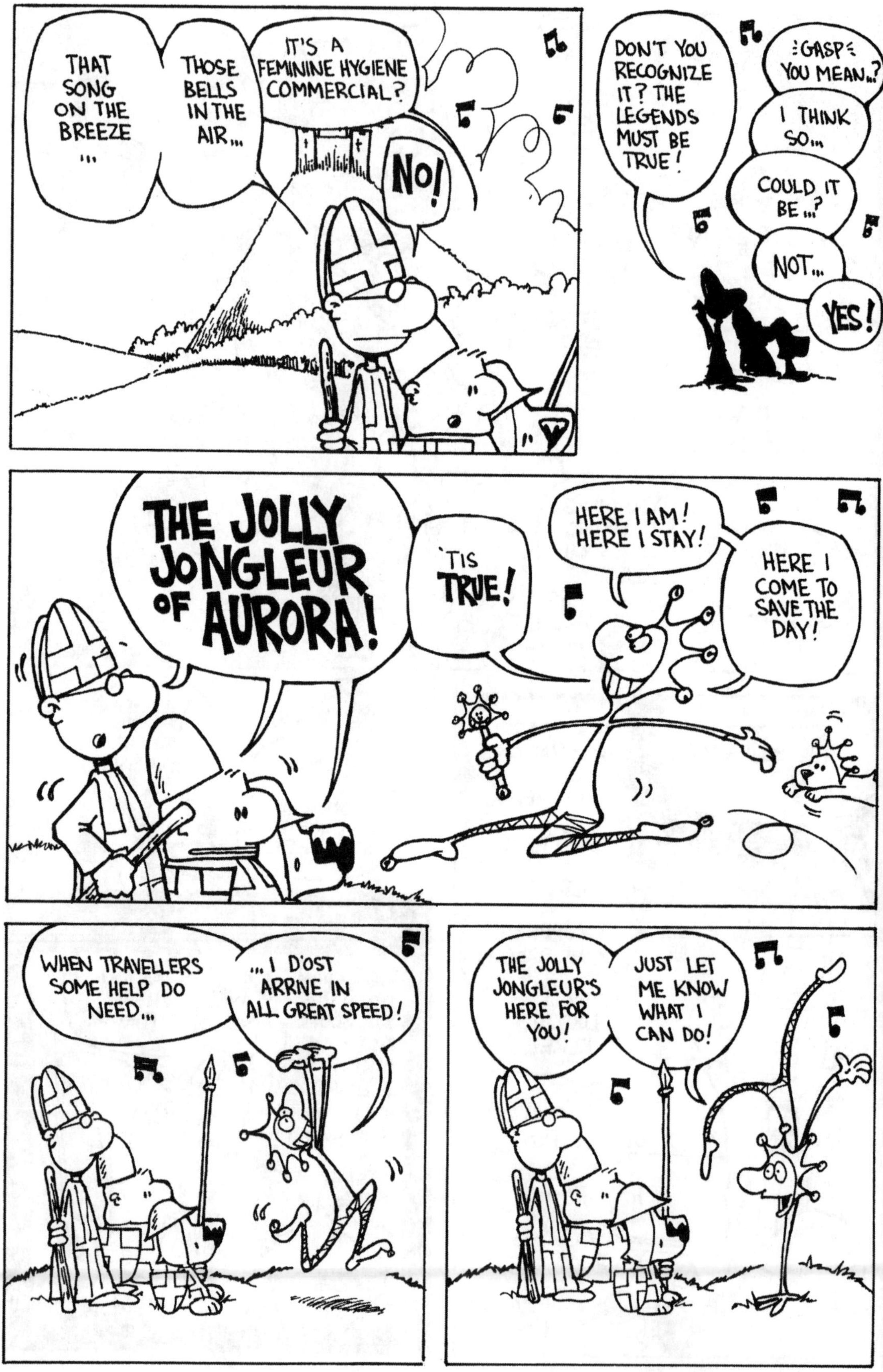
THAT SONG ON THE BREEZE ...
THOSE BELLS IN THE AIR...
IT'S A FEMININE HYGIENE COMMERCIAL?
NO!
DON'T YOU RECOGNIZE IT? THE LEGENDS MUST BE TRUE!
GASP YOU MEAN..?
I THINK SO...
COULD IT BE...?
NOT...
YES!
THE JOLLY JONGLEUR OF AURORA!
'TIS TRUE!
HERE I AM! HERE I STAY!
HERE I COME TO SAVE THE DAY!
WHEN TRAVELLERS SOME HELP DO NEED...
...I D'OST ARRIVE IN ALL GREAT SPEED!
THE JOLLY JONGLEUR'S HERE FOR YOU!
JUST LET ME KNOW WHAT I CAN DO!

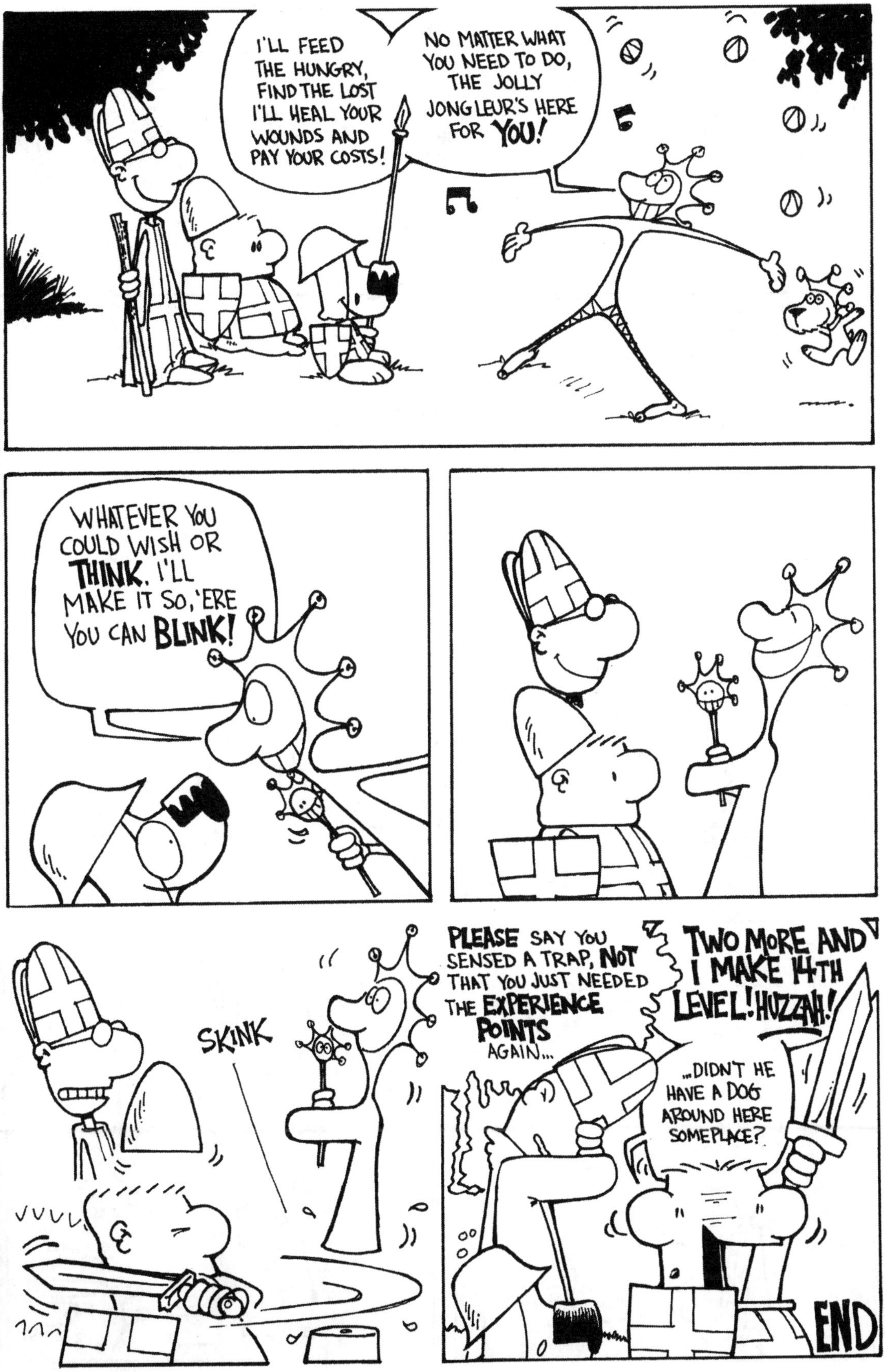

I'LL FEED THE HUNGRY, FIND THE LOST I'LL HEAL YOUR WOUNDS AND PAY YOUR COSTS!
NO MATTER WHAT YOU NEED TO DO, THE JOLLY JONGLEUR'S HERE FOR YOU!
WHATEVER YOU COULD WISH OR THINK, I'LL MAKE IT SO, 'ERE YOU CAN BLINK!
SKINK
PLEASE SAY YOU SENSED A TRAP, NOT THAT YOU JUST NEEDED THE EXPERIENCE POINTS AGAIN...
TWO MORE AND I MAKE 14TH LEVEL! HUZZAH!
...DIDN'T HE HAVE A DOG AROUND HERE SOMEPLACE?
END

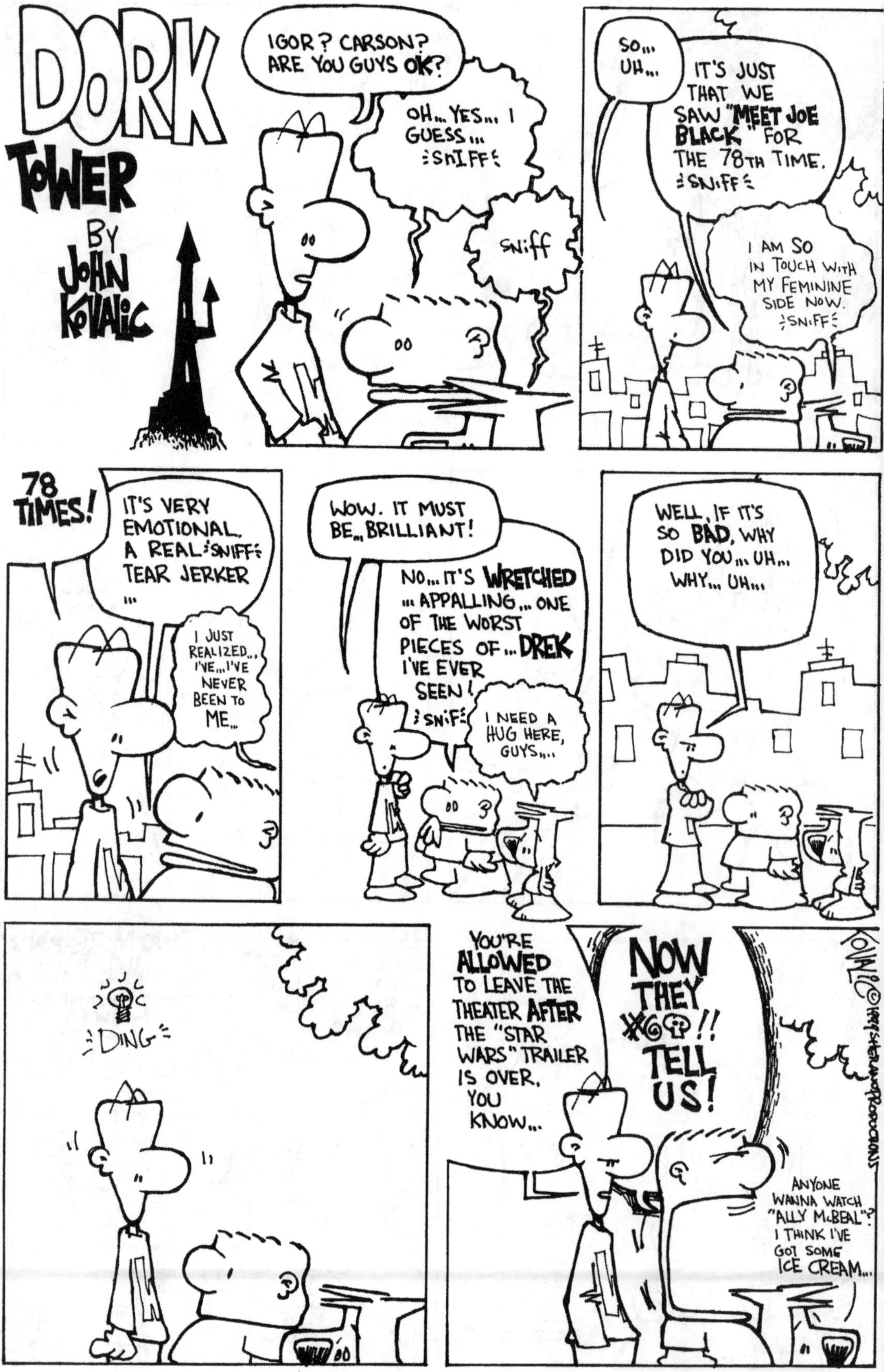
DORK TOWER
BY JOHN KOVALIC
IGOR? CARSON? ARE YOU GUYS OK?
OH... YES... I GUESS... ⁝SNIFF⁝
SNIFF
SO... UH...
IT'S JUST THAT WE SAW "MEET JOE BLACK" FOR THE 78TH TIME. ⁝SNIFF⁝
I AM SO IN TOUCH WITH MY FEMININE SIDE NOW. ⁝SNIFF⁝
78 TIMES!
IT'S VERY EMOTIONAL. A REAL ⁝SNIFF⁝ TEAR JERKER...
I JUST REALIZED... I'VE... I'VE NEVER BEEN TO ME...
WOW. IT MUST BE... BRILLIANT!
NO... IT'S WRETCHED... APPALLING... ONE OF THE WORST PIECES OF... DREK I'VE EVER SEEN! ⁝SNIF⁝
I NEED A HUG HERE, GUYS...
WELL, IF IT'S SO BAD, WHY DID YOU... UH... WHY... UH...
DING
YOU'RE ALLOWED TO LEAVE THE THEATER AFTER THE "STAR WARS" TRAILER IS OVER. YOU KNOW...
NOW THEY #@!! TELL US!
ANYONE WANNA WATCH "ALLY McBEAL"? I THINK I'VE GOT SOME ICE CREAM...
KOVALIC ©1999 SHETLAND PRODUCTIONS

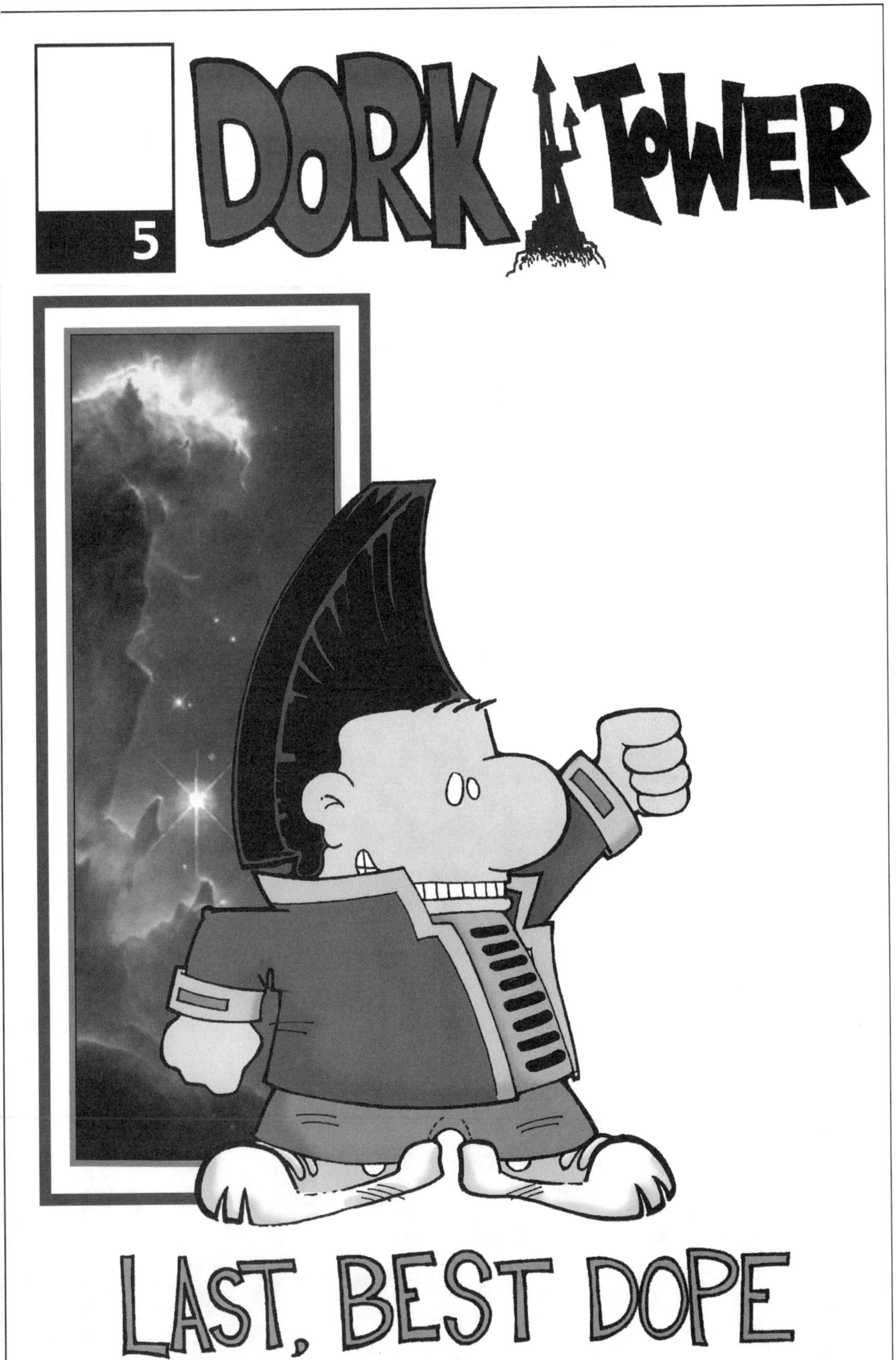
5
DORK TOWER
LAST, BEST DOPE

"On my world, there are books, thousands of pages, about the power of one mind to change the Universe, but none said it as clearly as this."

-Delenn to Sinclair in Babylon 5: "The Gathering"

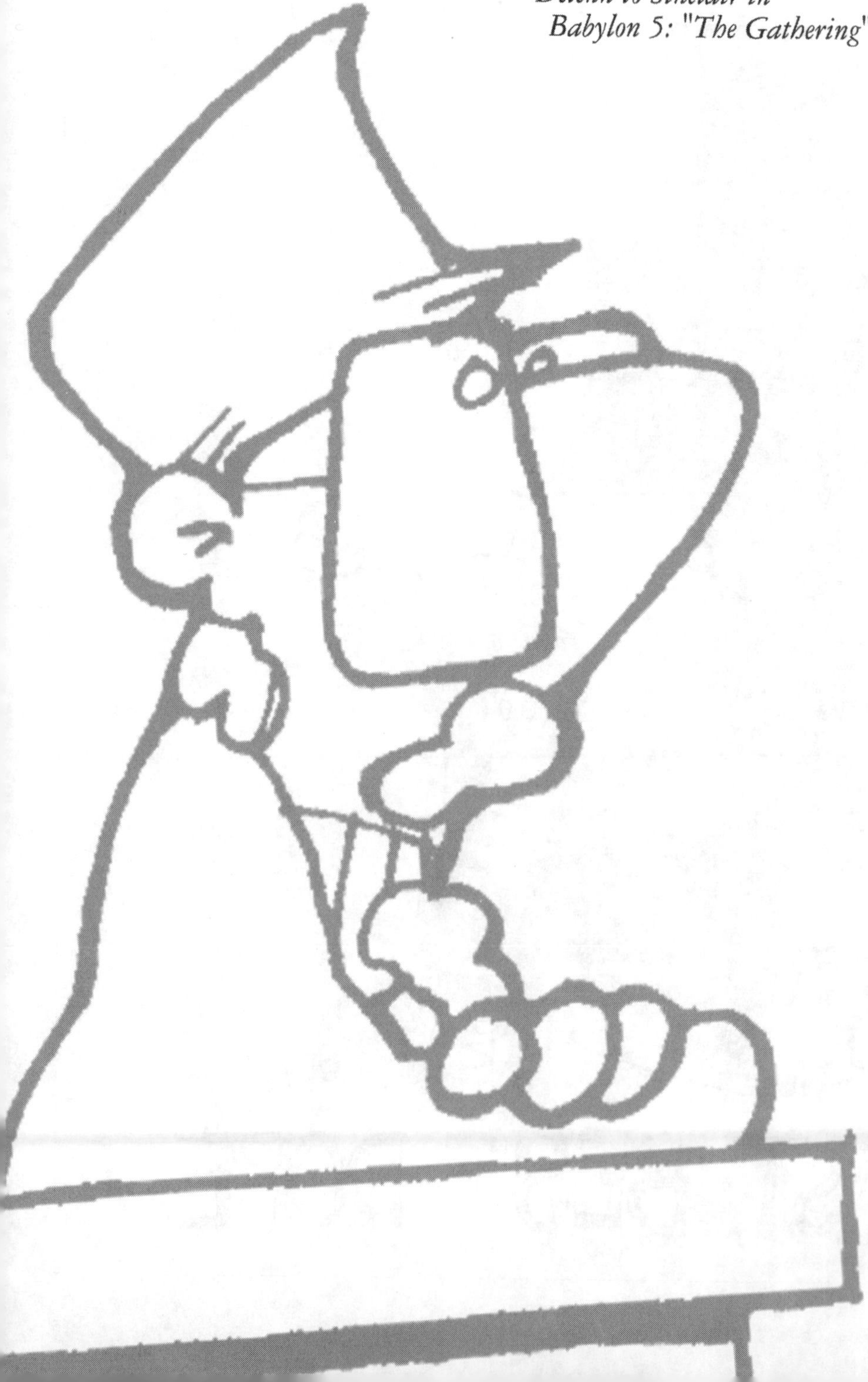

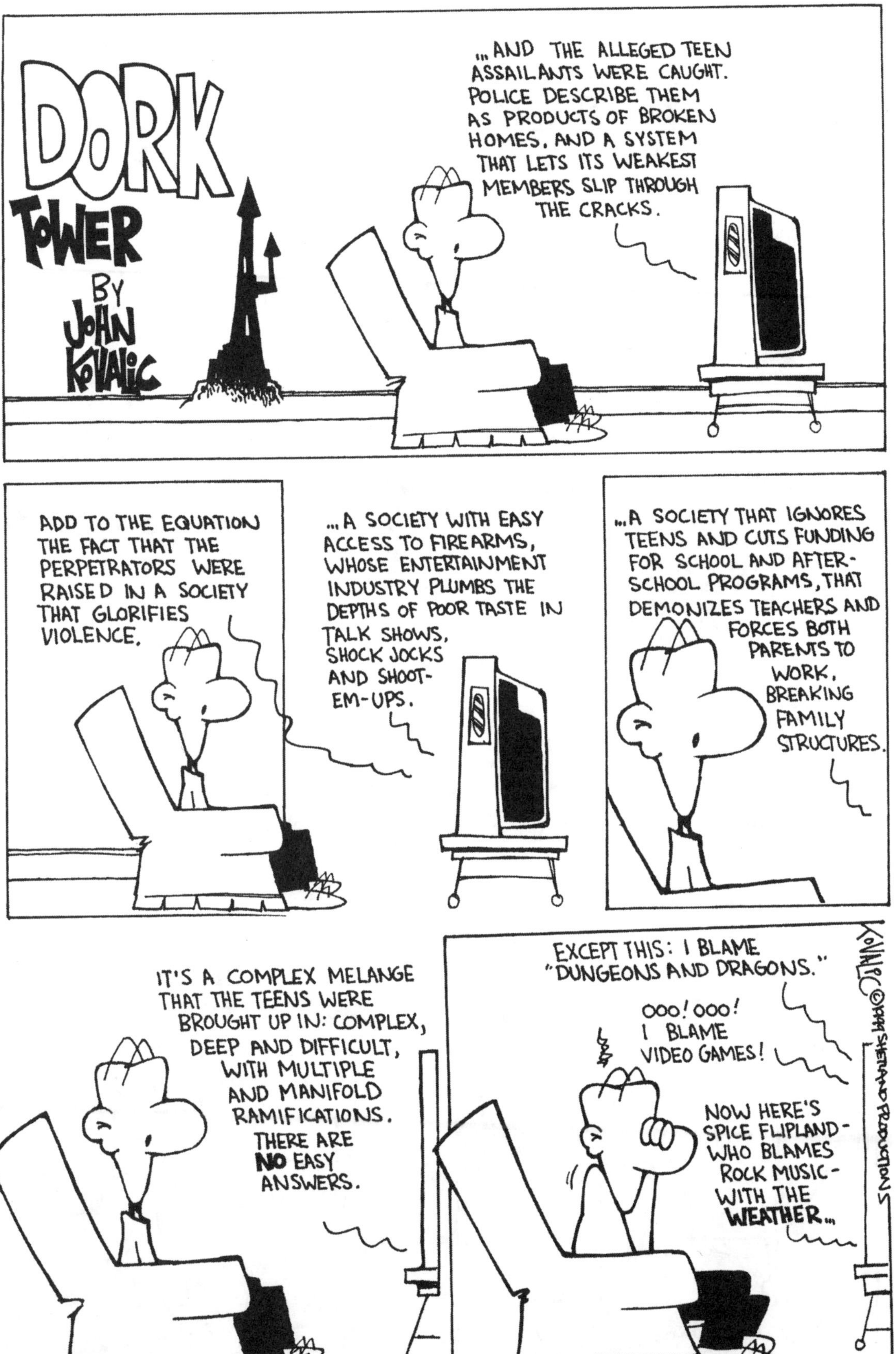
DORK TOWER
BY JOHN KOVALIC
...AND THE ALLEGED TEEN ASSAILANTS WERE CAUGHT. POLICE DESCRIBE THEM AS PRODUCTS OF BROKEN HOMES, AND A SYSTEM THAT LETS ITS WEAKEST MEMBERS SLIP THROUGH THE CRACKS.
ADD TO THE EQUATION THE FACT THAT THE PERPETRATORS WERE RAISED IN A SOCIETY THAT GLORIFIES VIOLENCE.
...A SOCIETY WITH EASY ACCESS TO FIREARMS, WHOSE ENTERTAINMENT INDUSTRY PLUMBS THE DEPTHS OF POOR TASTE IN TALK SHOWS, SHOCK JOCKS AND SHOOT-EM-UPS.
...A SOCIETY THAT IGNORES TEENS AND CUTS FUNDING FOR SCHOOL AND AFTER-SCHOOL PROGRAMS, THAT DEMONIZES TEACHERS AND FORCES BOTH PARENTS TO WORK, BREAKING FAMILY STRUCTURES.
IT'S A COMPLEX MELANGE THAT THE TEENS WERE BROUGHT UP IN: COMPLEX, DEEP AND DIFFICULT, WITH MULTIPLE AND MANIFOLD RAMIFICATIONS.
THERE ARE **NO** EASY ANSWERS.
EXCEPT THIS: I BLAME "DUNGEONS AND DRAGONS."
OOO! OOO! I BLAME VIDEO GAMES!
NOW HERE'S SPICE FLIPLAND - WHO BLAMES ROCK MUSIC - WITH THE **WEATHER**...
KOVALIC ©1999 SHETLAND PRODUCTIONS

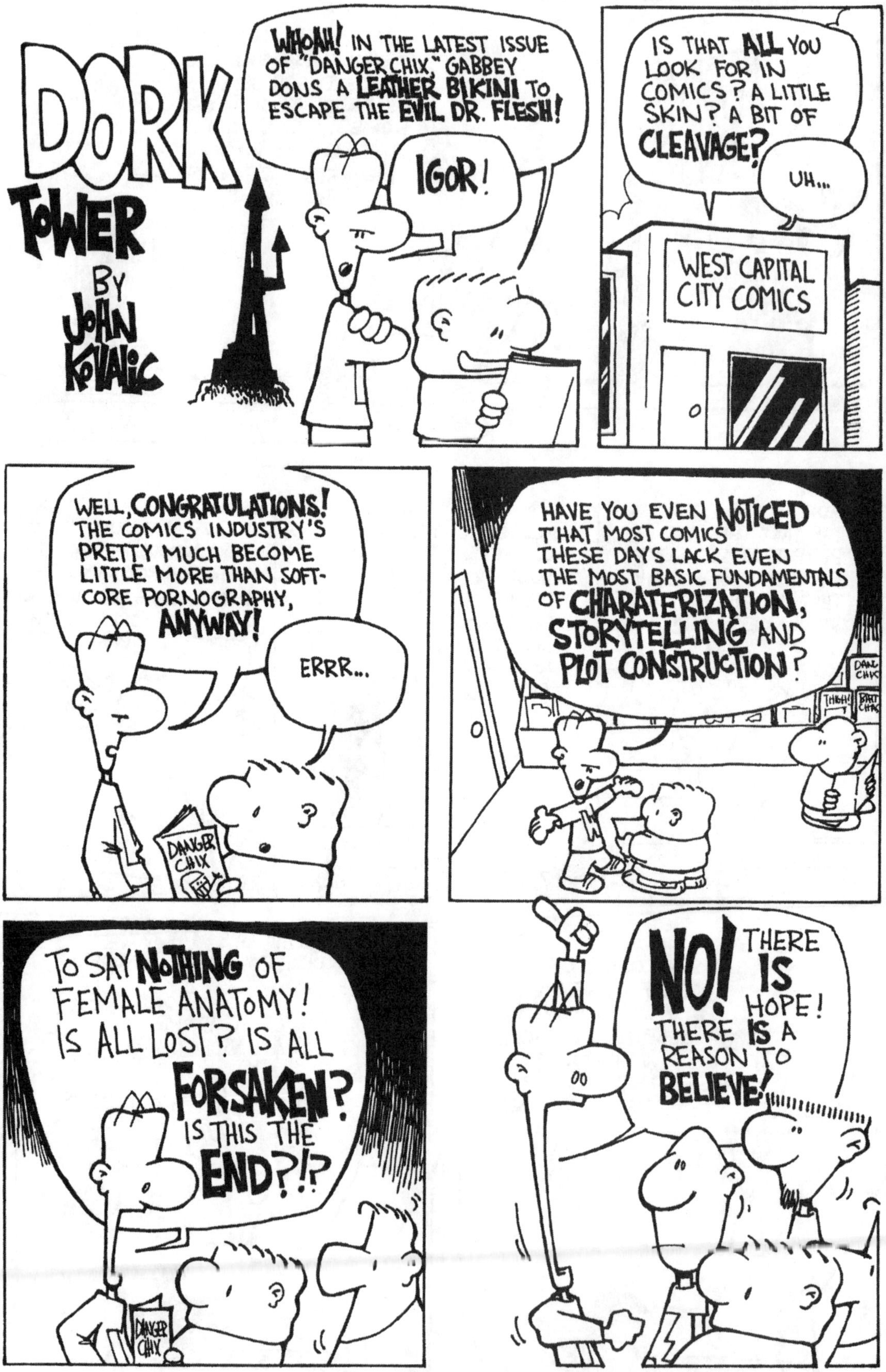
DORK TOWER
BY JOHN KOVALIC
WHOAH! IN THE LATEST ISSUE OF "DANGER CHIX," GABBEY DONS A LEATHER BIKINI TO ESCAPE THE EVIL DR. FLESH!
IGOR!
IS THAT ALL YOU LOOK FOR IN COMICS? A LITTLE SKIN? A BIT OF CLEAVAGE?
UH...
WEST CAPITAL CITY COMICS
WELL, CONGRATULATIONS! THE COMICS INDUSTRY'S PRETTY MUCH BECOME LITTLE MORE THAN SOFT-CORE PORNOGRAPHY, ANYWAY!
ERRR...
DANGER CHIX
HAVE YOU EVEN NOTICED THAT MOST COMICS THESE DAYS LACK EVEN THE MOST BASIC FUNDAMENTALS OF CHARATERIZATION, STORYTELLING AND PLOT CONSTRUCTION?
TO SAY NOTHING OF FEMALE ANATOMY! IS ALL LOST? IS ALL FORSAKEN? IS THIS THE END?!?
DANGER CHIX
NO! THERE IS HOPE! THERE IS A REASON TO BELIEVE!

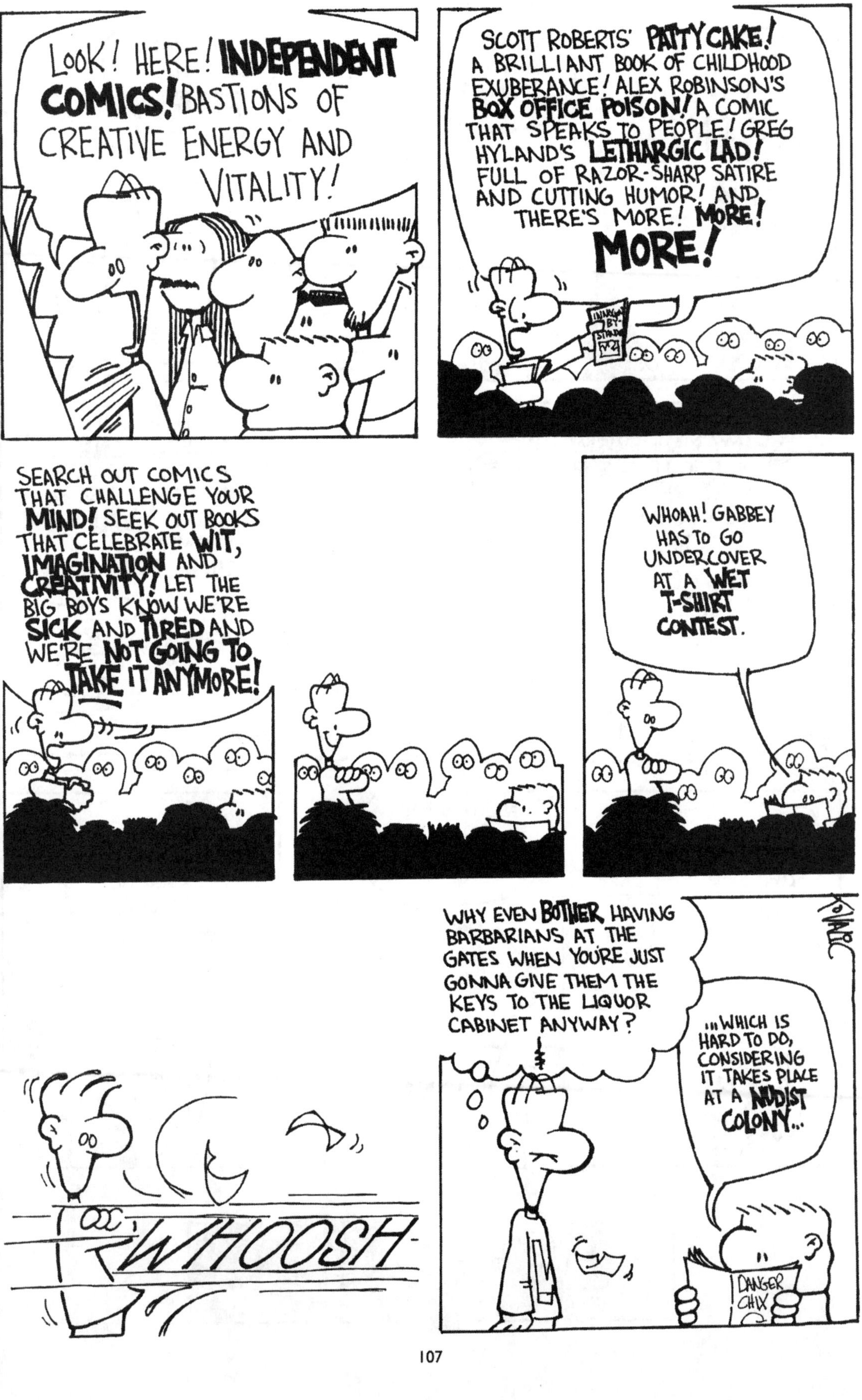
LOOK! HERE! INDEPENDENT COMICS! BASTIONS OF CREATIVE ENERGY AND VITALITY!
SCOTT ROBERTS' PATTY CAKE! A BRILLIANT BOOK OF CHILDHOOD EXUBERANCE! ALEX ROBINSON'S BOX OFFICE POISON! A COMIC THAT SPEAKS TO PEOPLE! GREG HYLAND'S LETHARGIC LAD! FULL OF RAZOR-SHARP SATIRE AND CUTTING HUMOR! AND THERE'S MORE! MORE! MORE!
BY-
SEARCH OUT COMICS THAT CHALLENGE YOUR MIND! SEEK OUT BOOKS THAT CELEBRATE WIT, IMAGINATION AND CREATIVITY! LET THE BIG BOYS KNOW WE'RE SICK AND TIRED AND WE'RE NOT GOING TO TAKE IT ANYMORE!
WHOAH! GABBEY HAS TO GO UNDERCOVER AT A WET T-SHIRT CONTEST.
WHOOSH
WHY EVEN BOTHER HAVING BARBARIANS AT THE GATES WHEN YOU'RE JUST GONNA GIVE THEM THE KEYS TO THE LIQUOR CABINET ANYWAY?
...WHICH IS HARD TO DO, CONSIDERING IT TAKES PLACE AT A NUDIST COLONY...
DANGER CHIX

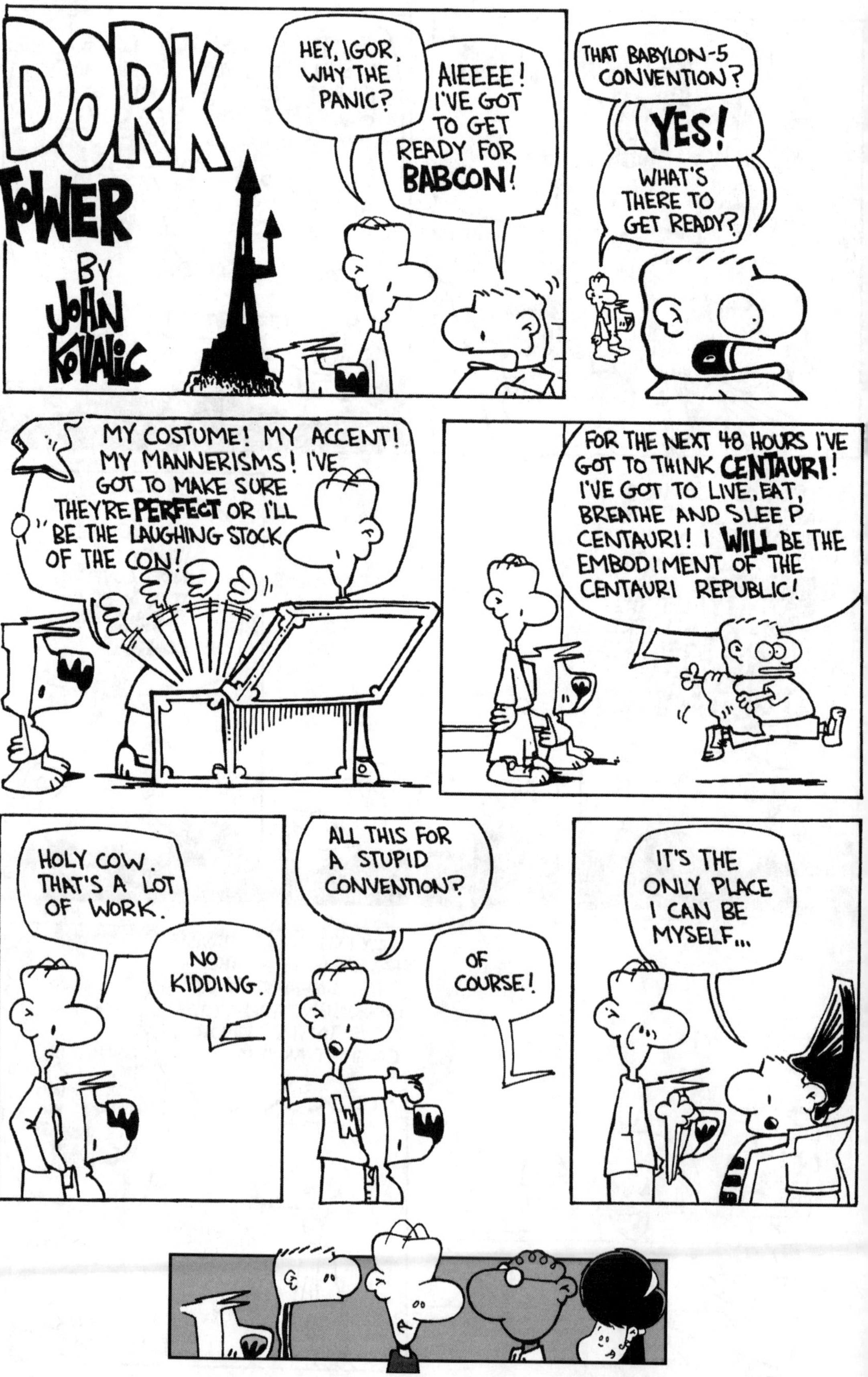
DORK TOWER
BY JOHN KOVALIC
HEY, IGOR. WHY THE PANIC?
AIEEEE! I'VE GOT TO GET READY FOR BABCON!
THAT BABYLON-5 CONVENTION?
YES!
WHAT'S THERE TO GET READY?
MY COSTUME! MY ACCENT! MY MANNERISMS! I'VE GOT TO MAKE SURE THEY'RE PERFECT OR I'LL BE THE LAUGHING STOCK OF THE CON!
FOR THE NEXT 48 HOURS I'VE GOT TO THINK CENTAURI! I'VE GOT TO LIVE, EAT, BREATHE AND SLEEP CENTAURI! I WILL BE THE EMBODIMENT OF THE CENTAURI REPUBLIC!
HOLY COW. THAT'S A LOT OF WORK.
NO KIDDING.
ALL THIS FOR A STUPID CONVENTION?
OF COURSE!
IT'S THE ONLY PLACE I CAN BE MYSELF...

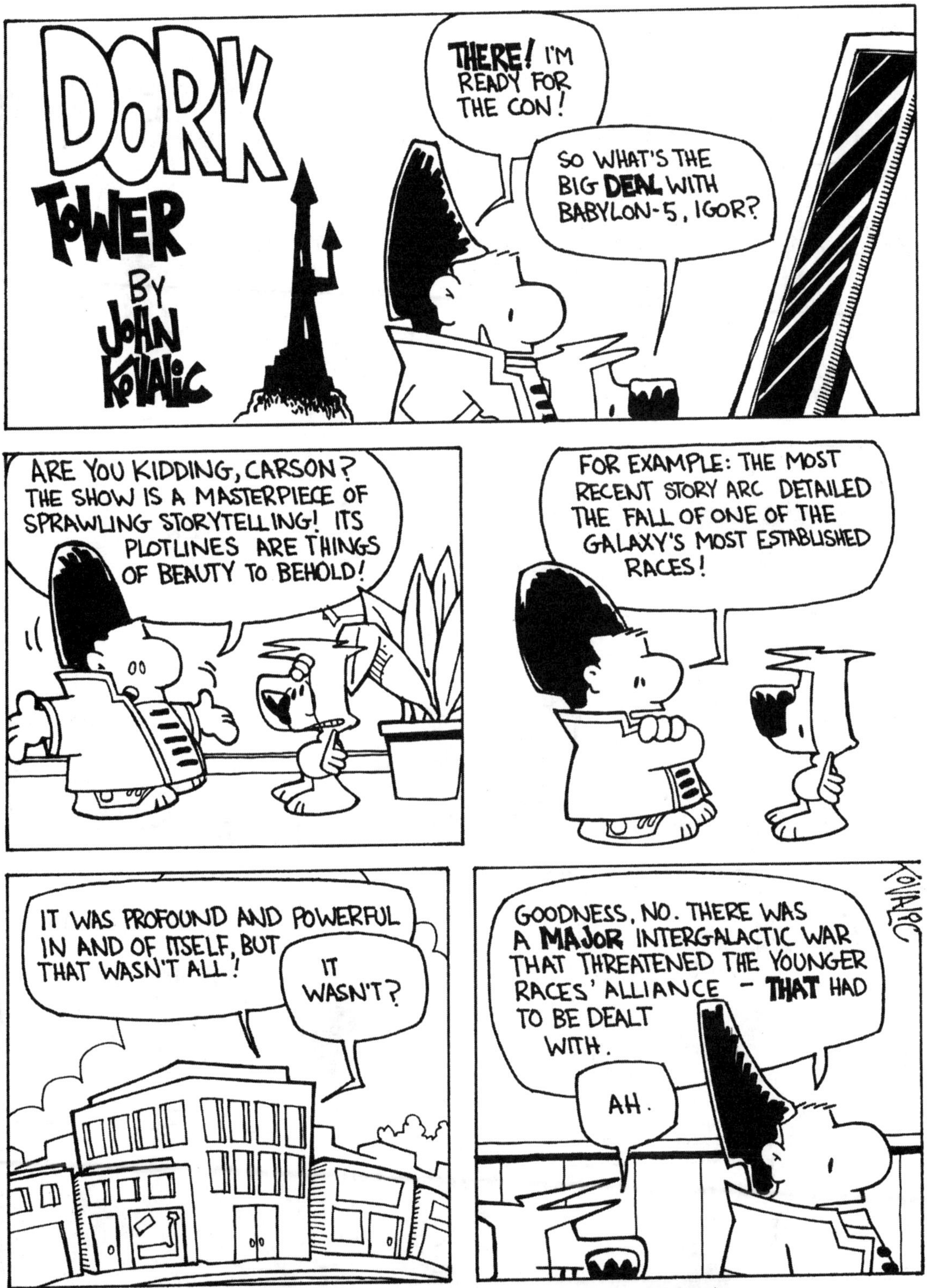
DORK TOWER
BY JOHN KOVALIC
THERE! I'M READY FOR THE CON!
SO WHAT'S THE BIG DEAL WITH BABYLON-5, IGOR?
ARE YOU KIDDING, CARSON? THE SHOW IS A MASTERPIECE OF SPRAWLING STORYTELLING! ITS PLOTLINES ARE THINGS OF BEAUTY TO BEHOLD!
FOR EXAMPLE: THE MOST RECENT STORY ARC DETAILED THE FALL OF ONE OF THE GALAXY'S MOST ESTABLISHED RACES!
IT WAS PROFOUND AND POWERFUL IN AND OF ITSELF, BUT THAT WASN'T ALL!
IT WASN'T?
GOODNESS, NO. THERE WAS A MAJOR INTERGALACTIC WAR THAT THREATENED THE YOUNGER RACES' ALLIANCE — THAT HAD TO BE DEALT WITH.
AH.
KOVALIC

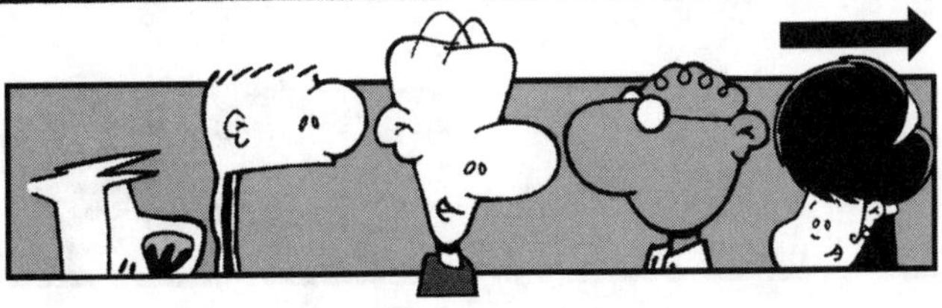

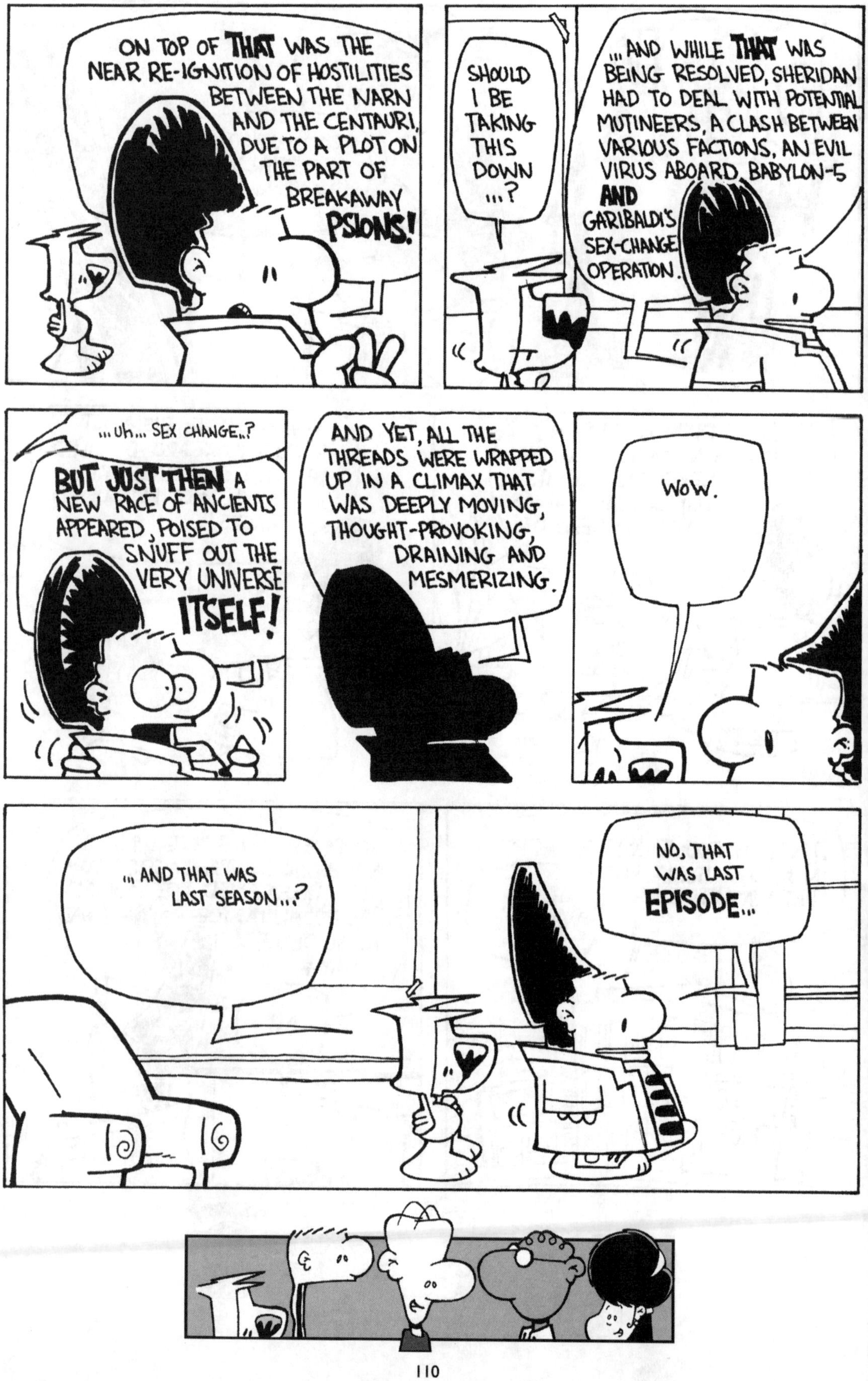
ON TOP OF THAT WAS THE NEAR RE-IGNITION OF HOSTILITIES BETWEEN THE NARN AND THE CENTAURI, DUE TO A PLOT ON THE PART OF BREAKAWAY PSIONS!
SHOULD I BE TAKING THIS DOWN ...?
... AND WHILE THAT WAS BEING RESOLVED, SHERIDAN HAD TO DEAL WITH POTENTIAL MUTINEERS, A CLASH BETWEEN VARIOUS FACTIONS, AN EVIL VIRUS ABOARD BABYLON-5 AND GARIBALDI'S SEX-CHANGE OPERATION.
... uh... SEX CHANGE..?
BUT JUST THEN A NEW RACE OF ANCIENTS APPEARED, POISED TO SNUFF OUT THE VERY UNIVERSE ITSELF!
AND YET, ALL THE THREADS WERE WRAPPED UP IN A CLIMAX THAT WAS DEEPLY MOVING, THOUGHT-PROVOKING, DRAINING AND MESMERIZING.
WoW.
... AND THAT WAS LAST SEASON..?
NO, THAT WAS LAST EPISODE...

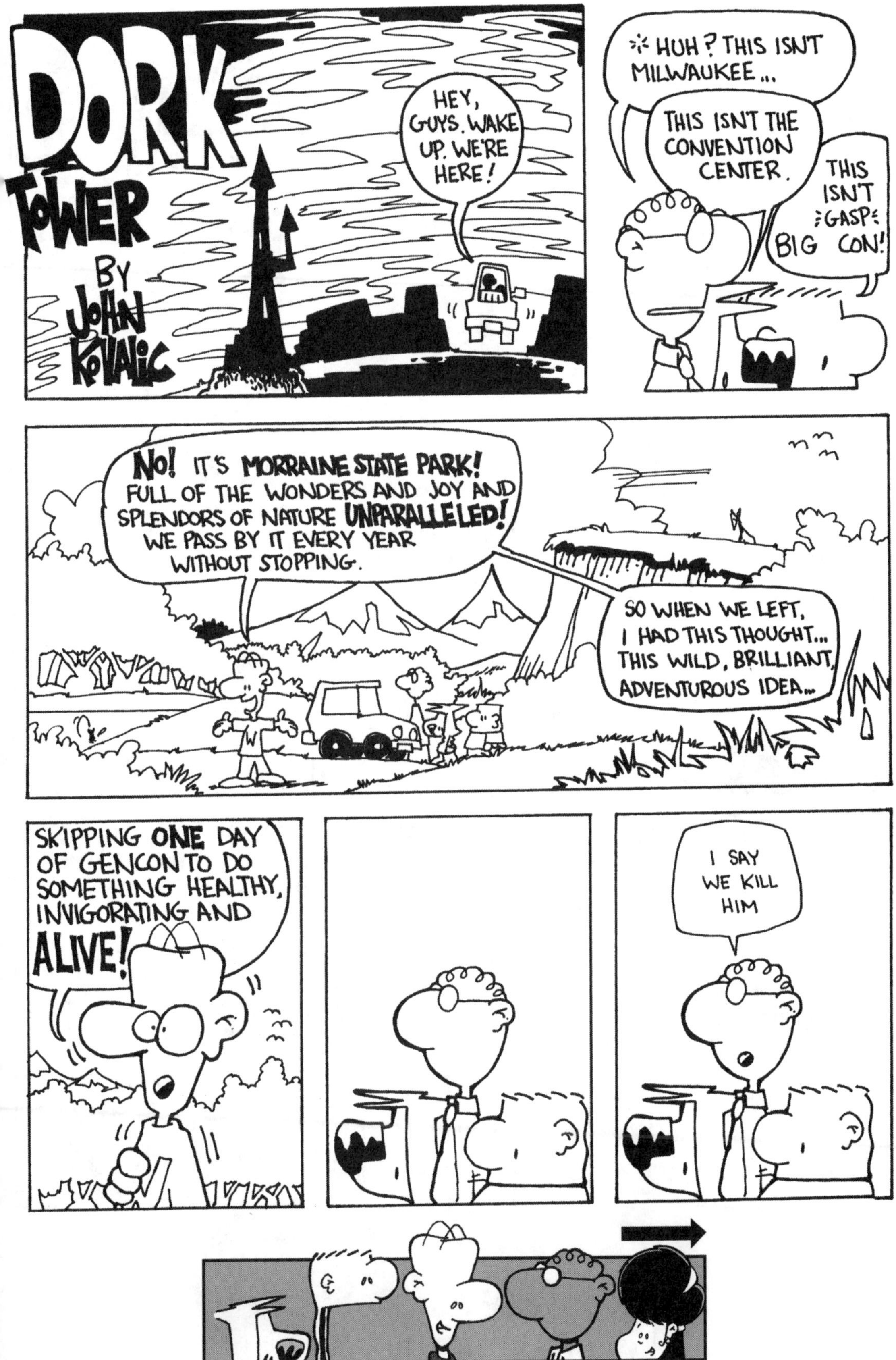
DORK TOWER
BY JOHN KOVALIC
HEY, GUYS. WAKE UP. WE'RE HERE!
HUH? THIS ISN'T MILWAUKEE...
THIS ISN'T THE CONVENTION CENTER.
THIS ISN'T *GASP* BIG CON!
NO! IT'S MORRAINE STATE PARK! FULL OF THE WONDERS AND JOY AND SPLENDORS OF NATURE UNPARALLELED! WE PASS BY IT EVERY YEAR WITHOUT STOPPING.
SO WHEN WE LEFT, I HAD THIS THOUGHT... THIS WILD, BRILLIANT, ADVENTUROUS IDEA...
SKIPPING ONE DAY OF GENCON TO DO SOMETHING HEALTHY, INVIGORATING AND ALIVE!
I SAY WE KILL HIM

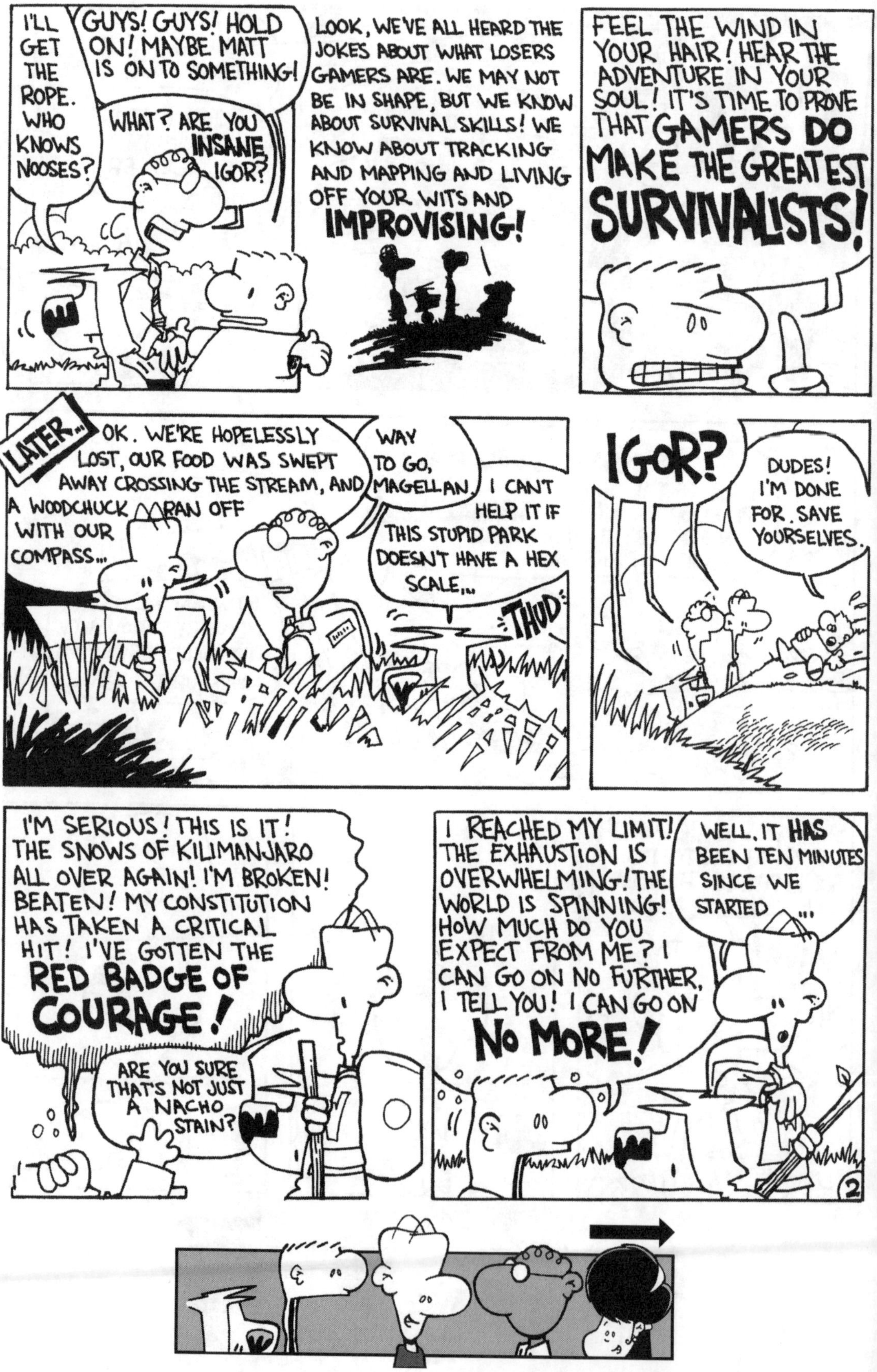
I'LL GET THE ROPE. WHO KNOWS NOOSES?
GUYS! GUYS! HOLD ON! MAYBE MATT IS ON TO SOMETHING!
WHAT? ARE YOU INSANE, IGOR?
LOOK, WE'VE ALL HEARD THE JOKES ABOUT WHAT LOSERS GAMERS ARE. WE MAY NOT BE IN SHAPE, BUT WE KNOW ABOUT SURVIVAL SKILLS! WE KNOW ABOUT TRACKING AND MAPPING AND LIVING OFF YOUR WITS AND IMPROVISING!
FEEL THE WIND IN YOUR HAIR! HEAR THE ADVENTURE IN YOUR SOUL! IT'S TIME TO PROVE THAT GAMERS DO MAKE THE GREATEST SURVIVALISTS!
LATER...
OK. WE'RE HOPELESSLY LOST, OUR FOOD WAS SWEPT AWAY CROSSING THE STREAM, AND A WOODCHUCK RAN OFF WITH OUR COMPASS...
WAY TO GO, MAGELLAN.
I CAN'T HELP IT IF THIS STUPID PARK DOESN'T HAVE A HEX SCALE...
THUD
IGOR?
DUDES! I'M DONE FOR. SAVE YOURSELVES.
I'M SERIOUS! THIS IS IT! THE SNOWS OF KILIMANJARO ALL OVER AGAIN! I'M BROKEN! BEATEN! MY CONSTITUTION HAS TAKEN A CRITICAL HIT! I'VE GOTTEN THE RED BADGE OF COURAGE!
ARE YOU SURE THAT'S NOT JUST A NACHO STAIN?
I REACHED MY LIMIT! THE EXHAUSTION IS OVERWHELMING! THE WORLD IS SPINNING! HOW MUCH DO YOU EXPECT FROM ME? I CAN GO ON NO FURTHER, I TELL YOU! I CAN GO ON NO MORE!
WELL, IT HAS BEEN TEN MINUTES SINCE WE STARTED...
2

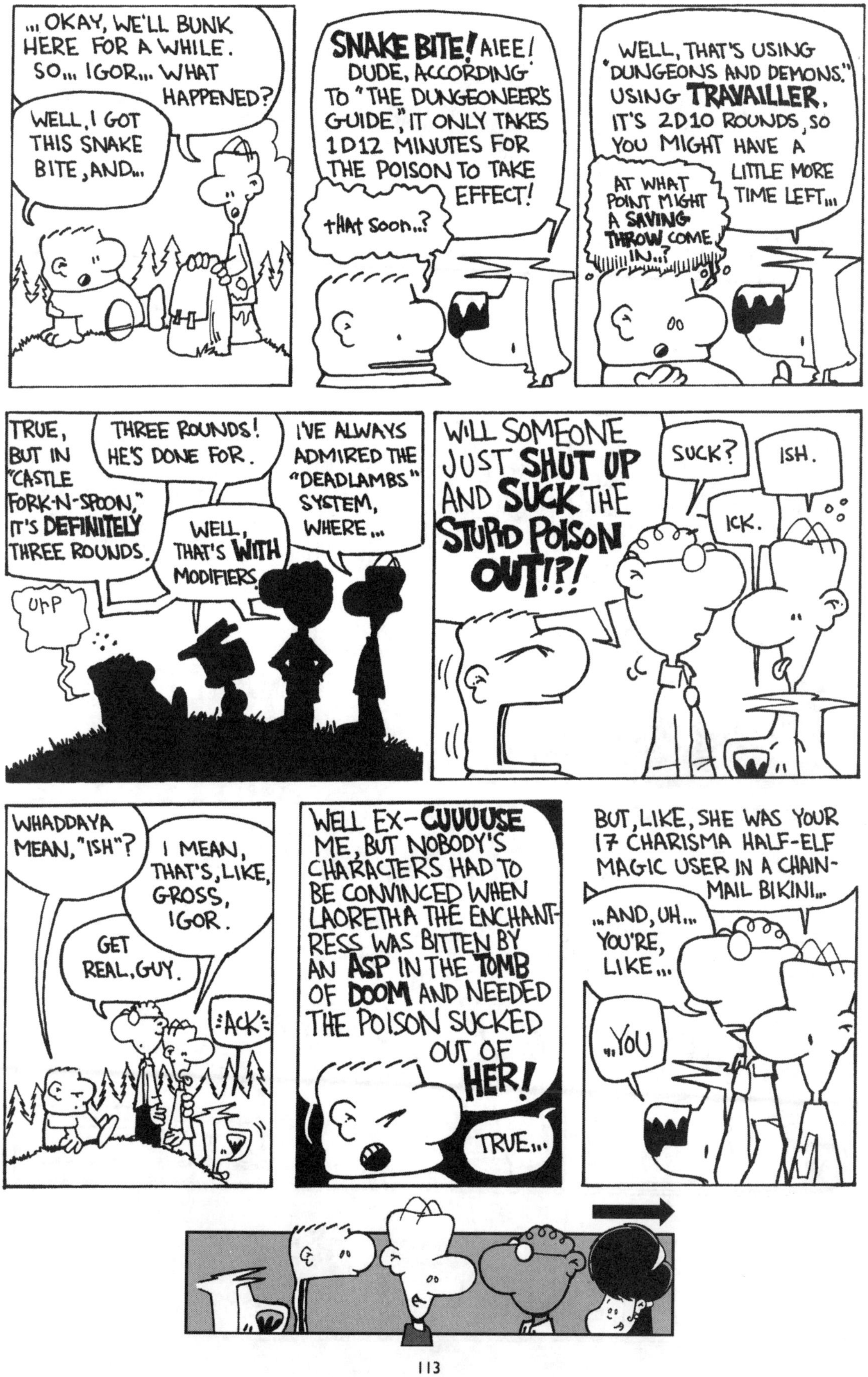
...OKAY, WE'LL BUNK HERE FOR A WHILE. SO... IGOR... WHAT HAPPENED?
WELL, I GOT THIS SNAKE BITE, AND...
SNAKE BITE! AIEE! DUDE, ACCORDING TO "THE DUNGEONEER'S GUIDE," IT ONLY TAKES 1D12 MINUTES FOR THE POISON TO TAKE EFFECT!
THAT SOON..?
WELL, THAT'S USING "DUNGEONS AND DEMONS." USING TRAVAILLER, IT'S 2D10 ROUNDS, SO YOU MIGHT HAVE A LITTLE MORE TIME LEFT...
AT WHAT POINT MIGHT A SAVING THROW COME IN..?
TRUE, BUT IN "CASTLE FORK-N-SPOON," IT'S DEFINITELY THREE ROUNDS.
THREE ROUNDS! HE'S DONE FOR.
WELL, THAT'S WITH MODIFIERS.
I'VE ALWAYS ADMIRED THE "DEADLAMBS" SYSTEM, WHERE...
UHP
WILL SOMEONE JUST SHUT UP AND SUCK THE STUPID POISON OUT!?!
SUCK?
ICK.
ISH.
WHADDAYA MEAN, "ISH"?
I MEAN, THAT'S, LIKE, GROSS, IGOR.
GET REAL, GUY.
ACK
WELL EX-CUUUUSE ME, BUT NOBODY'S CHARACTERS HAD TO BE CONVINCED WHEN LAORETHA THE ENCHANTRESS WAS BITTEN BY AN ASP IN THE TOMB OF DOOM AND NEEDED THE POISON SUCKED OUT OF HER!
TRUE...
BUT, LIKE, SHE WAS YOUR 17 CHARISMA HALF-ELF MAGIC USER IN A CHAIN-MAIL BIKINI...
...AND, UH... YOU'RE, LIKE...
...YOU

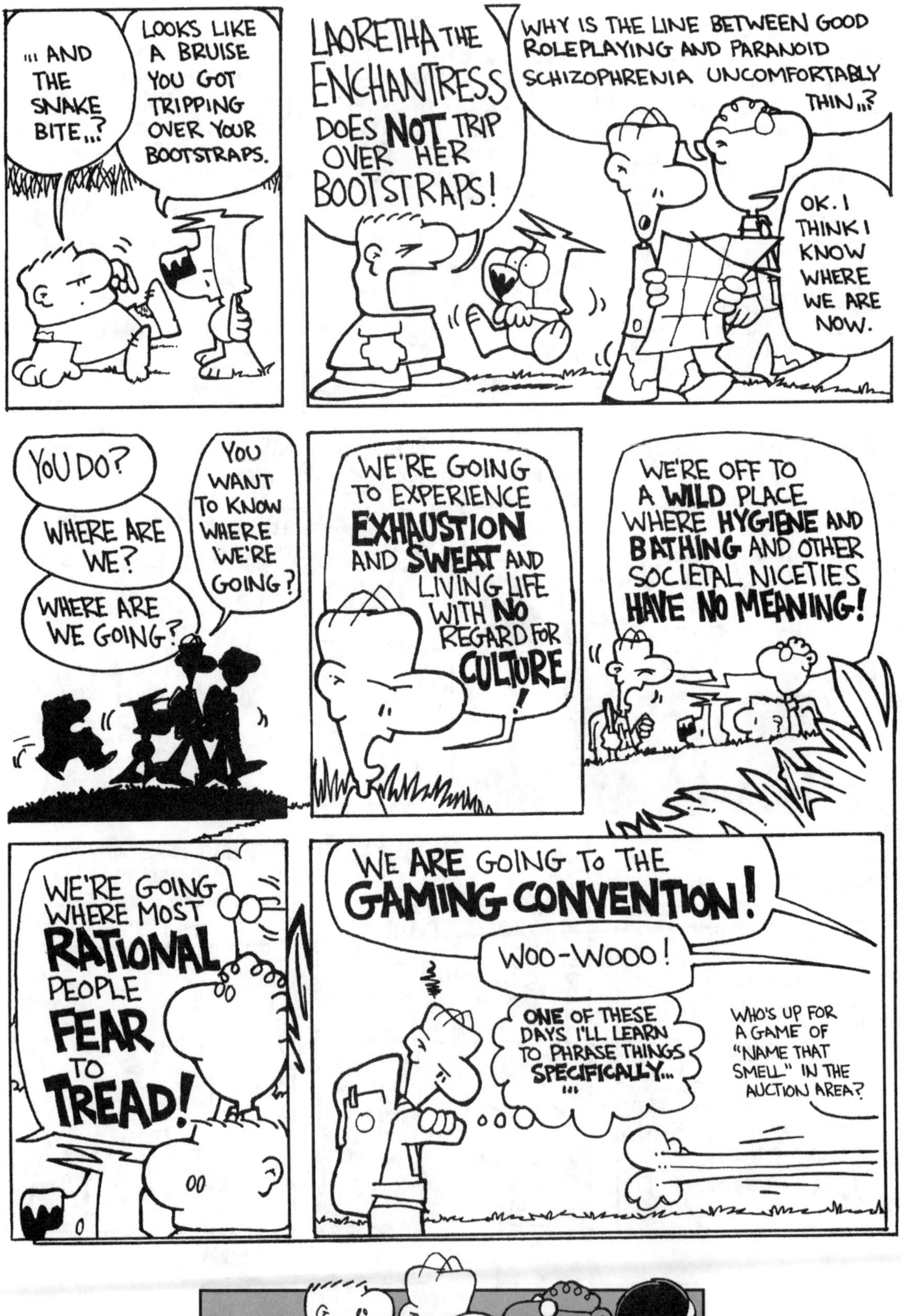
... AND THE SNAKE BITE...?
LOOKS LIKE A BRUISE YOU GOT TRIPPING OVER YOUR BOOTSTRAPS.
LAORETHA THE ENCHANTRESS DOES NOT TRIP OVER HER BOOTSTRAPS!
WHY IS THE LINE BETWEEN GOOD ROLEPLAYING AND PARANOID SCHIZOPHRENIA UNCOMFORTABLY THIN...?
OK. I THINK I KNOW WHERE WE ARE NOW.
YOU DO?
WHERE ARE WE?
WHERE ARE WE GOING?
YOU WANT TO KNOW WHERE WE'RE GOING?
WE'RE GOING TO EXPERIENCE EXHAUSTION AND SWEAT AND LIVING LIFE WITH NO REGARD FOR CULTURE!
WE'RE OFF TO A WILD PLACE WHERE HYGIENE AND BATHING AND OTHER SOCIETAL NICETIES HAVE NO MEANING!
WE'RE GOING WHERE MOST RATIONAL PEOPLE FEAR TO TREAD!
WE ARE GOING TO THE GAMING CONVENTION!
WOO-WOOO!
ONE OF THESE DAYS I'LL LEARN TO PHRASE THINGS SPECIFICALLY...
...
WHO'S UP FOR A GAME OF "NAME THAT SMELL" IN THE AUCTION AREA?

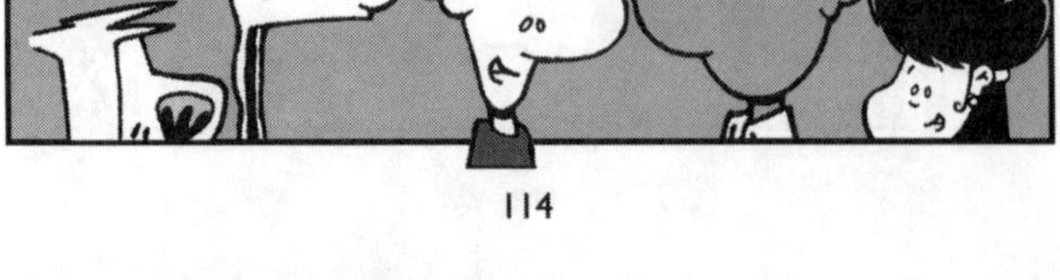

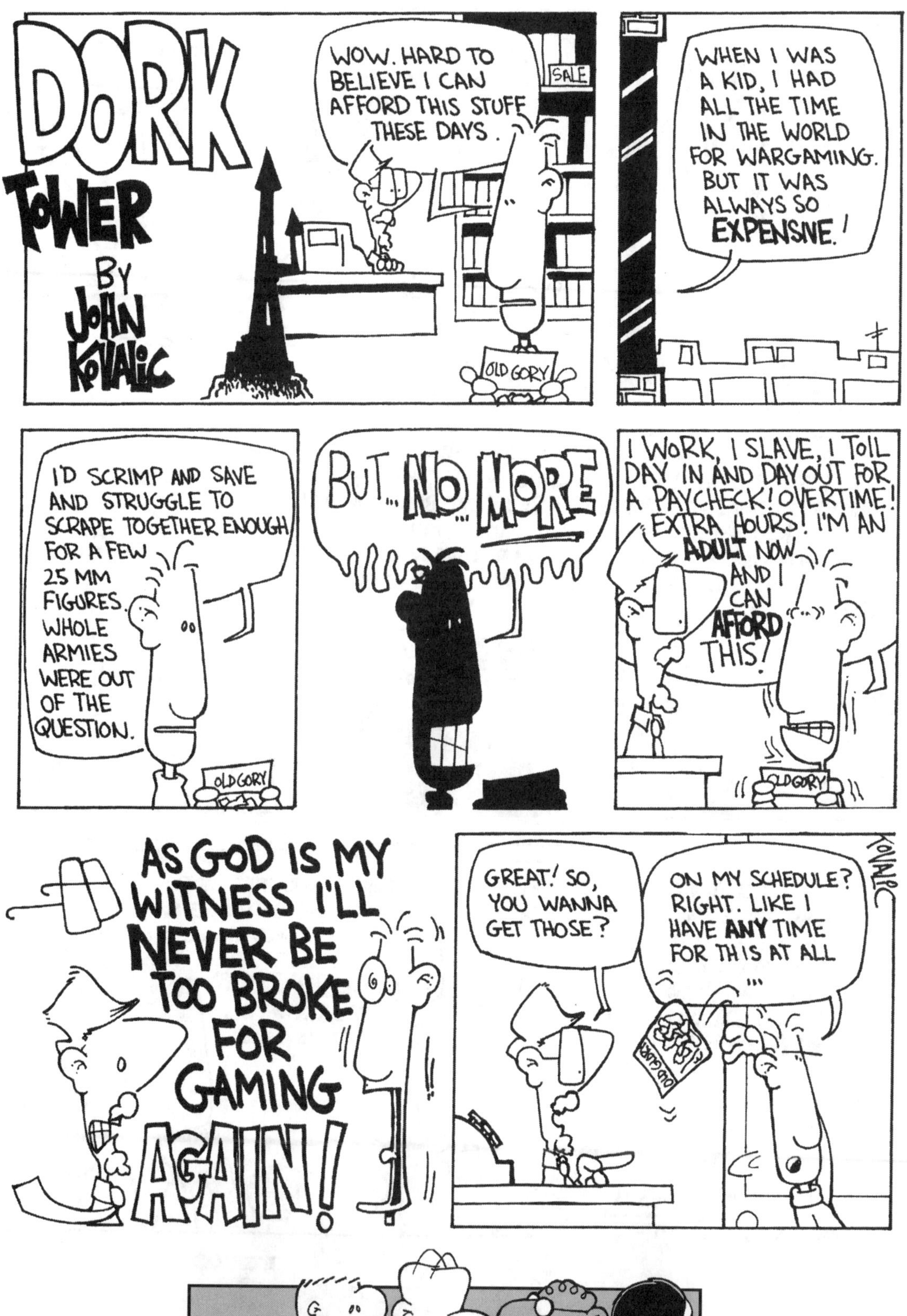
DORK TOWER
BY JOHN KOVALIC
WOW. HARD TO BELIEVE I CAN AFFORD THIS STUFF THESE DAYS.
SALE
OLD GORY
WHEN I WAS A KID, I HAD ALL THE TIME IN THE WORLD FOR WARGAMING. BUT IT WAS ALWAYS SO EXPENSIVE!
I'D SCRIMP AND SAVE AND STRUGGLE TO SCRAPE TOGETHER ENOUGH FOR A FEW 25 MM FIGURES. WHOLE ARMIES WERE OUT OF THE QUESTION.
OLD GORY
BUT... NO... MORE
I WORK, I SLAVE, I TOIL DAY IN AND DAY OUT FOR A PAYCHECK! OVERTIME! EXTRA HOURS! I'M AN ADULT NOW AND I CAN AFFORD THIS!
OLD GORY
AS GOD IS MY WITNESS I'LL NEVER BE TOO BROKE FOR GAMING AGAIN!
KOVALIC
GREAT! SO, YOU WANNA GET THOSE?
ON MY SCHEDULE? RIGHT. LIKE I HAVE ANY TIME FOR THIS AT ALL ...
OLD GORY

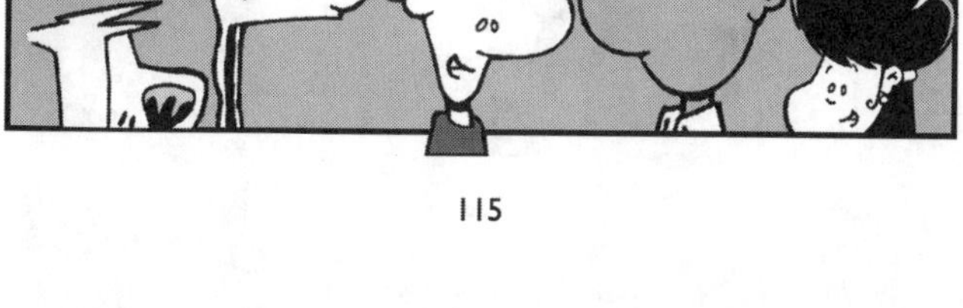

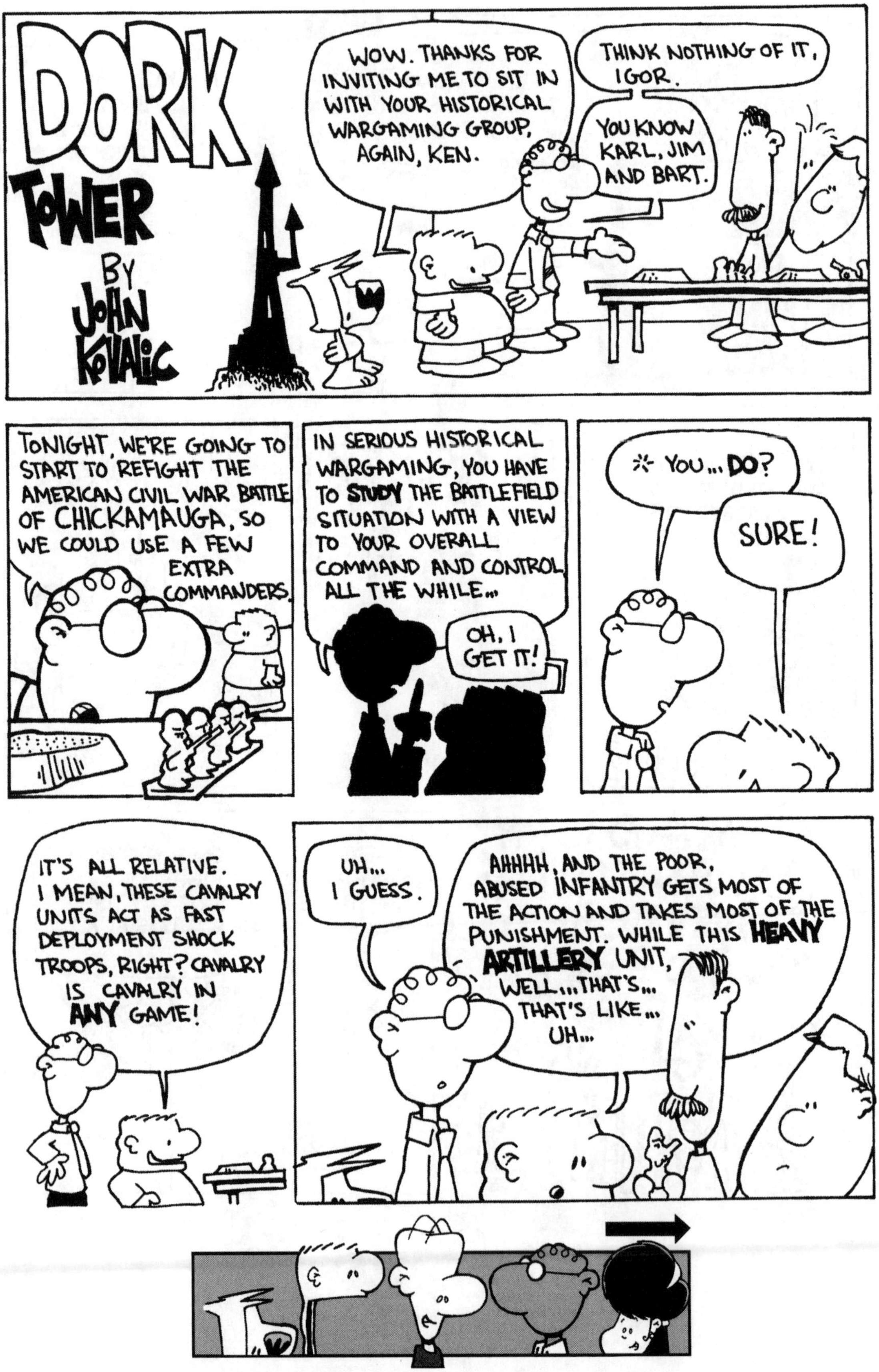
DORK TOWER
BY JOHN KOVALIC
WOW. THANKS FOR INVITING ME TO SIT IN WITH YOUR HISTORICAL WARGAMING GROUP, AGAIN, KEN.
THINK NOTHING OF IT, IGOR.
YOU KNOW KARL, JIM AND BART.
TONIGHT, WE'RE GOING TO START TO REFIGHT THE AMERICAN CIVIL WAR BATTLE OF CHICKAMAUGA, SO WE COULD USE A FEW EXTRA COMMANDERS.
IN SERIOUS HISTORICAL WARGAMING, YOU HAVE TO STUDY THE BATTLEFIELD SITUATION WITH A VIEW TO YOUR OVERALL COMMAND AND CONTROL ALL THE WHILE...
OH, I GET IT!
YOU... DO?
SURE!
IT'S ALL RELATIVE. I MEAN, THESE CAVALRY UNITS ACT AS FAST DEPLOYMENT SHOCK TROOPS, RIGHT? CAVALRY IS CAVALRY IN ANY GAME!
UH... I GUESS.
AHHHH, AND THE POOR, ABUSED INFANTRY GETS MOST OF THE ACTION AND TAKES MOST OF THE PUNISHMENT. WHILE THIS HEAVY ARTILLERY UNIT, WELL... THAT'S... THAT'S LIKE... UH...

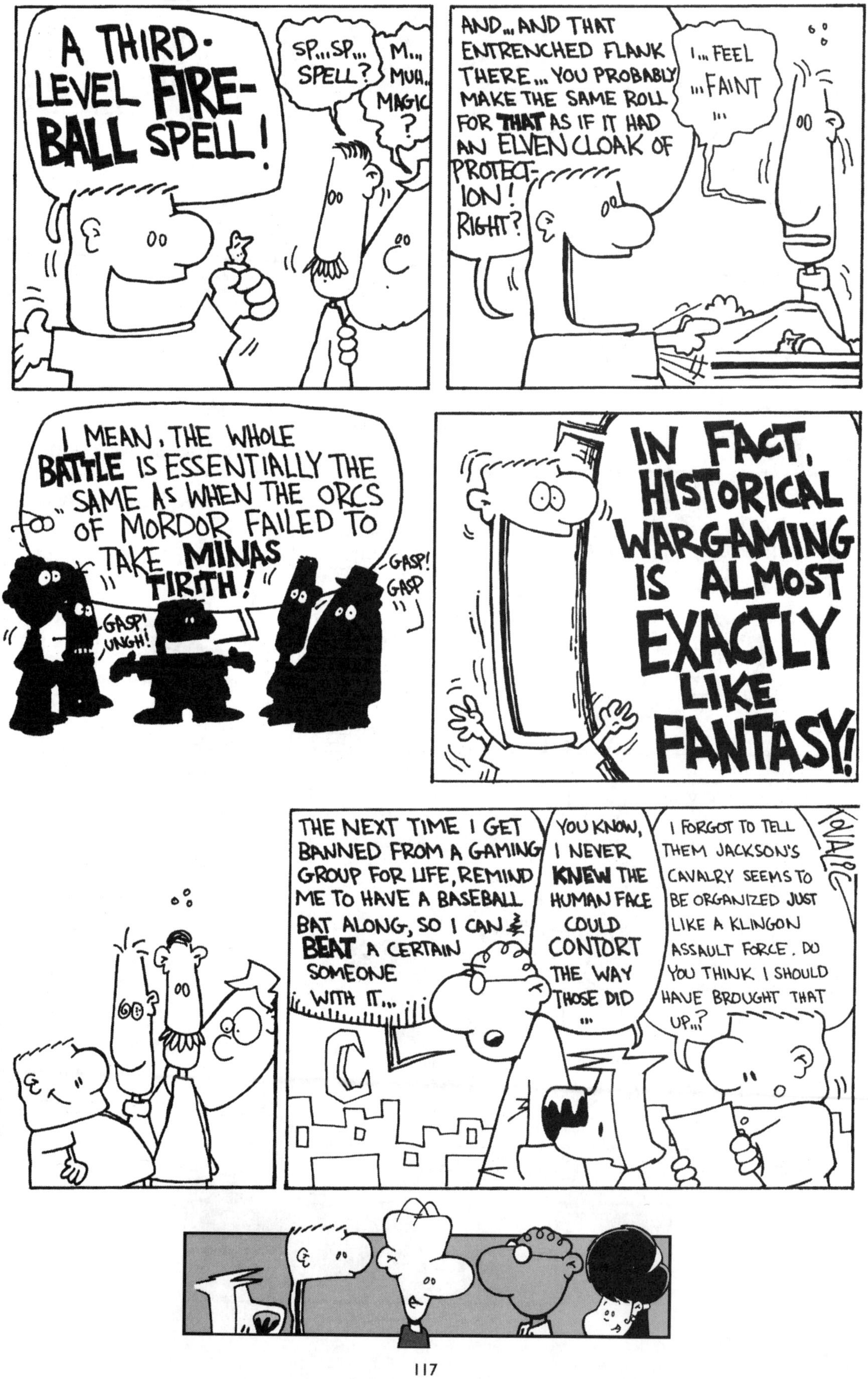
A THIRD-LEVEL FIRE-BALL SPELL!
SP... SP... SPELL?
M... MUH... MAGIC?
AND... AND THAT ENTRENCHED FLANK THERE... YOU PROBABLY MAKE THE SAME ROLL FOR THAT AS IF IT HAD AN ELVEN CLOAK OF PROTECT-ION! RIGHT?
I... FEEL ...FAINT ...
I MEAN, THE WHOLE BATTLE IS ESSENTIALLY THE SAME AS WHEN THE ORCS OF MORDOR FAILED TO TAKE MINAS TIRITH!
GASP! UNGH!
GASP! GASP
IN FACT, HISTORICAL WARGAMING IS ALMOST EXACTLY LIKE FANTASY!
THE NEXT TIME I GET BANNED FROM A GAMING GROUP FOR LIFE, REMIND ME TO HAVE A BASEBALL BAT ALONG, SO I CAN BEAT A CERTAIN SOMEONE WITH IT...
YOU KNOW, I NEVER KNEW THE HUMAN FACE COULD CONTORT THE WAY THOSE DID ...
I FORGOT TO TELL THEM JACKSON'S CAVALRY SEEMS TO BE ORGANIZED JUST LIKE A KLINGON ASSAULT FORCE. DO YOU THINK I SHOULD HAVE BROUGHT THAT UP...?
KOVALIC

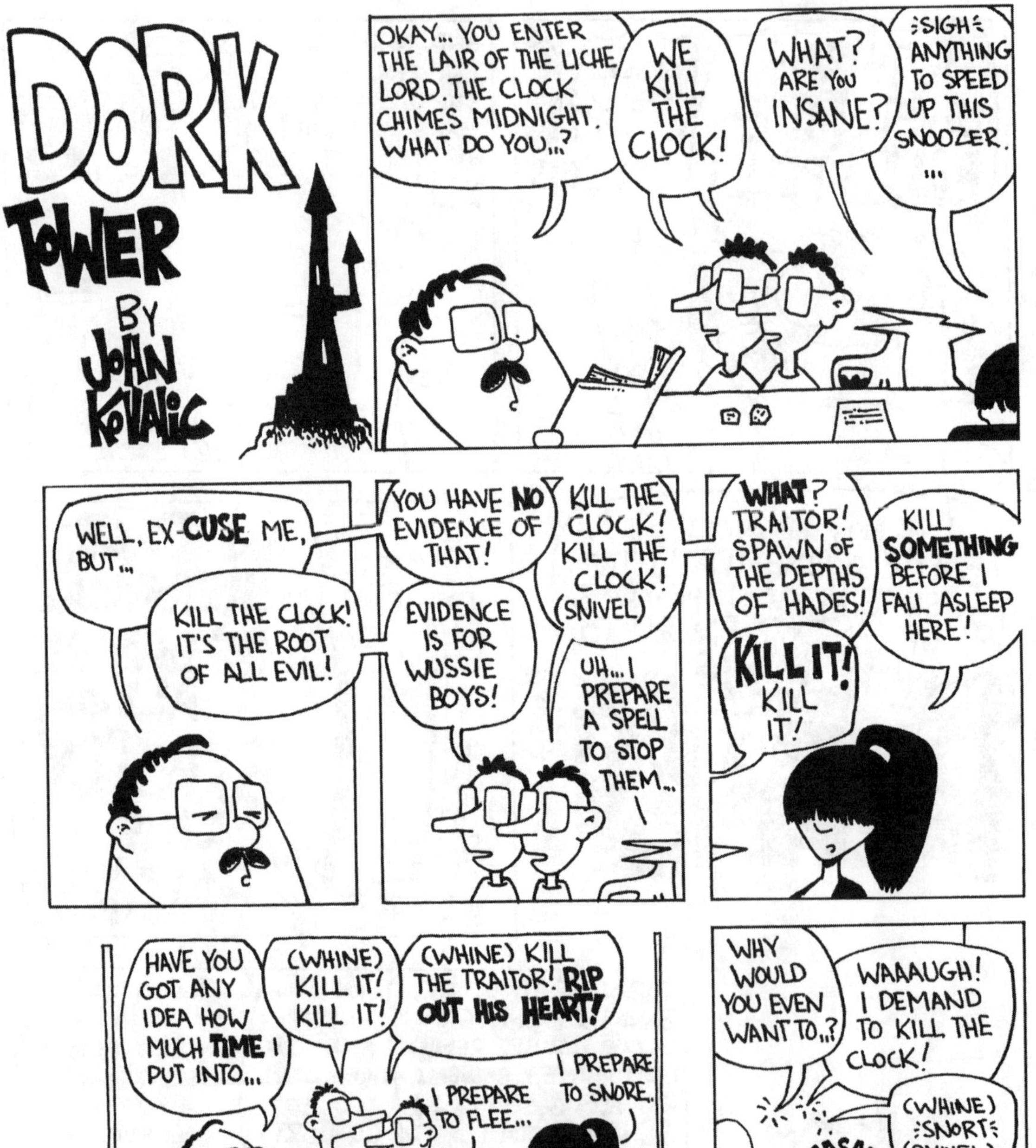
DORK TOWER
BY JOHN KOVALIC
OKAY... YOU ENTER THE LAIR OF THE LICHE LORD. THE CLOCK CHIMES MIDNIGHT. WHAT DO YOU...?
WE KILL THE CLOCK!
WHAT? ARE YOU INSANE?
≑SIGH≑ ANYTHING TO SPEED UP THIS SNOOZER. ...
WELL, EX-CUSE ME, BUT...
KILL THE CLOCK! IT'S THE ROOT OF ALL EVIL!
YOU HAVE NO EVIDENCE OF THAT!
EVIDENCE IS FOR WUSSIE BOYS!
KILL THE CLOCK! KILL THE CLOCK! (SNIVEL)
UH... I PREPARE A SPELL TO STOP THEM...
WHAT? TRAITOR! SPAWN OF THE DEPTHS OF HADES!
KILL IT! KILL IT!
KILL SOMETHING BEFORE I FALL ASLEEP HERE!
HAVE YOU GOT ANY IDEA HOW MUCH TIME I PUT INTO...
(WHINE) KILL IT! KILL IT!
(WHINE) KILL THE TRAITOR! RIP OUT HIS HEART!
I PREPARE TO FLEE...
I PREPARE TO SNORE.
WHY WOULD YOU EVEN WANT TO...?
WAAAUGH! I DEMAND TO KILL THE CLOCK!
(WHINE) ≑SNORT≑ (SNIVEL)
PEGASAURUS GAMES

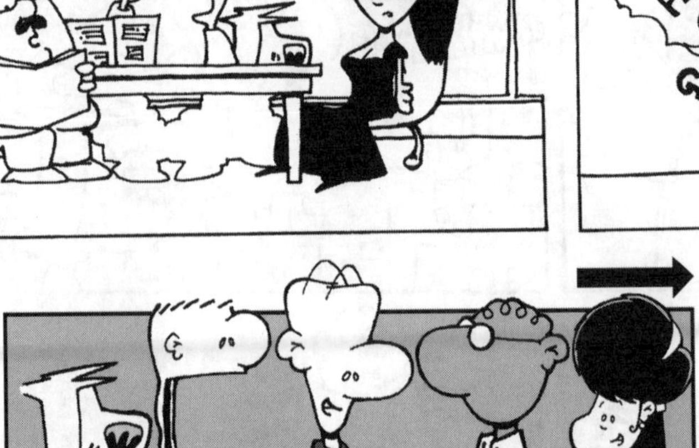

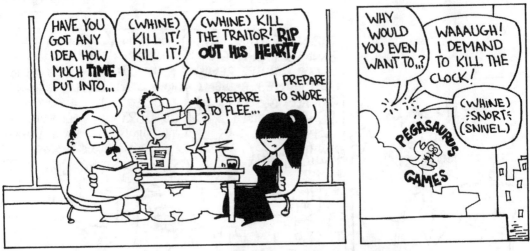

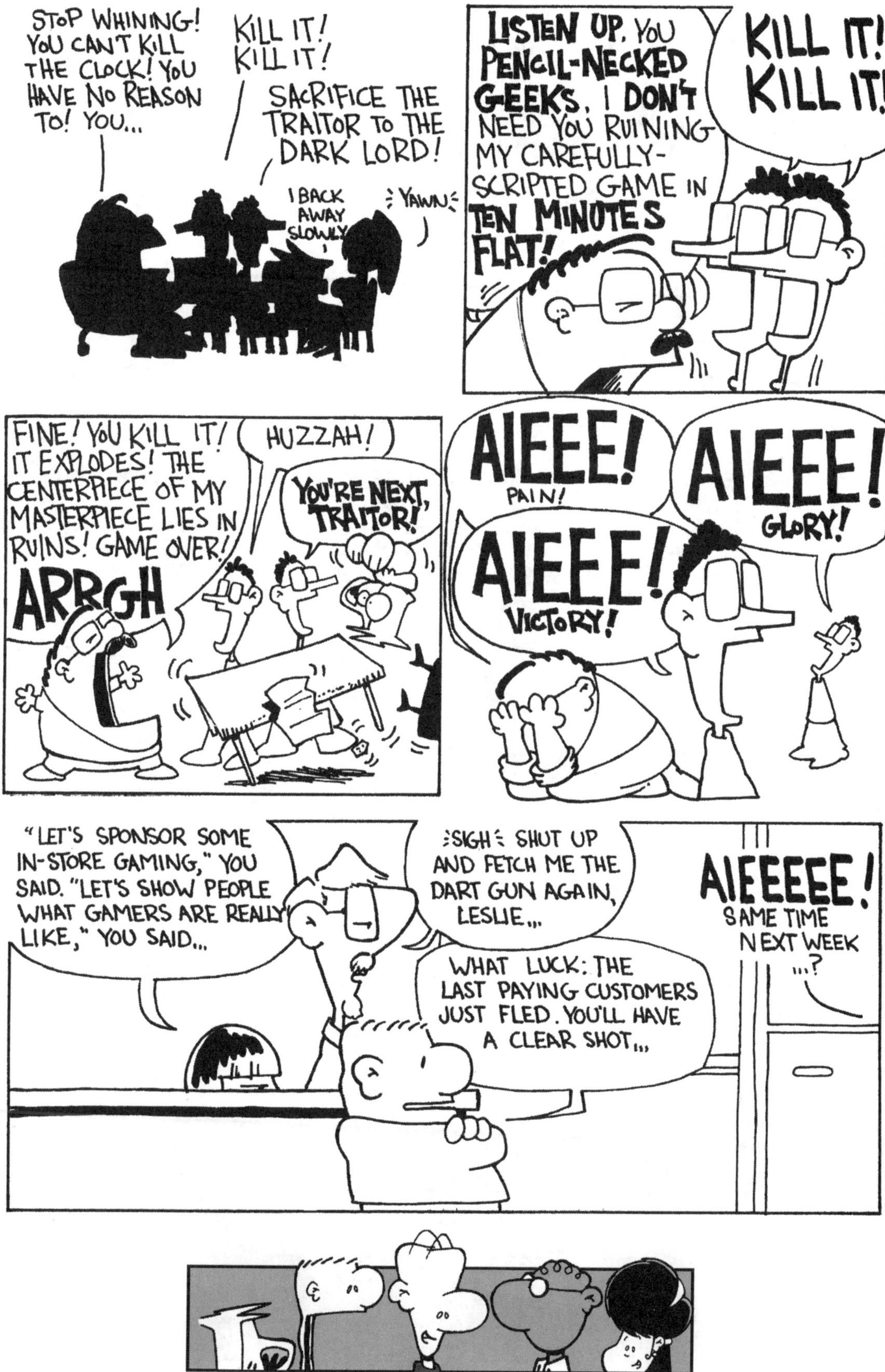
STOP WHINING! YOU CAN'T KILL THE CLOCK! YOU HAVE NO REASON TO! YOU...
KILL IT! KILL IT!
SACRIFICE THE TRAITOR TO THE DARK LORD!
I BACK AWAY SLOWLY
YAWN
LISTEN UP, YOU PENCIL-NECKED GEEKS, I DON'T NEED YOU RUINING MY CAREFULLY-SCRIPTED GAME IN TEN MINUTES FLAT!
KILL IT! KILL IT!
FINE! YOU KILL IT! IT EXPLODES! THE CENTERPIECE OF MY MASTERPIECE LIES IN RUINS! GAME OVER!
ARRGH
HUZZAH!
YOU'RE NEXT, TRAITOR!
AIEEE! PAIN!
AIEEE! GLORY!
AIEEE! VICTORY!
"LET'S SPONSOR SOME IN-STORE GAMING," YOU SAID. "LET'S SHOW PEOPLE WHAT GAMERS ARE REALLY LIKE," YOU SAID...
SIGH SHUT UP AND FETCH ME THE DART GUN AGAIN, LESLIE...
WHAT LUCK: THE LAST PAYING CUSTOMERS JUST FLED. YOU'LL HAVE A CLEAR SHOT...
AIEEEEE!
SAME TIME NEXT WEEK ...?

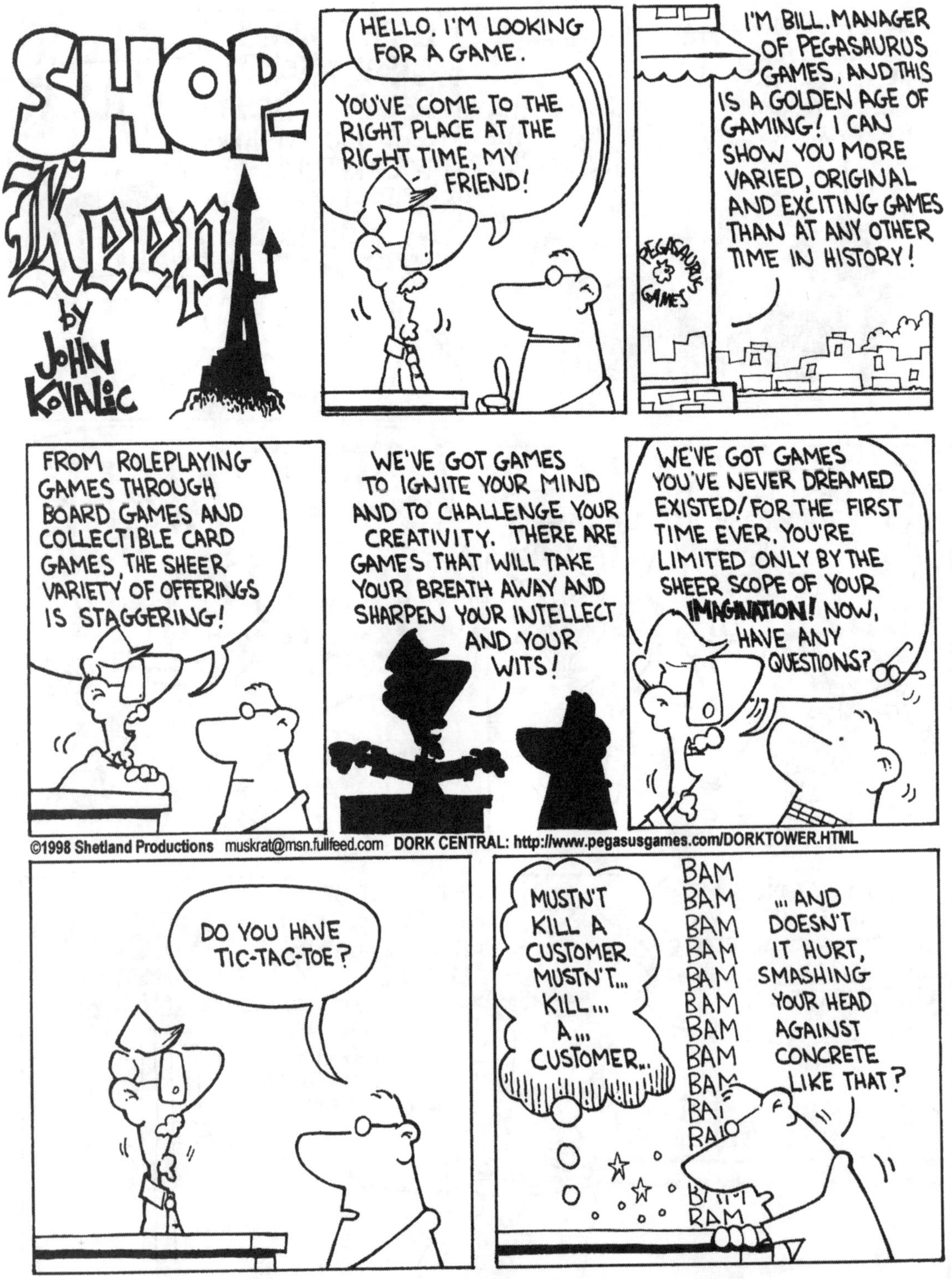
SHOP-Keep
by JOHN KOVALIC
HELLO, I'M LOOKING FOR A GAME.
YOU'VE COME TO THE RIGHT PLACE AT THE RIGHT TIME, MY FRIEND!
I'M BILL, MANAGER OF PEGASAURUS GAMES, AND THIS IS A GOLDEN AGE OF GAMING! I CAN SHOW YOU MORE VARIED, ORIGINAL AND EXCITING GAMES THAN AT ANY OTHER TIME IN HISTORY!
PEGASAURUS GAMES
FROM ROLEPLAYING GAMES THROUGH BOARD GAMES AND COLLECTIBLE CARD GAMES, THE SHEER VARIETY OF OFFERINGS IS STAGGERING!
WE'VE GOT GAMES TO IGNITE YOUR MIND AND TO CHALLENGE YOUR CREATIVITY. THERE ARE GAMES THAT WILL TAKE YOUR BREATH AWAY AND SHARPEN YOUR INTELLECT AND YOUR WITS!
WE'VE GOT GAMES YOU'VE NEVER DREAMED EXISTED! FOR THE FIRST TIME EVER, YOU'RE LIMITED ONLY BY THE SHEER SCOPE OF YOUR IMAGINATION! NOW, HAVE ANY QUESTIONS?
©1998 Shetland Productions muskrat@msn.fullfeed.com DORK CENTRAL: http://www.pegasusgames.com/DORKTOWER.HTML
DO YOU HAVE TIC-TAC-TOE?
MUSTN'T KILL A CUSTOMER. MUSTN'T... KILL... A... CUSTOMER...
BAM BAM BAM BAM BAM BAM BAM BAM
... AND DOESN'T IT HURT, SMASHING YOUR HEAD AGAINST CONCRETE LIKE THAT?

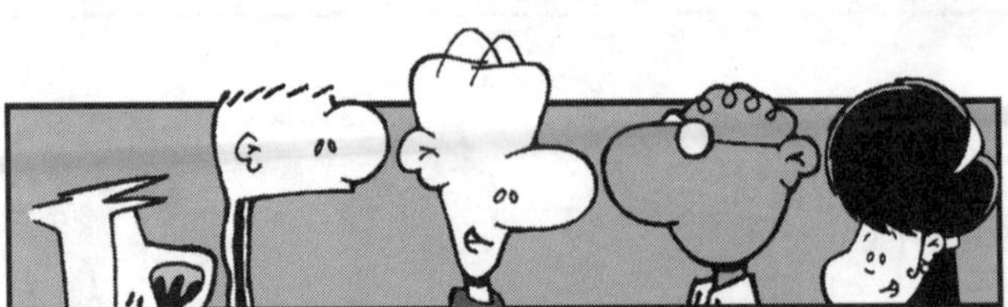

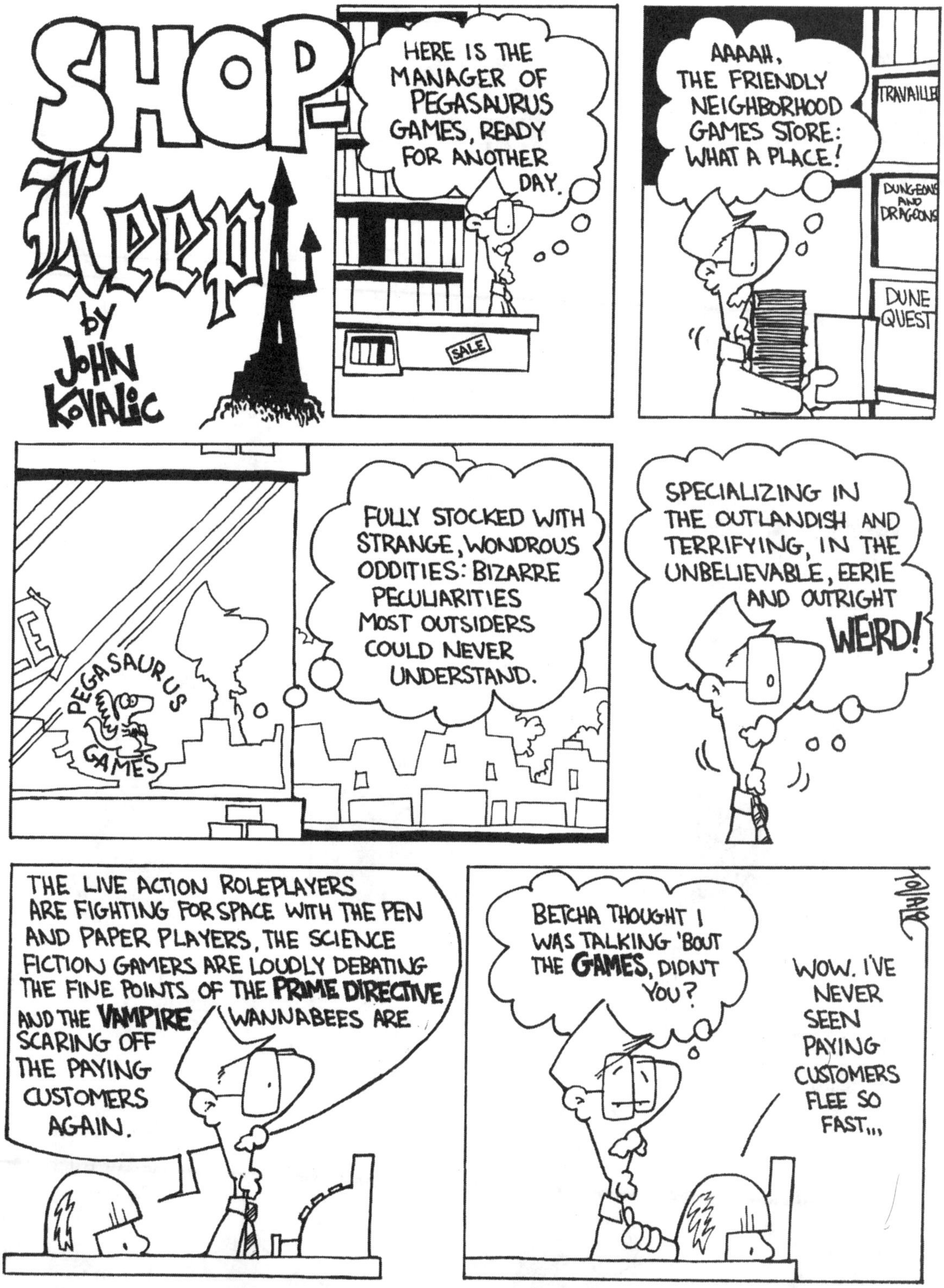
SHOP-Keep
by John Kovalic
HERE IS THE MANAGER OF PEGASAURUS GAMES, READY FOR ANOTHER DAY.
SALE
AAAAH, THE FRIENDLY NEIGHBORHOOD GAMES STORE: WHAT A PLACE!
DUNGEONS AND DRAGONS
DUNE QUEST
PEGASAURUS GAMES
FULLY STOCKED WITH STRANGE, WONDROUS ODDITIES: BIZARRE PECULIARITIES MOST OUTSIDERS COULD NEVER UNDERSTAND.
SPECIALIZING IN THE OUTLANDISH AND TERRIFYING, IN THE UNBELIEVABLE, EERIE AND OUTRIGHT WEIRD!
THE LIVE ACTION ROLEPLAYERS ARE FIGHTING FOR SPACE WITH THE PEN AND PAPER PLAYERS, THE SCIENCE FICTION GAMERS ARE LOUDLY DEBATING THE FINE POINTS OF THE PRIME DIRECTIVE AND THE VAMPIRE WANNABEES ARE SCARING OFF THE PAYING CUSTOMERS AGAIN.
BETCHA THOUGHT I WAS TALKING 'BOUT THE GAMES, DIDN'T YOU?
WOW. I'VE NEVER SEEN PAYING CUSTOMERS FLEE SO FAST...
KOVALIC

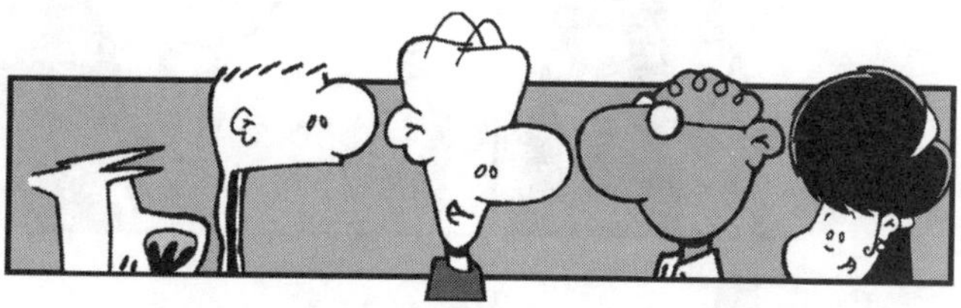

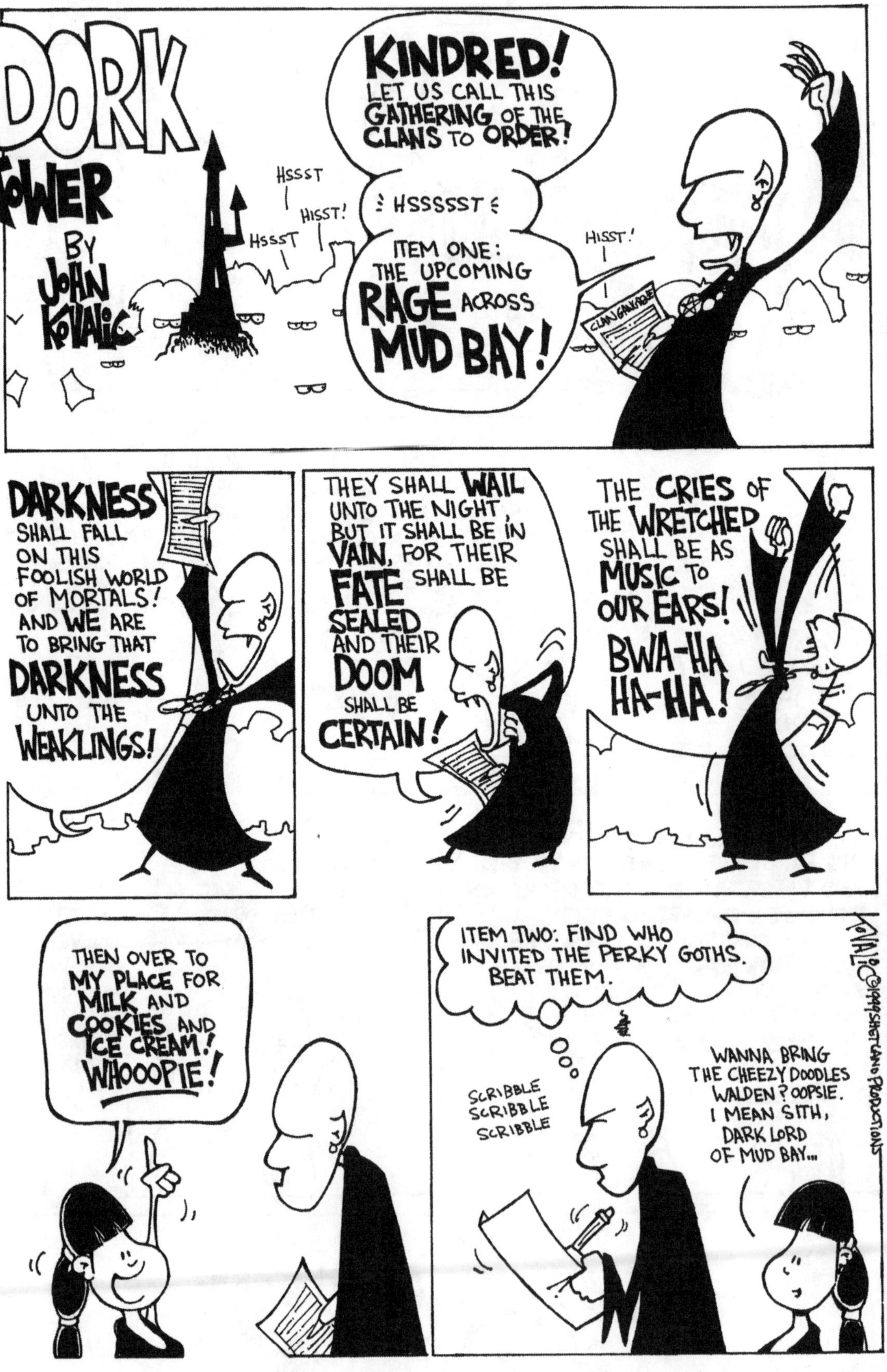
DORK TOWER
BY JOHN KOVALIC
KINDRED! LET US CALL THIS GATHERING OF THE CLANS TO ORDER!
HSSST
HISST!
HSSST
HSSSSST
HISST!
ITEM ONE: THE UPCOMING RAGE ACROSS MUD BAY!
CLAN GATHERING
DARKNESS SHALL FALL ON THIS FOOLISH WORLD OF MORTALS! AND WE ARE TO BRING THAT DARKNESS UNTO THE WEAKLINGS!
THEY SHALL WAIL UNTO THE NIGHT, BUT IT SHALL BE IN VAIN, FOR THEIR FATE SHALL BE SEALED AND THEIR DOOM SHALL BE CERTAIN!
THE CRIES OF THE WRETCHED SHALL BE AS MUSIC TO OUR EARS!
BWA-HA HA-HA!
THEN OVER TO MY PLACE FOR MILK AND COOKIES AND ICE CREAM! WHOOOPIE!
ITEM TWO: FIND WHO INVITED THE PERKY GOTHS. BEAT THEM.
SCRIBBLE SCRIBBLE SCRIBBLE
WANNA BRING THE CHEEZY DOODLES WALDEN? OOPSIE. I MEAN SITH, DARK LORD OF MUD BAY...
KOVALIC ©1999 SHETLAND PRODUCTIONS

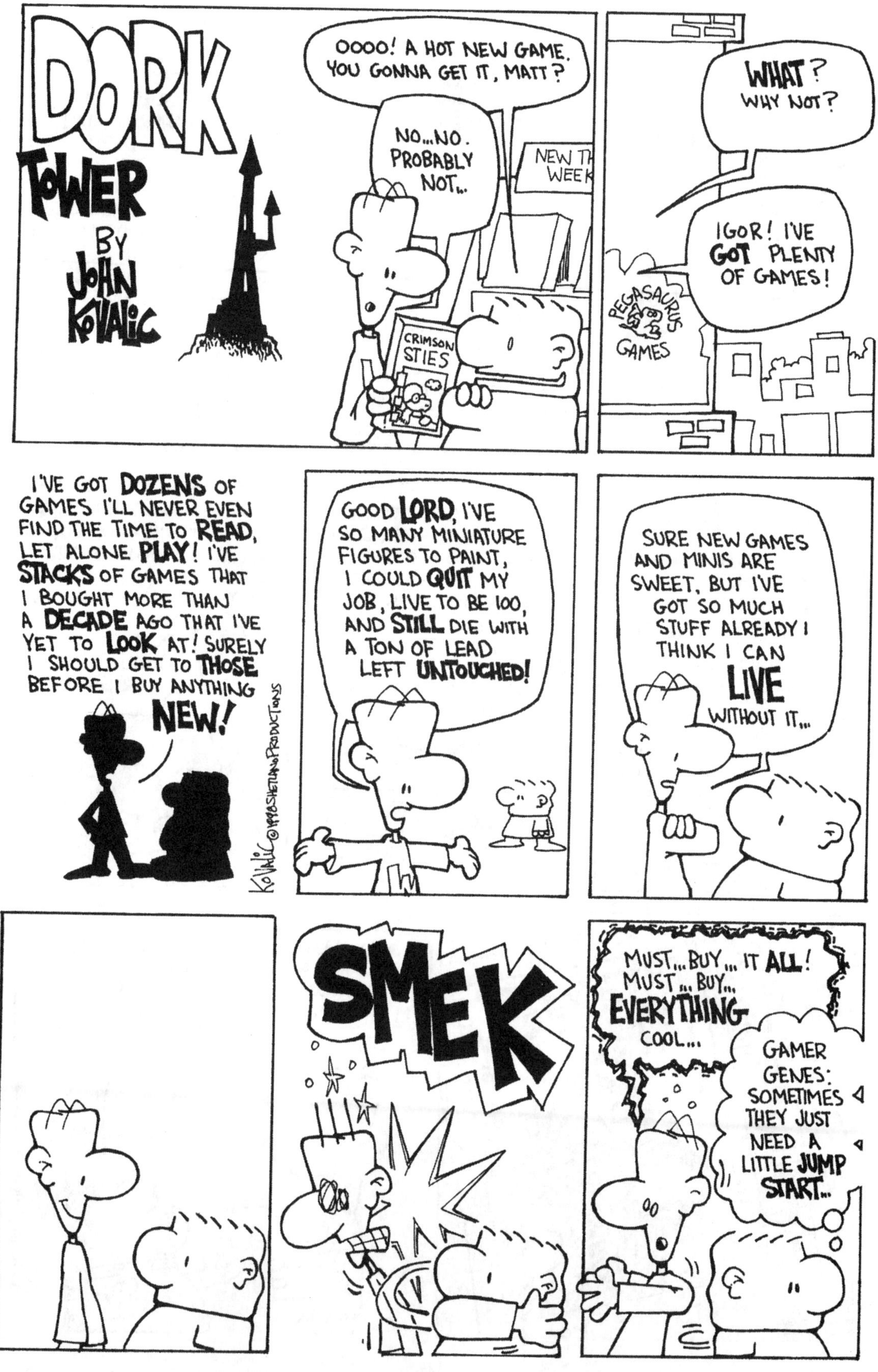
DORK TOWER
BY JOHN KOVALIC
OOOO! A HOT NEW GAME. YOU GONNA GET IT, MATT?
NO... NO. PROBABLY NOT...
NEW TH WEEK
CRIMSON STIES
WHAT? WHY NOT?
IGOR! I'VE GOT PLENTY OF GAMES!
PEGASAURUS GAMES
I'VE GOT DOZENS OF GAMES I'LL NEVER EVEN FIND THE TIME TO READ, LET ALONE PLAY! I'VE STACKS OF GAMES THAT I BOUGHT MORE THAN A DECADE AGO THAT I'VE YET TO LOOK AT! SURELY I SHOULD GET TO THOSE BEFORE I BUY ANYTHING NEW!
KOVALIC ©1998 SHETLAND PRODUCTIONS
GOOD LORD, I'VE SO MANY MINIATURE FIGURES TO PAINT, I COULD QUIT MY JOB, LIVE TO BE 100, AND STILL DIE WITH A TON OF LEAD LEFT UNTOUCHED!
SURE NEW GAMES AND MINIS ARE SWEET, BUT I'VE GOT SO MUCH STUFF ALREADY I THINK I CAN LIVE WITHOUT IT...
SMEK
MUST... BUY... IT ALL! MUST... BUY... EVERYTHING COOL...
GAMER GENES: SOMETIMES THEY JUST NEED A LITTLE JUMP START...

DORK TOWER BY JOHN KOVALIC

OK... DOES EVERYBODY HAVE THEIR NEW CHARACTERS READY FOR ME TO SEE?

OOO! OOO! ME FIRST!

OKAY, SO YOU **MAY** NOTICE THAT THIS CHARACTER IS A BIT MORE POWERFUL THAN MOST. BUT BY DEFTLY TAKING A SERIES OF MINOR QUIRKS, DISADVANTAGES AND HINDERANCES, I WAS ABLE TO RAISE MY POINT TOTAL BY FIVE **HUNDRED** PERCENT!

WHICH ALLOWED ME TO CREATE DEATHGRIPPE, THE CYBORG ASSASSIN, WITH INFRA-RED VISION, LIGHTNING-FAST REFLEXES AND A MASSIVE **TECH LEVEL 15 PLASMA RIFLE!!**

HE'S ALSO GOT PERSONAL BODY ARMOR, SUPER STRONG SYNTH SKIN AND LASER-LIKE MARKSMANSHIP, AS WELL AS CONCUSSION BOMBS, HYPER NUNCHAKU, THE "KILLER GRIP" SKILL AND WANG-CHUNG EVIL EYE!

THIS CHARACTER **MAY** SEEM A BIT EXTREME AND **MAY** BE A BIT SUPERHUMAN, BUT IT **IS** GOING BY THE RULES, IF YOU KNOW HOW TO TWEAK THEM, CARESS THEM AND PLAY THEM JUUUUUST RIGHT!

GTH	18
NCE	14
TY	13
M	17
N	19
A	15

AIEEEEE!!

Character Sketch

CONSIDERING WE'RE PLAYING "BUNNIES AND BURROWS," I'M IMPRESSED...

OOPSIE! I FORGOT TO DRAW IN THE RABBIT EARS. AND THE THERMONUCLEAR GRENADE LAUNCHER...

124

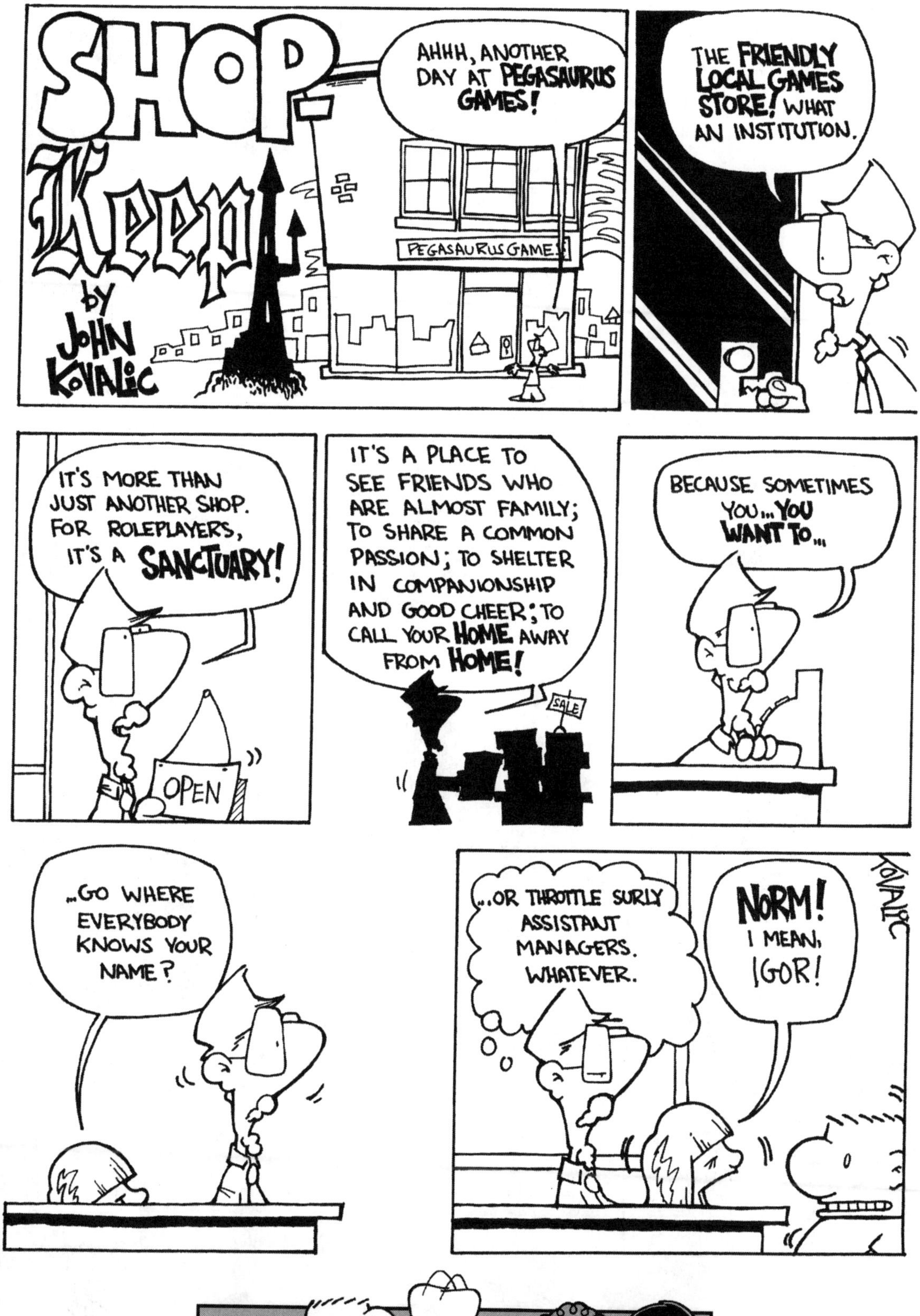
SHOP-Keep
by JOHN KOVALIC
AHHH, ANOTHER DAY AT PEGASAURUS GAMES!
PEGASAURUS GAMES
THE FRIENDLY LOCAL GAMES STORE! WHAT AN INSTITUTION.
IT'S MORE THAN JUST ANOTHER SHOP. FOR ROLEPLAYERS, IT'S A SANCTUARY!
OPEN
IT'S A PLACE TO SEE FRIENDS WHO ARE ALMOST FAMILY; TO SHARE A COMMON PASSION; TO SHELTER IN COMPANIONSHIP AND GOOD CHEER; TO CALL YOUR HOME AWAY FROM HOME!
SALE
BECAUSE SOMETIMES YOU... YOU WANT TO...
...GO WHERE EVERYBODY KNOWS YOUR NAME?
...OR THROTTLE SURLY ASSISTANT MANAGERS. WHATEVER.
NORM! I MEAN, IGOR!
KOVALIC

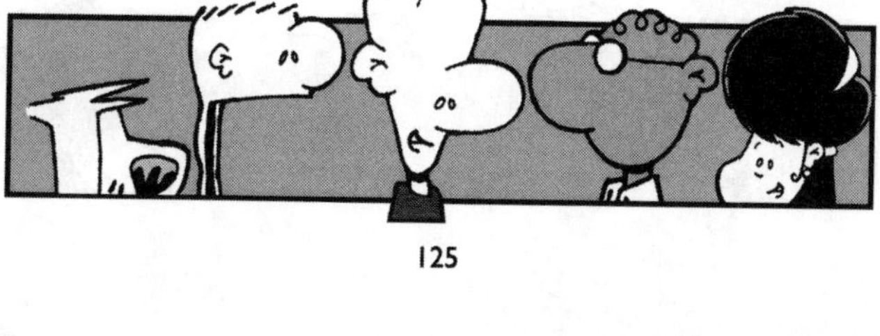

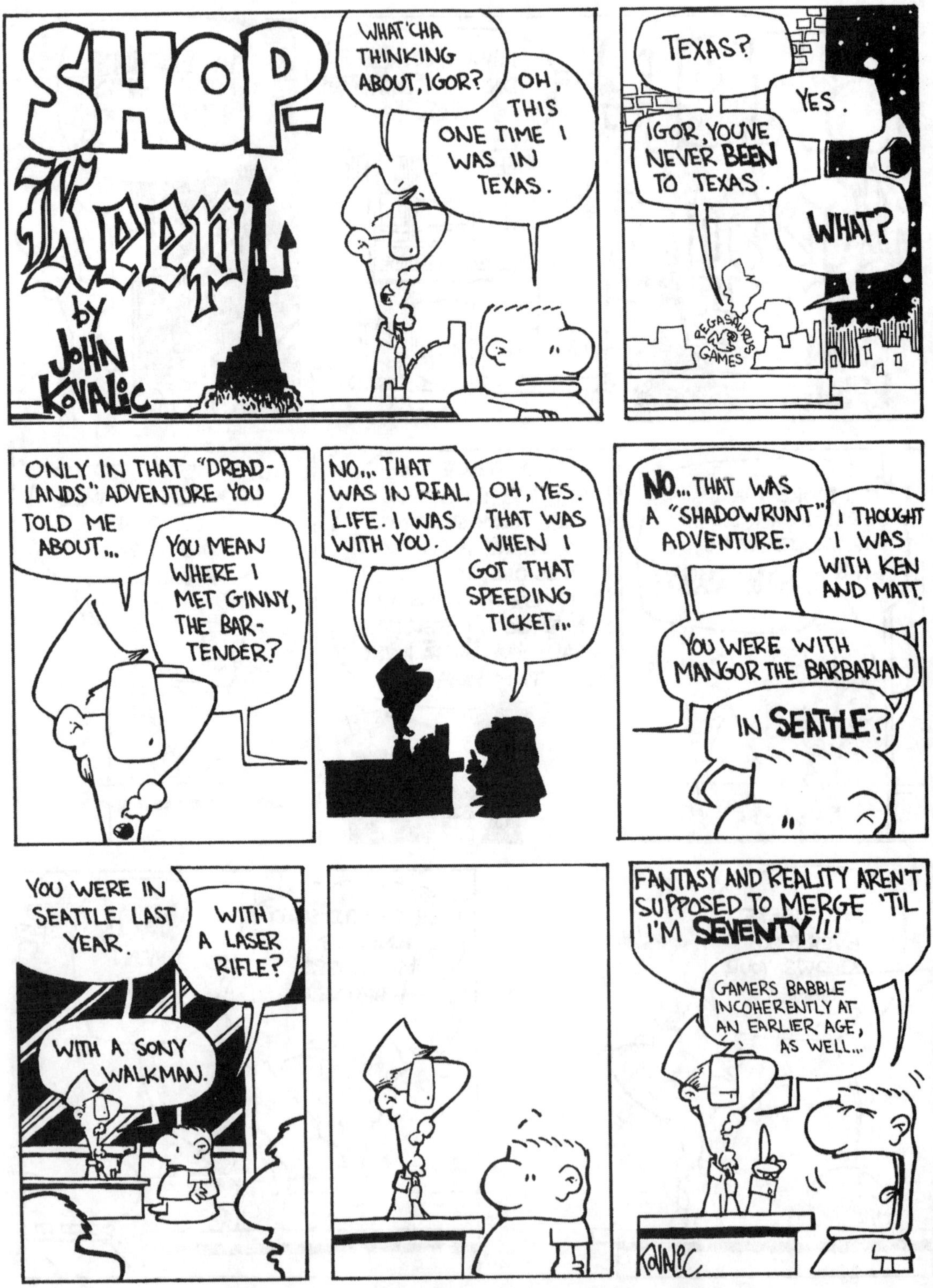
SHOP-Keep
by JOHN KOVALIC
WHAT'CHA THINKING ABOUT, IGOR?
OH, THIS ONE TIME I WAS IN TEXAS.
TEXAS?
YES.
IGOR, YOU'VE NEVER BEEN TO TEXAS.
WHAT?
PEGASAURUS GAMES
ONLY IN THAT "DREAD-LANDS" ADVENTURE YOU TOLD ME ABOUT...
YOU MEAN WHERE I MET GINNY, THE BAR-TENDER?
NO... THAT WAS IN REAL LIFE. I WAS WITH YOU.
OH, YES. THAT WAS WHEN I GOT THAT SPEEDING TICKET...
NO... THAT WAS A "SHADOWRUNT" ADVENTURE.
I THOUGHT I WAS WITH KEN AND MATT.
YOU WERE WITH MANGOR THE BARBARIAN
IN SEATTLE?
YOU WERE IN SEATTLE LAST YEAR.
WITH A LASER RIFLE?
WITH A SONY WALKMAN.
FANTASY AND REALITY AREN'T SUPPOSED TO MERGE 'TIL I'M SEVENTY!!!
GAMERS BABBLE INCOHERENTLY AT AN EARLIER AGE, AS WELL...
KOVALIC

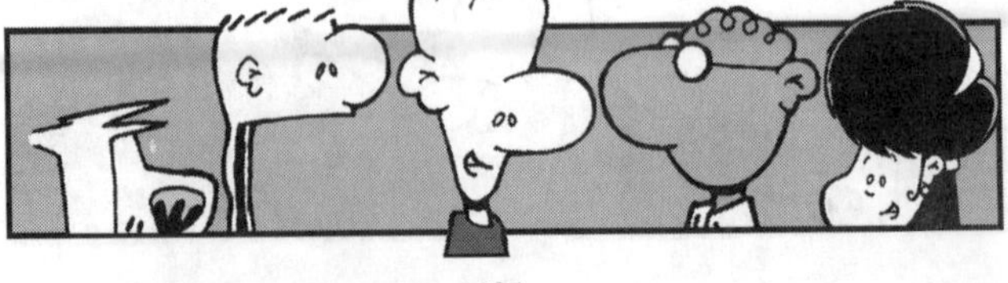

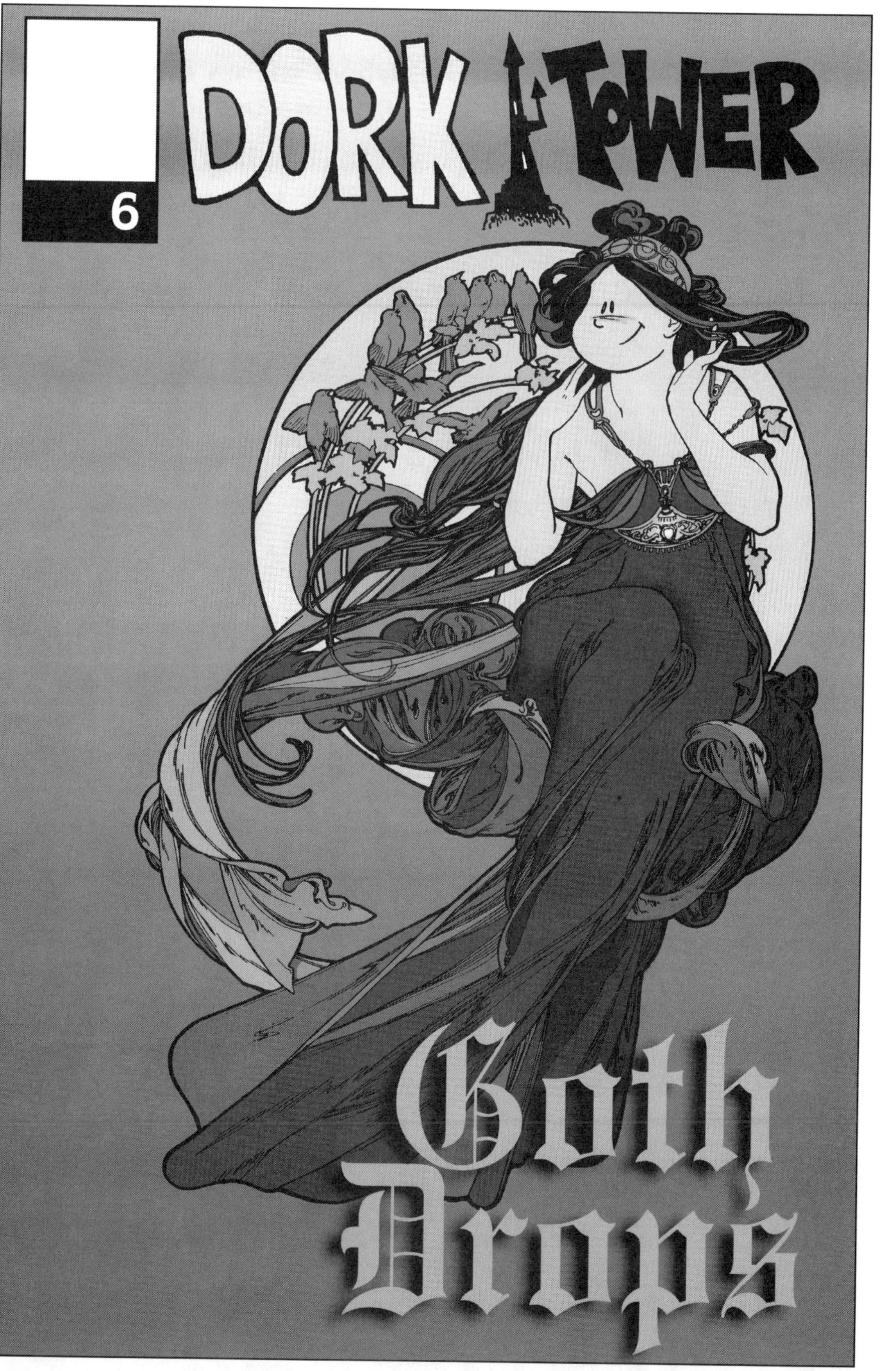
6
DORK TOWER
Goth Drops

"Take me out tonight, where there's music and there are people who are young and alive..."

-The Smiths: "There is a Light That Never Goes Out"

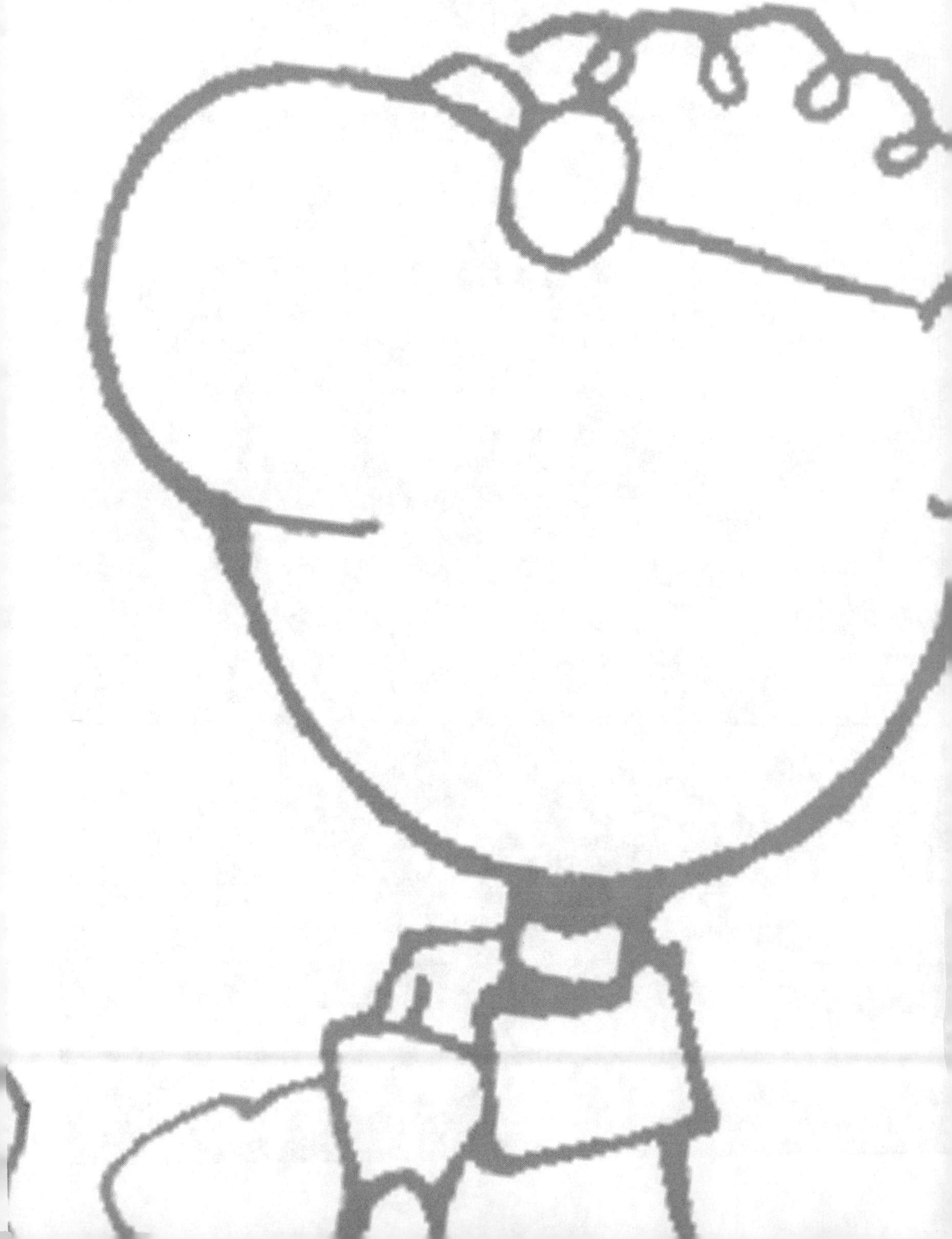

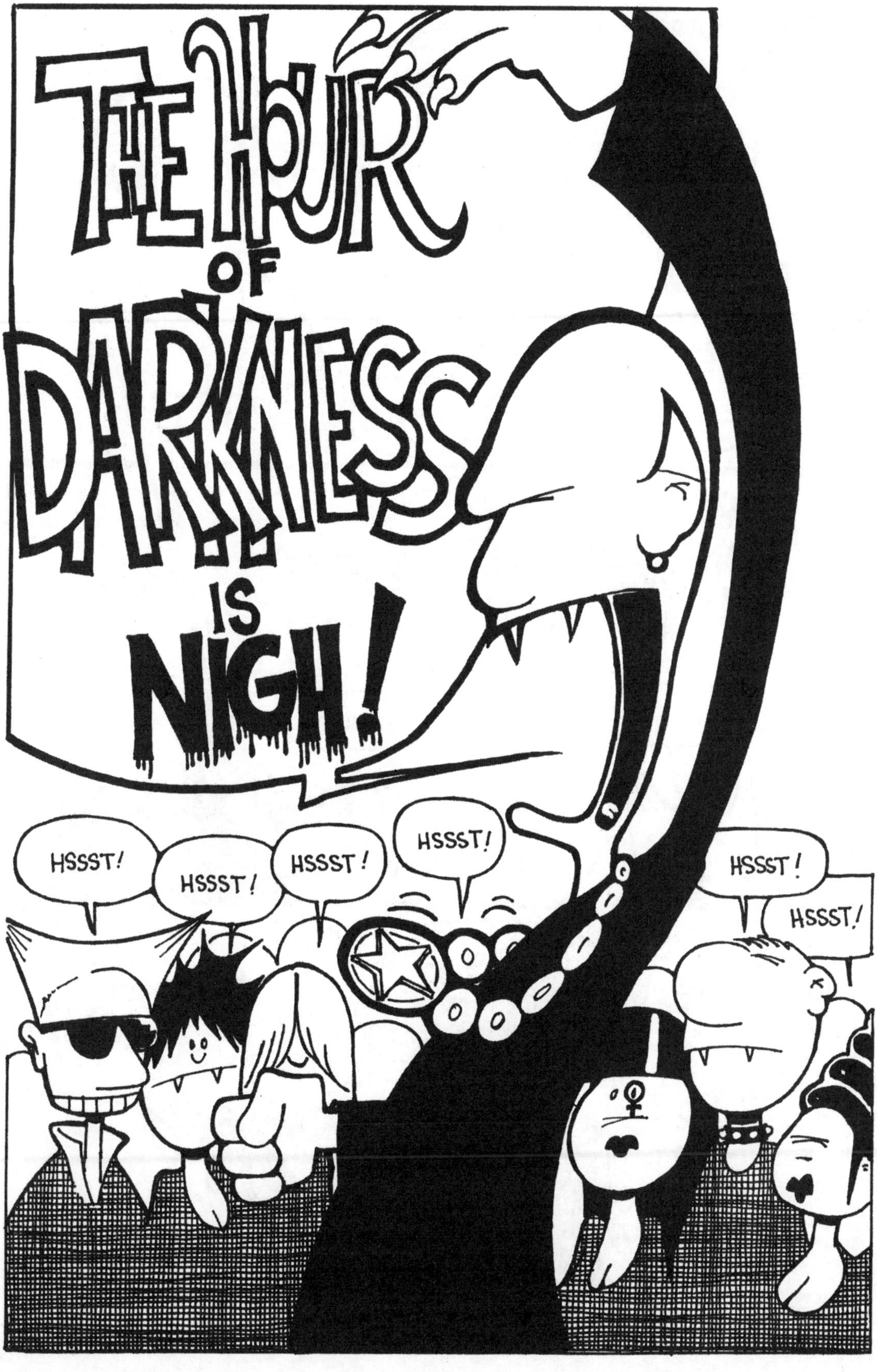
THE HOUR OF DARKNESS IS NIGH!
HSSST!
HSSST!
HSSST!
HSSST!
HSSST!
HSSST!

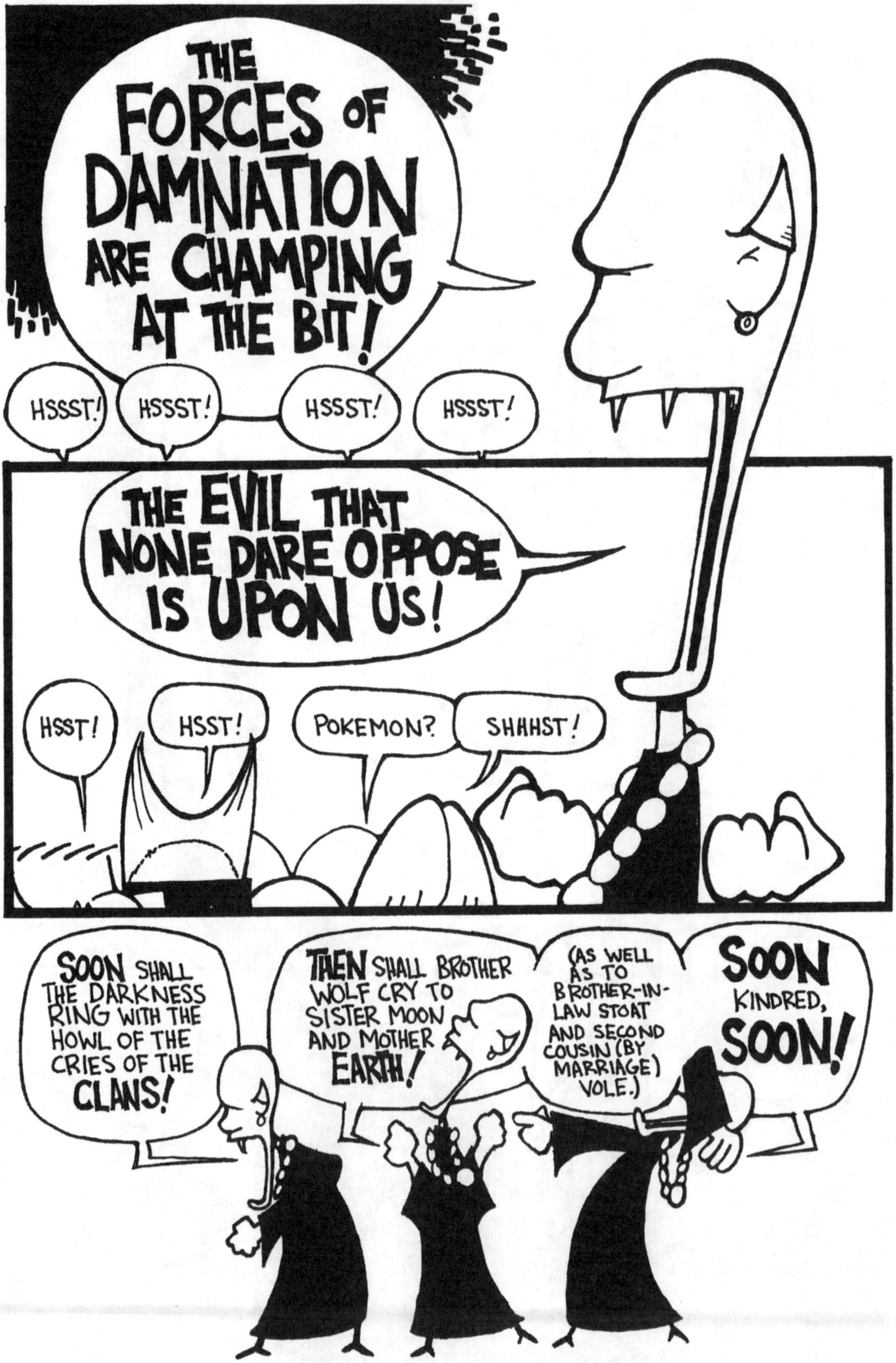
THE FORCES OF DAMNATION ARE CHAMPING AT THE BIT!
HSSST!
HSSST!
HSSST!
HSSST!
THE EVIL THAT NONE DARE OPPOSE IS UPON US!
HSST!
HSST!
POKEMON?
SHHHST!
SOON SHALL THE DARKNESS RING WITH THE HOWL OF THE CRIES OF THE CLANS!
THEN SHALL BROTHER WOLF CRY TO SISTER MOON AND MOTHER EARTH!
(AS WELL AS TO BROTHER-IN-LAW STOAT AND SECOND COUSIN (BY MARRIAGE) VOLE.)
SOON KINDRED, SOON!

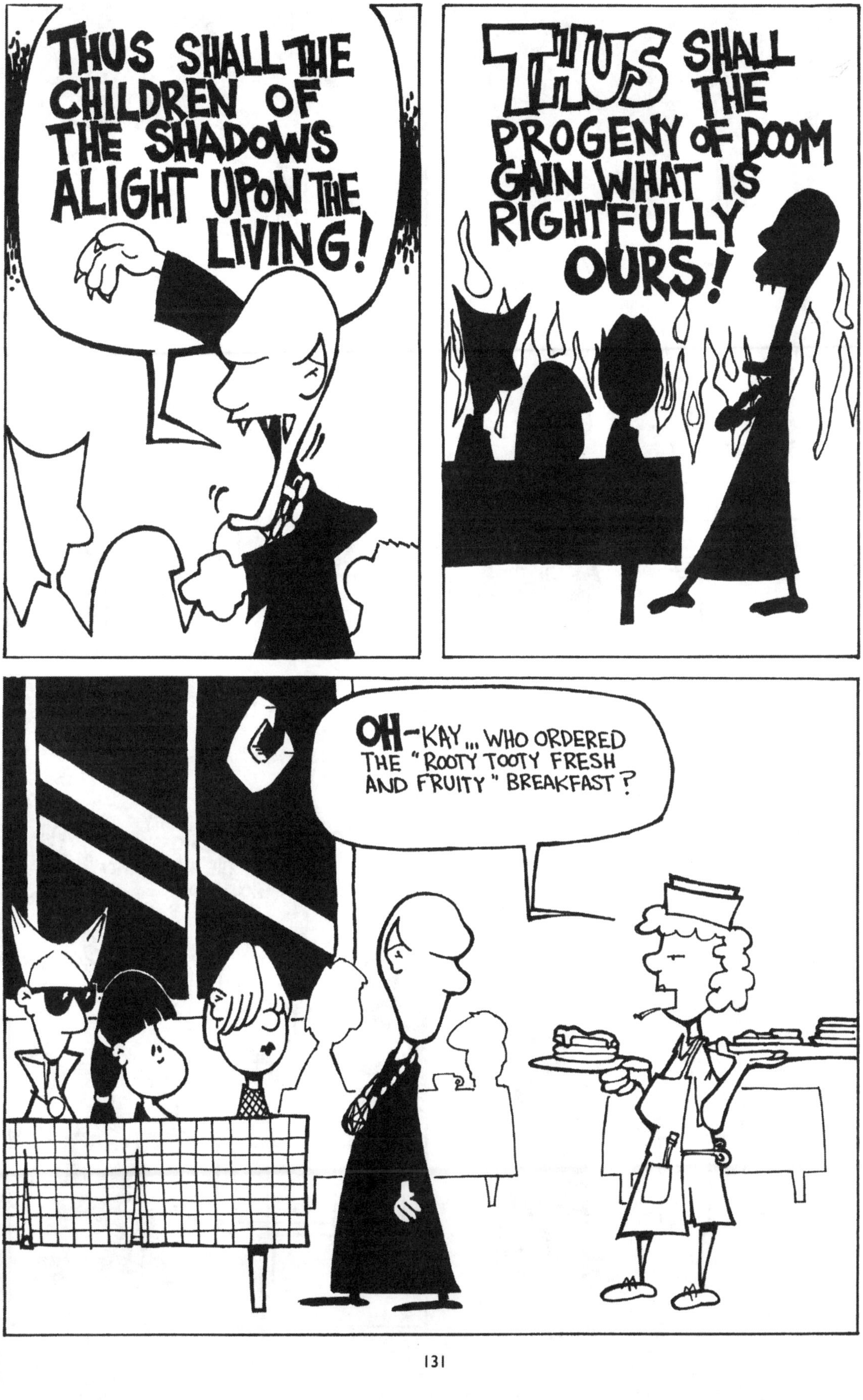
THUS SHALL THE CHILDREN OF THE SHADOWS ALIGHT UPON THE LIVING!
THUS SHALL THE PROGENY OF DOOM GAIN WHAT IS RIGHTFULLY OURS!
OH-KAY... WHO ORDERED THE "ROOTY TOOTY FRESH AND FRUITY" BREAKFAST?

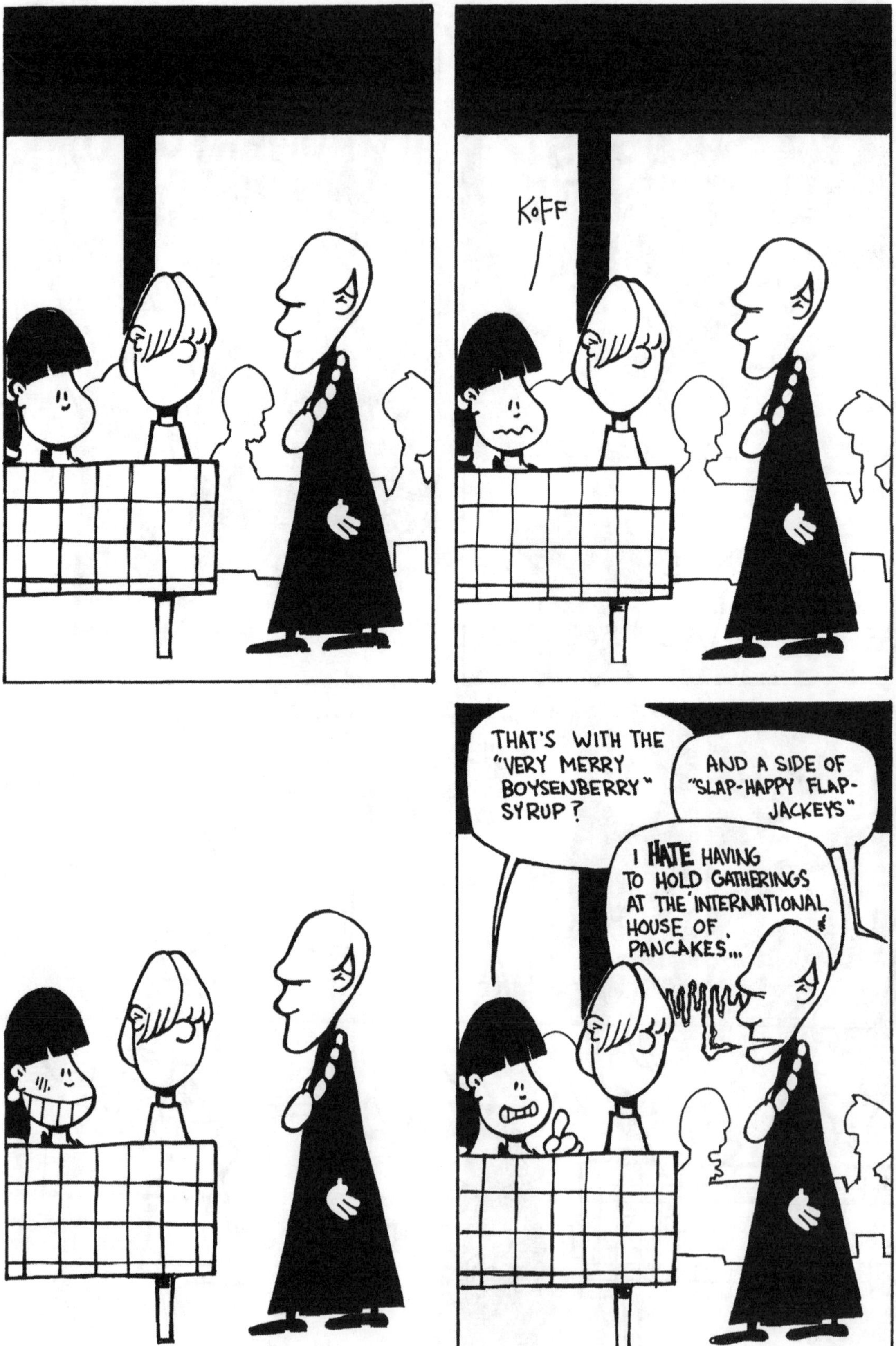
KoFF
THAT'S WITH THE "VERY MERRY BOYSENBERRY" SYRUP?
AND A SIDE OF "SLAP-HAPPY FLAP-JACKEYS"
I HATE HAVING TO HOLD GATHERINGS AT THE 'INTERNATIONAL HOUSE OF PANCAKES'...

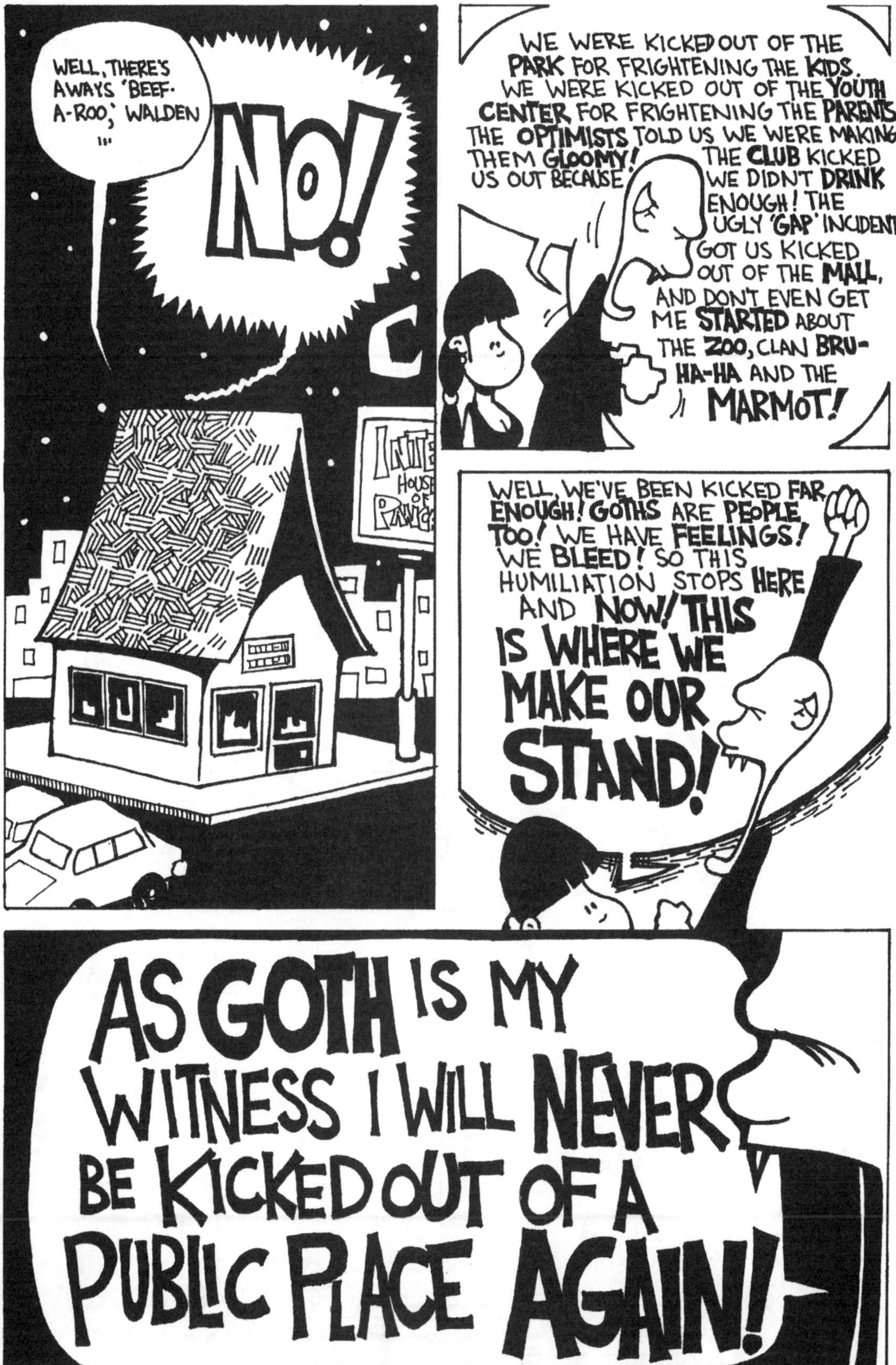

WELL, THERE'S AWAYS 'BEEF-A-ROO,' WALDEN ...
NO!
WE WERE KICKED OUT OF THE PARK FOR FRIGHTENING THE KIDS. WE WERE KICKED OUT OF THE YOUTH CENTER FOR FRIGHTENING THE PARENTS! THE OPTIMISTS TOLD US WE WERE MAKING THEM GLOOMY! THE CLUB KICKED US OUT BECAUSE WE DIDN'T DRINK ENOUGH! THE UGLY 'GAP' INCIDENT GOT US KICKED OUT OF THE MALL, AND DON'T EVEN GET ME STARTED ABOUT THE ZOO, CLAN BRU-HA-HA AND THE MARMOT!
WELL, WE'VE BEEN KICKED FAR ENOUGH! GOTHS ARE PEOPLE, TOO! WE HAVE FEELINGS! WE BLEED! SO THIS HUMILIATION STOPS HERE AND NOW! THIS IS WHERE WE MAKE OUR STAND!
AS GOTH IS MY WITNESS I WILL NEVER BE KICKED OUT OF A PUBLIC PLACE AGAIN!

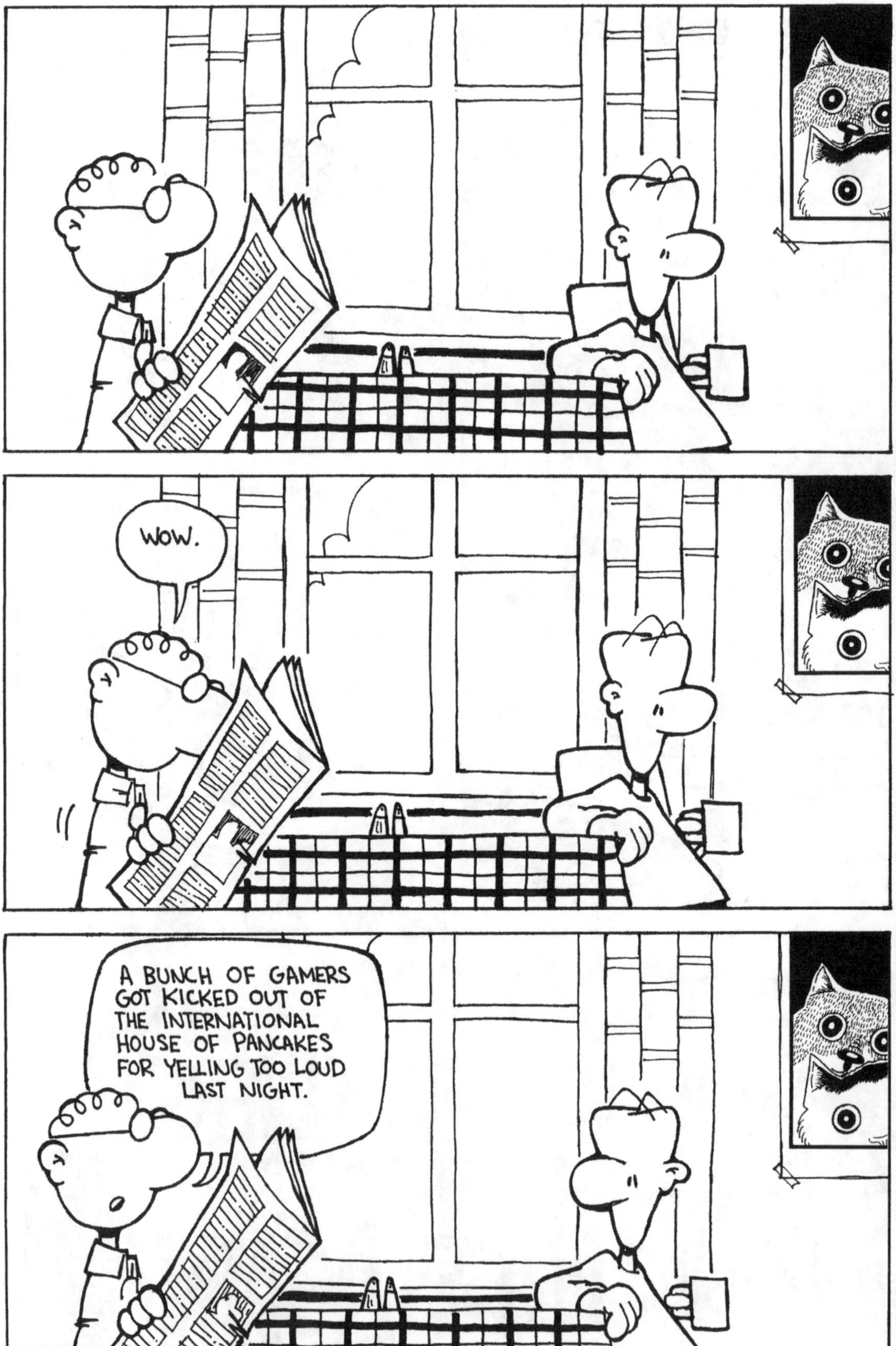
WOW.
A BUNCH OF GAMERS GOT KICKED OUT OF THE INTERNATIONAL HOUSE OF PANCAKES FOR YELLING TOO LOUD LAST NIGHT.

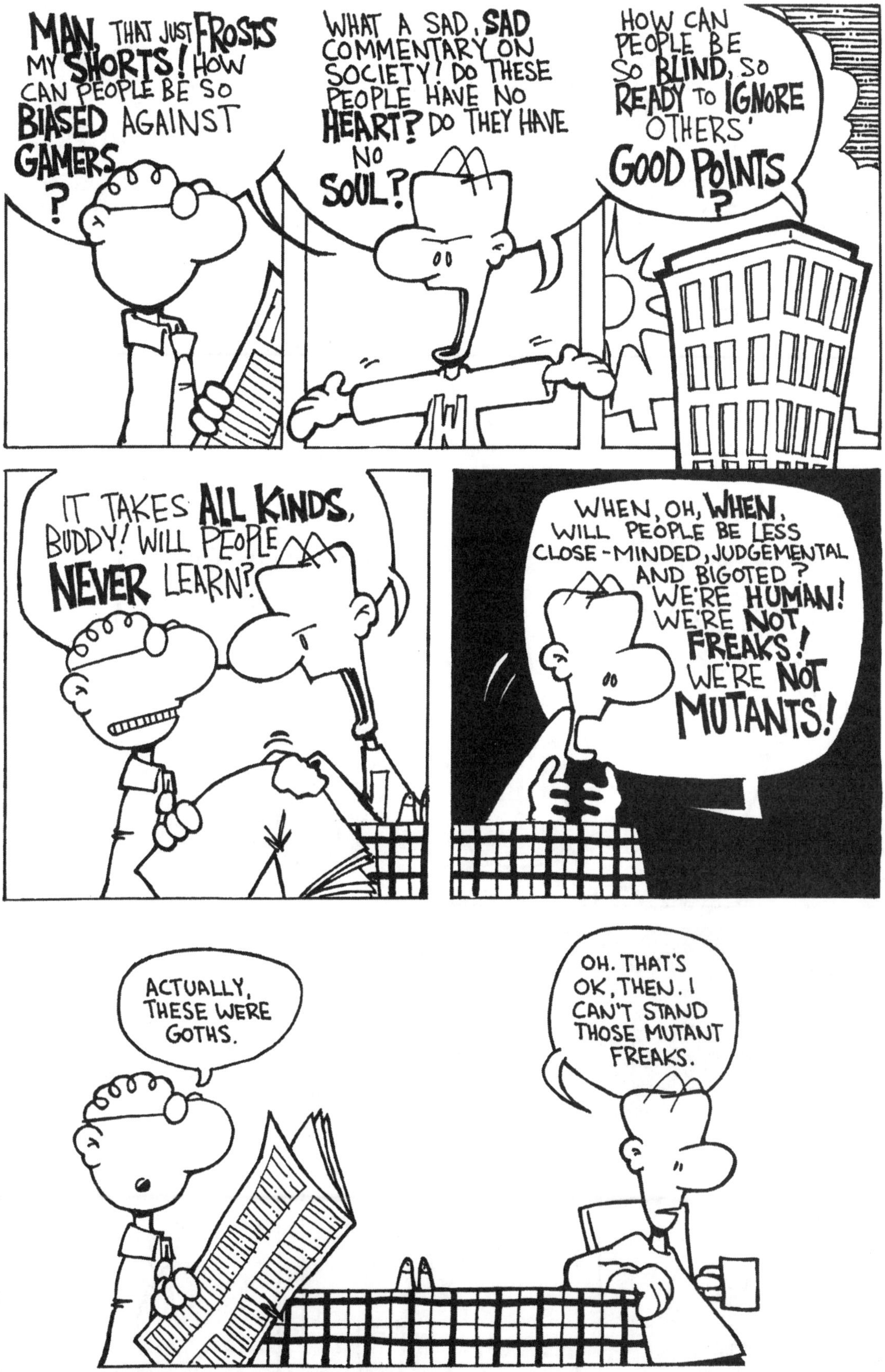
MAN, THAT JUST FROSTS MY SHORTS! HOW CAN PEOPLE BE SO BIASED AGAINST GAMERS ?
WHAT A SAD, SAD COMMENTARY ON SOCIETY! DO THESE PEOPLE HAVE NO HEART? DO THEY HAVE NO SOUL?
HOW CAN PEOPLE BE SO BLIND, SO READY TO IGNORE OTHERS' GOOD POINTS ?
IT TAKES ALL KINDS, BUDDY! WILL PEOPLE NEVER LEARN?
WHEN, OH, WHEN, WILL PEOPLE BE LESS CLOSE-MINDED, JUDGEMENTAL AND BIGOTED? WE'RE HUMAN! WE'RE NOT FREAKS! WE'RE NOT MUTANTS!
ACTUALLY, THESE WERE GOTHS.
OH. THAT'S OK, THEN. I CAN'T STAND THOSE MUTANT FREAKS.

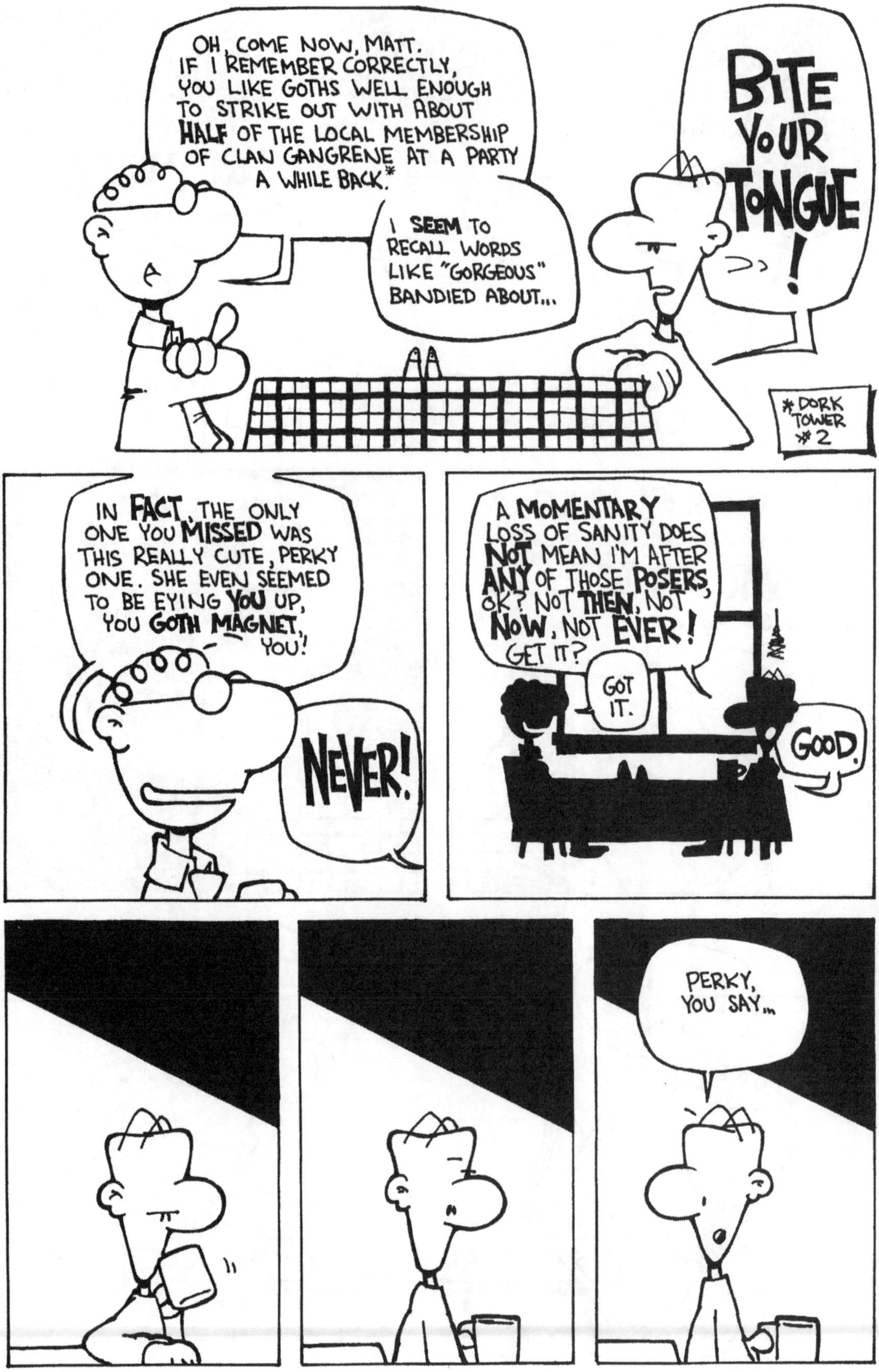
OH, COME NOW, MATT. IF I REMEMBER CORRECTLY, YOU LIKE GOTHS WELL ENOUGH TO STRIKE OUT WITH ABOUT HALF OF THE LOCAL MEMBERSHIP OF CLAN GANGRENE AT A PARTY A WHILE BACK.*
I SEEM TO RECALL WORDS LIKE "GORGEOUS" BANDIED ABOUT...
BITE YOUR TONGUE!
*DORK TOWER #2
IN FACT, THE ONLY ONE YOU MISSED WAS THIS REALLY CUTE, PERKY ONE. SHE EVEN SEEMED TO BE EYING YOU UP, YOU GOTH MAGNET, YOU!
NEVER!
A MOMENTARY LOSS OF SANITY DOES NOT MEAN I'M AFTER ANY OF THOSE POSERS, OK? NOT THEN, NOT NOW, NOT EVER! GET IT?
GOT IT.
GOOD.
PERKY, YOU SAY...

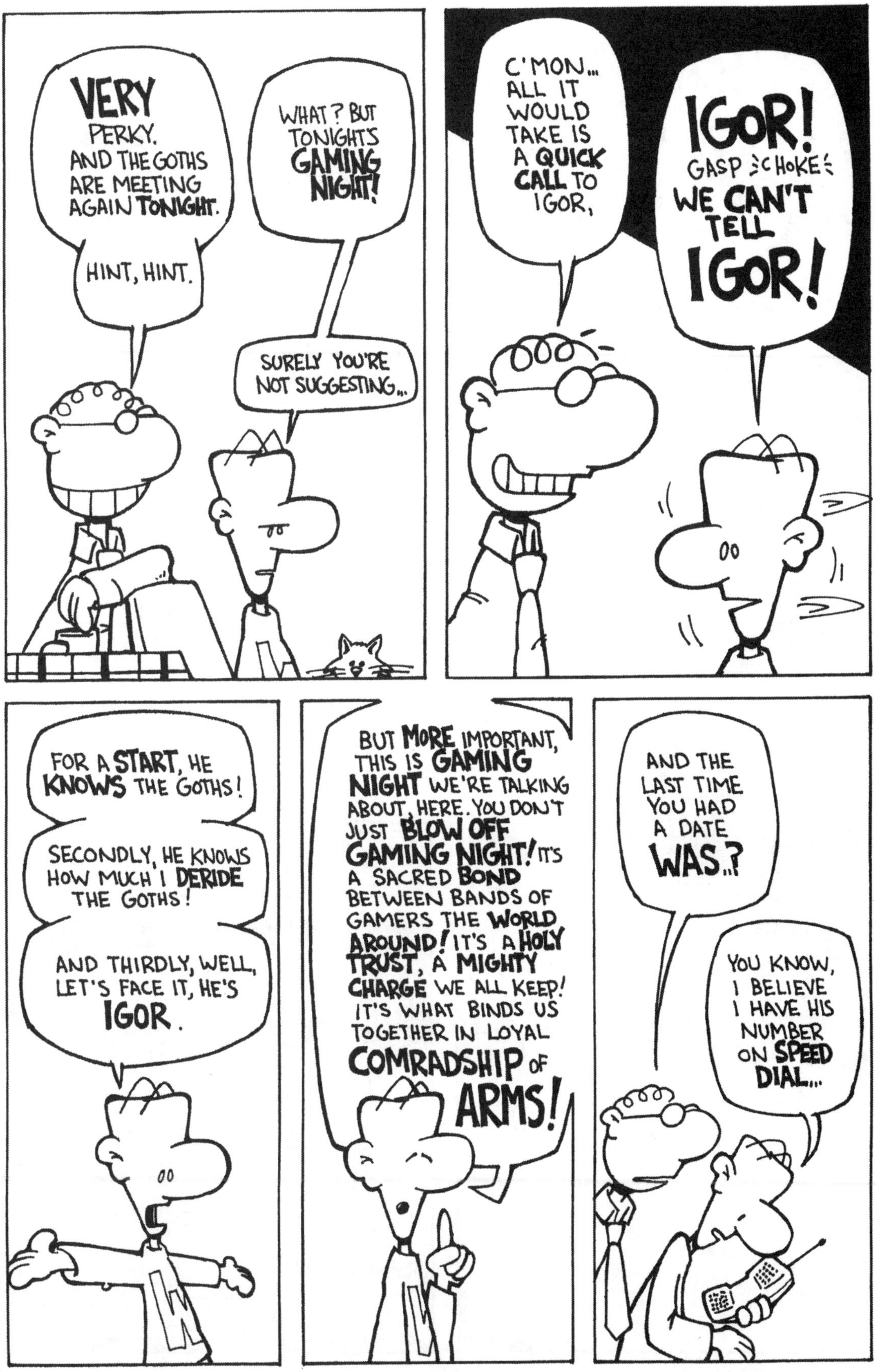
VERY PERKY. AND THE GOTHS ARE MEETING AGAIN TONIGHT.
HINT, HINT.
WHAT? BUT TONIGHT'S GAMING NIGHT!
SURELY YOU'RE NOT SUGGESTING...
C'MON... ALL IT WOULD TAKE IS A QUICK CALL TO IGOR,
IGOR! GASP CHOKE WE CAN'T TELL IGOR!
FOR A START, HE KNOWS THE GOTHS!
SECONDLY, HE KNOWS HOW MUCH I DERIDE THE GOTHS!
AND THIRDLY, WELL, LET'S FACE IT, HE'S IGOR.
BUT MORE IMPORTANT, THIS IS GAMING NIGHT WE'RE TALKING ABOUT, HERE. YOU DON'T JUST BLOW OFF GAMING NIGHT! IT'S A SACRED BOND BETWEEN BANDS OF GAMERS THE WORLD AROUND! IT'S A HOLY TRUST, A MIGHTY CHARGE WE ALL KEEP! IT'S WHAT BINDS US TOGETHER IN LOYAL COMRADSHIP OF ARMS!
AND THE LAST TIME YOU HAD A DATE WAS..?
YOU KNOW, I BELIEVE I HAVE HIS NUMBER ON SPEED DIAL...

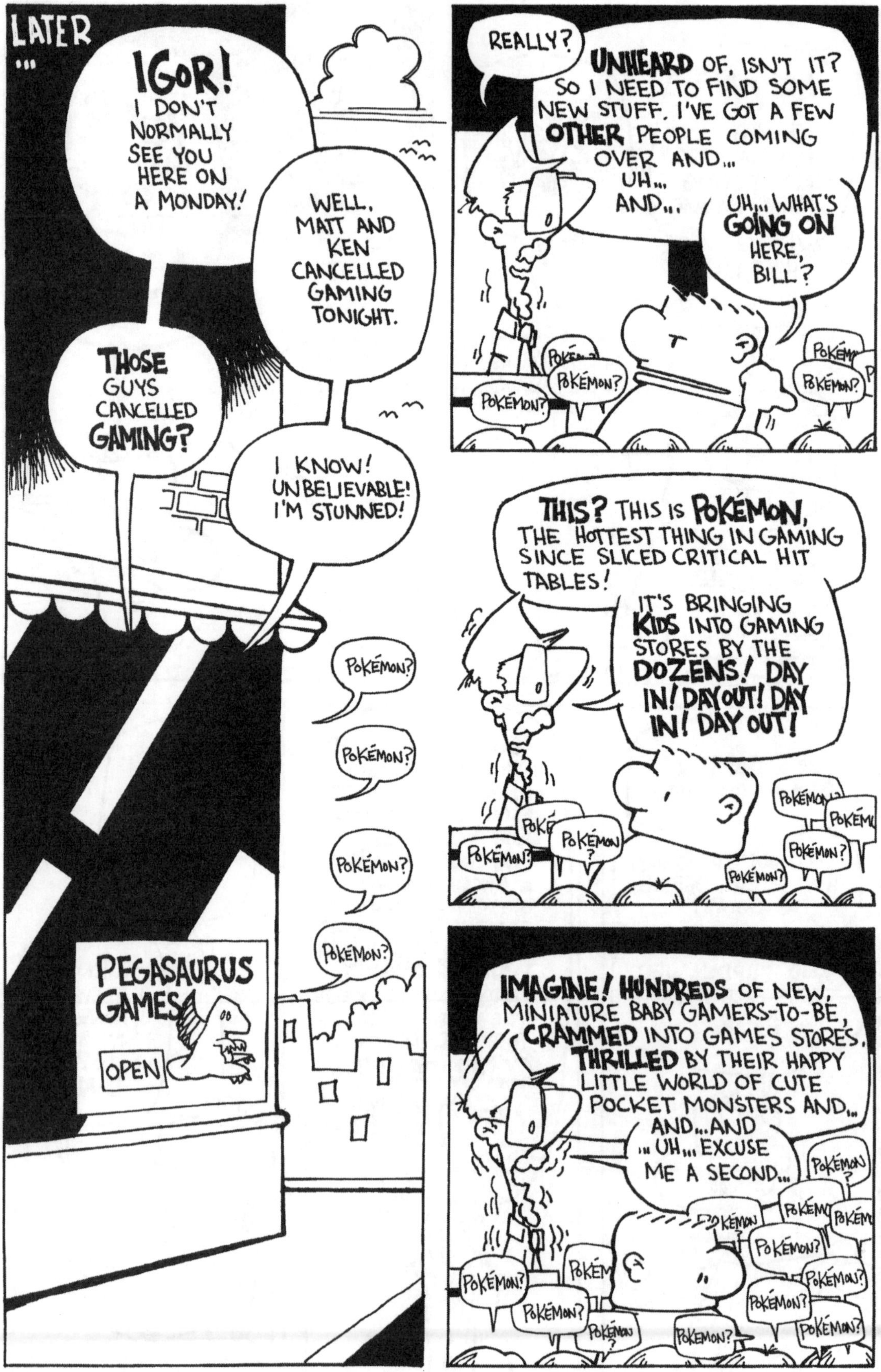
LATER ...
IGOR! I DON'T NORMALLY SEE YOU HERE ON A MONDAY!
WELL, MATT AND KEN CANCELLED GAMING TONIGHT.
THOSE GUYS CANCELLED GAMING?
I KNOW! UNBELIEVABLE! I'M STUNNED!
POKÉMON?
POKÉMON?
POKÉMON?
POKÉMON?
PEGASAURUS GAMES
OPEN
REALLY?
UNHEARD OF, ISN'T IT? SO I NEED TO FIND SOME NEW STUFF. I'VE GOT A FEW OTHER PEOPLE COMING OVER AND... UH... AND...
UH... WHAT'S GOING ON HERE, BILL?
POKÉMON?
POKÉMON?
POKÉMON?
THIS? THIS IS POKÉMON, THE HOTTEST THING IN GAMING SINCE SLICED CRITICAL HIT TABLES!
IT'S BRINGING KIDS INTO GAMING STORES BY THE DOZENS! DAY IN! DAY OUT! DAY IN! DAY OUT!
POKÉMON?
POKÉMON?
POKÉMON?
IMAGINE! HUNDREDS OF NEW, MINIATURE BABY GAMERS-TO-BE, CRAMMED INTO GAMES STORES, THRILLED BY THEIR HAPPY LITTLE WORLD OF CUTE POCKET MONSTERS AND... AND...AND
... UH... EXCUSE ME A SECOND...
POKÉMON?
POKÉMON?
POKÉMON?
POKÉMON?
POKÉMON?
POKÉMON?
POKÉMON?
POKÉMON?

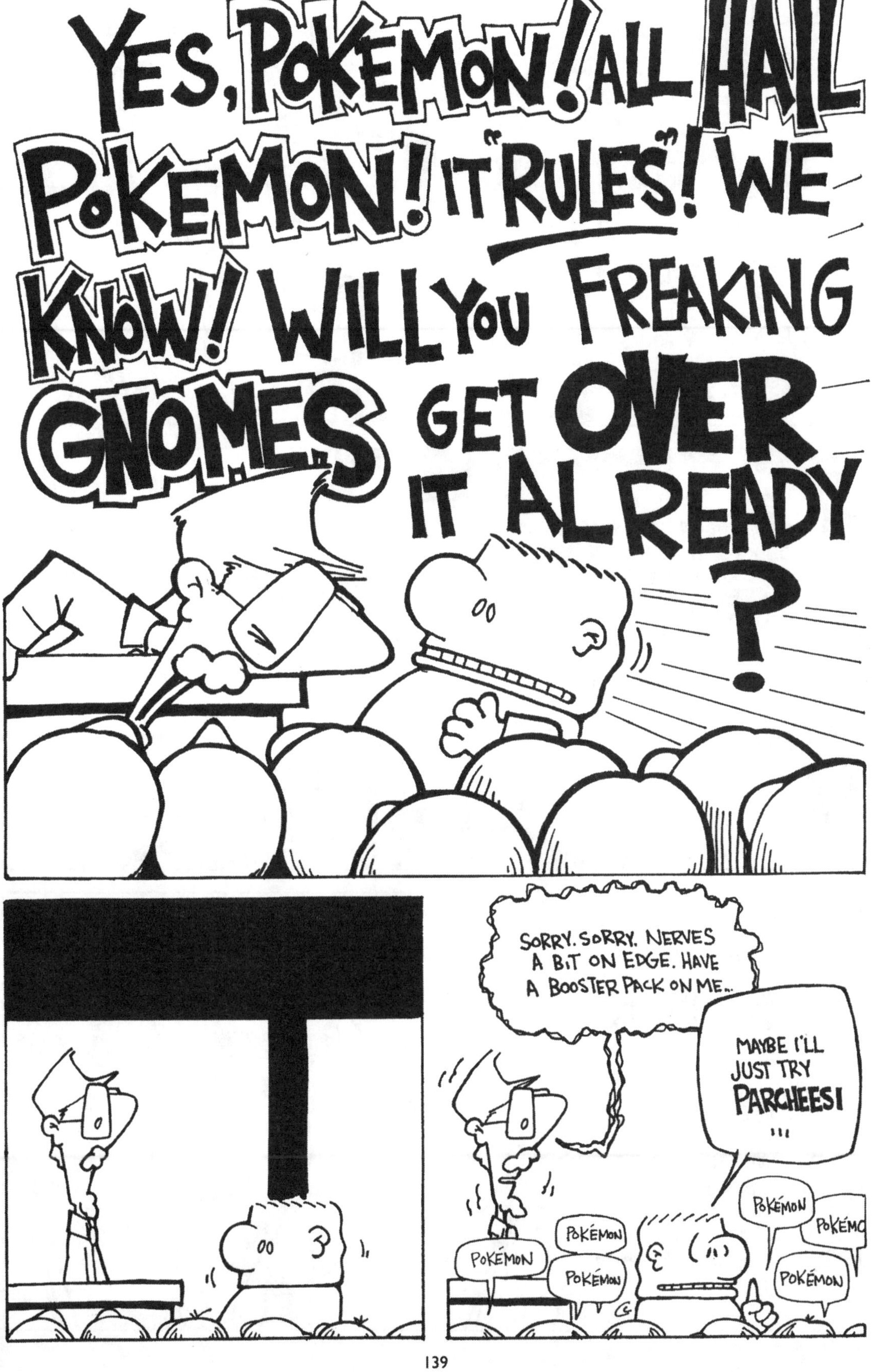
YES, POKEMON! ALL HAIL POKEMON! IT "RULES"! WE KNOW! WILL YOU FREAKING GNOMES GET OVER IT ALREADY?
SORRY. SORRY. NERVES A BIT ON EDGE. HAVE A BOOSTER PACK ON ME..
MAYBE I'LL JUST TRY PARCHEESI ...
POKÉMON
POKÉMON
POKÉMON
POKÉMON
POKÉMON
POKÉMON

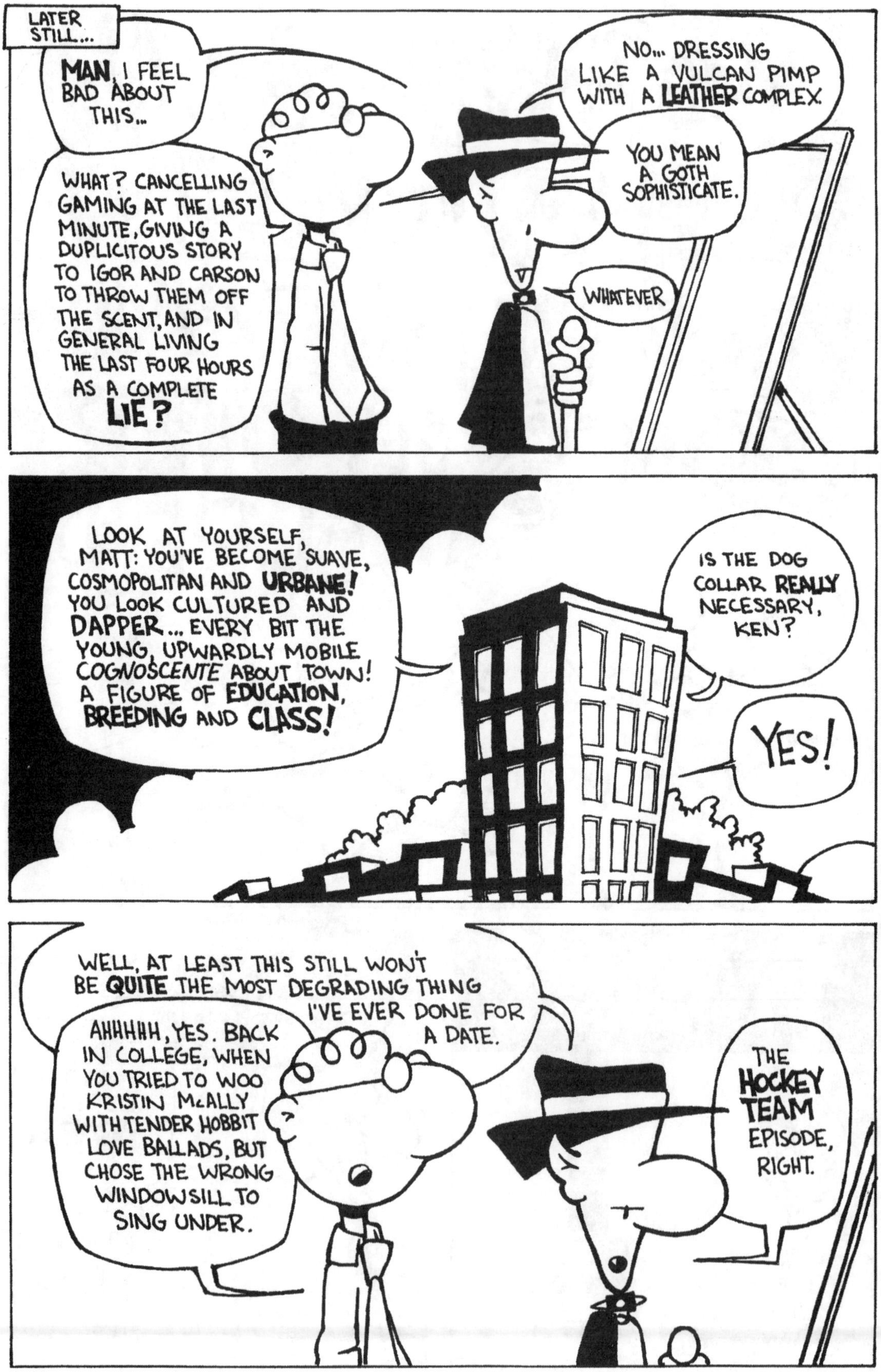
LATER STILL...
MAN, I FEEL BAD ABOUT THIS...
WHAT? CANCELLING GAMING AT THE LAST MINUTE, GIVING A DUPLICITOUS STORY TO IGOR AND CARSON TO THROW THEM OFF THE SCENT, AND IN GENERAL LIVING THE LAST FOUR HOURS AS A COMPLETE LIE?
NO... DRESSING LIKE A VULCAN PIMP WITH A LEATHER COMPLEX.
YOU MEAN A GOTH SOPHISTICATE.
WHATEVER
LOOK AT YOURSELF, MATT: YOU'VE BECOME SUAVE, COSMOPOLITAN AND URBANE! YOU LOOK CULTURED AND DAPPER... EVERY BIT THE YOUNG, UPWARDLY MOBILE COGNOSCENTE ABOUT TOWN! A FIGURE OF EDUCATION, BREEDING AND CLASS!
IS THE DOG COLLAR REALLY NECESSARY, KEN?
YES!
WELL, AT LEAST THIS STILL WON'T BE QUITE THE MOST DEGRADING THING I'VE EVER DONE FOR A DATE.
AHHHHH, YES. BACK IN COLLEGE, WHEN YOU TRIED TO WOO KRISTIN McALLY WITH TENDER HOBBIT LOVE BALLADS, BUT CHOSE THE WRONG WINDOWSILL TO SING UNDER.
THE HOCKEY TEAM EPISODE, RIGHT.

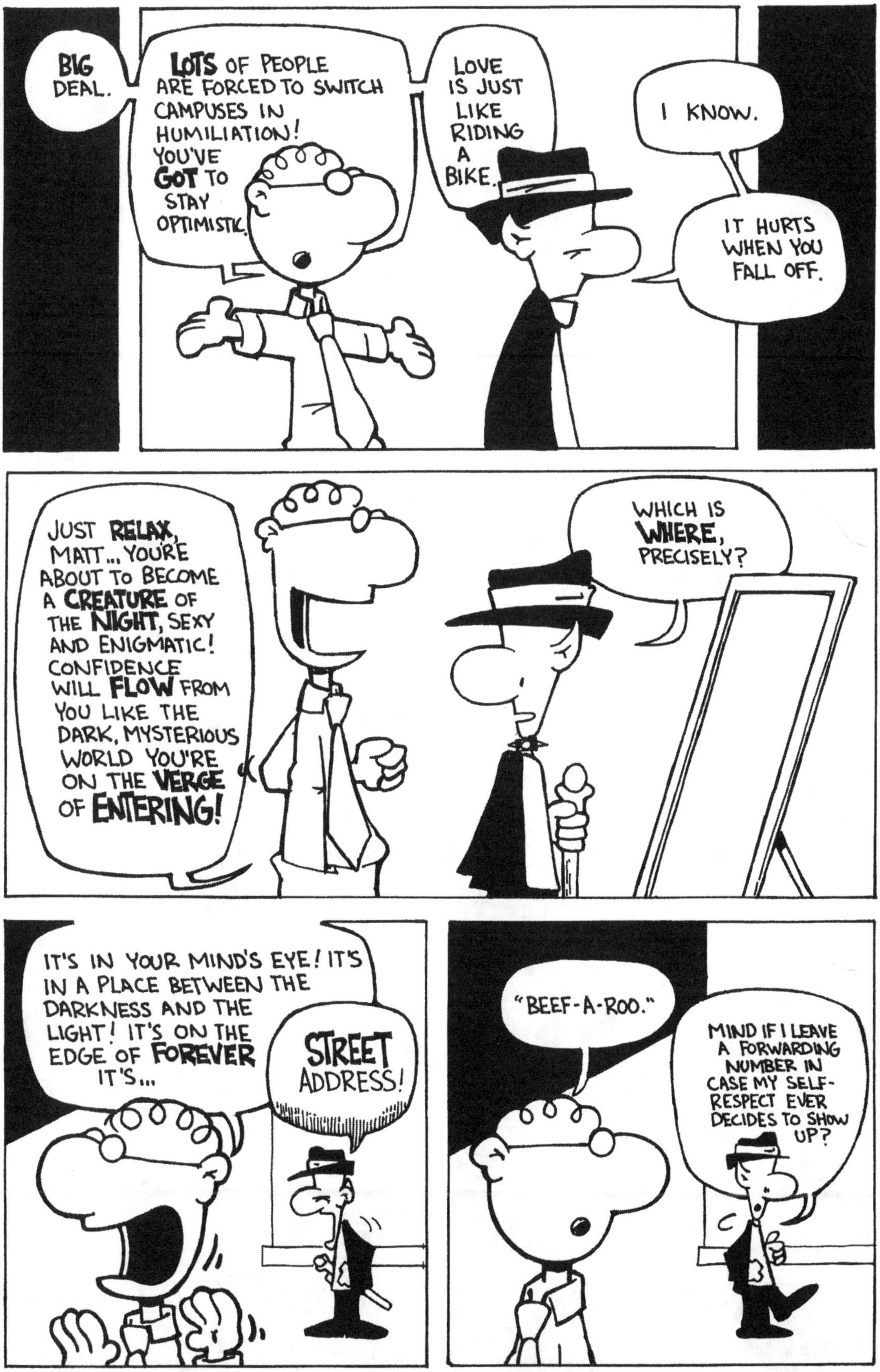
BIG DEAL.
LOTS OF PEOPLE ARE FORCED TO SWITCH CAMPUSES IN HUMILIATION! YOU'VE GOT TO STAY OPTIMISTIC.
LOVE IS JUST LIKE RIDING A BIKE.
I KNOW.
IT HURTS WHEN YOU FALL OFF.
JUST RELAX, MATT... YOU'RE ABOUT TO BECOME A CREATURE OF THE NIGHT, SEXY AND ENIGMATIC! CONFIDENCE WILL FLOW FROM YOU LIKE THE DARK, MYSTERIOUS WORLD YOU'RE ON THE VERGE OF ENTERING!
WHICH IS WHERE, PRECISELY?
IT'S IN YOUR MIND'S EYE! IT'S IN A PLACE BETWEEN THE DARKNESS AND THE LIGHT! IT'S ON THE EDGE OF FOREVER IT'S...
STREET ADDRESS!
"BEEF-A-ROO."
MIND IF I LEAVE A FORWARDING NUMBER IN CASE MY SELF-RESPECT EVER DECIDES TO SHOW UP?

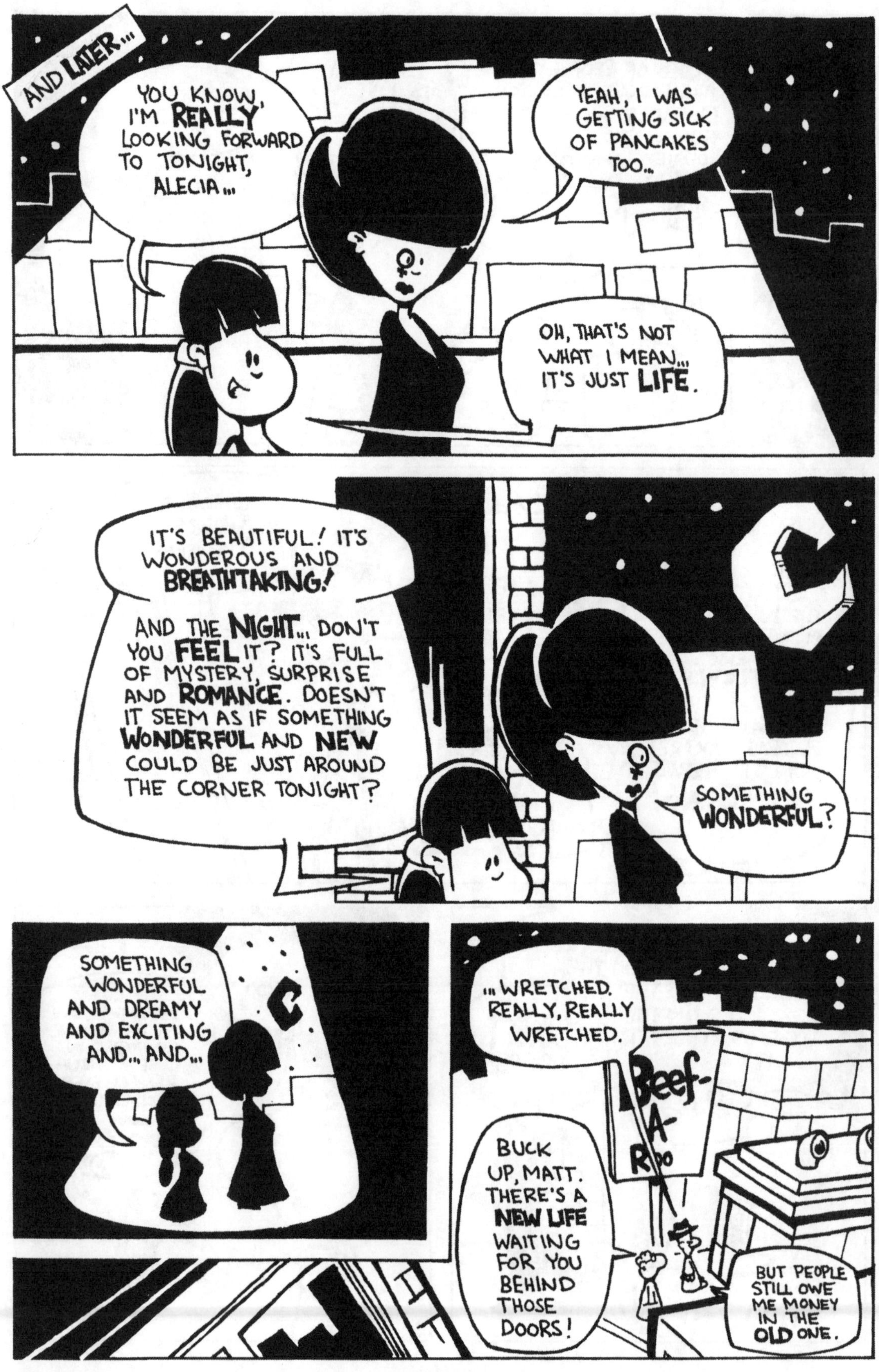
AND LATER...
YOU KNOW, I'M REALLY LOOKING FORWARD TO TONIGHT, ALECIA...
YEAH, I WAS GETTING SICK OF PANCAKES TOO...
OH, THAT'S NOT WHAT I MEAN... IT'S JUST LIFE.
IT'S BEAUTIFUL! IT'S WONDEROUS AND BREATHTAKING!
AND THE NIGHT... DON'T YOU FEEL IT? IT'S FULL OF MYSTERY, SURPRISE AND ROMANCE. DOESN'T IT SEEM AS IF SOMETHING WONDERFUL AND NEW COULD BE JUST AROUND THE CORNER TONIGHT?
SOMETHING WONDERFUL?
SOMETHING WONDERFUL AND DREAMY AND EXCITING AND... AND...
...WRETCHED. REALLY, REALLY WRETCHED.
Beef-A-Roo
BUCK UP, MATT. THERE'S A NEW LIFE WAITING FOR YOU BEHIND THOSE DOORS!
BUT PEOPLE STILL OWE ME MONEY IN THE OLD ONE.

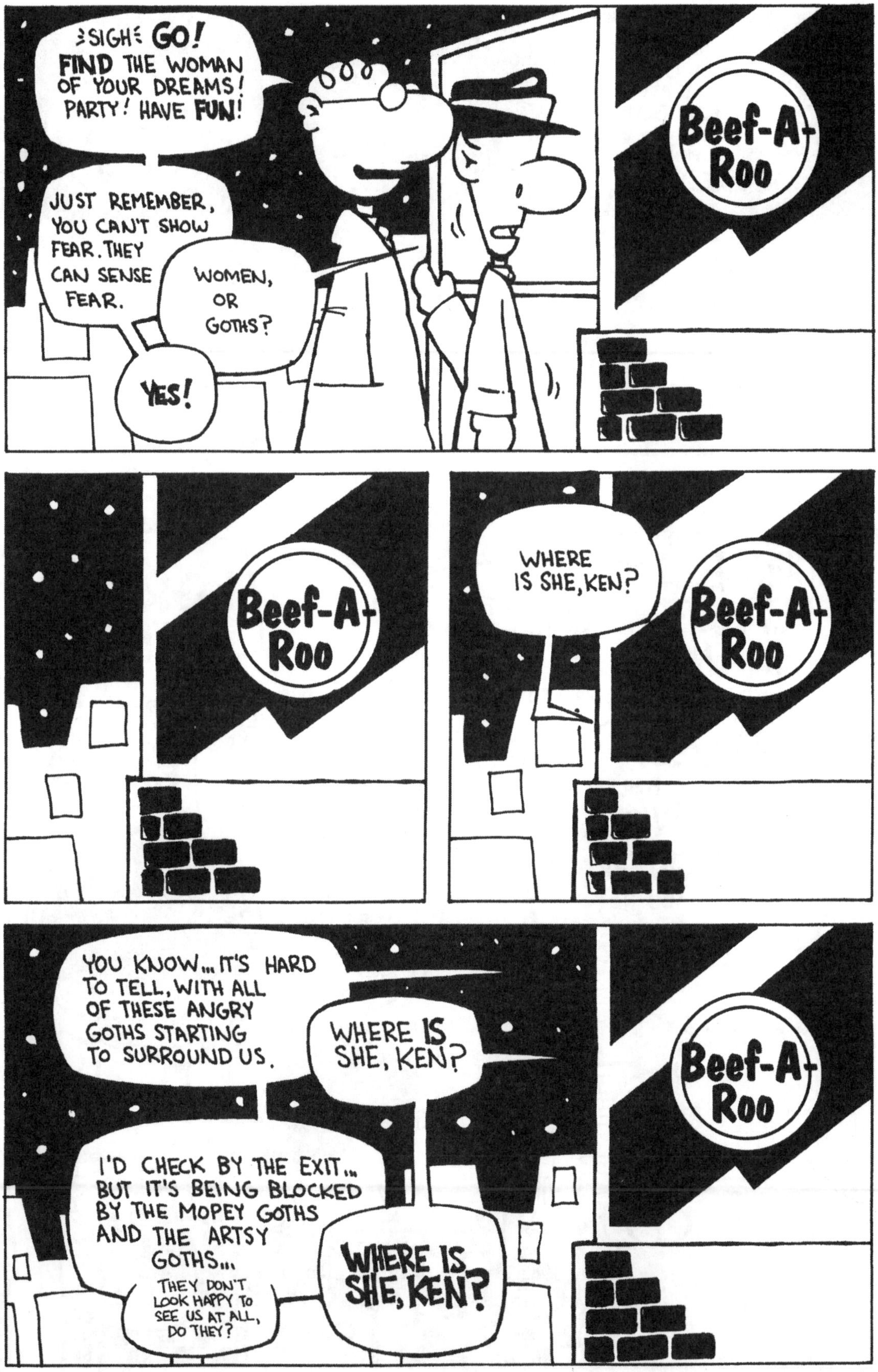

SIGH GO! FIND THE WOMAN OF YOUR DREAMS! PARTY! HAVE FUN!
JUST REMEMBER, YOU CAN'T SHOW FEAR. THEY CAN SENSE FEAR.
WOMEN, OR GOTHS?
YES!
Beef-A-Roo
Beef-A-Roo
WHERE IS SHE, KEN?
Beef-A-Roo
YOU KNOW... IT'S HARD TO TELL, WITH ALL OF THESE ANGRY GOTHS STARTING TO SURROUND US.
WHERE IS SHE, KEN?
I'D CHECK BY THE EXIT... BUT IT'S BEING BLOCKED BY THE MOPEY GOTHS AND THE ARTSY GOTHS...
THEY DON'T LOOK HAPPY TO SEE US AT ALL, DO THEY?
WHERE IS SHE, KEN?
Beef-A-Roo

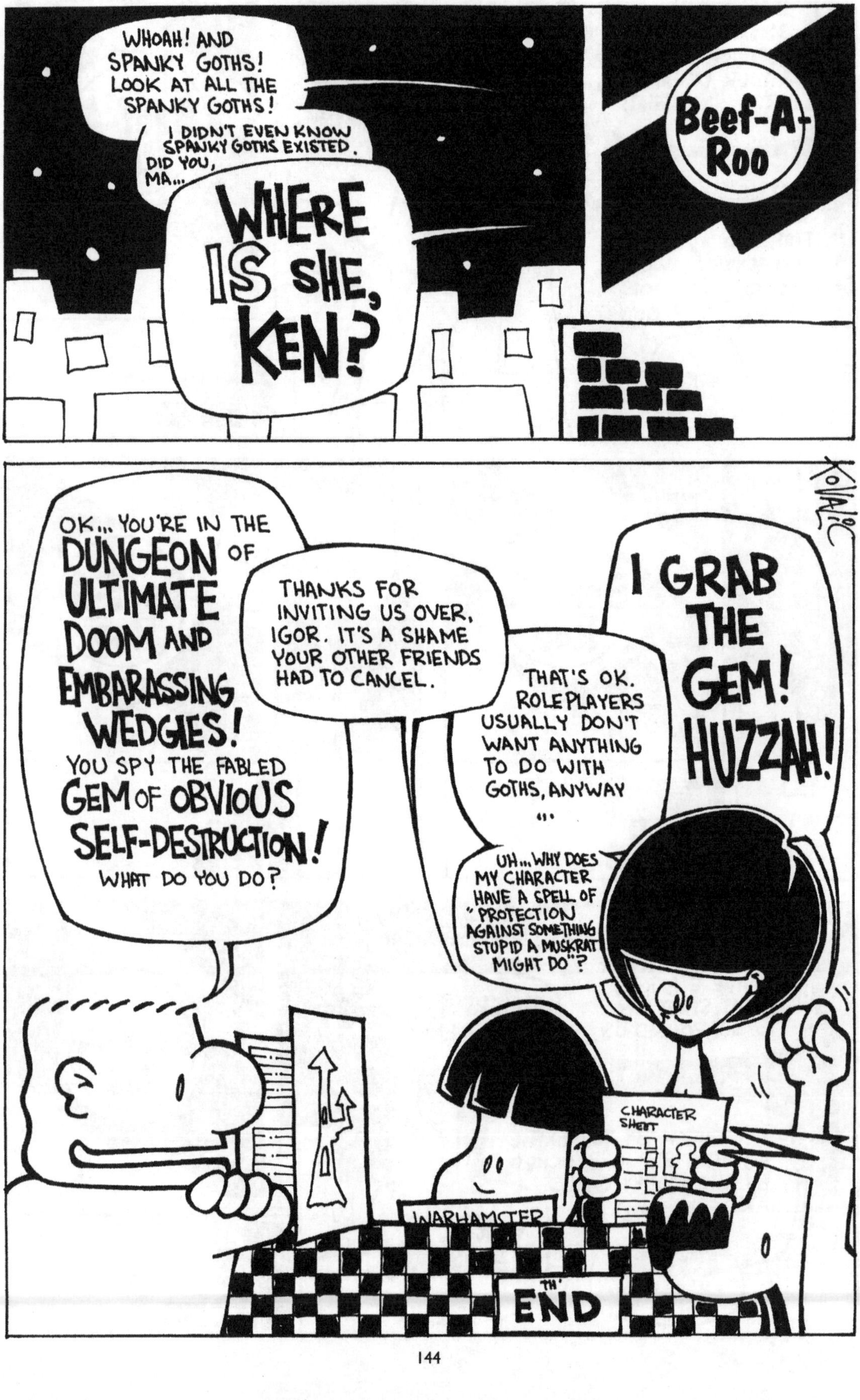
WHOAH! AND SPANKY GOTHS! LOOK AT ALL THE SPANKY GOTHS!
I DIDN'T EVEN KNOW SPANKY GOTHS EXISTED. DID YOU, MA...
WHERE IS SHE, KEN?
Beef-A-Roo
KOVALIC
OK... YOU'RE IN THE DUNGEON OF ULTIMATE DOOM AND EMBARASSING WEDGIES! YOU SPY THE FABLED GEM OF OBVIOUS SELF-DESTRUCTION! WHAT DO YOU DO?
THANKS FOR INVITING US OVER, IGOR. IT'S A SHAME YOUR OTHER FRIENDS HAD TO CANCEL.
THAT'S OK. ROLEPLAYERS USUALLY DON'T WANT ANYTHING TO DO WITH GOTHS, ANYWAY
...
I GRAB THE GEM! HUZZAH!
UH... WHY DOES MY CHARACTER HAVE A SPELL OF "PROTECTION AGAINST SOMETHING STUPID A MUSKRAT MIGHT DO"?
CHARACTER SHEET
WARHAMSTER
TH' END

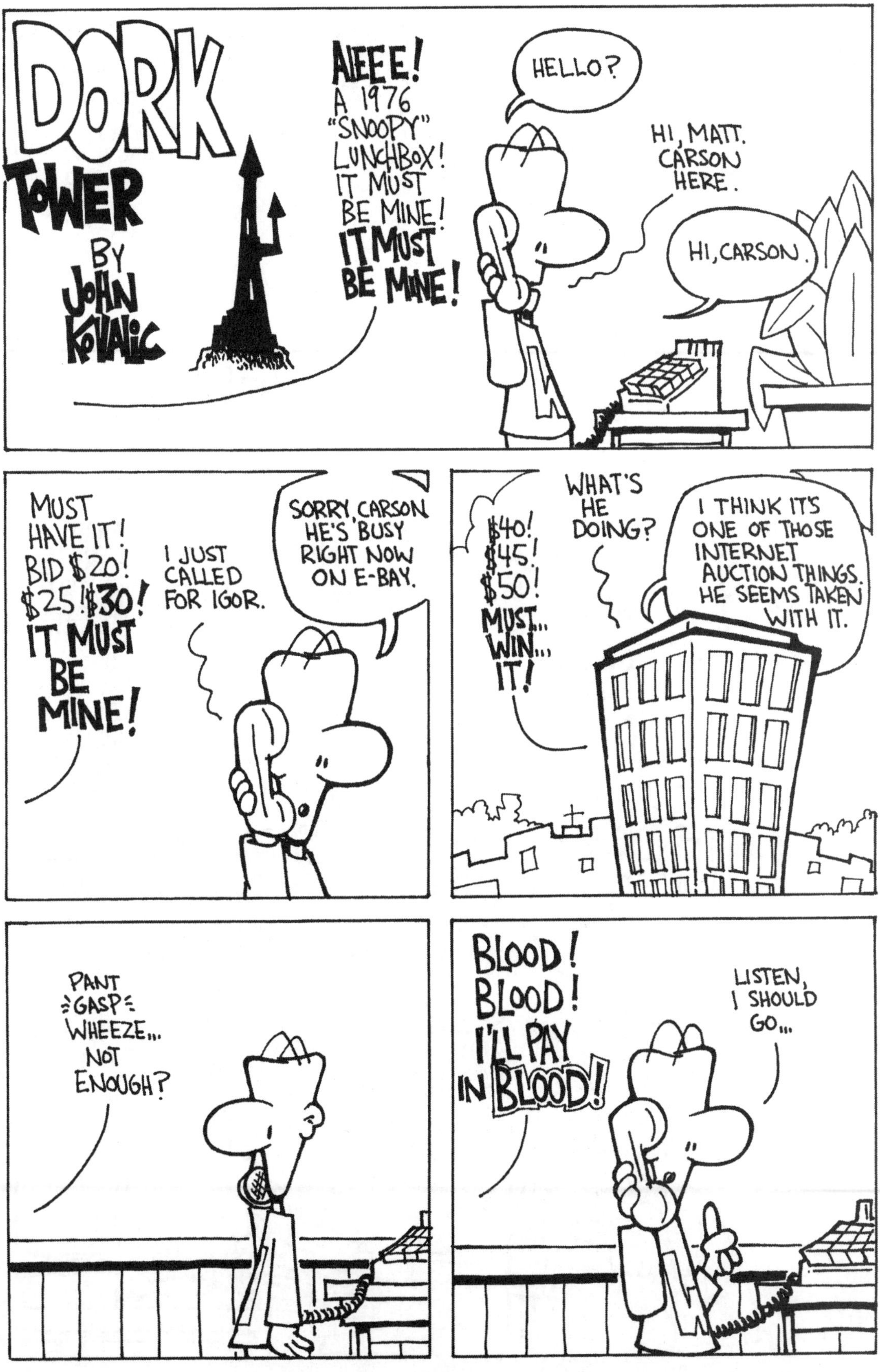
DORK TOWER
BY JOHN KOVALIC
AIEEE! A 1976 "SNOOPY" LUNCHBOX! IT MUST BE MINE! IT MUST BE MINE!
HELLO?
HI, MATT. CARSON HERE.
HI, CARSON.
MUST HAVE IT! BID $20! $25! $30! IT MUST BE MINE!
I JUST CALLED FOR IGOR.
SORRY, CARSON HE'S BUSY RIGHT NOW ON E-BAY.
$40! $45! $50! MUST... WIN... IT!
WHAT'S HE DOING?
I THINK IT'S ONE OF THOSE INTERNET AUCTION THINGS. HE SEEMS TAKEN WITH IT.
PANT GASP WHEEZE... NOT ENOUGH?
BLOOD! BLOOD! I'LL PAY IN BLOOD!
LISTEN, I SHOULD GO...

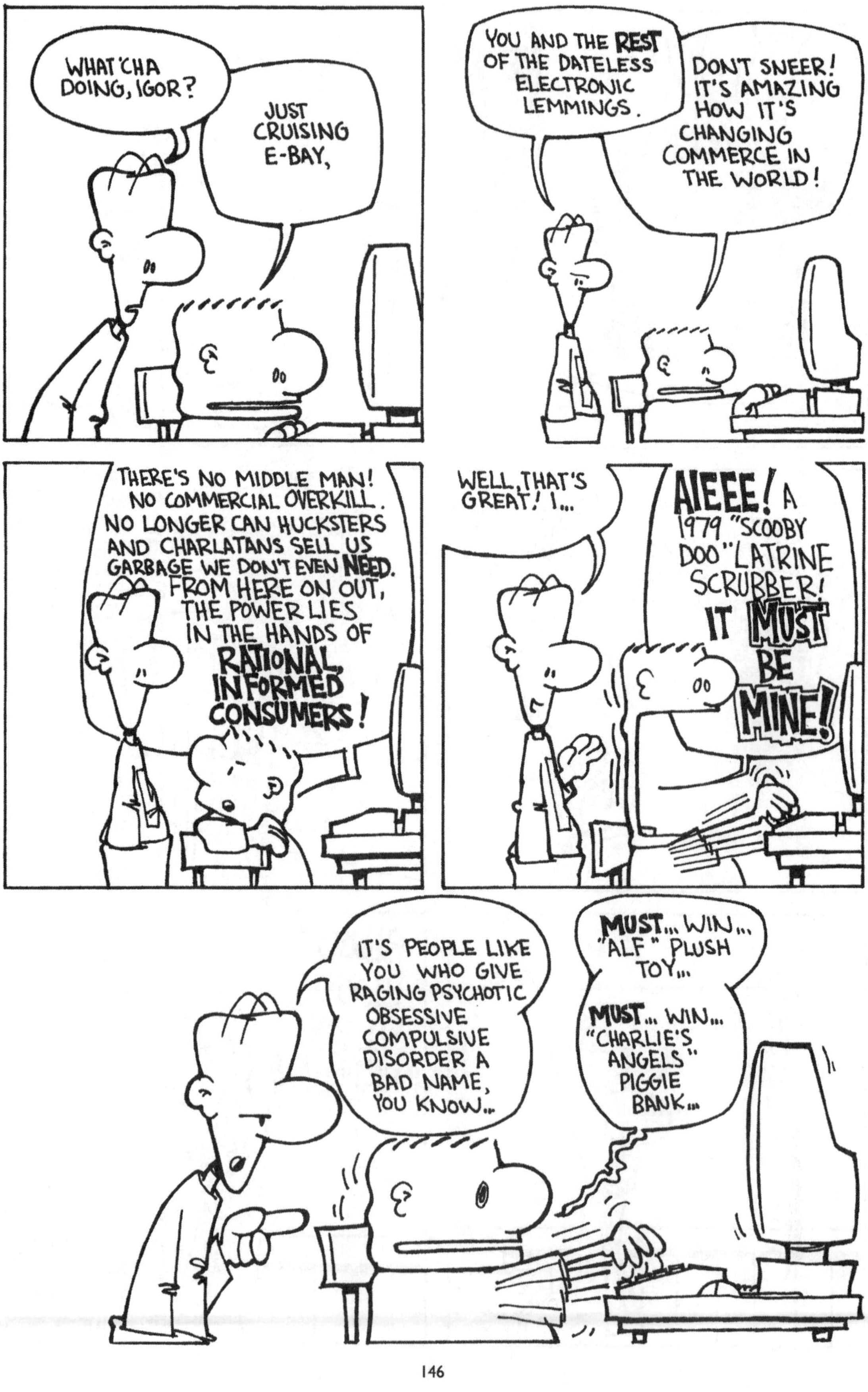
WHAT'CHA DOING, IGOR?
JUST CRUISING E-BAY,
YOU AND THE REST OF THE DATELESS ELECTRONIC LEMMINGS.
DON'T SNEER! IT'S AMAZING HOW IT'S CHANGING COMMERCE IN THE WORLD!
THERE'S NO MIDDLE MAN! NO COMMERCIAL OVERKILL. NO LONGER CAN HUCKSTERS AND CHARLATANS SELL US GARBAGE WE DON'T EVEN NEED. FROM HERE ON OUT, THE POWER LIES IN THE HANDS OF RATIONAL, INFORMED CONSUMERS!
WELL, THAT'S GREAT! I...
AIEEE! A 1979 "SCOOBY DOO" LATRINE SCRUBBER! IT MUST BE MINE!
IT'S PEOPLE LIKE YOU WHO GIVE RAGING PSYCHOTIC OBSESSIVE COMPULSIVE DISORDER A BAD NAME, YOU KNOW...
MUST... WIN... "ALF" PLUSH TOY...
MUST... WIN... "CHARLIE'S ANGELS" PIGGIE BANK...

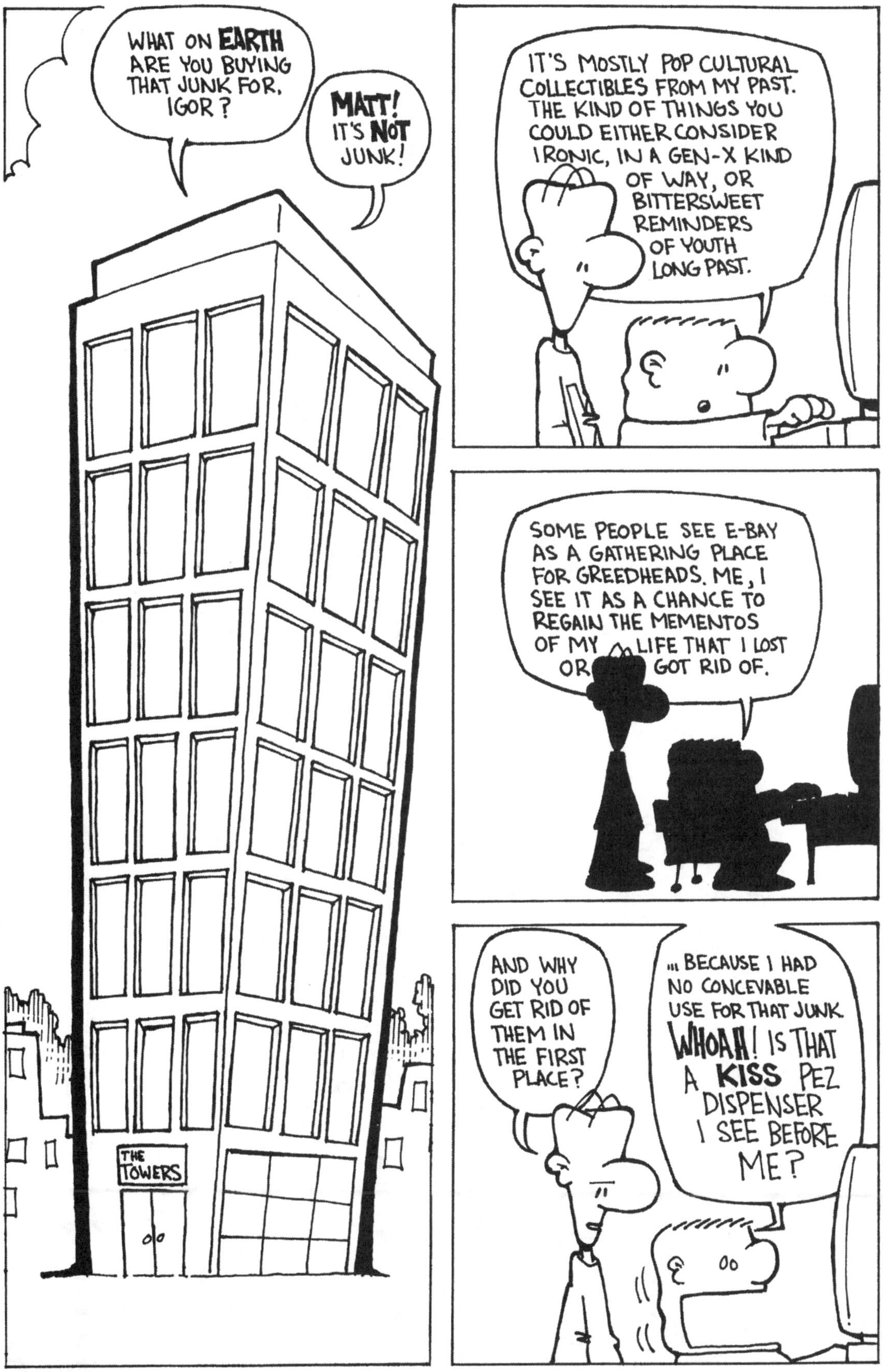
WHAT ON EARTH ARE YOU BUYING THAT JUNK FOR, IGOR?
MATT! IT'S NOT JUNK!
THE TOWERS
IT'S MOSTLY POP CULTURAL COLLECTIBLES FROM MY PAST. THE KIND OF THINGS YOU COULD EITHER CONSIDER IRONIC, IN A GEN-X KIND OF WAY, OR BITTERSWEET REMINDERS OF YOUTH LONG PAST.
SOME PEOPLE SEE E-BAY AS A GATHERING PLACE FOR GREEDHEADS. ME, I SEE IT AS A CHANCE TO REGAIN THE MEMENTOS OF MY LIFE THAT I LOST OR GOT RID OF.
AND WHY DID YOU GET RID OF THEM IN THE FIRST PLACE?
...BECAUSE I HAD NO CONCEVABLE USE FOR THAT JUNK. WHOAH! IS THAT A KISS PEZ DISPENSER I SEE BEFORE ME?

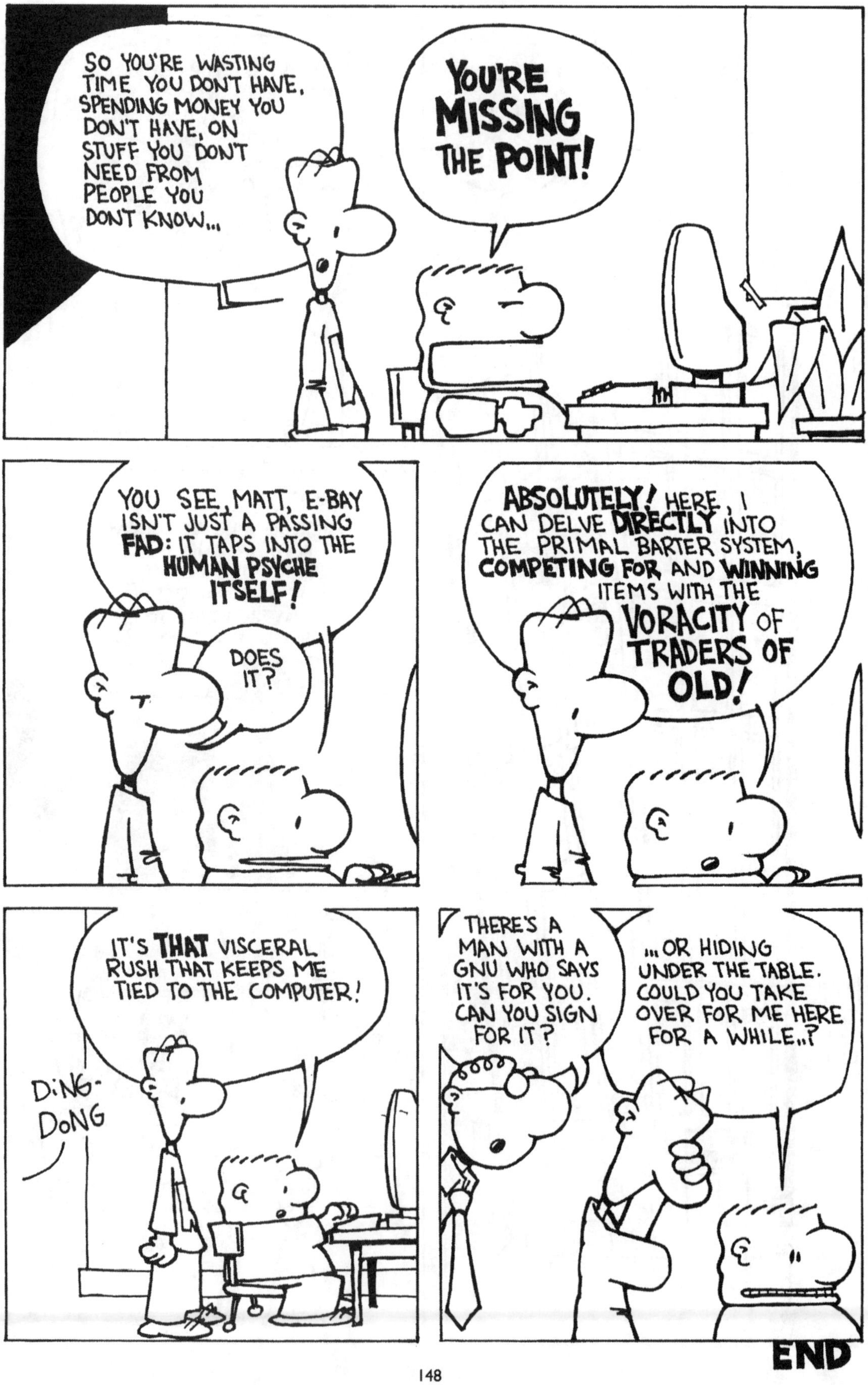
SO YOU'RE WASTING TIME YOU DON'T HAVE, SPENDING MONEY YOU DON'T HAVE, ON STUFF YOU DON'T NEED FROM PEOPLE YOU DON'T KNOW...
YOU'RE MISSING THE POINT!
YOU SEE, MATT, E-BAY ISN'T JUST A PASSING FAD: IT TAPS INTO THE HUMAN PSYCHE ITSELF!
DOES IT?
ABSOLUTELY! HERE, I CAN DELVE DIRECTLY INTO THE PRIMAL BARTER SYSTEM, COMPETING FOR AND WINNING ITEMS WITH THE VORACITY OF TRADERS OF OLD!
IT'S THAT VISCERAL RUSH THAT KEEPS ME TIED TO THE COMPUTER!
DING-DONG
THERE'S A MAN WITH A GNU WHO SAYS IT'S FOR YOU. CAN YOU SIGN FOR IT?
...OR HIDING UNDER THE TABLE. COULD YOU TAKE OVER FOR ME HERE FOR A WHILE..?
END

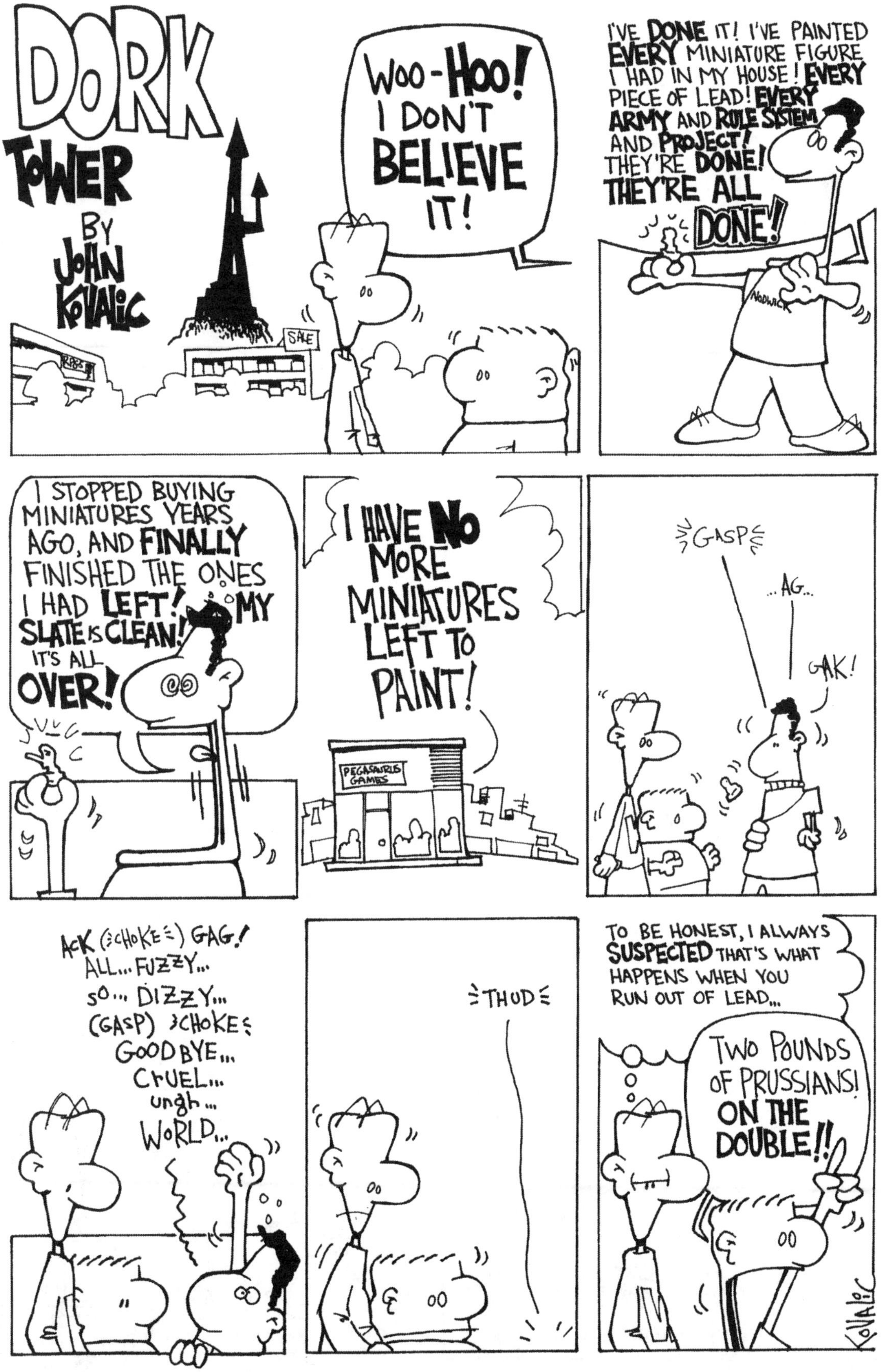
DORK TOWER
BY JOHN KOVALIC
RPGs
SALE
WOO-HOO! I DON'T BELIEVE IT!
I'VE DONE IT! I'VE PAINTED EVERY MINIATURE FIGURE I HAD IN MY HOUSE! EVERY PIECE OF LEAD! EVERY ARMY AND RULE SYSTEM AND PROJECT! THEY'RE DONE! THEY'RE ALL DONE!
NODWICK
I STOPPED BUYING MINIATURES YEARS AGO, AND FINALLY FINISHED THE ONES I HAD LEFT! MY SLATE IS CLEAN! IT'S ALL OVER!
I HAVE NO MORE MINIATURES LEFT TO PAINT!
PEGASAURUS GAMES
GASP
... AG...
GAK!
ACK (CHOKE) GAG! ALL... FUZZY... SO... DIZZY... (GASP) CHOKE GOODBYE... CRUEL... UNGH... WORLD...
THUD
TO BE HONEST, I ALWAYS SUSPECTED THAT'S WHAT HAPPENS WHEN YOU RUN OUT OF LEAD...
TWO POUNDS OF PRUSSIANS! ON THE DOUBLE!!
KOVALIC

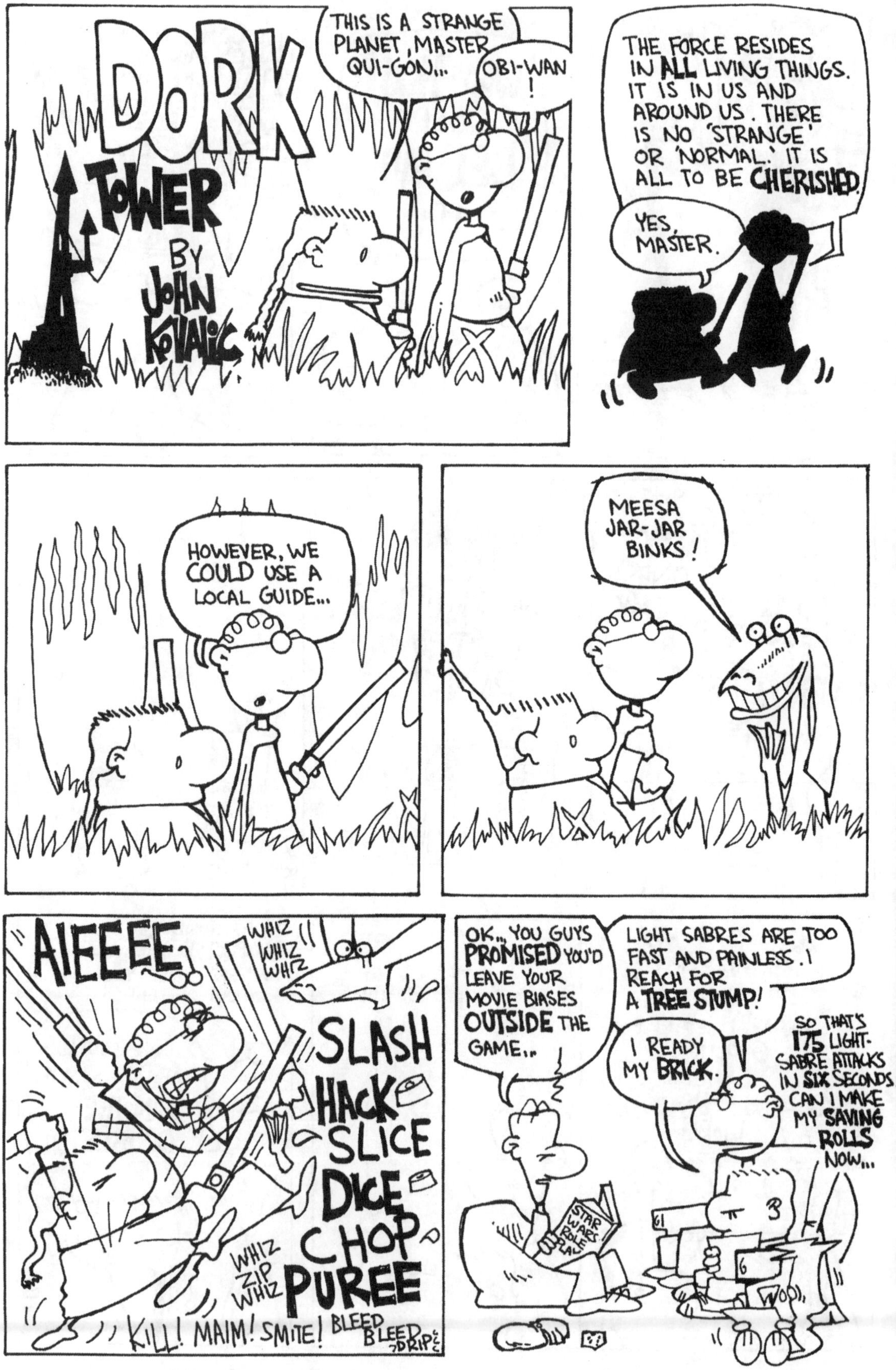
DORK TOWER
BY JOHN KOVALIC
THIS IS A STRANGE PLANET, MASTER QUI-GON...
OBI-WAN!
THE FORCE RESIDES IN ALL LIVING THINGS. IT IS IN US AND AROUND US. THERE IS NO 'STRANGE' OR 'NORMAL.' IT IS ALL TO BE CHERISHED.
YES, MASTER.
HOWEVER, WE COULD USE A LOCAL GUIDE...
MEESA JAR-JAR BINKS!
AIEEEE
WHIZ WHIZ WHIZ
SLASH
HACK
SLICE
DICE
CHOP
PUREE
WHIZ ZIP WHIZ
KILL! MAIM! SMITE! BLEED BLEED DRIP
OK... YOU GUYS PROMISED YOU'D LEAVE YOUR MOVIE BIASES OUTSIDE THE GAME...
LIGHT SABRES ARE TOO FAST AND PAINLESS. I REACH FOR A TREE STUMP!
I READY MY BRICK.
SO THAT'S 175 LIGHT-SABRE ATTACKS IN SIX SECONDS. CAN I MAKE MY SAVING ROLLS NOW...
STAR WARS ROLE PLAY

ESCAPE FROM DORK TOWER

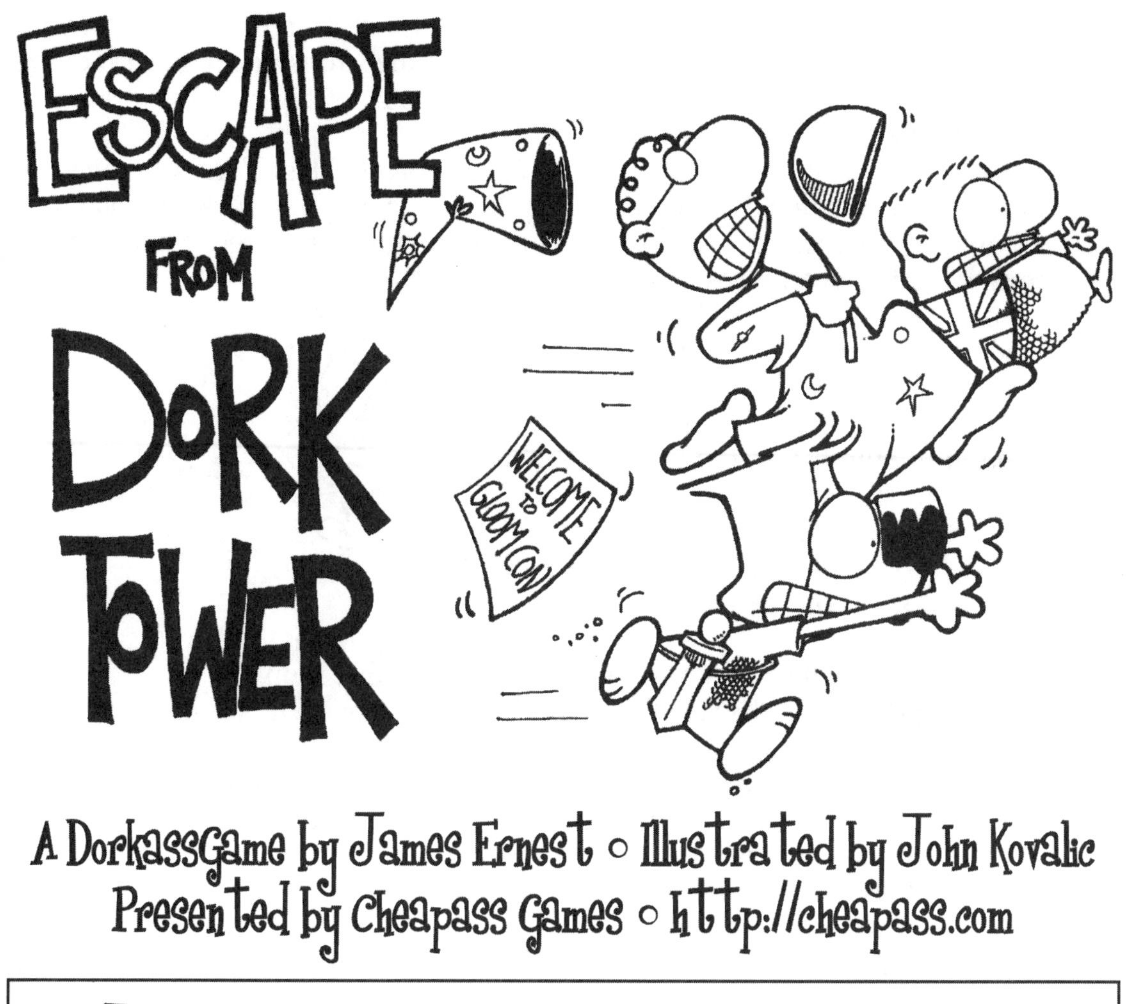
WELCOME TO GLOOMCON

A Dorkassgame by James Ernest ○ Illustrated by John Kovalic
Presented by Cheapass Games ○ http://cheapass.com

Welcome to GloomCon, a dreary little convention where you and your lifeless friends have made the fatal error of signing up for a LARP called "Escape from Dork Tower." It's a live-action role-playing game that takes you all over the hotel, playing tic-tac-toe for "combat" and collecting "magic beans" for use in your "quest" to save the "princess" from the "Evil sorcerer" who's locked her up in his "tower." In other words, it's even stupider than you thought.

The winner of today's game gets to participate in the all-day "Escape from Dork Tower" adventure/tournament tomorrow, which is a punishment you now desperately want to avoid. However, there's only one creature left, he's been worn down to one hit point, and no one who's still alive has any desire to kill it.

So, run away! If the Monster catches you, you'll be forced to fight it, and you'll win the game automatically. And if you win, you'll be stuck playing this all again tomorrow, which basically means you lose.

The Rules:

Players: 3-6
Playing Time: 15-30 Minutes
You Need: A Pawn for every player, some Pennies, one 6-sided die, and one Master Pawn to represent the Monster.
The Board: The board represents the convention area of the hotel. It is composed of 25 rooms separated by 42 doorways.
To Begin: Determine a first player by some random method, and then place your Pawns on the numbered rooms surrounding the Ballroom, starting with the player who will go first. In other words, Player 1 starts on the "1," Player 2 on "2," and so on.

Start the Monster in the Ballroom (the center of the board, labeled "Escape From Dork Tower").

Place pennies across some of the doorways, as shown by the circles on the board. These pennies represent tables, which block off the doorways they cover. The tables will move around throughout the game, and the number and starting configuration of the tables will vary depending on how many people are playing.

Now you're ready to play!

On Every Turn: Roll the die, and take that many steps from room to room. After each step you take, the Monster will take one step towards you by the shortest open path. So, if you roll a 5, both you and the Monster will take 5 steps. If the Monster ever catches you, you lose!

How You Move: *You can move into any empty* room, through any open doorway.

You can't move through a table.

You can't move into an occupied room.

You must take a step if you can.

If you are blocked off completely (which is highly unlikely), you must count off "pauses" for each step remaining in your move, so the Monster can keep moving towards you.

Moving the Tables: You can move one table after taking a step. After you move into a room, you may move a table from

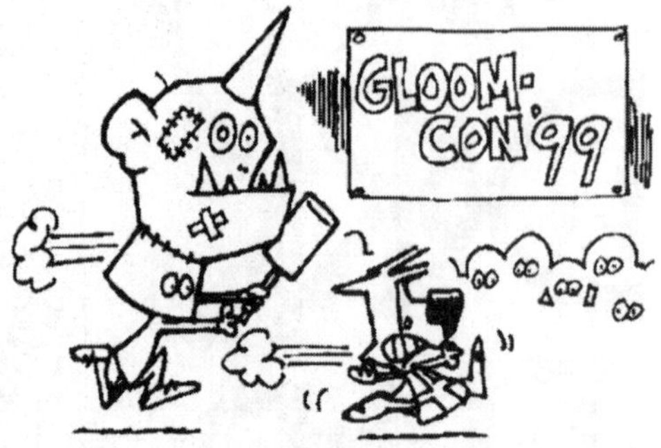
GLOOM-
CON'99

any doorway in that room to any other doorway in that room.

You can't move a table before you take a step. In other words, when you start your turn, you can't move a table in your current location to open up a new exit; you must move one step first, through an open door.

How the Monster Moves: The Monster takes each step right after you do. He can't move through tables, but he can move through other players. However, he can only catch the player who is currently active; the inactive players are "out of game," and so he can't see them. The Monster always tries to take the shortest path towards you. If the best route is blocked, he moves along the shortest unblocked route. If there are two or more equivalent moves, the Monster will randomly pick one. You can do this by rolling the die, or by letting someone who's not paying much attention pick a route. If there is no open path to you (which is unlikely) then the Monster does not move. If you and the Monster start a turn on the same space, he can't catch you just yet, because you're still "out of game." In this case, you've got just one step to throw a table in his way!

Winning: There isn't a winner in this game, just one loser. When the Monster catches up to you, you win, which means you lose, because everybody else goes away happy. If you have a competitive streak, keep score over a series of games. The losers get 1 mark for each loss, and the player with the fewest marks wins.

Strategy: It's very hard for the Monster to catch you unless you run into a dead end, or get stuck in a corner. Therefore, to isolate someone, players must try to build dead ends for others by moving the tables, and by using themselves as roadblocks. Remember, players can't run through other players, but the Monster can. So, cluster around the player you want to catch, and trap him.

Where to put the tables: For 5 or 6 players, place 12 tables on the doors marked with white dots. For 3 or 4 players, place 4 additional tables on the doors marked "T."

If there are more than 6 players: You can start extra players in the outside corners. Starting at the upper left, and proceeding clockwise, number the corners 7, 8, 9, and 10. Remove the tables from every occupied corner.

Escape from Dork Tower ©1999 Cheapass Games. A game by James Ernest, illustrated by John Kovalic with help from Toivo Rovainen, Joshua Howard, Jeff Vogel, Dave Howell, and a punch bowl full of timid and retiring guinea pigs.

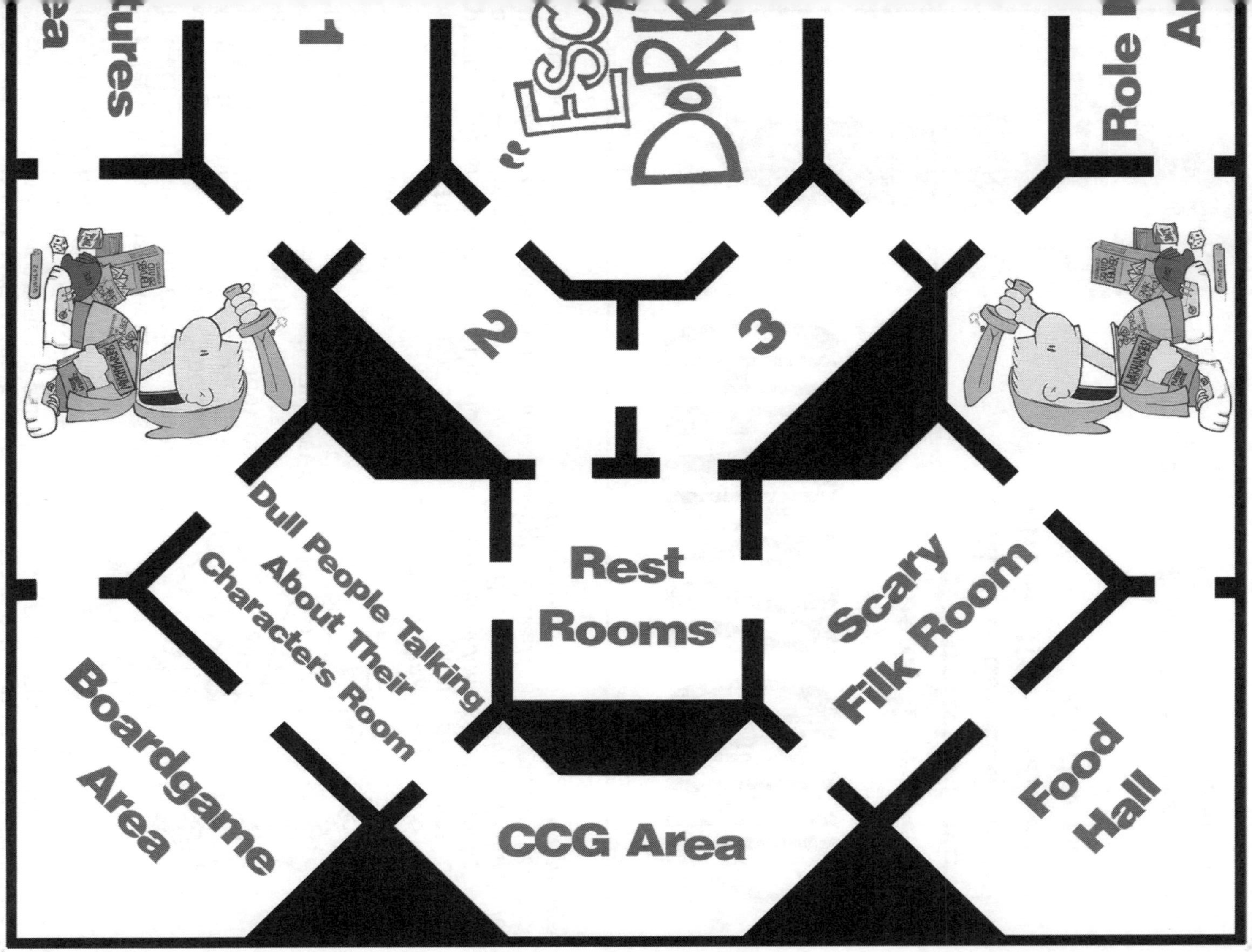

tures
ea
1
2
3
"ESC
DORK
Role
A
Dull People Talking
About Their
Characters Room
Rest
Rooms
Scary
Filk Room
Boardgame
Area
CCG Area
Food
Hall

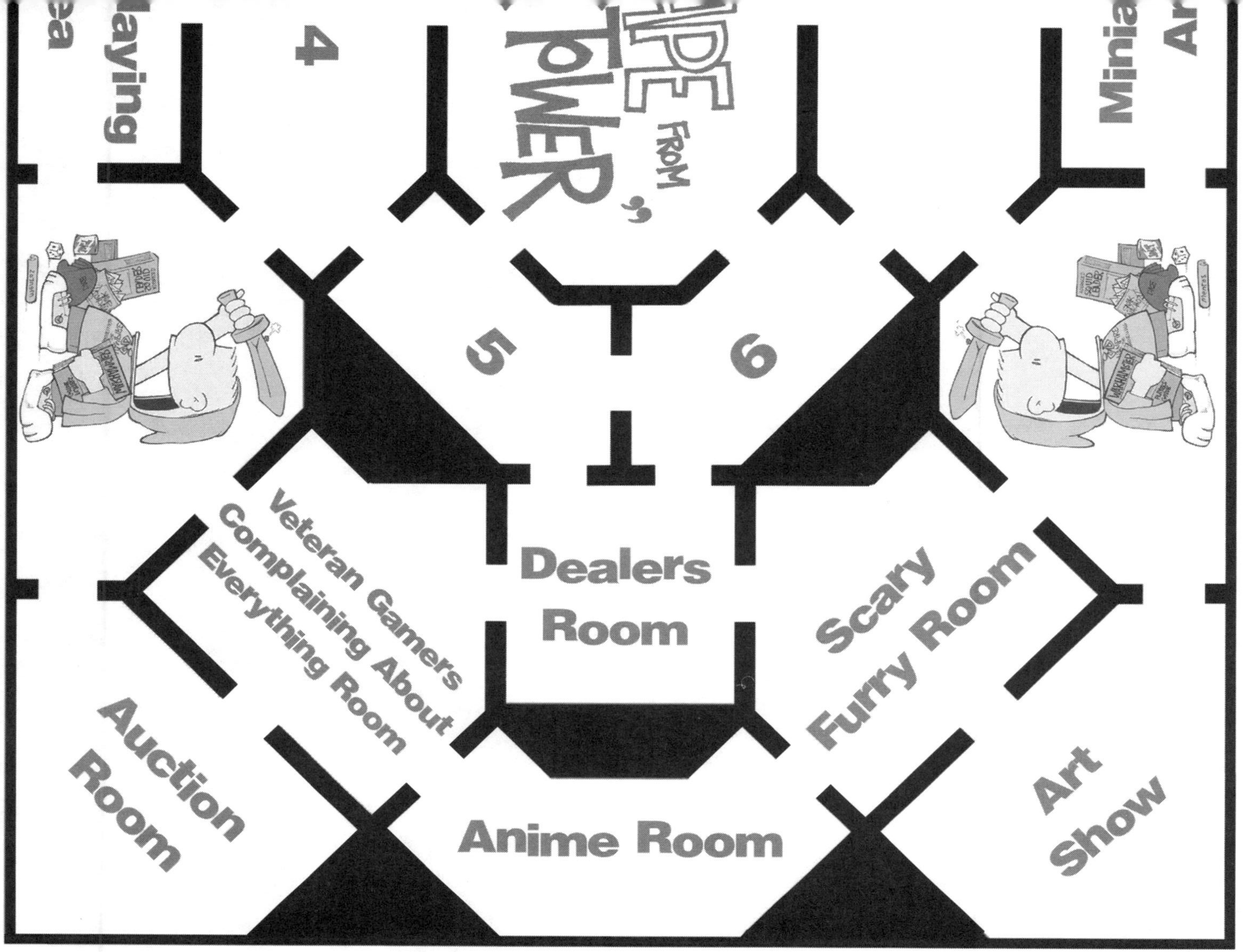
laying
ea
4
APE FROM
TOWER"
Minia
Ar
5
6
Dealers
Room
Veteran Gamers
Complaining About
Everything Room
Scary
Furry Room
Auction
Room
Anime Room
Art
Show

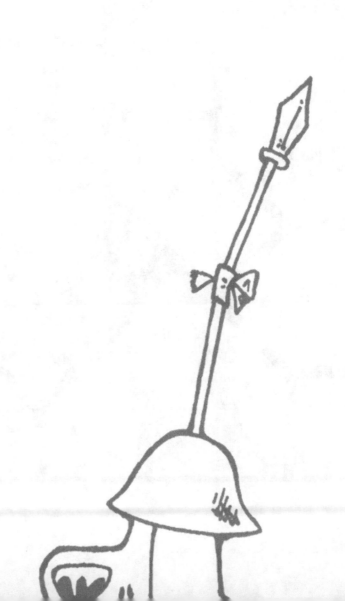

ACKNOWLEDGEMENTS

The number of people I have to thank is simply staggering to me. My family, first and foremost, and my friends. My readers (thank you thank you thank you). My gaming group (Lory, Randy, Terry, Krista (MIA) and Dino (MIA)) in general, and Scott Olman (the real Igor) and Bill Bodden (the real Pegasaurus Bill) in particular. Everyone at Pegasus Games, The Last Square, Castle Perilous, the Source, Capital City Comics, Westfield Comics, Etc., 20th Century Books, Star Clipper and Dreamhaven Comics. Everyone at the late, lamented Shadis magazine for starting this whole thing in the first place - DJ, Rob, Jim, Marcello, Cris, Maureen and the Z-Man - it was like family, guys, and I miss you. Dave Gross and everyone at Dragon Magazine for being so freaking great, and Larry Smith for dragging me there in the first place. Which is to say nothing of the folks at Pyramid and Scrye magazines these days. Steve Jackson Games, Cheapass Games and The Army of Dorkness (you know who you are). Dave Sim, Terry Moore, Phil & Kaja Foglio, Mike Baron, Gary Gygax, Steve Jackson and Jolly Blackburn, for being great guys. The folks on the Dork Tower mailing lists and at the Dork Tower Yahoo club. Bruce McLean and the crew at the Millfield Newspaper. Alex Robinson, Scott Roberts and all the others whose work keeps me going. Mark, Al and Cathy at Out of the Box. Phil Reed. Jon and Phil at Corsair. Everyone else whom I've forgotten as I sit here typing this, blown away by it all.

Last -- and far from least -- I wouldn't here if it wasn't for the help of my partners in crime, Aaron Williams and Liz Fulda.

Blame them. And my cats.

John Kovalic

About the Author

John Kovalic was born in Manchester, England, in 1962. Dork Tower began in SHADIS magazine in 1996, and the multi-Origins award-nominated Dork Tower comic book was launched in June 1998. The first issue sold out in eight weeks to fantastic reviews and tremendous industry buzz. John's award-winning editorial cartoons appear everywhere from his hometown WISCONSIN STATE JOURNAL and CAPITAL TIMES (Madison, WI) to the NEW YORK TIMES and the WASHINGTON POST. His other creations include SnapDragons and Newbies (with Liz Rathke), Wild Life, Beached, the Unspeakable Oaf and many others.

One of the first cartoonists to put their work on the internet, his self-produced World Wide Web site, kovalic.com, has received numerous national and international kudos. If you ask him nicely, he'll tell you how he helped create GAMES Magazine's 1999 Party Game of the Year, the international best-selling, award-winning "Apples to Apples." He may even tell you how he once ended up in the pages of the National Enquirer.

His degree was in Economics with a minor in Astrophysics. In his spare time, John searches for spare time.

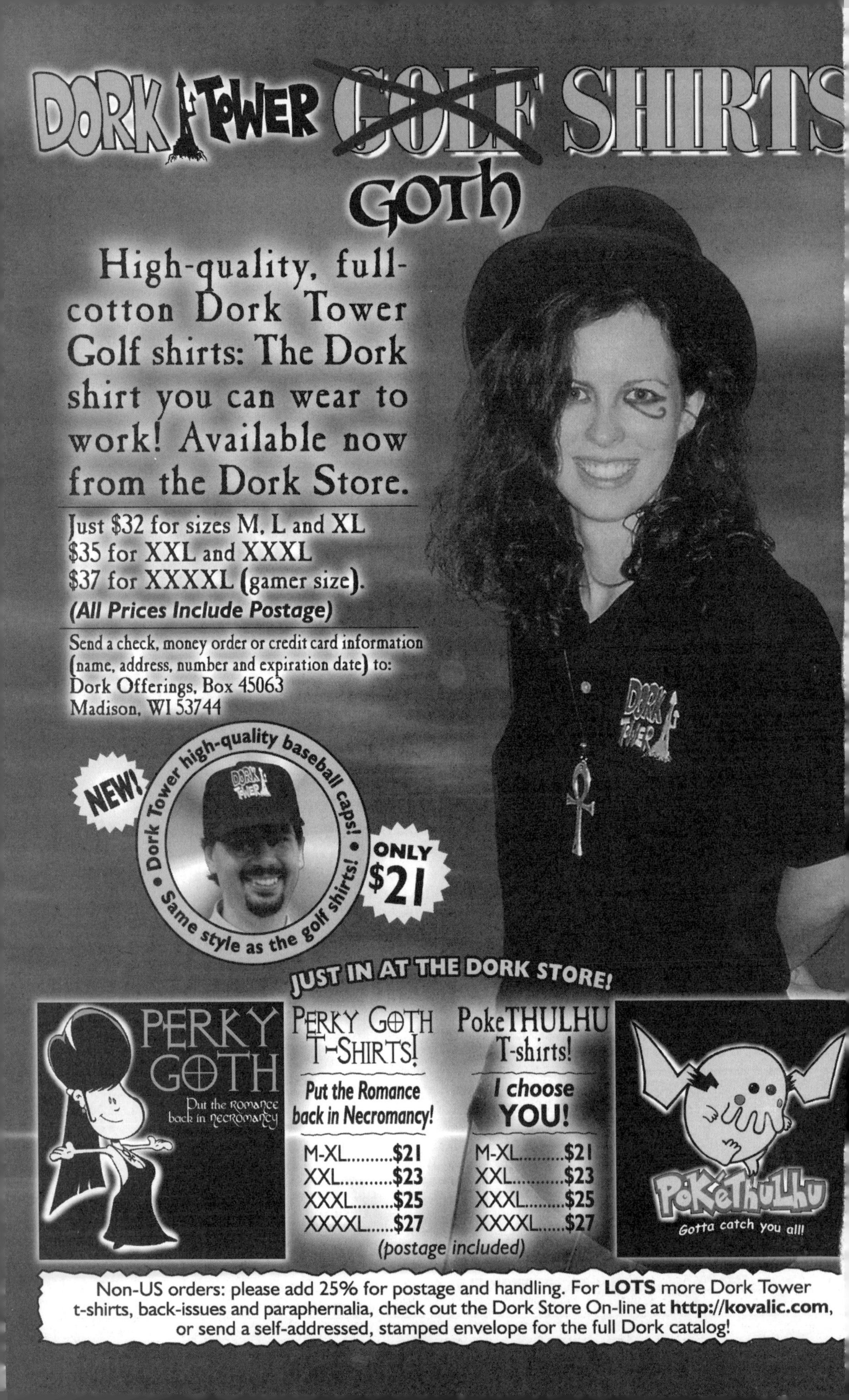

DORK TOWER GOLF SHIRTS
GOTH
High-quality, full-cotton Dork Tower Golf shirts: The Dork shirt you can wear to work! Available now from the Dork Store.
Just $32 for sizes M, L and XL
$35 for XXL and XXXL
$37 for XXXXL (gamer size).
(All Prices Include Postage)
Send a check, money order or credit card information (name, address, number and expiration date) to:
Dork Offerings, Box 45063
Madison, WI 53744
NEW!
Dork Tower high-quality baseball caps! • Same style as the golf shirts! •
ONLY $21
JUST IN AT THE DORK STORE!
PERKY GOTH
Put the Romance back in Necromancy
PERKY GOTH T-SHIRTS!
Put the Romance back in Necromancy!
M-XL..........$21
XXL...........$23
XXXL.........$25
XXXXL......$27
PokeTHULHU T-shirts!
I choose YOU!
M-XL..........$21
XXL...........$23
XXXL.........$25
XXXXL......$27
(postage included)
PoKeThULhU
Gotta catch you all!
Non-US orders: please add 25% for postage and handling. For LOTS more Dork Tower t-shirts, back-issues and paraphernalia, check out the Dork Store On-line at http://kovalic.com, or send a self-addressed, stamped envelope for the full Dork catalog!